Risk Assessment and Countermeasures for Cybersecurity

Mohammed Amin Almaiah
The University of Jordan, Amman, Jordan

Yassine Maleh
Sultan Moulay Slimane University, Morocco

Abdalwali Alkhassawneh
King Faisal University, Saudi Arabia

IGI Global
PUBLISHER of TIMELY KNOWLEDGE

A volume in the Advances in IT Standards and Standardization Research (AITSSR) Book Series

Published in the United States of America by
IGI Global
Information Science Reference (an imprint of IGI Global)
701 E. Chocolate Avenue
Hershey PA, USA 17033
Tel: 717-533-8845
Fax: 717-533-8661
E-mail: cust@igi-global.com
Web site: http://www.igi-global.com

Library of Congress Cataloging-in-Publication Data

CIP Pending

Risk Assessment and Countermeasures for Cybersecurity
Mohammed Almaiah, Yassine Maleh, Abdalwali Alkhassawneh
2024 Information Science Reference

ISBN: 979-8-3693-2691-6
eISBN: 979-8-3693-2692-3

This book is published in the IGI Global book series Advances in IT Standards and Standardization Research (AITSSR) (ISSN: 1935-3391; eISSN: 1935-3405)

British Cataloguing in Publication Data
A Cataloguing in Publication record for this book is available from the British Library.

All work contributed to this book is new, previously-unpublished material. The views expressed in this book are those of the authors, but not necessarily of the publisher.

For electronic access to this publication, please contact: eresources@igi-global.com.

Advances in IT Standards and Standardization Research (AITSSR) Book Series

Kai Jakobs
RWTH Aachen University, Germany

ISSN:1935-3391
EISSN:1935-3405

Mission

IT standards and standardization are a necessary part of effectively delivering IT and IT services to organizations and individuals, as well as streamlining IT processes and minimizing organizational cost. In implementing IT standards, it is necessary to take into account not only the technical aspects, but also the characteristics of the specific environment where these standards will have to function.

The **Advances in IT Standards and Standardization Research (AITSSR) Book Series** seeks to advance the available literature on the use and value of IT standards and standardization. This research provides insight into the use of standards for the improvement of organizational processes and development in both private and public sectors.

Coverage

- Management of Standards
- Prescriptive Theory of Standardization
- Technological innovation and standardization
- Descriptive Theory of Standardization
- Standards in the Public Sector
- Standards and Technology Transfer
- Tools and Services Supporting Improved Standardization
- National, regional, international, and corporate standards strategies
- Analyses of Standards-Setting Processes, Products, and Organization
- Impacts of Market-Driven Standardization and Emerging Players

IGI Global is currently accepting manuscripts for publication within this series. To submit a proposal for a volume in this series, please contact our Acquisition Editors at Acquisitions@igi-global.com or visit: http://www.igi-global.com/publish/.

The Advances in IT Standards and Standardization Research (AITSSR) Book Series (ISSN 1935-3391) is published by IGI Global, 701 E. Chocolate Avenue, Hershey, PA 17033-1240, USA, www.igi-global.com. This series is composed of titles available for purchase individually; each title is edited to be contextually exclusive from any other title within the series. For pricing and ordering information please visit http://www.igi-global.com/book-series/advances-standards-standardization-research/37142. Postmaster: Send all address changes to above address.

Titles in this Series

For a list of additional titles in this series, please visit: www.igi-global.com/book-series/advances-standards-standardization-research/37142

Examining the Rapid Advance of Digital Technology in Africa
Lloyd G. Adu Amoah (University of Ghana, Ghana)
Engineering Science Reference • copyright 2024 • 369pp • H/C (ISBN: 9781668499627) • US $235.00 (our price)

Modernizing Enterprise IT Audit Governance and Management Practices
Manish Gupta (University at Buffalo, SUNY, USA) and Raj Sharman (University at Buffalo, SUNY, USA)
Engineering Science Reference • copyright 2023 • 318pp • H/C (ISBN: 9781668487662) • US $250.00 (our price)

Handbook of Research on Evolving Designs and Innovation in ICT and Intelligent Systems for Real-World Applications
Kandarpa Kumar Sarma (Gauhati University, India) Navajit Saikia (Assam Engineering College, India) and Mridusmita Sharma (Gauhati University, India)
Engineering Science Reference • copyright 2022 • 312pp • H/C (ISBN: 9781799897958) • US $380.00 (our price)

Digital Transformation for Promoting Inclusiveness in Marginalized Communities
Munyaradzi Zhou (Midlands State University, Zimbabwe) Gilbert Mahlangu (Midlands State University, Zimbabwe) and Cyncia Matsika (Midlands State University, Zimbabwe)
Engineering Science Reference • copyright 2022 • 311pp • H/C (ISBN: 9781668439012) • US $260.00 (our price)

The Strategies of Informing Technology in the 21st Century
Andrew Targowski (Independent Researcher, USA)
Engineering Science Reference • copyright 2022 • 557pp • H/C (ISBN: 9781799880363) • US $240.00 (our price)

Developing Countries and Technology Inclusion in the 21st Century Information Society
Alice S. Etim (Winston Salem State University, USA)
Information Science Reference • copyright 2021 • 318pp • H/C (ISBN: 9781799834687) • US $205.00 (our price)

IT Auditing Using a System Perspective
Robert Elliot Davis (Walden University, USA)
Information Science Reference • copyright 2020 • 260pp • H/C (ISBN: 9781799841982) • US $215.00 (our price)

Handbook of Research on the Evolution of IT and the Rise of E-Society
Maki Habib (The American University in Cairo, Egypt)
Information Science Reference • copyright 2019 • 602pp • H/C (ISBN: 9781522572145) • US $245.00 (our price)

IGI Global
PUBLISHER of TIMELY KNOWLEDGE

701 East Chocolate Avenue, Hershey, PA 17033, USA
Tel: 717-533-8845 x100 • Fax: 717-533-8661
E-Mail: cust@igi-global.com • www.igi-global.com

Table of Contents

Section 2
Machine Intelligence Applications in Cyber Risk Management

Section 3
Advanced Techniques for Network Security and Data Protection

Detailed Table of Contents

Section 1
Risk Assessment and Mitigation Strategies

In the evolving realm of online social networks (OSNs), assessing cybersecurity risks and implementing effective countermeasures are crucial for practitioners. This chapter confronts this challenge, beginning with an extensive literature review that explores the range of threats, vulnerabilities, and attacks prevalent in OSNs. It differentiates between general cybersecurity risks and those unique to OSNs, with a special focus on user-side vulnerabilities. The chapter critically analyzes risk assessment and security assessment, highlighting their distinct yet interconnected roles in cybersecurity. Various risk assessment methods are evaluated for their applicability to OSNs, alongside a discussion of both technical and non-technical countermeasures for risk mitigation. Concluding with key findings and future research directions, this chapter offers a comprehensive guide for understanding and tackling the complex cybersecurity challenges in online social networks.

This study is placed within the framework of cybersecurity, particularly with regard to the identification of advanced persistent threats (APT). The research that resulted in this publication examines the MICTIC framework, confirming its validity and suggesting an expansion to make assigning APTs easier. The authors outline the rationale behind this approach and provide evidence for it in this study. Additionally, the MICTIC is presented layer by layer, and the expanded version is put to the test by having around 50 academics and researchers from universities complete a survey. They choose to do it in addition to the extension request since the MICTIC hasn't been verified on its own. Attribution is crucial because it identifies the person who launched an APT-style assault or encouraged one. However, the very existence of advanced attribution systems may serve as a warning against such assaults in the future.

Many consider the internet a safe environment for sharing information and performing online transactions. However, they are unaware of the cyberattacks that occur in the cyber environment. People are vulnerable to cyberattacks such as stealing of data and identity theft that cause financial loss and mental distress. Thus, cybersecurity that protects computer systems is considered vital to combat cyberattacks. This chapter aims to review strategies that can combat cyberattacks systematically. The results of this chapter showed an overview of the reviewed literature about authorship, geographical distribution of the studies, applied methods, types of respondents involved, types of strategies used to combat cyberattacks, and main study findings. Twenty-one studies met the authors' inclusion criteria. The findings highlighted that good governance, strategic partnership, perceived threat, coping appraisal, perceived cultural values, attitude, and technology efficacy are the strategies adopted by organisations and individuals to combat cyberattacks.

Online social networks (OSNs) are platforms on the web that have seen significant growth. They allow people to connect, interact, and share information with others over the internet. These platforms have become an essential part of people's daily lives, serving as the primary means of communication for individuals worldwide. However, despite the significant benefits these platforms offer, they face privacy concerns such as identity theft and misuse of users' sensitive information. This chapter aims to provide a comprehensive review of the various privacy weaknesses in OSNs, along with an exploration of the existing mechanisms and techniques used to safeguard users' data within this dynamic environment. The review is based on the rigorous Kitchenham protocol and performs a comprehensive assessment of 26 journal articles, published in the last five years. This study serves as a valuable resource for researchers and developers seeking to enhance the privacy preservation of OSNs.

Section 2
Machine Intelligence Applications in Cyber Risk Management

In the meticulously networked world of today, cybersecurity is a primary concern for firms operating in various industries. The cornerstone for protecting sensitive information and fending off cyber threats is administrative compliance. This chapter delves into the important area of risk assessment in cybersecurity, emphasizing administrative compliance as a primary concern. It promotes the use of a robust compliance administration system in order to effectively manage compliance complexity. Through the coordination of such a system, enterprises may competently investigate administrative situations, ready their cybersecurity defenses, and preserve the accuracy of their data. This strategy strengthens firms' overall resilience against evolving cyber threats while also addressing immediate compliance challenges.

Memory analysis is important in malware detection because it may capture a wide range of traits and behaviors. As aspects of technology evolve, so do the strategies used by malicious who aim to compromise the security and integrity of digital systems. This study investigates the classification of cyberattacks into malicious and benign. A specific malware memory dataset, MalMemAnalogy-2022, was created to test and evaluate this framework. In this chapter, a set of machine learning algorithms was used, including support vector machine (SVM), K nearest neighbor (KNN), and random forest (RF). To ensure promising performance, especially in identifying important features, the random forest method was used to select the most important features, which achieves the best results and avoids features of little importance. The random forest algorithm achieved 99.9% accuracy, precision, recall, and f1-score. The present approach can detect and mitigate malicious cyber-attacks significantly improving the security framework for end-users by detecting memory malware using machine learning.

Effective surveillance of cybersecurity is essential for safeguarding the security of computer networks. Nevertheless, due to the increasing scope, complexity, and amount of data created by computer networks, cybersecurity monitoring has become a more intricate issue. The difficulty of correctly and effectively monitoring computer network cybersecurity is a challenge faced by traditional approaches examining a greater quantity of data. Hence, using deep learning models to oversee computer network cybersecurity becomes necessary. This chapter introduces a technique for overseeing the cybersecurity of computer networks by using deep learning knowledge about models. The combination of CNN (convolutional neural networks) and LSTM (long short-term memory) models is used for monitoring the cybersecurity of computer networks. This combination enhances the accuracy of classifying network cybersecurity problems. The CICIDS2017 dataset is used for training and evaluating the suggested model.

The work aims to improve model resilience and accuracy in machine learning (ML) by addressing data poisoning attacks. Data poisoning attacks are a type of adversarial attack where malicious data is injected into the training data set to manipulate the machine learning model's output, compromising model performance and security. To tackle this, a multi-faceted approach is proposed, including data assessment and cleaning, detecting attacks using outlier and anomaly detection techniques. The authors also train robust models using techniques such as adversarial training, regularization, and data diversification. Additionally, they use ensemble methods that combine the strengths of multiple models, as well as Gaussian processes and Bayesian optimization to improve resilience to attacks. The work aims to contribute to machine learning security by providing an integrated solution for addressing data poisoning attacks and advancing the understanding of adversarial attacks and defenses in the machine learning community.

Section 3
Advanced Techniques for Network Security and Data Protection

Since the beginning of the digital era, there has been an increasing focus on picture security since it is a crucial medium for the transfer of information. In this regard, the study develops a hybrid cloud and half-tensor compression-aware technology network image security transmission technique. Following an introduction to the fundamentals of cryptography and its use in the encryption of images, the relevant compression perception methods are expounded upon. In order to further secure the security of network pictures during transmission, the research then suggests the half-tensor product compression perception approach and integrates this technique with the hybrid cloud idea to build a new image encryption and decryption algorithm. According to the findings, the suggested method obtains the greatest peak signal-to-noise ratio value of 31.89 and structural similarity index value of 0.97, respectively. In addition, the lowest values for the times spent on encryption and decryption are 2.128 and 0.288, respectively, indicating that these techniques need less time than others.

Wireless sensor networks (WSNs) are important in various applications, including environmental monitoring, healthcare, and industrial automation. However, the energy constraints of sensor nodes present significant challenges in deploying robust security mechanisms, such as intrusion detection systems (IDS). The method involves using data aggregation, node selection, and energy harvesting techniques to reduce energy consumption while maintaining the accuracy of the IDS. The effectiveness of the proposed approach is evaluated using simulation experiments. This chapter offers a promising solution for providing effective and energy-efficient intrusion detection in ZigBee-based WSNs. The study found that applying machine learning techniques, specifically SFA, can significantly improve the energy efficiency of Zigbee protocol in wireless sensor networks. Results indicate that using these techniques energy consumption is up to 95.42% and 190 μW / node, IDS prediction ratio is 98.5%, and accuracy is 99.5% while maintaining network performance.

Jamming is the most critical security threat because the rapid development of new technology, such as smart mobile devices, and ad hoc networks have drawn a lot of interest from the academic community in recent years. Ad hoc protocols represent an important role in the efficient transmission of data across mobile ad hoc protocols (MANET). The choice of a suitable routing protocol is influenced by several variables, including network structure, scalability, mobility, and reliability. In this chapter, the authors employed three protocols: dynamic source routing (DSR), optimized link state routing (OLSR), and temporally ordered routing algorithm (TORA) routing protocols, including distance-vector, link-state, and hybrid protocols are thoroughly analyzed under jamming attack with an emphasis on their advantages, disadvantages, and practical uses. This chapter focuses on these protocols' applicability for various network scenarios with attacks using the network simulator OPNET 14.5.

Preface

Welcome to *Risk Assessment and Countermeasures for Cybersecurity*, a comprehensive compilation edited by Mohammed Amin Almaiah, Yassine Maleh, and Abdalwali Lutfi. In this volume, our aim is to provide a systematic exploration of essential cybersecurity concepts, methodologies, and technologies.

Cybersecurity is an ever-evolving field, crucial for safeguarding our digital world against a myriad of threats. This book is meticulously crafted to address a wide spectrum of topics, ranging from risk assessment to the deployment of cutting-edge security countermeasures.

Our primary objective is to serve as a catalyst for advancing knowledge in cybersecurity. We invite scientists, researchers, academics, developers, policymakers, and cybersecurity practitioners to delve into the wealth of insights presented within these pages.

From academia to industry, from theoretical frameworks to real-world applications, this book offers valuable resources for anyone engaged in the pursuit of securing digital assets and infrastructure.

The topics covered in this book span various domains including machine learning, artificial intelligence, big data, cloud computing, digital forensics, cryptography, and more. Each chapter is crafted to provide both theoretical foundations and practical insights, making it accessible to a diverse audience.

Whether you are a seasoned cybersecurity analyst, a postgraduate student exploring emerging trends, or a policymaker shaping the future of digital governance, we believe you will find this book to be a valuable resource in your endeavors.

We extend our gratitude to all the contributors who have shared their expertise and insights, helping to enrich the discourse surrounding cybersecurity. It is our sincere hope that this book will foster further collaboration and innovation in the ongoing quest to secure our digital landscape.

ORGANIZATION OF THE BOOK

Section 1: Risk Assessment and Mitigation Strategies

In "A Deep Dive into Cybersecurity Risk Assessment and Countermeasures in Online Social Networks" by Zineddine, Yousra Belfaik, and Yassine SADQI, the authors meticulously explore the landscape of cybersecurity risks within online social networks (OSNs). They conduct an extensive literature review to delineate the threats and vulnerabilities unique to OSNs, while also discussing various risk assessment methods and both technical and non-technical countermeasures for risk mitigation. This chapter serves as a comprehensive guide for practitioners seeking to understand and address the complex cybersecurity challenges specific to online social networks.

"Identification of Advancing Persistent Risks: Expanding the MICTIC Model", by Virendra Kumar Yadav, Shelendra Pal, Raghavendra R. Jain, Aishwary Awasthi, Laxmi Bewoor, Adapa Gopi, Sabyasachi Pramanikcontributes to the field of cybersecurity, specifically focusing on Advanced Persistent Threats (APT) identification. The research detailed in this publication evaluates the effectiveness of the MICTIC Framework and proposes an extension to facilitate APT attribution. We provide a comprehensive overview of our approach and offer empirical evidence to support its efficacy. Furthermore, we dissect the MICTIC Framework layer by layer and assess its expanded version through a survey involving approximately 50 academics and researchers from various universities.

"Strategies to Combat Cyberattacks: A Systematic Review" by Malathi Letchumanan and Rohaidah Kamaruddin conducts a systematic review of strategies to combat cyberattacks. Analyzing a range of literature, the chapter highlights key strategies adopted by organizations and individuals to mitigate cyber threats, emphasizing the importance of good governance, strategic partnerships, and technology efficacy in bolstering cybersecurity defenses.

"Privacy-Preserving Techniques for Online Social Networks Data" by Yousra Belfaik et al. examines the privacy concerns inherent in online social networks (OSNs) and explores existing mechanisms for safeguarding user data. Through a comprehensive review of recent literature, the chapter provides insights into privacy weaknesses in OSNs and offers valuable recommendations for researchers and developers aiming to enhance privacy preservation in these platforms.

Section 2: Machine Intelligence Applications in Cyber Risk Management

In "Securing the Future: Unveiling Risks and Safeguarding Strategies in Machine Learning-Powered Cybersecurity", by C.V. Suresh Babu and Rahul A, the authors delve into the critical domain of cybersecurity risk assessment, with a particular focus on administrative compliance. They advocate for the implementation of a robust compliance management system to handle compliance intricacies effectively. By adopting such a system, organizations can efficiently address administrative issues, fortify their cybersecurity posture, and maintain data integrity. This approach enhances overall organizational resilience against emerging cyber threats while tackling immediate compliance hurdles.

"Improving Memory Malware Detection in Machine Learning with Random Forest-Based Feature Selection" by Qais Al-Na'amneh et al. addresses the critical issue of memory malware detection. By employing machine learning algorithms, particularly the random forest method for feature selection, the chapter achieves remarkable accuracy in identifying malicious cyber-attacks, significantly enhancing security frameworks for end-users.

Dharmesh Dhabliya et al. present a "Deep Learning-Based Methodology for Tracking Cybersecurity in Networked Computers", leveraging deep learning models, specifically CNN (Convolutional Neural Networks) and LSTM (Long Short-Term Memory), to monitor cybersecurity in computer networks. By utilizing these advanced techniques, the chapter enhances the accuracy of classifying network cybersecurity issues, showcasing the potential of deep learning in bolstering network security.

In "Enhancing Algorithmic Resilience against Data Poisoning Using CNN: Data Poisoning", by Jayapradha et al., the authors aim to bolster the resilience and accuracy of Machine Learning (ML) models by addressing data poisoning attacks, which manipulate training datasets to compromise model output. Their approach includes data evaluation, outlier detection, and robust model training techniques such as adversarial training and ensemble methods. By offering an integrated solution, they seek to advance ML security and deepen understanding of adversarial attacks and defenses.

Section 3: Advanced Techniques for Network Security and Data Protection

"HtStego as a Utility Used for Halftone Steganography", by Sabyasachi Pramanik, introduces a free and open-source steganography tool capable of concealing plaintext payloads within halftone images. It also provides a utility for extracting these payloads from the concealed images. Notably, the utility enhances payload security by distributing payloads across multiple outputs, preventing unauthorized extraction and obviating the need for the original image during retrieval. Moreover, the utility includes quantitative assessments of image quality, demonstrating the efficacy of the steganography technique presented in this study.

"Enhancing 2D Logistic Chaotic Map for Gray Image Encryption" by Qais Alnaamneh et al. delves into the realm of image encryption using chaos theory. Employing a two-dimensional logistic chaotic map, the chapter proposes a secure cipher for encrypting images, ensuring both confusion and diffusion. Through rigorous evaluation using various metrics, the researchers demonstrate the efficacy of their encryption method in safeguarding image data against differential attacks.

"An Approach for Safe Network Image Communication Using Hybrid Cloud and Half Tensor Product Compression Perception" by Madhura K et al. introduces a novel technique for securing network image transmission. The chapter combines cryptography fundamentals with compression perception methods, proposing a hybrid cloud and half-tensor compression-aware technology. By integrating these approaches, the researchers demonstrate enhanced image encryption and decryption algorithms, achieving superior performance metrics compared to existing methods.

KEERTHIKA et al. presents an "Enhancing Energy Efficiency in Intrusion Detection Systems for Wireless Sensor Networks through Zigbee Protocol". This chapter offers a promising solution for providing effective and energy-efficient intrusion detection in ZigBee-based WSNs. The study found that applying machine learning techniques, specifically SFA, can significantly improve the energy efficiency of Zigbee protocol in Wireless Sensor Networks. Results indicate that using these techniques energy consumption is up to 95.42% and 190 μW / node, IDS prediction ratio is 98.5% and accuracy is 99.5% while maintaining network performance.

"Simulation of Routing Protocols for Jamming Attacks in Mobile Ad-Hoc Network", by Al-Na'amneh et al. focuses on these protocols' applicability for various network scenarios with attacks using the network simulator OPNET 14. 5.

IN CONCLUSION

In the ever-evolving landscape of cybersecurity, our edited reference book, *Risk Assessment and Countermeasures for Cybersecurity*, seeks to provide a comprehensive resource for practitioners, researchers, and academics alike. Throughout the chapters, our esteemed contributors have delved into various facets of cybersecurity, ranging from risk assessment methodologies to innovative countermeasures against emerging threats.

From the exploration of cybersecurity risks in online social networks to the development of novel encryption techniques for network image communication, each chapter offers valuable insights and practical solutions to address the complex challenges facing cybersecurity professionals today. By leveraging advanced technologies such as deep learning and chaos theory, our contributors have demonstrated the potential for innovation in safeguarding digital assets and infrastructure.

Moreover, our book underscores the interdisciplinary nature of cybersecurity, bringing together expertise from fields such as machine learning, cryptography, and network security. By fostering collaboration and knowledge exchange among diverse stakeholders, we aim to advance the collective understanding and capabilities in cybersecurity research and practice.

As we conclude this preface, we extend our sincere appreciation to all the authors who have contributed their expertise and insights to this volume. It is our hope that *Risk Assessment and Countermeasures for Cybersecurity* will serve as a valuable resource for years to come, inspiring further exploration and innovation in the ongoing mission to secure our digital future.

Mohammed Amin Almaiah
The University of Jordan, Amman, Jordan

Yassine Maleh
Sultan Moulay Slimane University, Morocco

Abdalwali Alkhassawneh
King Faisal University, Saudi Arabia

Section 1

Risk Assessment and Mitigation Strategies

Chapter 1
A Deep Dive Into Cybersecurity Risk Assessment and Countermeasures in Online Social Networks

Abdelhadi Zineddine
https://orcid.org/0009-0000-8188-1353
Department of Computer Sciences, Sultan Moulay Slimane University, Morocco

Yousra Belfaik
https://orcid.org/0009-0000-6270-882X
Department of Computer Sciences, Sultan Moulay Slimane University, Morocco

Yassine Sadqi
https://orcid.org/0000-0002-0772-9916
Department of Computer Sciences, Sultan Moulay Slimane University, Morocco

ABSTRACT

In the evolving realm of online social networks (OSNs), assessing cybersecurity risks and implementing effective countermeasures are crucial for practitioners. This chapter confronts this challenge, beginning with an extensive literature review that explores the range of threats, vulnerabilities, and attacks prevalent in OSNs. It differentiates between general cybersecurity risks and those unique to OSNs, with a special focus on user-side vulnerabilities. The chapter critically analyzes risk assessment and security assessment, highlighting their distinct yet interconnected roles in cybersecurity. Various risk assessment methods are evaluated for their applicability to OSNs, alongside a discussion of both technical and non-technical countermeasures for risk mitigation. Concluding with key findings and future research directions, this chapter offers a comprehensive guide for understanding and tackling the complex cybersecurity challenges in online social networks.

DOI: 10.4018/979-8-3693-2691-6.ch001

INTRODUCTION

In the digital era, online social networks (OSNs) have become integral to our daily communication, information exchange, and even identity management. However, this widespread integration of OSNs into various facets of our lives brings with it an array of cybersecurity risks that cannot be overlooked. This introduction section aims to provide a detailed overview of these risks, emphasizing the threats, vulnerabilities, and potential cyberattacks that jeopardize user data security and privacy.

OSNs are rich repositories of personal information, making them attractive targets for cybercriminals. Threats in these platforms range from identity theft and data breaches to more sophisticated forms of cyberattacks such as social engineering and phishing (Sahoo & Gupta, 2019). For instance, a common tactic employed by attackers is creating fake profiles to disseminate malware through seemingly innocuous links or messages. Additionally, vulnerabilities such as weak encryption or flawed authentication processes can expose user data to unauthorized access (Space, 2018). A notable example was the 2018 Facebook data breach, where attackers exploited vulnerabilities in the platform's code to access over 50 million accounts (Cadwalladr & Graham-Harrison, 2018).

Furthermore, the use of OSNs as identity providers (IDPs) presents a unique cybersecurity challenge. Many websites allow users to log in using their OSN credentials, offering convenience and reducing the burden of managing multiple accounts (Corre et al., 2017). However, this interconnectivity can also be a liability. If an attacker compromises a user's OSN account, they potentially gain access to a multitude of other services linked to that account. A case in point is the "Single Sign-On" feature used by many websites, which, while convenient, can create a domino effect of security vulnerabilities if the OSN account is compromised (Kontaxis et al., 2011).

In addition, it is clear that cyberattacks are no longer focused on the weaknesses of organizations, but on the vulnerabilities of users within OSNs. While companies are increasingly bolstering their cybersecurity infrastructure, individual users often remain the weakest link. For example, users may unknowingly expose sensitive information through oversharing on social media or fall prey to phishing scams cleverly disguised as genuine communications (Kwak et al., 2020). This trend was evident in the series of "spear phishing" attacks that targeted high-profile Twitter accounts in 2020, exploiting human vulnerabilities rather than system flaws (Witman & Mackelprang, 2022).

The research gap addressed in this chapter pertains to the distinct challenges associated with cybersecurity risk assessment within the realm of OSNs. The primary objective of the chapter is to bridge a deficiency in the existing literature by conducting a thorough exploration of cybersecurity risks inherent in online social networks, coupled with an assessment of various methods tailored to this environment. It underscores the significance of differentiating between general cybersecurity risks and those specific to OSNs, with a pronounced emphasis on vulnerabilities stemming from user-side factors. The chapter not only contributes to a comprehensive review of the current state of knowledge but also engages in a critical analysis of the distinct roles played by risk assessment and security assessment in the cybersecurity of OSNs. Furthermore, the research aims to scrutinize both technical and non-technical countermeasures for mitigating risks in OSNs. Ultimately, the chapter offers a holistic guide for comprehending and tackling the intricate cybersecurity challenges unique to the domain of OSNs.

The structure of the remaining chapter is organized as follows: Section 2 presents a comprehensive literature review, providing an overview of the existing research. It covers a broad spectrum of threats, vulnerabilities, attacks, and their impacts specifically associated with Online Social Networks (OSNs). In Section 3, we delve into the concept of Cybersecurity Risks, examining it from both general and

OSN-specific perspectives and highlighting various user vulnerabilities that could lead to increased cybersecurity risks. Section 4 elaborates on the critical distinction between risk assessment and security assessment, shedding light on their unique roles and methodologies within the cybersecurity domain. Section 5 focuses on risk mitigation, exploring an array of both technical and non-technical countermeasures. The final section concludes the chapter, summarizing the key findings, discussing the implications, and suggesting potential future directions for research and practice in the field of cybersecurity risk assessment in online social networks.

BACKGROUND AND KNOWLEDGE

This section is designed to provide a comprehensive overview of the cybersecurity environment specific to OSNs. We will explore the evolution of these networks, their significance in modern communication, and the various types of cyberattacks that uniquely target or exploit these platforms. This knowledge serves as a critical backdrop for the subsequent discussions on cybersecurity risks, assessments, and mitigation strategies tailored to the unique environment of OSNs.

Evolution and Significance of OSNs

In this subsection, we delve into the evolution and growing significance of Online Social Networks (OSNs) in the fabric of modern communication. We trace the journey of OSNs from their inception as platforms for personal interaction to their current status as multifaceted ecosystems integral to various aspects of daily life, including socializing, business, and politics. This exploration not only highlights the transformative impact of OSNs on global communication and public opinion but also sheds light on the immense volumes of personal and sensitive data they manage. By understanding the developmental trajectory and the pivotal role of OSNs, we lay the groundwork for comprehending the unique cybersecurity challenges they present.

- Evolution of Online Social Networks (OSNs): The inception and evolution of Online Social Networks (OSNs) mark a significant transformation in digital communication. Originating as platforms for personal interactions, OSNs have burgeoned into complex ecosystems integral for not just socializing but also for business, politics, and more. They have become pivotal in shaping public opinion, marketing strategies, and even global events. This evolution reflects in the data they generate and manage, turning them into vast repositories of personal and sensitive information (Kim et al., 2013).
- The Importance of OSNs in Modern Communication: OSNs have transcended their original purpose, becoming crucial in various aspects of daily life. They connect individuals across the globe, facilitate business operations, and have become primary sources for news and information. This centrality in communication underscores the richness of data they hold, which includes detailed user profiles, their interactions, preferences, and behaviors (Barreda et al., 2015).
- Basic Concepts of Cybersecurity: Understanding cybersecurity involves comprehending the measures taken to protect systems, networks, and data from digital attacks. It encompasses various domains, including data protection, network security, and information security. The core principles

of cybersecurity, such as confidentiality, integrity, and availability (CIA), form the foundation of understanding how data and systems are protected (Kaur et al., 2021).

- Common Cybersecurity Threats and Vulnerabilities: The digital landscape is fraught with a variety of threats such as malware, phishing, and ransomware, which pose significant risks to any digital platform. In the context of OSNs, these threats take on unique forms like account hijacking and privacy breaches (Humayun et al., 2020). This distinct environment of OSNs, characterized by vast user interactions and data exchange, presents unique vulnerabilities and challenges.
- Cybersecurity Challenges Unique to OSNs: OSNs present specific cybersecurity challenges, such as securing vast amounts of user data, ensuring privacy, and preventing unauthorized access. These platforms are not just at risk from general cybersecurity threats but also face unique challenges like social engineering tailored to their social aspects. The recent high-profile incidents in OSNs highlight the real-world implications of these cybersecurity challenges (Gupta et al., 2018).
- Regulatory and Ethical Considerations: The increasing significance of OSNs has led to heightened regulatory and ethical considerations. Data protection laws like GDPR and CCPA have been implemented to safeguard user privacy and data. Ethical considerations are paramount in managing these platforms, encompassing aspects like data ownership, user privacy, and the ethical use of data (Determann, 2019).

Types of Cyberattacks Related to OSNs

In this subsection, we focus on various cyberattacks that are particularly relevant to OSNs, highlighting their methods and impacts.

- Account Hijacking: This involves unauthorized access and control over a user's social network account. Attackers often exploit weak passwords or social engineering tactics to gain access and may use the hijacked account for spreading malware, scams, or misinformation (Thomas et al., 2014).
- Identity Theft: This refers to the malicious acquisition and use of someone's personal information, typically for financial gain or to impersonate the victim on social networks. Identity thieves may gather personal information from social media profiles to impersonate or defraud victims (Bilge et al., 2009).
- Phishing Attacks: Phishing in OSNs involves tricking users into revealing sensitive information (like passwords or credit card numbers) by masquerading as a trustworthy entity in an electronic communication, often through direct messages or posts (Gao et al., 2011).
- Social Engineering: This is the psychological manipulation of people into performing actions or divulging confidential information. In OSNs, it often involves tactics like pretexting, baiting, or tailgating, exploiting the social aspect of these platforms (Krombholz et al., 2015).
- Third-party Application: These attacks exploit vulnerabilities in third-party applications integrated with OSNs. Malicious apps might harvest user data or spread malware under the guise of legitimate services (Manikandan & Kaladevi, 2017).
- Data Breaches: Data breaches in OSNs involve unauthorized access to or disclosure of personal data. These can occur through hacking attacks, improper disposal of data, or inadequate security measures (Syed & Dhillon, 2015).

- Malware Distribution: Malware distribution in OSNs involves spreading malicious software through these platforms. Attackers may use compromised accounts or social engineering tactics to spread links to malware-infested websites or direct malware downloads (Javed, 2019).

This section provides a succinct overview of the evolution, importance, and unique cybersecurity challenges of OSNs, including specific types of cyberattacks. This background sets the stage for a detailed exploration of cybersecurity risk assessment in OSNs in the subsequent sections of the chapter.

LITERATURE REVIEW

The landscape of cybersecurity in online social networks (OSNs) is complex and continuously evolving. This literature review examines a selection of scientific research studies that contribute significantly to the understanding of threats, vulnerabilities, attacks, and the impacts these have on users and organizations within OSNs. These following works collectively offer a multifaceted perspective on cybersecurity challenges in social media and online networks.

General Cybersecurity Challenges in OSNs

The cybersecurity landscape within online social networks (OSNs) presents a complex array of challenges, ranging from data breaches to sophisticated malware attacks. This subsection collates pivotal studies that shed light on these overarching security concerns.

Several studies have shed light on the growing challenges of privacy and security in online social networks (OSNs). Jain et al. highlight the exponential rise of OSNs and the corresponding escalation of privacy and security concerns, particularly regarding the vast amount of user information stored within these platforms (Jain et al., 2021). Similarly, Zhang et al. delve into the inherent design conflicts in OSNs, where balancing social interaction with robust privacy and security measures presents a significant challenge (Zhang et al., 2010). In addition, Kayes & Iamnitchi offer a comprehensive review of solutions to these pressing issues, focusing on privacy-preserving techniques that can effectively counter common threats like Sybil attacks (Kayes & Iamnitchi, 2017).

Further, Majeed et al. address securing personal user information against privacy attacks, reviewing various solutions for protecting user data (Majeed et al., 2022). Bhattacharya et al., in their Wiley Online Library article, present a taxonomy of security attacks in OSNs, emphasizing machine learning-based defenses (Bhattacharya et al., 2023). Additional perspectives are offered by Sahoo & Gupta and Ali et al., focusing on user-centric security issues and privacy concerns like surveillance, respectively (Sahoo & Gupta, 2018) (Ali et al., 2018). Lastly, Rao et al. discuss the dynamic nature of cybersecurity challenges in OSNs, highlighting a range of evolving threats (Rao et al., 2021).

User Awareness and Human Factors in OSN Security Risks

Understanding user behavior and raising awareness are crucial in mitigating cybersecurity risks in OSNs. This subsection explores research focused on these human-centric aspects of cybersecurity.

In their study, Jain et al. highlight the impact of OSNs' popularity on security and privacy concerns. They specifically link user connectivity within these networks to potential risks, underscoring the interplay between widespread OSN usage and increased vulnerability to security breaches (Jain et al., 2021). Complementing this perspective, Fire et al. address the crucial gap in user awareness. Their research illuminates the importance of user education in bolstering OSN security, particularly against threats like identity theft (Fire et al., 2014).

Pham et al. explore the dynamics between users' information-sharing behavior and their awareness of data collection practices in OSNs. Their study sheds light on how users' decisions to share information are influenced by their understanding of data collection processes, which in turn affects their vulnerability to security risks (Pham et al., 2023).

Pollini et al. adopt a holistic approach in examining human factors in cybersecurity. Their research delves into the cognitive characteristics and motivations of end-users, analyzing how these human elements impact security within OSNs (Pollini et al., 2022). Similarly, Barati provides a comprehensive analysis of the various security and privacy threats encountered by users of social networks. The study emphasizes the critical need to understand user behavior patterns to effectively assess and address these threats (Barati, 2022).

Metalidou et al. discuss how human weaknesses can inadvertently compromise organizational security. Their focus on the human factor highlights the broader implications of individual behaviors on the security posture of organizations (Metalidou et al., 2014). In a related vein, Molok et al. draw attention to the risks associated with the inadvertent leakage of sensitive information through OSNs. They emphasize the potential consequences, such as the loss of trade secrets or personal employee details (Molok et al., 2018).

Cengiz et al. observe a worrying trend of increasing attacks that exploit both system vulnerabilities and user-induced weaknesses. This observation points to the evolving nature of cyber threats in OSNs, where user behavior plays a significant role in shaping hackers' strategies (Cengiz et al., 2022). Finally, Herath et al. present a secondary research study on recommended cybersecurity practices for social media users. Their study follows a structured methodological approach, emphasizing the user's role in dealing with cyber risks in social media usage (Herath et al., 2022).

Protective Strategies in OSN Cybersecurity

Developing effective strategies to combat cybersecurity challenges in OSNs is essential. This subsection reviews research focusing on innovative solutions and future-oriented defensive techniques.

Shinde et al. emphasize the significance of incorporating cutting-edge technologies such as blockchain in AI applications. They argue that this integration is crucial in effectively combating identity theft and data breaches in OSNs, offering a novel approach to reinforcing network security. Their research underscores the potential of blending blockchain's security features with AI's analytical capabilities to create more robust protection mechanisms in the digital landscape of social media (Shinde et al., 2021).

Nawaz et al. present a comprehensive approach to addressing the security challenges in OSNs. Their research spans a broad spectrum, covering aspects ranging from user behavior dynamics to the implementation of defensive techniques. By providing an all-encompassing overview, they highlight the multifaceted nature of cybersecurity in OSNs and the need for diverse strategies to safeguard these platforms effectively (Nawaz et al., 2023).

Further contributing to the discourse on user-centric cybersecurity strategies, Albladi & Weir delve into the specifics of countering social engineering attacks in OSNs. They advocate for targeted training and awareness programs as key tools in combating these types of attacks. Their work suggests that enhancing user awareness and education can significantly reduce the susceptibility of individuals to manipulation and deceit commonly employed in social engineering (Albladi & Weir, 2020).

Lastly, Sarker et al. explore the role of artificial intelligence (AI) in fortifying internet-connected systems, including OSNs. They highlight AI's potential in identifying and mitigating various security risks, emphasizing its growing importance in the development of advanced cybersecurity strategies. This study points towards AI's capacity to adapt and respond to the evolving landscape of cyber threats, making it an indispensable tool in the ongoing battle against digital security breaches (Sarker et al., 2021).

This structured review of literature delineates the multifaceted nature of cybersecurity in OSNs, from general challenges and user awareness to innovative protective strategies. It underscores the continuous need for research that adapts to and addresses the dynamic and complex challenges of cybersecurity in online social networks. Although existing research delves into various cybersecurity aspects of online

Table 1. Comparative analysis of main themes in existing related work and our chapter

Paper Reference	OSN Cybersecurity Risks	OSN User Vulnerabilities	Risk vs. Security Assessment	Countermeasures for OSN Risks	
				Technical	Non-Technical
(Zhang et al., 2010)	✓	✓		✓	
(Fire et al., 2014)	✓	✓		✓	✓
(Metalidou et al., 2014)		✓			✓
(Kayes & Iamnitchi, 2017)	✓	✓		✓	✓
(Sahoo & Gupta, 2018)	✓	✓			✓
(Ali et al., 2018)	✓	✓		✓	✓
(Molok et al., 2018)	✓		✓	✓	
(Albladi & Weir, 2020)		✓	✓	✓	
(Rao et al., 2021)		✓		✓	
(Jain et al., 2021)	✓	✓		✓	✓
(Shinde et al., 2021)	✓			✓	
(Sarker et al., 2021)	✓			✓	
(Pollini et al., 2022)	✓	✓	✓		✓
(Cengiz et al., 2022)	✓	✓			
(Barati, 2022)	✓	✓		✓	
(Herath et al., 2022)	✓	✓			
(Majeed et al., 2022)		✓		✓	
(Bhattacharya et al., 2023)	✓	✓		✓	
(Pham et al., 2023)		✓	✓	✓	
(Nawaz et al., 2023)	✓	✓		✓	
Our chapter	✓	✓	✓	✓	✓

social networks (OSNs), highlighting the necessity for robust security measures and user behavior understanding, it often overlooks a critical area: the effectiveness of cybersecurity risk assessment methods. This chapter aims to bridge this gap by evaluating existing risk assessment methods and their ability to mitigate threats unique to these virtual social networks. Table 1 illustrates the key differences between the focal points discussed in the preceding related work within this section and the topics presented in this chapter.

CYBERSECURITY RISKS: GENERAL VS. ONLINE SOCIAL NETWORKS

In this section, we delve into the intricate world of cybersecurity risks, drawing a comparison between the general cybersecurity landscape and the unique challenges presented by online social networks (OSNs). This comparative analysis is crucial in understanding how the risks in OSNs differ and sometimes intensify compared to those in other digital environments, necessitating tailored strategies for mitigation.

Cybersecurity Risks: A General context

The exploration of cybersecurity risks in a general context begins with understanding the wide array of threats and vulnerabilities that exist across various digital platforms and systems. This realm is vast and diverse, encompassing risks that can compromise the confidentiality, integrity, and availability (CIA) of information systems and data (Hubbard & Seiersen, 2023). Threats such as malware, including viruses, worms, and Trojan horses, represent just a facet of this landscape. They have the potential to infiltrate systems to steal or corrupt data, disrupt operations, or even hold systems hostage for ransom (Ryan, 2021). Another prevalent threat is phishing and social engineering, where deceptive tactics are employed to trick users into revealing sensitive information or clicking on malicious links. Furthermore, software vulnerabilities form a critical component of these risks, providing hackers with potential unauthorized access to systems and data. Each of these following threats, among others, poses significant challenges to maintaining a secure digital environment, requiring continuous vigilance and adaptive security measures.

- Malware: This category includes viruses, worms, and Trojan horses, which are designed to infiltrate and damage systems, steal sensitive data, or hold systems hostage (ransomware). For example, the WannaCry ransomware attack in 2017 demonstrated how quickly malware could spread globally, crippling thousands of organizations (Mohurle & Patil, 2017).
- Phishing and Social Engineering: These techniques deceive users into disclosing sensitive information or clicking malicious links, often using emails or messages that appear legitimate. The 2016 incident involving a phishing email sent to the Hillary Clinton presidential campaign is a notable example, leading to a significant data breach (McFaul & Bronte Kass, 2019).
- Software Vulnerabilities: Flaws and weaknesses in software can be exploited by hackers to gain unauthorized access. The Equifax breach of 2017, where personal data of millions was compromised, was attributed to exploiting a vulnerability in website software (Zou et al., 2018).

Cybersecurity Risks in Online Social Networks

When shifting focus to online social networks, the cybersecurity risks take on a more specific and sometimes more complex dimension. OSNs are characterized by their vast user bases and the wealth of personal data that users share, making them attractive targets for a variety of cyber threats (Atri et al., 2023). These networks face unique challenges such as account access issues, where hackers gain control of user accounts to impersonate them, spread misinformation, or access sensitive data. Data breaches in this context can have far-reaching consequences, given the personal nature of the information stored on these platforms. Social engineering attacks also take on a new form in OSNs, exploiting the social aspect of these networks to manipulate users' trust. Additionally, the propagation of malware through shared links, attachments, and embedded content is a significant risk, leveraging the interconnectedness and virality inherent in OSNs. Understanding these following specific risks is essential for developing effective strategies to protect users and maintain the integrity of these digital social spaces.

- Account access: Attackers often target user accounts to impersonate them, disseminate misinformation, or access sensitive data. The Twitter Bitcoin scam of 2020, where high-profile accounts were hacked to promote a cryptocurrency scam, illustrates this risk (Buttan, 2020).
- Data Breaches: OSNs are treasure troves of personal data, making them prime targets for breaches. This can lead to severe consequences like identity theft, financial fraud, and reputational damage (Syed & Dhillon, 2015).
- Social Engineering Attacks: The interactive nature of OSNs makes them ideal for spreading misinformation and deceptive content, exploiting users' trust (Krombholz et al., 2015). An example is the spread of fake news during political elections, manipulating public opinion.
- Malware Propagation: OSNs enable the rapid spread of malware through shared links, attachments, and embedded content, as seen in various instances where malicious links disguised as popular videos or news stories have spread malware (Chen et al., 2017).

Key OSNs User Vulnerabilities

Users of online social networks (OSNs) face a range of vulnerabilities that can expose them to a variety of cybersecurity risks. These vulnerabilities result from a combination of factors, including the inherent nature of OSNs, and user behavior. The main vulnerabilities associated with OSN users include:

- Oversharing of Personal Information: OSNs encourage users to share personal information, such as their names, addresses, birthdays, interests, and even intimate details of their lives. This wealth of personal data can be used for malicious purposes, such as identity theft, targeted advertising, and social engineering attacks (Paullet & Pinchot, 2012).
- Weak Password Practices: Many OSN users employ weak or easily guessable passwords, making their accounts susceptible to brute-force attacks and credential stuffing. Additionally, users often reuse passwords across multiple accounts, increasing the risk of compromise if one account is breached (Franchi et al., 2015).
- Clicking on Malicious Links: OSNs are rife with malicious links, often disguised as genuine links, that can lead users to phishing websites or malware-infected pages. Unintentional clicks on these links can result in data breaches, malware infections, and financial losses (Alghamdi et al., 2016).

- Lack of Awareness and Education: Many OSN users lack sufficient understanding of cybersecurity risks and best practices. This can make them more vulnerable to phishing scams, social engineering attacks, and other online threats (Fire et al., 2014).
- Trusting Third-party Apps and Extensions: Users often grant permissions to third-party apps and extensions on OSNs without fully understanding the potential risks. These apps may collect personal data, track user activity, or even inject malware into the user's environment (Cheng et al., 2013) .

Understanding these varied cybersecurity risks, both in a general context and specifically in OSNs, is vital for developing effective strategies to combat them. This section not only highlights the myriad of threats that users and organizations face in digital spaces but also underscores the unique and heightened risks present within OSNs. The subsequent sections of the chapter will delve into risk assessment methodologies and solutions tailored for these environments.

RISK ASSESSMENT VS. SECURITY ASSESSMENT: UNVEILING THE DISTINCTION

In this pivotal section, the chapter clarify the often-confused concepts of risk assessment and security assessment within the realm of cybersecurity. Understanding the nuances between these two assessments is critical for developing a comprehensive security strategy. Furthermore, the table 2 summarize these key distinctions between these two crucial concepts.

Risk Assessment

Risk assessment in cybersecurity is a focused and systematic process, aimed at identifying, analyzing, and evaluating potential risks and vulnerabilities that could impact an organization's assets, operations, or information systems. The focus here is on uncovering potential threats and the weaknesses that could be exploited, with the goal of understanding the likelihood and potential impact of these risks (Choi et al., 2004). For instance, in a risk assessment scenario, a company might evaluate the likelihood of a data breach or unauthorized access to their cloud storage services, considering factors like cloud service provider vulnerabilities, data encryption methods, and access control policies (Latif et al., 2014). The ultimate purpose of this assessment is to help organizations prioritize risks and make informed decisions on where to allocate resources for effective risk mitigation, thereby enabling a strategic approach to managing cybersecurity threats.

Security Assessment

On the other hand, security assessment encompasses a broader scope compared to risk assessment. It involves a comprehensive evaluation of an organization's existing security controls, policies, procedures, and overall security posture to ensure the confidentiality, integrity, and availability of information (Morison et al., 2004). For example, a security assessment for a company using cloud storage services would include reviewing the implemented security measures like firewalls, intrusion detection systems, and the frequency and thoroughness of security audits. It also involves assessing the adherence of employees to

Table 2. Summarizing key distinctions between risk assessment vs. security assessment

Feature	Risk Assessment	Security Assessment
Focus	***Proactive, assessing all types of risks.***	Reactive, focused on security threats and vulnerabilities.
Scope	***Broader, encompassing all business areas and assets.***	***Narrower, focused on information systems and data.***
Methodology	***Qualitative and quantitative analysis of threats, vulnerabilities, and impacts.***	***Technical testing and evaluation of security controls and systems.***
Output	***Prioritized list of risks with mitigation strategies.***	***Detailed report on security vulnerabilities and recommendations for improvement.***

security protocols and procedures. The primary purpose of a security assessment is to determine how well these security measures are implemented and whether they are effective in protecting the organization against identified and potential threats (Zineddine et al., 2024). This process includes examining the technical, physical, and administrative aspects of security, ensuring a comprehensive evaluation of the organization's security health and readiness (Szczepaniuk et al., 2020).

Risk Assessment Methods Applicability

Risk assessment methods involve systematic processes and techniques used to identify, analyze, and evaluate potential risks in various contexts (Punt et al., 2011). The applicability of these methods is crucial to ensure they are suitable and effective for the specific context or industry in question. Evaluating this applicability criteria involves meticulous consideration of the following steps:

- Context Understanding: Comprehend the specific environment or sector in which the risk assessment method will be applied. For instance, the method applicable in a healthcare setting might differ from that in a financial institution.
- Method Suitability: Assess whether the chosen method aligns with the unique characteristics of the organization or industry. This includes considering the nature of data, user behavior, and prevalent threat types.
- Resource Evaluation: Determine if the organization has the necessary resources, including technical expertise and tools, to effectively implement and sustain the chosen risk assessment method.
- Regulatory Compliance: Ensure that the method adheres to relevant legal and regulatory requirements. For example, methods used in data protection must comply with regulations like GDPR or HIPAA.
- Effectiveness Review: Regularly review and update the risk assessment methodology to adapt to evolving threats and changes in the organization's structure or technology.

By delineating the distinctions between risk assessment and security assessment, this section emphasizes the importance of both in a comprehensive cybersecurity strategy. While risk assessment is more about identifying and understanding potential risks, security assessment is about evaluating and improving existing security measures. Both are integral to a robust cybersecurity framework, and their effective implementation is key to safeguarding organizational assets and information systems.

MITIGATING CYBERSECURITY RISKS IN OSNS: SOLUTIONS AND COUNTERMEASURES

In addressing cybersecurity risks within online social networks (OSNs), it is imperative to deploy a range of countermeasures. These measures, vital for safeguarding user data, preventing cyber-attacks, maintaining platform integrity, and ensuring regulatory compliance, can be broadly categorized into technical and non-technical approaches. This chapter section presents a detailed description of these various countermeasures, highlighting their objectives and the specific threats they address, which are then summarized in Table 3.

Technical Countermeasures

Technical countermeasures form the backbone of cybersecurity defense in OSNs. These following measures involve direct interventions in the digital infrastructure, employing advanced technologies and tools to protect against cyber threats. They are designed to secure the network, systems, and data from various forms of cyberattacks, ranging from data breaches to malware dissemination. The effectiveness of these countermeasures lies in their ability to adapt and respond to evolving threats, ensuring robust defense mechanisms are in place to protect both the security and privacy of OSN users.

- Encryption Technologies: End-to-end encryption (e.g., as employed by messaging apps like WhatsApp) serves as a crucial technical countermeasure. Encrypting the data during transmission ensures that messages remain confidential, and readable only by the sender and receiver (Schillinger & Schindelhauer, 2019). This technology is particularly effective in protecting data privacy against threats like data interception and safeguarding personal and sensitive information circulating on online social networks (OSNs).
- Secure Authentication Mechanisms: Platforms like Facebook have adopted Two-factor authentication (2FA) to bolster account security. This measure adds a layer beyond traditional passwords, often requiring a code sent to the user's phone or email. It addresses the threat of unauthorized account access, a common issue in OSNs, where attackers often exploit weak or stolen passwords to gain control of user accounts (Joe & Ramakrishnan, 2017).
- Regular Software Updates and Patch Management: The implementation of automatic software updates in social media apps exemplifies this countermeasure. These updates are essential for fixing security vulnerabilities and enhancing existing security features. Regular patch management mitigates the risk posed by software vulnerabilities, which, if left unaddressed, can be exploited by cybercriminals to gain unauthorized access, disrupt functionality, or even steal sensitive data (Jain et al., 2021).
- AI-based Threat Detection Systems: Social networks like Twitter utilize machine learning algorithms to proactively detect and respond to security threats. These AI-based systems are adept at identifying patterns indicative of spam, malicious activity, or other security threats, addressing issues such as automated attacks and the distribution of malicious content (Gera & Sinha, 2022) .

Non-Technical Countermeasures

While technical solutions are crucial, non-technical countermeasures are equally important in the cybersecurity landscape of OSNs. These following measures focus on the human aspect of cybersecurity - from user behavior and awareness to policy adherence and collaborative efforts. They encompass educational programs, policy enforcement, and community-driven initiatives, all aimed at creating a more secure and aware user base and ensuring compliance with regulatory standards. Non-technical countermeasures address the social and organizational elements of cybersecurity, complementing technical strategies to form a comprehensive defense system.

- User Education and Awareness Programs: Cybersecurity awareness campaigns, like those conducted by LinkedIn, play a significant role in mitigating risks. These programs aim to educate users about common threats such as phishing scams and encourage safe online practices (Ikhalia et al., 2018). By increasing user awareness, these campaigns target social engineering attacks, which exploit user ignorance and trust.
- Community Reporting and Moderation Tools: The "Report" feature in Facebook is an excellent example of empowering users to contribute to platform security. These tools allow the community to flag inappropriate or harmful content, effectively combatting the spread of misinformation and harmful content (Edelson et al., 2020). Such features rely on user participation to maintain a secure and trustworthy online environment.
- Policy and Regulation Compliance: Adherence to data protection laws, such as the General Data Protection Regulation (GDPR), is a non-technical but essential aspect of cybersecurity. By complying with these regulations, OSNs ensure the protection of user data and privacy rights, addressing risks like privacy violations and data misuse (Voloch et al., 2023). This compliance not only safeguards user information but also reinforces the trust users place in these platforms.

Table 3. Summary of the various countermeasures, their description and the threats addressed

Countermeasure Type	Tool/Approach	Description	Threat/Attack Addressed
Technical	*End-to-End Encryption*	*Encrypt messages between sender and receiver*	*Data Interception*
	Two-Factor Authentication	*Additional security layer beyond passwords*	*Unauthorized Access*
	Software Updates	*Regular updates to fix vulnerabilities*	*Software Vulnerabilities*
	AI-based Threat Detection	*Machine learning for detecting spam/ malicious acts*	*Automated Attacks, Spam*
Non-Technical	*User Education Programs*	*Campaigns to educate users about cyber threats*	*Social Engineering*
	Community Reporting Tools	*User-enabled reporting of inappropriate content*	*Harmful Content, Misinformation*
	GDPR Compliance	*Adhering to data protection regulations*	*Privacy Violations, Data Misuse*
	Public-Private Collaboration	*Collaboration for enhanced security intelligence*	*Coordinated Cyber Attacks*

- Public-Private Collaboration for Security: Collaborations between social media companies and cybersecurity firms exemplify this countermeasure. These partnerships enhance threat intelligence and response capabilities, addressing sophisticated cyber threats like coordinated cyber-attacks and advanced persistent threats (Zrahia, 2018). Such collaborations leverage external expertise and resources, bolstering the security posture of OSNs.

This diverse array of technical and non-technical countermeasures underlines the multifaceted approach required to effectively mitigate cybersecurity risks in OSNs. While technical measures provide the necessary infrastructure and defense mechanisms, non-technical strategies cultivate an informed and vigilant user base and an environment of compliance and collaboration. Together, they form a comprehensive defense against the myriad of cybersecurity challenges faced in the dynamic world of online social networks.

CONCLUSION: KEY FINDINGS AND FUTURE DIRECTIONS

This chapter has effectively set the stage for a comprehensive exploration of cybersecurity risks, encompassing both the general digital landscape and the specific challenges within online social networks (OSNs). It underscores the increasing reliance and dependence on OSNs, paralleled by a surge in cybersecurity threats that target user data. A thorough literature review was conducted, shedding light on a broad spectrum of threats, vulnerabilities, attacks, and their impacts specifically related to OSNs. The chapter then adeptly distinguished between general cybersecurity risks and those peculiar to OSNs, spotlighting challenges such as account access issues, data breaches, social engineering attacks, and malware propagation.

Crucially, the chapter delved into the critical distinction between risk assessment and security assessment, illuminating their distinct roles and methodologies within the realm of cybersecurity. This delineation is pivotal for understanding strategic approaches to managing cybersecurity threats. The chapter also scrutinized various risk assessment methods, evaluating their relevance and efficacy in the context of OSNs. Moreover, it addressed risk mitigation by examining a range of both technical and non-technical countermeasures, highlighting their indispensable role in safeguarding user data, thwarting cyber-attacks, and upholding the integrity of OSN platforms.

The insights gleaned from this chapter bear significant implications for both practitioners and researchers in the field of cybersecurity. For practitioners, the exhaustive overview of risks and countermeasures provides a valuable guide to fortify cybersecurity strategies in OSNs. It emphasizes the importance of implementing robust technical solutions in tandem with proactive non-technical strategies, such as user education and policy compliance. For researchers, the chapter uncovers gaps in existing research on cybersecurity risk assessment in OSNs, and accentuates the nature of cybersecurity threats in these constantly evolving platforms. The in-depth analysis of risk assessment methodologies lays a solid groundwork for future scientific exploration in the cybersecurity domain.

Looking forward, the chapter identifies multiple avenues for continued research and practical application. As cyber threats persistently evolve, especially within the milieu of OSNs, ongoing research is essential to stay abreast of these changes and to develop innovative solutions. The integration of emerging technologies like blockchain and quantum computing could significantly enhance OSN cybersecurity. Similarly, the development and implementation of advanced AI and machine learning tools for real-time threat detection and response in OSNs represent a promising area of research. Additionally, studies focusing on the behavioral aspects of OSN users are crucial, as they can offer deeper insights into how user behavior influences cybersecurity risks and the effectiveness of various countermeasures. This comprehensive approach underscores the continued need for research that adapts and responds to the dynamic challenges of cybersecurity in online social networks.

REFERENCES

Albladi, S. M., & Weir, G. R. S. (2020). Sarker. *Cybersecurity*, *3*(1), 7. doi:10.1186/s42400-020-00047-5

Alghamdi, B., Watson, J., & Xu, Y. (2016). Toward detecting malicious links in online social networks through user behavior. *2016 IEEE/WIC/ACM International Conference on Web Intelligence Workshops (WIW)*, 5–8. 10.1109/WIW.2016.014

Ali, S., Islam, N., Rauf, A., Din, I. U., Guizani, M., & Rodrigues, J. J. (2018). Privacy and security issues in online social networks. *Future Internet*, *10*(12), 114. doi:10.3390/fi10120114

Atri, R., Prabhu, S., & Cherady, J. (2023). Study of cyber security threats to online social networks. *AIP Conference Proceedings*, *2736*(1), 060004. doi:10.1063/5.0171142

Barati, R. (2022). Security Threats and Dealing with Social Networks. *SN Computer Science*, *4*(1), 9. doi:10.1007/s42979-022-01434-0

Barreda, A. A., Bilgihan, A., Nusair, K., & Okumus, F. (2015). Generating brand awareness in online social networks. *Computers in Human Behavior*, *50*, 600–609. doi:10.1016/j.chb.2015.03.023

Bhattacharya, M., Roy, S., Chattopadhyay, S., Das, A. K., & Shetty, S. (2023). A comprehensive survey on online social networks security and privacy issues: Threats, machine learning-based solutions, and open challenges. *Security and Privacy*, *6*(1), e275. doi:10.1002/spy2.275

Bilge, L., Strufe, T., Balzarotti, D., & Kirda, E. (2009). All your contacts are belong to us: automated identity theft attacks on social networks. *Proceedings of the 18th International Conference on World Wide Web*, 551–560. 10.1145/1526709.1526784

Buttan, D. (2020). *Hacking the Human Brain: Impact of Cybercriminals Evoking Emotion for Financial Profit*. Utica College.

Cadwalladr, C., & Graham-Harrison, E. (2018). Revealed: 50 million Facebook profiles harvested for Cambridge Analytica in major data breach. *The Guardian, 17*(1), 22.

Cengiz, A. B., Kalem, G., & Boluk, P. S. (2022). Herath. *IEEE Access : Practical Innovations, Open Solutions*, *10*, 57674–57684. doi:10.1109/ACCESS.2022.3177652

Chen, Y., Mao, Y., Leng, S., Wei, Y., & Chiang, Y. (2017). Malware propagation analysis in message-recallable online social networks. *2017 IEEE 17th International Conference on Communication Technology (ICCT)*, 1366–1371.

Cheng, Y., Park, J., & Sandhu, R. (2013). Preserving user privacy from third-party applications in online social networks. *Proceedings of the 22nd International Conference on World Wide Web*, 723–728. 10.1145/2487788.2488032

Choi, H.-H., Cho, H.-N., & Seo, J.-W. (2004). Risk assessment methodology for underground construction projects. *Journal of Construction Engineering and Management*, *130*(2), 258–272. doi:10.1061/(ASCE)0733-9364(2004)130:2(258)

Corre, K., Barais, O., Sunyé, G., Frey, V., & Crom, J.-M. (2017). Why can't users choose their identity providers on the web? *Proceedings on Privacy Enhancing Technologies. Privacy Enhancing Technologies Symposium*, *2017*(3), 72–86. doi:10.1515/popets-2017-0029

Determann, L. (2019). Healthy Data Protection. *Michigan Technology Law Review*, *26*, 229.

Edelson, L., Lauinger, T., & McCoy, D. (2020). A security analysis of the Facebook ad library. *2020 IEEE Symposium on Security and Privacy (SP)*, 661–678. 10.1109/SP40000.2020.00084

Fire, M., Goldschmidt, R., & Elovici, Y. (2014). Online social networks: Threats and solutions. *IEEE Communications Surveys and Tutorials*, *16*(4), 2019–2036. doi:10.1109/COMST.2014.2321628

Franchi, E., Poggi, A., & Tomaiuolo, M. (2015). Information and password attacks on social networks: An argument for cryptography. *Journal of Information Technology Research*, *8*(1), 25–42. doi:10.4018/JITR.2015010103

Gao, H., Hu, J., Huang, T., Wang, J., & Chen, Y. (2011). Security Issues in Online Social Networks. *IEEE Internet Computing*, *15*(4), 56–63. doi:10.1109/MIC.2011.50

Gera, S., & Sinha, A. (2022). T-Bot: AI-based social media bot detection model for trend-centric twitter network. *Social Network Analysis and Mining*, *12*(1), 76. doi:10.1007/s13278-022-00897-6

Gupta, T., Choudhary, G., & Sharma, V. (2018). A Survey on the Security of Pervasive Online Social Networks (POSNs). *Journal of Internet Services and Information Security*, *8*(2), 48–86. doi:10.22667/JISIS.2018.05.31.048

Herath, T. B., Khanna, P., & Ahmed, M. (2022). Cybersecurity practices for social media users: A systematic literature review. *Journal of Cybersecurity and Privacy*, *2*(1), 1–18. doi:10.3390/jcp2010001

Hubbard, D. W., & Seiersen, R. (2023). *How to Measure Anything in Cybersecurity Risk*. John Wiley & Sons. doi:10.1002/9781119892335

Humayun, M., Niazi, M., Jhanjhi, N. Z., Alshayeb, M., & Mahmood, S. (2020). Cyber security threats and vulnerabilities: A systematic mapping study. *Arabian Journal for Science and Engineering*, *45*(4), 3171–3189. doi:10.1007/s13369-019-04319-2

Ikhalia, E., Serrano, A., & Arreymbi, J. (2018). Deploying social network security awareness through Mass Interpersonal Persuasion (MIP). *International Conference on Cyber Warfare and Security.*

Jain, A. K., Sahoo, S. R., & Kaubiyal, J. (2021). Online social networks security and privacy: Comprehensive review and analysis. *Complex & Intelligent Systems*, *7*(5), 2157–2177. doi:10.1007/s40747-021-00409-7

Javed, A. (2019). *Understanding malware behaviour in online social networks and predicting cyber attack* [PhD, Cardiff University]. https://orca.cardiff.ac.uk/id/eprint/131640/

Joe, M. M., & Ramakrishnan, B. (2017). Novel authentication procedures for preventing unauthorized access in social networks. *Peer-to-Peer Networking and Applications*, *10*(4), 833–843. doi:10.1007/s12083-016-0426-7

Kaur, G., Habibi Lashkari, Z., Habibi Lashkari, A., Kaur, G., Habibi Lashkari, Z. & Habibi Lashkari, A. (2021). Introduction to Cybersecurity. *Understanding Cybersecurity Management in FinTech: Challenges, Strategies, and Trends*, 17–34.

Kayes, I., & Iamnitchi, A. (2017). Privacy and security in online social networks: A survey. *Online Social Networks and Media*, *3*, 1–21. doi:10.1016/j.osnem.2017.09.001

Kim, J., Leem, C., Kim, B., & Cheon, Y. (2013). Evolution of online social networks: A conceptual framework. *Asian Social Science*, *9*(4), 208. doi:10.5539/ass.v9n4p208

Kontaxis, G., Polychronakis, M., & Markatos, E. P. (2011). SudoWeb: Minimizing information disclosure to third parties in single sign-on platforms. *Information Security: 14th International Conference, ISC 2011, Xi'an, China, October 26-29, 2011 Proceedings*, *14*, 197–212.

Krombholz, K., Hobel, H., Huber, M., & Weippl, E. (2015). Advanced social engineering attacks. *Journal of Information Security and Applications*, *22*, 113–122. doi:10.1016/j.jisa.2014.09.005

Kwak, Y., Lee, S., Damiano, A., & Vishwanath, A. (2020). Why do users not report spear phishing emails? *Telematics and Informatics*, *48*, 101343. doi:10.1016/j.tele.2020.101343

Latif, R., Abbas, H., Assar, S., & Ali, Q. (2014). Cloud computing risk assessment: A systematic literature review. *Future Information Technology: FutureTech, 2013*, 285–295. doi:10.1007/978-3-642-40861-8_42

Majeed, A., Khan, S., & Hwang, S. O. (2022). A comprehensive analysis of privacy-preserving solutions developed for online social networks. *Electronics (Basel)*, *11*(13), 1931. doi:10.3390/electronics11131931

Manikandan, S. A., & Kaladevi, A. C. (2017). *Privacy Protection for Online Social Network Through Third Party Application Programming Interface* (SSRN Scholarly Paper No. 3125922). doi:10.2139/ssrn.3125922

McFaul, M. & Bronte, K. (2019). Understanding Putin's Intentions and Actions in the 2016 U.S. Presidential Election. *Securing American Elections*, 1.

Metalidou, E., Marinagi, C., Trivellas, P., Eberhagen, N., Skourlas, C., & Giannakopoulos, G. (2014). The human factor of information security: Unintentional damage perspective. *Procedia: Social and Behavioral Sciences*, *147*, 424–428. doi:10.1016/j.sbspro.2014.07.133

Mohurle, S., & Patil, M. (2017). A brief study of Wannacry Threat: Ransomware Attack 2017. *International Journal of Advanced Research in Computer Science*, *8*(5), 1938–1940. doi:10.26483/ijarcs.v8i5.4021

Molok, N. N. A., Ahmad, A., & Chang, S. (2018). A case analysis of securing organisations against information leakage through online social networking. *International Journal of Information Management*, *43*, 351–356. doi:10.1016/j.ijinfomgt.2018.08.013

Morison, K., Wang, L., & Kundur, P. (2004). Power system security assessment. *IEEE Power & Energy Magazine*, *2*(5), 30–39. doi:10.1109/MPAE.2004.1338120

Nawaz, N. A., Ishaq, K., Farooq, U., Khalil, A., Rasheed, S., Abid, A., & Rosdi, F. (2023). A comprehensive review of security threats and solutions for the online social networks industry. *PeerJ. Computer Science*, *9*, e1143. doi:10.7717/peerj-cs.1143 PMID:37346522

Paullet, K., & Pinchot, J. (2012). Cybercrime: the unintentional effects of oversharing information on Facebook. *Proceedings of the Conference on Information Systems Applied Research ISSN, 2167*, 1508.

Pham, T. H., Phan, T.-A., Trinh, P.-A., Mai, X. B. & Le, Q.-C. (2023). Information security risks and sharing behavior on OSN: the impact of data collection awareness. *Journal of Information, Communication and Ethics in Society*.

Pollini, A., Callari, T. C., Tedeschi, A., Ruscio, D., Save, L., Chiarugi, F., & Guerri, D. (2022). Leveraging human factors in cybersecurity: An integrated methodological approach. *Cognition Technology and Work*, *24*(2), 371–390. doi:10.1007/s10111-021-00683-y PMID:34149309

Punt, A., Schiffelers, M.-J. W., Horbach, G. J., van de Sandt, J. J., Groothuis, G. M., Rietjens, I. M., & Blaauboer, B. J. (2011). Evaluation of research activities and research needs to increase the impact and applicability of alternative testing strategies in risk assessment practice. *Regulatory Toxicology and Pharmacology*, *61*(1), 105–114. doi:10.1016/j.yrtph.2011.06.007 PMID:21782875

Rao, S., Verma, A. K., & Bhatia, T. (2021). Evolving cyber threats, combating techniques, and open issues in online social networks. In *Handbook of research on cyber crime and information privacy* (pp. 219–235). IGI Global.

Ryan, M. (2021). *Ransomware Revolution: The Rise of a Prodigious Cyber Threat* (Vol. 85). Springer International Publishing. doi:10.1007/978-3-030-66583-8

Sahoo, S. R. & Gupta, B. B. (2018). Security issues and challenges in online social networks (OSNs) based on user perspective. *Computer and Cyber Security*, 591–606.

Sahoo, S. R., & Gupta, B. B. (2019). Classification of various attacks and their defence mechanism in online social networks: A survey. *Enterprise Information Systems*, *13*(6), 832–864. doi:10.1080/17517575.2019.1605542

Sarker, I. H., Furhad, M. H., & Nowrozy, R. (2021). Ai-driven cybersecurity: An overview, security intelligence modeling and research directions. *SN Computer Science*, *2*(3), 1–18. doi:10.1007/s42979-021-00557-0

Schillinger, F., & Schindelhauer, C. (2019). End-to-end encryption schemes for online social networks. *Security, Privacy, and Anonymity in Computation, Communication, and Storage: 12th International Conference, SpaCCS 2019, Atlanta, GA, USA, July 14–17, 2019 Proceedings*, *12*, 133–146.

Shinde, R., Patil, S., Kotecha, K., & Ruikar, K. (2021). Blockchain for securing ai applications and open innovations. *Journal of Open Innovation*, *7*(3), 189. doi:10.3390/joitmc7030189

Space, M. (2018). The Dark Side of Social Media: A Reality Becoming More Contemporary by the Day. *Asian Social Science*, *14*(1).

Syed, R. & Dhillon, G. (2015). *Dynamics of Data Breaches in Online Social Networks: Understanding Threats to Organizational Information Security Reputation*. Academic Press.

Szczepaniuk, E. K., Szczepaniuk, H., Rokicki, T., & Klepacki, B. (2020). Information security assessment in public administration. *Computers & Security*, *90*, 101709. doi:10.1016/j.cose.2019.101709

Thomas, K., Li, F., Grier, C., & Paxson, V. (2014). Consequences of Connectivity: Characterizing Account Hijacking on Twitter. *Proceedings of the 2014 ACM SIGSAC Conference on Computer and Communications Security*, 489–500. 10.1145/2660267.2660282

Voloch, N., Gal-Oz, N. & Gudes, E. (2023). *A Privacy Providing Context-based Trust Model for OSN and its Relation to GDPR*. Academic Press.

Witman, P. D. & Mackelprang, S. (2022). The 2020 Twitter Hack--So Many Lessons to Be Learned. *Journal of Cybersecurity Education, Research and Practice, 2021*(2).

Zhang, C., Sun, J., Zhu, X., & Fang, Y. (2010). Privacy and security for online social networks: Challenges and opportunities. *IEEE Network*, *24*(4), 13–18. doi:10.1109/MNET.2010.5510913

Zineddine, A., Chakir, O., Sadqi, Y., Maleh, Y., Gaba, G. S., Gurtov, A., & Dev, K. (2024). A systematic review of cybersecurity assessment methods for HTTPS. *Computers & Electrical Engineering*, *115*, 109137. doi:10.1016/j.compeleceng.2024.109137

Zou, Y., Mhaidli, A. H., McCall, A., & Schaub, F. (2018). "I've Got Nothing to Lose": Consumers' Risk Perceptions and Protective Actions after the Equifax Data Breach. *Fourteenth Symposium on Usable Privacy and Security (SOUPS 2018)*, 197–216.

Zrahia, A. (2018). Threat intelligence sharing between cybersecurity vendors: Network, dyadic, and agent views. *Journal of Cybersecurity*, *4*(1), tyy008. doi:10.1093/cybsec/tyy008

Chapter 2
Identification of Advancing Persistent Risks: Expanding the MICTIC Model

Virendra Kumar Yadav
Swiss School of Business and Management, Switzerland

Shelendra Pal
Teerthanker Mahaveer University, India

Raghavendra R.
https://orcid.org/0000-0003-3538-2339
Jain University, India

Aishwary Awasthi
Sanskriti University, India

Laxmi Bewoor
Vishwakarma Institute of Information Technology, India

Adapa Gopi
Koneru Lakshmaiah Education Foundation, India

Sabyasachi Pramanik
https://orcid.org/0000-0002-9431-8751
Haldia Institute of Technology, India

ABSTRACT

This study is placed within the framework of cybersecurity, particularly with regard to the identification of advanced persistent threats (APT). The research that resulted in this publication examines the MICTIC framework, confirming its validity and suggesting an expansion to make assigning APTs easier. The authors outline the rationale behind this approach and provide evidence for it in this study. Additionally, the MICTIC is presented layer by layer, and the expanded version is put to the test by having around 50 academics and researchers from universities complete a survey. They choose to do it in addition to the extension request since the MICTIC hasn't been verified on its own. Attribution is crucial because it identifies the person who launched an APT-style assault or encouraged one. However, the very existence of advanced attribution systems may serve as a warning against such assaults in the future.

DOI: 10.4018/979-8-3693-2691-6.ch002

1. INTRODUCTION

Cyber adversaries have evolved from traditional cyberthreats to more sophisticated, intricate, focused, and well-planned assaults. These actors began breaking into the networks of big corporations and classified organizations by using evasive cyber methods and Advanced Persistent Threat (APT) vectors. Attacks have become more sophisticated in recent times, displaying traits like "big target" and "long term". These persistent attacks are commonly known as Advanced Persistent Threats (APT) and are occasionally funded by nation-state governments. An APT is not just a sophisticated attack; it is also a combination of well-known and highly skilled techniques used to accomplish a particular and valuable goal. As of right now, no technology can guarantee that an APT assault would be prevented; worse, by the time the attack is discovered, it is already too late. While new technologies like virtualization and cloud computing are very beneficial to computer networks, they also pose a significant challenge to classic and non-traditional cybersecurity measures like APT security. It is difficult to defend against APT attacks; strategies that integrate disparate technologies into one cohesive whole are needed. The Attribution of the APTs, or figuring out who sponsored and requested the APT, is even more difficult. As stated in the research work's Introduction, it is a complicated combination of operations, many of which are non-technological, whose favorable outcomes are always difficult to achieve. Unlike traditional worms or viruses, an APT typically consists of stealthy, targeted attacks that are information-or data-focused. Since it always modifies its tactics before and during attacks, uses users as an entry point, and hides its tracks well, it defies all the rules that conventional attackers follow. As a result, many conventional security measures fail to contain this threat. This paper's goal is to offer guidance on how to implement appropriate security in the Attribution segment of APT, rather than to debate a definition. By including two additional layers, the proposed MICTI Framework with extension seeks to facilitate the APT Attribution. This Framework is unique in that it combines technological and non-technological systems to accomplish its objectives. Therefore, the goal of this extension is to be scientifically developed in order to provide a more thorough solution for the APT Attribution step. Therefore, the main goals of this study and publication are to validate the MICTIC Framework technically and scientifically and to help accomplish more clear APT attribution by adding two additional levels to the Framework. The structure of this article is as follows: topic number two discusses the research background, including the issue of APT, the literature review, and the discussion of the problem under analysis; topic number three explains the research methodology; topic number four directly refers to the Framework Extension proposal, breaking it down layer by layer; topic number five discusses the validation of the Framework and results are analyzed; and finally, the conclusion.

2. LITERATURE REVIEW

The work and methodology of Barbara Kitchenham were followed in conducting the systematic review of the literature.

The following were identified as research issues that the literature review was to address, and it is these questions that this systematic review aims to address:

- Q1: What distinguishes an APT from a traditional cybersecurity attack?
- Q2: Exists a strategy to fight against APT?

Table 1. APT attacks and conventional threats

Feature	APT Attacks	Typical Malware Attacks
Definition	An APT is a targeted, sophisticated and very organized attack. (e.g., Stuxnet)	Malware is a malicious program used for attacking and disabling a system (e.g., ransomware)
Attack	Organized crime and government players groups	A cracker (a hacker in illegal activities)
Target	Diplomatic organizations, the information technology industry, and other sectors	Any personal or business computer
Purpose	Filter sensitive data or harm a specific target	Personal acknowledgment
Attack Lifecycle	Keeps possible persistence using different mechanisms	Ends when detected by the security system (e.g., anti-virus software)

- Q3: Is there a role for Advanced Persistent Security (APS) in thwarting Advanced Persistent Threats?
- Q4: How does the APT Assignment fit into the MICTIC Framework? Is there room for improvement?

It was discovered that the following search term might be utilized in search engines:

("Attribution" OR "APT") AND ("MICTIC" OR "APT" OR "Attribution") AND ("Advanced Persistent Threat" OR "Cybersecurity" OR "Cyber Security" OR "Internet Security") The databases that were searched were the following ones: The EBSCO website (https://www.ebsco.com); IEEE XPLORE (https://ieeexplore.ieee.org); IEEE XPLORE EXTENDED DIV (https://ieeexplore.ieee.org/), the search string was split in this database specifically for this query. Science@Direct (http://www.sciencedirect.com); Scopus (http://www.scopus.com)

it was discovered during protocol implementation that the topic of advanced persistent threat attribution is not well covered in peer-reviewed literature. As stated in the beginning, the development of this study was primarily motivated by two of the eight publications that were located explicitly on the APT Attribution. For this reason, it is crucial that the current effort use texts categorized as "gray literature." However, a selection and quality attribution procedure was utilized to ensure the authenticity of the papers used. In this study, we used the Vahid Garousi et al. approach for the usage of gray literature.

Three levels may be used to indicate the quality and ensuing credibility of gray literature, according to a research by Garousi. Each of these "grey" layers stands for a different degree of credibility. Layer one represents the highest degree of trust, while Layer Three represents the lowest amount of credibility. This terminological idea may be illustrated as follows:

a) Tier 1 (High Credibility): Government reports, white papers, books, and periodicals.
b) Tier 2 (Moderate Credibility): New papers, presentations, videos, annual reports, etc.
c) Low Credibility Tier 3: Emails, Tweets, blogs, etc.

Table 1 provides a clear summary of the distinctions between APT attacks and traditional threats.

According to C. Jiageng, an APT is someone who possesses a high level of sophistication and specialization in their potential resources. This allows them to take advantage of opportunities for success through a variety of attack possibilities, such as information infrastructure, data mining, organization, or reserving these possibilities for future attacks. This definition of APT is provided by the National Institute of Standards and Technology. According to Ussath, there has been a notable surge in the quantity of APT campaigns that have been identified and made public. In order to compromise their targets, the majority of these operations use complex strategies, techniques, and processes. APT operations usually have the primary objective of exfiltrating sensitive information (Bodeau, D.J. 2018) or intellectual property. Most security systems are unable to identify or stop these kinds of assaults because of their complexity.

As stated by L. Advanced Persistent risks (APT) are a class of new risks to cyber-physical systems that have specific characteristics, according to Huang. APTs have defined targets and adequate knowledge of system design, valuable assets, and even protection methods, in contrast to lone opportunistic attackers. Attackers are able to modify their approach and render intrusion detection systems, firewalls, and encryption inoperable. APTs might pose as reputable users who have been using the victim's system for a long time, in contrast to attackers who delete data from computers. Researchers and security professionals have suggested the existence of APT models, such the NSA/CSS cyber threat technical framework, Lockheed-Martin's Cyber Kill Chain, and MITRE's ATT&CK, which break down the infiltration process into a series of steps. In order to locate important targets, a threat actor gathers insider or open source information during the reconnaissance phase. Once the attacker has a private key, he gains ground. From there, he advances in privileges, spreads laterally across the cyber network, and ultimately gains access to confidential data or does physical harm. A physical system's static autonomous protection is unable to thwart cyber network intrusions. The idea of defensive in Depth (DiD), or multi-stage defensive strategies spanning layers, is a product of APT's multi-phase characteristic. At every level of APT, a system defender has to implement defensive countermeasures and take into account the interdependencies and linkages among these layers on a whole Additionally, this author claims that since APT is sneaky and cunning, early detection of APT—that is, before attackers reach the final stage—is still an unresolved issue despite being effective—that is, with a low percentage of false alarms and missed detections. Attackers have to go through many stages of undetected assaults in order to accomplish their goals. In order to reach the target system and conduct out their illegal activities, these several procedures include setting up backup points, scanning the internal network, and moving laterally inside the network from one system to another. Typically, these phases include breaking into a network system, then increasing privileges to get access to the victim system if necessary, breaking into sensitive systems, and sending data to the attackers' command and control center via the Internet. Once the assault is over, the attackers have two options: they may remain and continue their malicious attacks on other network systems, or they can leave the system once it has been cleaned up, depending on the funding source's criteria. The assaults are conducted using many phases and models in order to achieve success. Attack techniques may vary and include the use of many vectors, such as digital and physical, complicating the work of any detection system that may be in place. Criminal investigations are often used to look into the perpetrators of conventional crimes. Attribution is often saved for APT (Chen, P. 2014) monitoring, or cyber espionage. For underdeveloped and rising nations, investing a few million dollars in the development of APT tools may provide greater results than protracted and costly research programs. Technical information theft might significantly advance a country's development goals. Given this chance, it is not unexpected that a number of APT groups have been deployed to North Korea, China, India, Pakistan, Iran, and security corporations. The prohibitions against implanting devices to destroy vital infrastructure, such as electricity and telecommunications networks, during peacetime may and could be drastically reduced by plausible denial capability. These statically positioned implants have the potential to be utilized against an opponent in a confrontation as a means of coercion or perhaps serious injury. Thus, a major obstacle is the capacity to designate a state, and prior to that, the capacity to identify implants prior to their use for sabotage. For this reason, attribution is crucial. APT would be a low-risk method in the absence of attribution.

The following are the responses we can currently provide to the research questions.

Q1: What distinguishes an APT from a traditional cybersecurity attack? An impartial analysis of the material reviewed leads to the conclusion that there is a significant distinction between an APT and a traditional cybersecurity assault (Jeun, I et al. 2014).

Q2: Is there a way to fight against APT? Based on the reviewed literature, it is determined that identifying an APT at the outset of an attack is very challenging for a security system since APTs employ tools designed specifically for this purpose rather than pre-known signatures.

Q3: How significant is an APS for the defense against an APT? A well-implemented APS may be beneficial for the prevention of APT since it does behavior analysis rather than just signature analysis, despite the paucity of research on the subject.

Q4: How does the APT Assignment relate to the MICTIC Framework? Is there room for improvement?

There is significantly less literature accessible in regards to APT Assignment. The body of research on this subject is rather thin. Nevertheless, the available data suggests that the MICTIC Framework is among the few approaches that may help with the Assignment. The Framework can be made better by include more levels. All things considered, we can infer from the RSL that APTs are now the most sophisticated cyberthreat and are very challenging to identify. This assault is not like the conventional attacks at all. APT deliberately creates attacks using methods and tools. There is no publicly available, scientifically verified framework for the allocation of APT.

It supports the production of a framework, allowing for the creation of an extension from the MICTIC Framework and moving on to its scientific validation after that artifact has been created.

3. METHODOLOGY

Design Science Research (DSR) is the scientific research approach used. The DSR methodology, primarily in the epistemological aspect and the framework derived from the work "The Science of the Artificial" by Herbert Simon, with the adaptations and proposals of Ken Peffers, is where we find the appropriate foundations for the development of the artifacts of this research as the ideal means to produce scientific knowledge. According to Peffers, an artifact need not only be a physical object; it can also be something created abstractly, such as artificiality; in other words, abstractions can also be artifacts. In this case, the artifact that will be created during the research and using the scientific method is primarily a framework, or a conceptual roadmap that will support and direct the goals of the study. K. proposed the Design Science Research Methodology (DSRM) approach. The process will be as follows: (1) issue description; (2) literature study; (3) presentation of potential solutions; (4) development; (5) assessment; (6) best solution choice; (7) reflection and learning; and (8) presentation of outcomes, in accordance with Pefferset al. We shall constantly keep K's model in mind while we conduct our study. In the context of this paper, DSR commits to two main goals: first, solving a practical problem in a high-specificity context through an artifact; second, producing new scientific knowledge. The DSR will consist of two related research cycles: the "Design Cycle" (Quintero-Bonill et al. 2020), which focuses on designing the artifact to solve the main goal (the MICTIC Framework with extension); the "Knowledge Cycle", on the other hand, focuses on elaborating conjectural theories related to the human (significantly important in the primary purpose of our study) and organizational aspects.

Figure 1. The design science research methodology (DSRM)

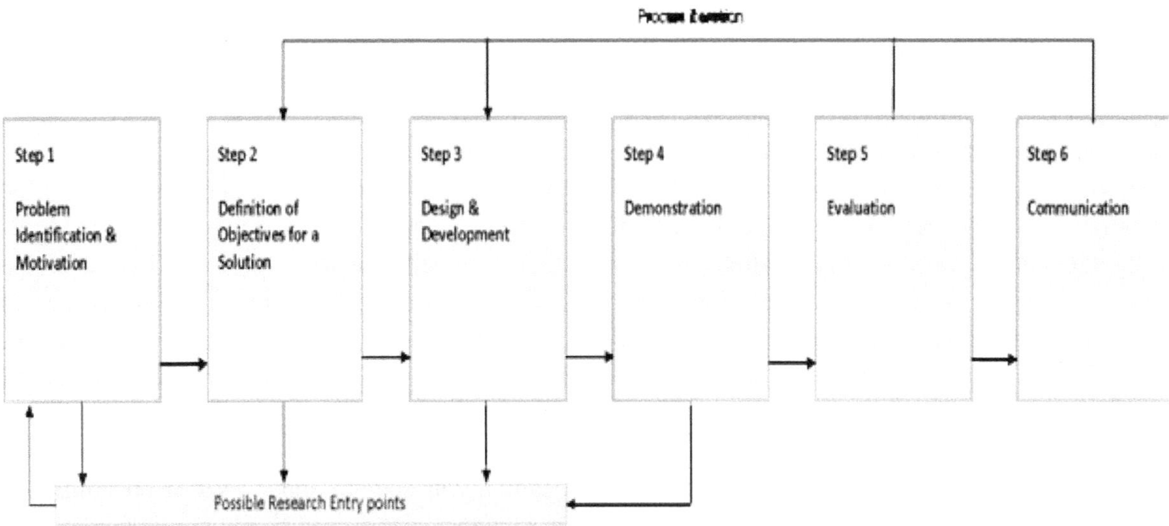

A proposed global model will incorporate the MICTIC framework with an extension, which assigns an APT. The MICTIC Framework was previously mentioned by T. Steffens, but it has not been scientifically validated. This work develops new layers and validates them scientifically. This will enable the attribution engine, or simply put, attribution needs to be taken into consideration to work better. In this case, attribution is directly related to the first layer of the aforementioned framework extension, which is the analysis of the general behavior of a sample of a system.

The second layer of the Framework extension—which includes everything pertaining to social engineering—will be created in the background. An a priori vector that is undeniably difficult and demands the most objective configuration conceivable, along with the building of links and correlations between actions and artifacts in a system where many participants may already be taken into account and where an APT event is anticipated to transpire.

Regarding the second section of the framework extension work, many situations and components are taken into consideration. The examination of all the components engaged in a process connected to an APT, rather than just the Attribution, is necessary to address the problem of social engineering. The development of the two MICTIC Framework levels in abstract terms, where there is a direct and dynamic interaction between the study objects and the actual world, is referred to as the qualitative element. The interpretation of phenomena and the attribution of meaning are fundamental to the qualitative research process, and this also holds true for the conceptualization of the whole APT attribution process. The proposed data analysis will be mostly inductive. On the other hand, these two artifacts will be inserted in a larger model whose goal is the defense and mitigation against APT. The goal is to conceptually develop two more layers at the level of one of the most well-known frameworks for obtaining APT attribution based on the existing literature. Once the model has been conceptualized and contextualized inside an anti-APT framework utilizing Attribution, it will proceed to a phase of qualitative study. A poll, to be completed anonymously by fifty experts, will be used to verify the plan.

In the context of cybersecurity and APTs, attribution is a highly specific situation. Its examination encompasses more than just technology. This is because it makes use of other non-technological systems such as: the analysis of facts (data related to the event, such as the time it took place, code syntax, i.e. the way the code is written, hypothetical motivations, social context of the target, etc.); social engineering (vulnerabilities caused by humans, both inside and outside, behavior analysis, obtaining privileged information about users from third parties, level of security culture on the part of users, relationship of users with other entities and companies, etc.); espionage (it may be necessary to use espionage methods to obtain data about the attackers, i.e. involve intelligence agencies to get facts and data confirmations); specific reasoning in relation to facts (correlation of data and cross-referencing of data, such as possible geo-location of the origin of attacks, similarity of the attack with other attacks, comparison of the tools used in the attack with other tools already used, checking whether there are attacks that have used the same tools, etc.) . As a consequence, adopting a particularly complicated combination of systems leads to Attribution. As a result, it has to be handled in a precise and thorough manner. The accurate attribution of an APT may be possible if all analytic methods are combined. The human mind is capable of hijacking logic all the time. It is presumed that someone is outside the home and rings the doorbell if we hear the doorbell ring (the observation) (explanation). The other theory that a switch or other component malfunctioned is tacitly ignored. More significantly, you operate under a set of presumptions and premises that you most likely aren't even aware of. One theory that may be put out is that animals never ring the doorbell; only people do. Another is that this is a deliberate action rather than an accident. The following explanation is significantly impacted by these presumptions: I want to talk to someone. Remember that finding a probable answer would often be impossible in the absence of premises. Since adductive reasoning depends on the premises, they have to be true! Despite the fact that a number of security firms, governmental bodies, and non-governmental groups provide attribution services, there is currently no published framework outlining the precise technical steps involved in attribution. Companies and agencies may already have internal procedures in place, even if they haven't made them public. Only the general technical method to accomplish these objectives is addressed in Thomas Rid and Ben Buchanan's Q model, which is largely focused on political considerations and whether the results of the allocation are to be revealed.

Our goal is not to provide a technological attribution system that is accepted by everybody. However, a framework aids in defining a common thread that preserves the potential of attribution for the purposes of this article. The MICTIC framework and its expansion are presented for this reason. We want to do a scientific verification and validation of the MICTIC framework, since it has never been published in a scientific publication before, as part of this project. Even when it comes to published publications on the topic, we could only locate one by Brandão, a peer-reviewed piece stressing the significance of this framework and outlining the potential benefit of expanding it.

This concept is predicated on the broad notion that sabotage and cyberespionage (Mauw, S. et al. 2005) are made up of several discrete elements. These are the resources, actions, and artifacts of an APT group, not phasing as in the cyber chain. The component names—Malware, Infrastructure, Control Servers, Telemetry, Intelligence, and Cui bono—combine to form the acronym MICTIC. It may be thought of as a more condensed version of the Diamond model, modified to better fit the specialized areas of knowledge held by Infosec analysts, while still adhering to the theory of work division within APT groups. Every component of MICTIC identifies a kind or source of important data that needs to be given credit. This often translates into tasks that an APT group's members or its sub-teams might be given.

On the attacker's end, this is the responsibility of the developers; on the information security side, this is the work of the malware analysts and inversion engineers.

Table 2. Extended framework MICTIC

	Aspect	Example
M	**Malware**	**Timestamps, Language Settings, Chains**
I	Infrastructure	WHOIS data links to private websites
C	Control Server	hard disk logs or source code
T	Telemetry	source IPs, working hours, and malware generation
I	Intelligence	intercepted communication
C	Cui bono	Geopolitical analysis of strategic motivation
A	Social Acceptance	Through incentives
C	International Cooperation	Sharing of information on APT identification

The infrastructure consists of renting and running servers that are used to download malicious code and exfiltrate data. It's said that many APT groups have committed members who maintain the infrastructure. When it comes to analysis, this is reflected by researchers who use publicly available services to track and monitor C&Cs. The control server aspect consists of the individual servers and the artifacts contained within. These are the main tools that the operators use when conducting real cyberespionage operations. Security companies can analyze telemetry, which is data on the (primarily manual) actions of operators within a target network. The 'intelligence' component includes additional sources that are accessible to government agencies. Last but not least, the cui bono aspect describes the task that is requested by the group state sponsor, which is typically a non-technical department. Within the INFOSEC community, this is addressed by the geopolitical analysis, which posits that the nation's strategic objectives coincide with the alleged attack activity. These elements are embodied in the following topics (though not necessarily in that order), and they define and characterize our Framework for attribution by outlining the evidence that can be found in each. It should be noted that these elements are involved in every stage of attribution that was previously discussed. The extended MICTIC framework can be used to make sure that all aspects of a cyber activity are covered and are also useful for defining work packages for a team of analysts. The stages structure the process of attribution regarding the order of analysis steps. For example, during phase 1 data collection, reverse engineers can concentrate on the malware component. Policy analysts can concentrate on the cui bono aspect while liaison officers utilize law enforcement to seize control servers. The process of attribution ought to encompass the maximum number of MICTIC extended aspects. The attribution hypothesis is supported with greater confidence the more sources of evidence there are, or the more evidence that has been demonstrated. The aspects are parallel rather than in any temporal or causal order. They call for distinct abilities and materials. As a result, various APT group sub-teams may even operate them. To define the monolithic or self-restraint nature of an intrusion set or APT group (as defined technically), a framework is a useful tool in this context.

4. MICTIC EXTENSIONS

Using incentives to promote social acceptance Actors who are rational respond to incentives. There is no incentive system in place on today's Internet to promote positive attribution practices and discourage negative ones. Methods to pinpoint the individuals accountable for the malevolent behavior both during and after the act are examples of positive forms of attribution. Erroneous attribution involves identifying the parties involved in interactions that are not malicious. There are very few incentives on the Internet today to deter crime and malicious behavior because the risks of being caught and given credit are low, while the rewards for malicious behavior are high. Users are not incentivized to accept attribution as a prerequisite for altering the reward system to reward good deeds.

There are very few incentives on the Internet today to deter crime and malicious behavior because the risks of being caught and receiving an assignment are low, while the rewards for malicious behavior are high. Additionally, there are no incentives for users to accept attribution, which is required to change the reward structure to reward good deeds. The average user does not understand the value of attribution. The majority of people are informed that the Internet is all about non-attribution, or anonymity, privacy, and repudiation. This ubiquitous notion is undoubtedly the secret to both malicious activity and the unrestricted flow of ideas. In order to increase value for the typical user and foster growth in individual, commercial, and governmental uses, and attribution can be used as a tool to create both positive and negative incentives. People need to have faith in the ability to identify, attribute, and prosecute instances of fraud and theft, as well as find value in dependable financial and business transactions.

- To manage the risk associated with malicious activities on the Internet that disrupt commercial interests, businesses need to implement a significant amount of policies, legal measures, and technical methods. This would suggest the presence of reasonably developed risk models, which would enable businesses to more effectively manage risk and, as a result, accomplish attribution with greater ease. • For both routine and emergency operations, governments are relying more and more on information technology (IT) and the Internet (Brandao, P.R et al. 2021). The core of many governments' internal communications, financial transactions, policy announcements, public relations, and emergency operations is provided by Internet technologies. They should also be highly interested in influencing employees' perspectives on the need to pay close attention to system anomalies that might be signs of cybercrime and to report these incidents right away, as this would help with attribution.

The importance of the world's information infrastructure makes it necessary to create incentives for stakeholders to use value-added techniques. More importantly, we felt that in order to achieve widespread acceptance and understanding, it was imperative that we begin sharing the importance of attribution.

Determining a set of online activities where something valuable to the user is at risk is the first step towards developing positive incentives for Internet users to take part in promoting and attributing, and eventually demanding, attribution of online actions. Online banking, online tax preparation, online health services, and the management of personal data are a few examples of these kinds of activities. We'll use online banking as an example to show one potential strategy. It is possible to create an online logical overlay that facilitates assignment amongst a group of online bank clients. That is to say, each user who chooses to participate in the attribution overlay bears full responsibility for all noteworthy actions taken by that user. Users now have a greater sense of accountability for their online behavior as a result. A system that allows online actions to be linked to a legitimate user will be valuable to well-intentioned users for applications where transaction accuracy is required. However, by supplying proof that the action was carried out outside of the community of members, the attribution override can facilitate an investigation and shield the user from fraudulent transactions, even though malicious actions carried out by a non-member may not always be linked to the perpetrator. Furthermore, if a user within the assignment overlay retracts an assigned action, the computer belonging to that user can be removed from the assignment overlay and examined for potential security breaches. The attribution overlay offers users protection of computers inside the attribution overlay, enhanced transactional accuracy, and defense against external threats on the Internet.

While not completely impervious to exploitation, the idea of overlapping attribution is a positive step in the right direction. The implementation will inevitably bring unexpected complexity and vulnerability, as is typically the case with security services, necessitating ongoing improvement. An assignment group administration procedure that grants each user a root of trust (RoT) is the foundation for one possible implementation of an assignment override.

4.1 Aspect of MICTIC Extension: International Cooperation

More technical cooperation is required than ever before, going well beyond current in-principle agreements, as a result of the proliferation of cyberattacks that cross multiple jurisdictions and the increasing demand for quick and precise attribution capabilities. While this kind of collaboration may still be in its early stages of CERT (Computer Emergency Response Teams) system development, it would be extremely helpful for cybersecurity overall even if it only directly benefits enhanced attribution. This capacity for multi-stakeholder technical research, engineering, and consulting would close some significant gaps by:

- Investigation and suggestion of optimal attribution methods;
- Continually bolstering a multilateral allocation capacity;
- Offering ongoing education and training to enable teams worldwide to collaborate on investigations and incident response;
- Offering recommendations for standardization and protocol enhancement in order to satisfy member nation requests for the tracking of attackers to international engineering organizations (like the IETF);
- collaborating with those creating laws and policies against cybercrime to ensure that technical and non-technical approaches are complimentary and support one another;
- Assist in ensuring that the technologies and attribution infrastructures used by cooperating entities are compatible;
- Assessing the results of the collaboration that law enforcement and technical bodies have already put into place in order to offer suggestions for ongoing development.
- Information exchange and collaboration on the following would ideally be part of such cooperation:
- Details about vulnerabilities;
- Information about incidents;
- New attribution and tracking methodologies and techniques, including software and hardware tools;
- Optimal Procedures
- Knowledge of current hacking tactics and capabilities (including ways to thwart attempts to establish attribution).

Additional desirable characteristics of a system for technical cooperation are:

Figure 2. Validating with the survey

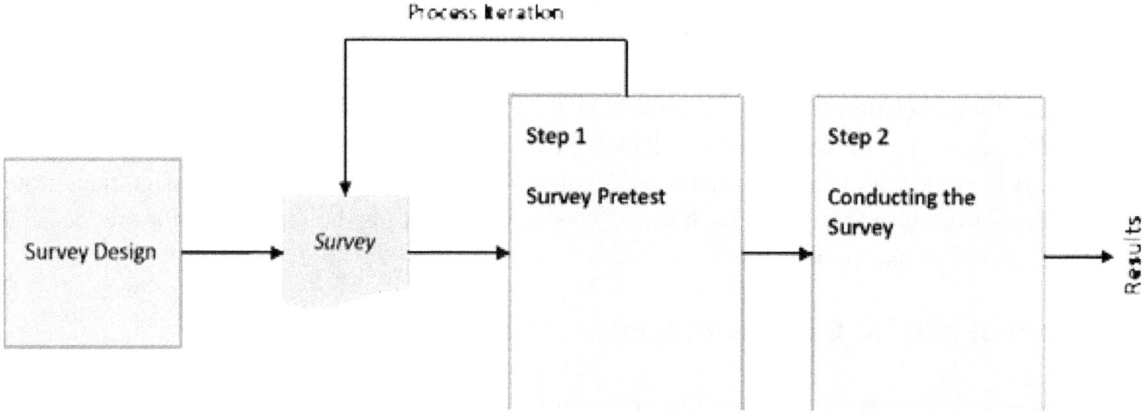

- The technical team's stability and continuity to build and preserve world-class experience, primarily because technical knowledge about attacker-defender resources and other technologies is highly perishable. In this case, informal cooperation is probably not appropriate.
- The volume of data that needs to be gathered. Technical difficulties might restrict the quantity of data gathered to facilitate attribution, but policy decisions about the conditions for collecting, storing, and using tracking data must be made clear;
- The quantity of data to be shared, along with the tools and procedures to be used, as well as the speed at which the data will be shared (a crucial factor since the data needs to be shared as soon as possible in order to cross-check data and be able to be attributed). The importance of this will grow as attribution procedures become more automated. Technical methods will need to take policy decisions about the degree of information sharing into account. Similar to how quick action is necessary due to the transient nature of evidence in cyberspace, a successful policy framework must include components of a multilateral (Saini, et al. 2008) technical assistance role;

5. VERIFICATION

We showcase the completed work on validation in this section. Utilizing a survey, the validation is accomplished.

The purpose of this survey is to validate the Framework and its extension from a technical and scientific standpoint. In order to prevent misunderstandings and create a diverse and impartial body for the artifact's validation, the questions were carefully crafted. This survey's questions were all verified in the Pre-Test.

For the survey, we used a two-step procedure, as Figure 2 shows.

The survey's questions were developed with the intention of facilitating its validation. The goal was to ascertain whether or not the pairs thought that the questions would ultimately enable the acquisition of a trustworthy validation result. As a result, the inquiries are restricted to the fundamental elements of the survey questions for validation. In order to employ the binary method, it was also intended to determine whether the questions were sufficiently objective. The questions were designed to elicit a

Table 3. Validation question areas for proposals

Analysis Vector	Description
Relevance	To what extent is the proposed framework relevant and/or important
Utility	The proposed Framework will be useful
Completeness	Classifying the framework in terms of completeness
Generic	Any other comments on the proposed Framework

viewpoint on each layer of the Framework as well as an overall assessment of its viability. The survey has been pre-tested after it was defined, and the findings of that process must be reflected in the survey. It is then put through another round of pretesting until it is deemed acceptable. In this scenario, step 2 is carried out, completing the survey and obtaining the data.

5.1 Survey Framework

As indicated in Table 3, we took into account six analysis vectors when designing the survey.

The following inquiries have been developed in light of those analysis areas:

- First Question: Can you define an Advanced Persistent Threat (APT) for me?

The purpose of the first question is to ascertain whether the respondents are familiar with the idea of APT, since they will be unable to respond to the subsequent inquiries if they are not. However, it also seeks to establish a proportionality viewpoint regarding respondents' ignorance of this kind of attack, given their employment in the information sciences.

- Second Question: Could you describe the APT Attribution phase? The purpose of the survey is to find out if the respondents who understood the meaning of APT were familiar with one of its phases—in this example, the Attribution. • Question 3: Is the data provided about the MICTIC Extended Framework sufficient and clear enough to make inferences about it? This inquiry guarantees that the data submitted for examination permits the objective drawing of conclusions. In other words, the data provided was clear and comprehensive enough for analysis.
- Question 4: Do you concur with the malware analysis performed on Layer 1 of the Framework?

As mentioned in Section 5.3, Layer 1 of the Framework reports to malware analysis. This question aims to verify the suggestions made regarding the analysis that should be done on malware in order to determine attribution.

- Question 5: Do you concur with the layer 2 of the Framework's attack infrastructure analysis?

It seeks to verify the choices made for layer 2 of the Framework (Batskih, A.V et al. 2020), which include active tracking, public data and tools, and attack infrastructure as seen from the attacker's point of view, all as means of incorporating an attribution analysis.

- Question 6: Do you concur with the Control Server Analysis, which was done on layer 3 of the Framework?

This inquiry concerns the use of Control Servers by attackers, their operation and analysis, and methods for doing so. The examination of these servers could, whenever feasible, enable a definitive approximation of the attack's attribution.

- Question 7: Do you concur with the analysis done on the Framework's Telemetry (Milko, D.S et al. 2021) layer?

This inquiry relates to the suggested creation of a telemetry analysis layer that would combine data from analysis and add it to the remaining data from the other layers in order to accomplish attribution.

- Question 8: Do you concur with the Intelligence Framework's layer 5 analyses?

The function of intelligence and espionage services is discussed in Question 8. Appreciating the important role that this kind of information acquisition plays in attribution—in many situations, it serves as one of the primary attribution tools.

- Question 9: Do you concur with the analysis conducted on Social Acceptance through Incentives, Layer 6 of the Framework (Framework Extension)? Regarding social acceptance through incentives, there may be some uncertainty because these are a subjective set of tools. This section was included in the MICTIC Framework extension already.
- Question 10: Do you concur with the analysis conducted on International Cooperation, Layer 7 of the Framework (Framework Extension)? In reference to the extra layer proposal, it is suggested to leverage integrated international cooperation in order to gather data in order to develop a model capable of constructing the attribution of an APT attack.
- Question 11: Do you think that including the two MICTIC Framework extension layers is relevant in order to obtain an APT Attribution? The purpose of the survey is to find out whether respondents think it's necessary to add two more layers to the MICTIC Framework in order to facilitate attribution.
- Question 12: Is the expanded MICTIC Framework and the way it was constructed and presented a vital tool for obtaining an APT Attribution in your opinion? It is clear that the goal is to determine whether the Framework's scope matters for an APT attribution.
- Question 13: Do you think there is scientific value to this paper on APT Attribution?

The purpose of this question is to provide a general assessment of the Framework's development, including its scope and scientific viability.

- Question 14: In what social and political contexts do you think this paper on the APT Attribution (Peace, C et al. 2017) is relevant? As with many attribution questions regarding the work's perceived social and political relevance, this one is more open to interpretation. This is due to the fact that attribution disputes can lead to a wide range of political concerns, including diplomatic disputes between nations.

Table 4. Survey questions

Question Nr.	Analysis Vector	Question
Q1	Generic	Do you know what an Advanced Persistent Threat (APT) is?
Q2	Utility	Do you know what the APT Attribution phase is?
Q3	Completeness	Is the information submitted regarding the MICTIC Extended Framework clear and sufficient to draw conclusions about it?
Q4	Relevance	Do you agree with the analysis carried out on layer 1 of the Framework: Malware Analysis?
Q5	Relevance	Do you agree with the analysis carried out on layer 2 of the Framework: Attack infrastructure?
Q6	Relevance	Do you agree with the analysis carried out on layer 3 of the Framework: Control Server Analysis?
Q7	Relevance	Do you agree with the analysis carried out on layer 4 of the Framework: Telemetry?
Q8	Relevance	Do you agree with the analysis on layer 5 of the Intelligence Framework?
Q9	Relevance	Do you agree with the analysis done on layer 6 of the Framework (Framework Extension): Social Acceptance through Incentives?
Q10	Relevance	Do you agree with the analysis done on layer 7 of the Framework (Framework Extension): International Cooperation?
Q11	Relevance	To achieve an APT Attribution, do you consider adding the two layers of the MICTIC Framework extension relevant?
Q12	Completeness/Utility	Do you consider the extended MICTIC Framework and how it was built/presented a critical tool to achieve an APT Attribution?
Q13	Relevance	Do you consider the proposal on APT Attribution scientifically relevant?
Q14	Relevance	Do you consider the proposal on the APT Attribution relevant in social and political terms?
Q15	Utility/Completeness	In general, do you consider the Framework with all the proposed layers well designed?

- Question 15: In general, do you think the Framework is well-designed with all of the suggested layers included?

Another last global issue is this one. Additionally, a general assessment of all the work submitted, including the proposal's architectural structure, is sought after. The idea behind these questions was to allow the survey questions to be validated. The objective was to ascertain whether the peers concurred that the questions would ultimately enable the acquisition of a trustworthy validation result. Additionally, the goal was to determine if the questions were objective enough to support the use of the binary method. As a result, only the questions that were inherent in the validation survey were asked. The survey questions are listed in Table 4 along with an indication of the corresponding analysis vector.

5.2 Pre-Test for the Survey

Preparing the pre-test for the Framework validation survey and its corresponding extension followed the best procedures. Table 5 presents the questions that were utilized, in accordance with their suggestions.

In Table 6, the pretest respondents' characterization is shown. To confirm the clarity and scientific objectivity of the questions used in the main survey, a pretest of the survey was conducted with ten in-

Table 5. Practice test items

Question Nr.	Question
Q1	Was the information submitted on the Framework sufficient to be analyzed in a way that could be evaluated??
Q2	The Framework information sent was clear and objective?
Q3	Is the number of questions sufficient to conclude on the importance, or not, of the Framework?
Q4	The information for each question is clear and unambiguous?
Q5	Are the questions logically well ordered?
Q6	Are the questions direct and concise?
Q7	Do the questions measure what is intended to be measured?
Q8	Are the questions free of unnecessary expressions and jargon?
Q9	Are the questions impartial?
Q10	Are the results obtained from the answers formulated mutually exclusive and exhaustive?
Q11	Do you consider the survey technically correct?

dividuals (all PhD holders in computer science, professors in higher education, and with more than 20 years of professional experience).

Every responder gave a "yes" response to every pretest question. Thus, it was feasible to draw the conclusion that the survey is acceptable and valid.

5.3 Carrying Out the Survey

We conducted the survey after validating it and by adhering to the procedures deemed necessary in this methodology. It has been conducted with 53 people, all of whom have PhDs in information technology.

The universe of respondents to the Framework validation survey with extension is described in Table 7.

Table 6. Pretest respondents' characteristics

Academic Degree	Profession/Institution	Teaching Area (T=Tecnol./ O=Other)	Years of Professional Practice
PhD	University Professor/ISTEC Lisboa	T	30
PhD	University Professor/ISTEC Lisboa	T	25
PhD	University Professor/ISTEC Lisboa	T	15
PhD	University Professor/ISTEC Lisboa	T	10
PhD	University Professor/Univ. Nova de Lisboa	T	13
PhD	University Professor/Univ. Évora	T	32
PhD	University Professor/Univ. Évora	T	31
PhD	University Professor/Univ. Lusíada	T	29
PhD	University Professor/Univ. Lusíada	T	14
PhD	University Professor /IP Luso Lisboa	T	16

Table 7. Analysis of the results

Questions	Analysis
Question 1	We have noticed seven respondents didn't know the concept, which is a significant percentage. Of these seven respondents who didn't know the APT concept, it is inferred that they were the ones who didn't answer the following questions.
Question 2	They know what an APT is and what Attribution means in the context of this threat. Therefore, they can understand the following questions as they relate directly to Attribution, i.e., knowing who the promoter is of the APT type attack.
Question 3	The result of the survey regarding this question has proven that the information provided was sufficient for the respective intended analysis.
Question 4	The answers to the survey regarding this question were all affirmative, thus validating the options presented.
Question 5	The answers were all affirmative; the respondents agreed with the formulations presented.
Question 6	The answers to the question were all positive, thus allowing this layer of the Framework to be validated.
Question 7	The answers to this question were all positive, thus allowing us to validate the proposed layer.
Question 8	All the respondents' answers to this question were positive, which validates the proposals outlined in this Framework layer.
Question 9	The answers to this one were all positive; that is, the relevance of this additional layer of the Framework was validated.
Question 10	The answers were all positive, which validates this proposal for the extra layer of the Framework.
Question 11	All the answers to this question were positive. This means that respondents consider the creation of these two layers both relevant and important.
Question 12	All responses were positive, meaning that the respondents validated the importance of the Framework extension
Question 13	All the answers were positive. This means that the respondents consider the work relevant and scientifically valid.
Question 14	All the answers were positive. This means that the respondents consider that the model presented could be important in both political and social terms if it allows an allocation to be more easily achieved.
Question 15	All respondents answered positively. This means they considered the work well integrated and well structured.

5.4 Analysis of the Results

We provide the findings of our study of the validation survey responses in this subject.

5.5 Results and Discussion

The process of attribution involves using adductive reasoning to determine which explanation best fits observations. In this work we submit for validation, we have highlighted that this technique is utilized to develop hypotheses regarding the persons, organization, or nation likely to be behind cyber-operations. The whole premise of what is put up for validation is that an APT is seen as an assault by a specific organization rather than a lone person. The underlying idea behind this may also be used to explain why An APT group's organizational structure will affect the traces and evidence it leaves behind. If the malicious software is obtained from an international provider, comparable family samples will be identified in divergent networks of victims, which cannot be explained by coherent cui bono. Assume that a single "quartermaster"-type entity oversees the infrastructures used by different units. In such scenario, intrusion sets will vary with respect to TTP and malware, but they will have similarities with regard to infrastructure setup. A variety of TTPs and malware will target the same businesses if a customer hires several freelancers, with certain TTPs having a strong correlation with malware. Just as programmers choose from a number of software design patterns to best fit a job, analysts may select from a range of group patterns to best match the data given. Law enforcement and intelligence techniques are the only ones who will finally be able to reveal the precise composition of the inner gang. Threat intelligence consumers and information security analysts will need to roughly identify the most likely group structures on the basis of technical facts. These findings will sadly only be made public in full in exceptional cases. Any subset of the MICTIC aspects—sponsors (cui bono), telemetry (operators), control servers (administrators), infrastructure (acquisition manager), and malware (developers)—can theoretically dictate group configurations. Here, we exclusively discuss configurations that either align with the infosec community's existing traditions or match the findings in reports and indictments. One effect of having thinner group arrangements is that campaigns or even events might include numerous teams. This makes logical sense when one imagines a fictitious attack including malware created by a foreign contractor and used by independent contractors while working for a federal agency. This work has been submitted for validation since the framework that has been described and its expansion may make it easier to pursue attribution in this situation. Based on the survey responses, the following conclusions can be made: with regard to the Framework and its extensions, the mechanisms and proposals for malware analysis are validated; the issue of the attack infrastructure and its tools is also validated; the analysis that needs to be done on the control servers is confirmed; the use of telemetry techniques is confirmed; and the significance of intelligence organizations' work, including espionage methods, is recognized. The Framework's two supplementary layers—social acceptability via rewards and international collaboration to gather data on APT attacks—has also been verified. To facilitate the award process and increase its potential political and social significance, the Framework's design and the work's applicability were confirmed. The work presented has been deemed legitimate in terms of its general and scientific significance.

6. CONCLUSION

Regarding the primary goal of this work, which is to help achieve simpler APT attribution by adding two new layers to the MICTIC Framework and validating it, protocols were designed and explained for every layer of the Framework, along with the addition of two new layers. It has been explained how malware analysis and functioning might implicate the attackers. Malware's creation for Attribution was explained in the malware analysis layer as a way for malware to take specificity into account while also assisting in the identification of a cybercriminal cell. It explained how malware may act as a source for analysts and stressed the need of examining the evidence gleaned from the unique circumstances surrounding tool advancements that support the assault. We have shown the usefulness and significance of controlling the control server, as well as how crucial it might be to locate that same server, at the attack infrastructure layer. The significance of making tools and information available to the public was outlined and explored. Active screening's significance was established and proven.

We discuss the APT approaches at the layer on control servers, as well as the significance of gathering data on these devices in order to accomplish attribution. We discuss how telemetry is crucial for analysts at the telemetry layer. Telemetry in the context of the MICTIC Framework pertains to the operators' manual actions, such deploying spear-phishing emails, downloading malware, or even doing diagonal actions. The perspective and operators using control servers are similar in this regard. Nevertheless, the data typology differs significantly from that acquired via C&C, leading to distinct analytical methodologies and tools. The intelligence layer has grown and shown how crucial the problem of ordered information is. These elements—espionage, counterintelligence, signals intelligence, cyber activity, human intelligence, and hacking back—may be crucial to winning an APT Award. Since these are espionage activities that provide Attribution information, a direct and inherent link has also been created between this layer and cui bono. From this point on, two entirely new layers were made in order to facilitate the easier acquisition of an APT Attribution in a summing with the earlier ones. Through incentives, we have established a layer of societal acceptability, with the main premise being that rational actors respond to incentives. Thus, rewards may encourage the gathering of data. The need to provide incentives for parties to use value-added attribution methodologies is dictated by the significance of the global information infrastructure. More significantly, in order to achieve widespread acceptance and understanding, it is imperative that we begin sharing the importance of Attribution. We have devised a system wherein identifying a collection of online behaviors in which something valuable to the user is at danger is the key to providing positive incentives for Internet users to engage in acquiring and finally demanding online share attribution. The second stratum put out was global collaboration. Achieving the Attribution—possibly even one of the most important levels of the whole model—requires international collaboration between all relevant entities, not just official bodies. The survey findings thoroughly confirmed the proposed Framework and the significance of the work to the problem of acquiring the Attribution.

This study uses a combination of non-technical and technology ways to objectively contribute to obtaining the APT attribution. Since an APT Attribution is a strong barrier to an APT group being discovered and having an Attribution given to it, it helps to achieve computer security environments. When hackers are discovered, they usually cease functioning; however, this is not always the case with unknown actors, who continue to strike for extended periods of time. As a result, our activity also helps to maintain cybersecurity generally. Future research should go more into the topic of using APS as a tool for identifying and averting APT assaults. The APS includes concepts like adversarial mindset, motivation, and the economics of cybercrime, criminal infrastructure, dark web, and the types of criminals that organizations face today. It also covers secure network design and implementation, including authentication, authorization, data and access integrity, network monitoring, and risk assessment. It is essential to develop new strategies to counter this very sophisticated danger. Thus, we think the development of APS frameworks in tandem with Attribution is the right course of action. Lastly, it is important to note that this is a very new field of study and that, as of right now; there are very few scholarly publications on APT Attribution. Due to this circumstance, it has become more difficult to find peer-reviewed scholarly publications on APT Attribution. Thus, a major contribution to the difficult scientific distribution of APT Attribution is made by the current study activity.

7. FUTURE RESEARCH DIRECTION

As cybercrime develops, more businesses will probably become victims, which might result in a rise in the use of ERPs. The public disclosure of advanced persistent threats by governments and major public companies may incentivize more corporations to include these dangers into their risk assessments. The following ideas are recommended for later investigation. Based on the quantity and kind of vulnerabilities revealed, comparing businesses using the original 1992 COSO model to businesses using an ERM model may help identify the sectors and characteristics that encourage the adoption of ERM. From a security perspective, comparing information security expenditures might result in a model budget; analyzing the frequency of outsourcing the information security function could provide insight into what functions well and poorly.

REFERENCES

Batskih, A. V., Drovnikova, I. G., Ovchinnikova, E. S., & Rogozin, E. A. (2020). *Analysis and classification of the main threats to information security of automated systems at the objects of informatiza tion of internal affairs bodies*. Bezopasnost Informatsionnykh Tekhnologiy. doi:10.26583/bit.2020.1.04

Bodeau, D. J. (2018). *Cyber Threat Modeling: Survey, Assessment, and Representative Framework*. HSSEDI.

Brandao, P. R., & Limonova, V. (2021). Defense methodologies against advanced persistent threats. *American Journal of Applied Sciences*, *18*(1), 207–212. Advance online publication. doi:10.3844/ajassp.2021.207.212

Chen, P. (2014). *A Study on Advanced Persistent Threats*. LNCS. doi:10.1007/978-3-662-44885-4_5

Jeun, I. (2012). A practical study on advanced persistent threats. In *Com puter Applications for Security*. Control and System Engineering. doi:10.1007/978-3-642-35264-5_21

Mauw, S., & Oostdijk, M. (2005). *Foundations of Attack Trees*. ICISC. doi:10.1007/11734727_17

Milko, D. S. (2021). Threat modeling expert system: Reasons for develop ment, method and implementation troubles. Modern technologies. Systemanalysis. *Modeling*, (D). Advance online publication. doi:10.26731/1813 9108.2021.2(70).182-189 123 372

Peace, C. (2017). *The risk matrix: uncertain results?* Policy Pract. Health Saf. doi:10.1080/14773996.2017.1348571

Quintero-Bonilla, S., Rey, T. J., & Park, A. M. (2020). A new proposal on the advanced persistent threat: A survey. *Applied Sciences (Basel, Switzerland)*, *10*(11), 3874. Advance online publication. doi:10.3390/app10113874

Saini, V. K., Duan, Q., & Paruchuri, V. (2008). Threat modeling using attack trees. *JCSC*, *23*(4), 124–131.

Chapter 3
Strategies to Combat Cyberattacks:
A Systematic Review

Malathi Letchumanan
https://orcid.org/0000-0001-5709-3787
Institute for Mathematical Research, Universiti Putra Malaysia, Malaysia

Rohaidah Kamaruddin
Universiti Putra Malaysia, Malaysia

ABSTRACT

Many consider the internet a safe environment for sharing information and performing online transactions. However, they are unaware of the cyberattacks that occur in the cyber environment. People are vulnerable to cyberattacks such as stealing of data and identity theft that cause financial loss and mental distress. Thus, cybersecurity that protects computer systems is considered vital to combat cyberattacks. This chapter aims to review strategies that can combat cyberattacks systematically. The results of this chapter showed an overview of the reviewed literature about authorship, geographical distribution of the studies, applied methods, types of respondents involved, types of strategies used to combat cyberattacks, and main study findings. Twenty-one studies met the authors' inclusion criteria. The findings highlighted that good governance, strategic partnership, perceived threat, coping appraisal, perceived cultural values, attitude, and technology efficacy are the strategies adopted by organisations and individuals to combat cyberattacks.

1. INTRODUCTION

Cyberattack is one of the serious issues for most of the countries around the globe. Governments of each country are trying very hard to protect their valuable data from being stolen by intruders (Senol & Karacuha, 2020). For instance, 10,790 cyberattack cases in Malaysia were reported in 2020 (MyCERT, 2021). Meanwhile, in 2020, the average data breach cost is estimated at $3.86 million in 524 organisa-

DOI: 10.4018/979-8-3693-2691-6.ch003

tions across 17 countries and regions and 17 industries in those countries (IBM, 2020). The statistics indicate that cybercrime incidents are increasing daily, and many countries, including developed nations, face difficulties overcoming cyberattacks.

The fundamental causes of cyberattacks are (i) inefficient laws and policies related to cybersecurity, (ii) technology shortages, (iii) lack of preparedness against attacks, (iv) lack of user training, and (v) lack of coordination between organisations (Senol & Karacuha, 2020). It is also highlighted that interest in cybersecurity issues often emphasises incidents and actions that must be taken after the attack. Surprisingly, prevention and investment in better cybersecurity measures always lagged. Therefore, effective strategies, policies, and measures are needed to prevent or reduce the impact before cybercrime incidents occur.

2. BACKGROUND

Current systematic reviews of cybersecurity mainly focus on identifying types of cybersecurity vulnerabilities (Humayun et al., 2020), approaches to evaluate cybersecurity awareness (Rahim et al., 2015), assess cyber situational awareness levels (Franke & Brynielsson, 2014), tools to evaluate and educate people about cybersecurity (Zhang-Kennedy & Chiasson, 2021), theories used to explain employees about cybersecurity awareness level and their behaviour (Lebek et al., 2014), security issues related to cyber-physical systems (Lun et al., 2016), identify vulnerabilities and attacks related to cross-site scripting (XSS) and assess approaches to handle self-adaptation in cyber-physical systems (CPS) (Muccini et al., 2016).

Humayun et al. (2020) examined the types of cybersecurity vulnerabilities and threats and the standard cyber-threat mitigation techniques various organisations use. The authors highlighted that the common cybersecurity threats reported were malware, phishing, and denial of service (DoS). Meanwhile, the authors also reported other vulnerabilities such as session hijacking, man-in-the-middle attacks, credential reuse, SQL injection attacks and cross-site scripting (XSS). In addition, the authors highlighted that the industries usually use a combination of mitigation techniques to combat cyber threats. For instance, many organisations use firewalls and IDs to protect Information Systems (IS) from vulnerabilities.

Another systematic review by Rahim et al. (2015) examined the security awareness and knowledge level of organisations, home users, higher learning institution students, novice Internet users and social networking users. The authors concluded that very few studies have evaluated cybersecurity awareness using the program evaluation technique, which focuses on assessing youngsters' cybersecurity awareness level and issues related to protecting the personal information of cyber users.

Franke and Brynielsson (2014) conducted a systematic review to examine cybersecurity situational awareness concepts, tools, architectures, and algorithms used to detect, measure, and protect systems from threats and exercises relating to increasing cyber situational awareness levels. Meanwhile, Zhang-Kennedy and Chiasson (2021) reviewed tools developed to assess cybersecurity awareness and educate non-expert end-users on cybersecurity. The authors reviewed current trends, the use of relevant instructional design principles, and the evidence of the tools' effectiveness.

Lebek et al. (2014) reviewed the theories that explain employees' cybersecurity awareness level and behaviour. The authors reported that behavioural and learning theories such as Theory of Reasoned Action/Theory of Planned Behavior (TRA/TPB) and General Deterrence Theory (GDT) were used to describe the employees' cybersecurity awareness level and behaviour. Level et al. (2014) reported that studies on assessing employees' cybersecurity awareness level and behaviour were mainly conducted using quantitative methods. The authors suggested using the triangulation method by combining self-reporting and observational sampling to obtain more reliable data.

Lun et al. (2016) systematically reviewed security issues related to cyber-physical systems. The authors concluded that research on security for cyber-physical systems mainly focused on power grids, attacks on sensors and their protection countermeasures. Meanwhile, Hydara (2015) initiated a systematic review to identify vulnerabilities and attacks related to cross-site scripting (XSS). The authors concluded that the available solutions to the counterattacks associated with XSS range from static analysis, dynamic analysis, secure programming and modelling.

Muccini et al. (2016) reviewed advanced methods for self-adaptation in cyber-physical systems (CPS). The authors concluded performance, flexibility and reliability are the three main issues associated with self-adaptation in CPS. Monitor-Analyze-Plan-Execute was used as the primary adaptation mechanism.

The existing review studies on cybersecurity have notable limitations. Previous review studies lacked a clear classification of strategies used to combat cyberattacks, and this may hinder cyber users from understanding and applying the existing approaches to overcome cyberattacks effectively. Additionally, they did not highlight strategies to combat cyberattacks from a general social sciences context that is believed to yield significant contributions to cyber users from both technical and non-technical backgrounds. Thus, this study systematically reviews the available strategies that can combat cyberattacks. The guiding question for this study is, "What are the strategies that can assist the cyber users to combat cyberattacks?". By conducting a comprehensive review, this study could provide valuable insights for educators, policymakers and researchers in the field of cybersecurity.

3. METHOD

The methodology used was a systematic literature review according to Prisma international standards (Moher et al., 2015). The objective was to identify relevant studies on strategies to increase cybersecurity awareness among cyber users. The review included resources from Scopus and journals related to cybersecurity.

3.1 PRISMA

The PRISMA Statement (Preferred Reporting Items for Systematic Reviews and Meta-Analyses) guided the review. PRISMA is often utilised in fields such as education, healthcare, agriculture, landscape, and design to guide the systematic review process. PRISMA generates systematic review reports based on clearly defined research questions and inclusion and exclusion criteria and examines large scientific research databases within a specified time. The PRISMA Statement enables a rigorous search of terms related to strategies used to combat cyberattacks.

3.2 Resources

Resources are from the Scopus journal database and Journals such as MIS Quarterly, Decision Support Systems, Information and Management, Information Systems Journal and Computers & Security.

Scopus provides access to journals on diverse subjects such as education, social science, agriculture, science, and technology.

3.3 Systematic Review Process

3.3.1 Identification

The review process was performed in June 2022. The researchers start the review by identifying keywords used for the search process. Keywords similar to and related to strategy, combat, and cybercrime were used (Table 1). The keywords were extracted from previous studies and thesaurus. At this stage, five duplicated articles were removed.

Table 1. Keywords and searching information strategy example

Databases	Keywords Used
Scopus	TITLE-ABS-KEY (*"strategy"* OR *"action"* OR *"approach"*) AND (*"combat"* OR *"overcome"* OR *"fight"* OR *"contest"*) AND (*"cybercrime"* OR *"cybercrime"* OR *"cyberattack"* OR *"cyber attack"* OR *"cyber offence"* OR *"cyber violation"*)

3.3.2 Screening

The exclusion or inclusion of papers was determined according to specific criteria described hereafter. First, concerning literature type, only article journals with empirical data were selected. This resulted in the exclusion of review articles, book series, books, chapters in books, and conference proceedings. Second, only articles published in English were considered. Thirdly, articles published for six years were selected (2017-2022), an adequate period to see the evolution of research related to strategies to combat cyberattacks as the cybercrime incidents have recently shown an accelerating pattern (Alshaikh, 2020).

Table 2. The inclusion and exclusion criteria

Criterion	Eligibility	Exclusion
Literature type	Journal (research articles)	Journals (systematic review), book series, book, chapter in book, conference proceeding
Language	English	Non-English
Timeline	Between 2017-2022	<2017

3.3.3 Data Abstraction and Analysis

The remaining articles were assessed and analysed. The studies related to the prespecified research question were focused and analysed. The data were extracted by reading the abstracts and full articles (in-depth) to determine the themes and sub-themes. Content analysis was used to identify themes related to strategies to combat cyberattacks among cyber users. The authors then organised sub-themes around the themes established by typology.

3.3.4 Thematic Analyses

The authors of this review article used an inductive lens to identify common themes using a process defined by Braun and Clarke (2006). It involves data familiarisation, coding, theme searching and review, and describing and naming themes. By following the process suggested by Braun and Clarke (2006). the following themes were extracted: (i) strategies adopted by organisations (ii) strategies adopted by individuals. Then, sub-themes were identified. The sub-themes were: (i)good governance, (ii) strategic partnership, (iii) perceived threat, (iv) coping appraisal, (v) perceived cultural values, (vi) attitude, and (vii) technology efficacy. Figure 1 shows the review process.

4. FINDINGS AND DISCUSSION

This study has reviewed a total of 21 articles. The reviewed articles showed that studies on strategies to overcome cybercrime have been conducted in most of the world but are more focused in North America, Europe, Africa, and Asia. The review highlighted that USA, Australia, United Kingdom, Belgium, Nigeria and South Korea are the main regions of research. The review showed that authors from Europe predominantly studied strategies to overcome cybercrime. It is not surprising, as the Cyberthreat Defense Report (2021) highlighted, that European countries, especially the UK, have a higher percentage of compromises, at least for one cyberattack incident. Meanwhile, many studies were also conducted in Africa since Africa is one of the fastest-growing regions in cybercrime activities (Kshetri, 2019). However, countries in these regions also seriously drafted measures and developed legislation to fight cyber threats (Kshetri, 2019). Countries in Asia, such as China, India, South Korea, and North America, have also seen an increase in cybercrime strategy research due to the increased penetration of IT use in these countries.

All studies reported information regarding sample characteristics. Most of the studies recruited respondents among employees (6 studies), followed by the public (3 studies), university students (3 studies), top management (3 studies), police officers (1 study), and a mixture of respondents (3 studies (employees and university students; employees and top management; police officers and public). One article each recruited respondents among IB users and online content providers. Most studies recruited employees from organisations as these groups of people are more vulnerable to cyber threats. Employee factors such as passive engagement, lack of cyber-threat knowledge, misdirected attention, and engaging in risky cybersecurity behaviours contribute to the increasing number of cybercrime incidents (Hadlington, 2018). Thus, it is unsurprising that most of this review's studies recruited employees. Meanwhile, few studies also focus on the public as their respondents. As the number of people in the general public relying on the Internet daily for routine activities increases, people are exposed to the perpetual risk of cyber-victimisation.

Interestingly, this review also showed that studies on strategies to overcome cybercrime also focused on specific groups such as policemen, university students, IB users, and online service providers. This is because frontline police officers are assumed to have a complete understanding of different modus operandi of cybercrime, have knowledge of the essential directions for investigation and evidence gathering, and are trained with adequate knowledge to advise the cybercrime victims (Hadlington et al., 2021). Meanwhile, cybercrime incidents among Internet banking users and social media users also show an increasing trend as these groups are vulnerable to many cybercrime incidents (Aribake & Aji, 2020). University students were selected as the respondents as they are perceived as a convenient sample and easy to approach. Figure 2 shows studies across continents, and Figure 3 shows the types of respondents.

Only one study in this review highlighted the different strategies adopted by male and female respondents. Anyone who uses cyberspace can become a victim of cybercrime regardless of sex, age, and educational background. However, it is essential to note that cybercriminals would like to target weak entities in a community where women are considered easily to become the target of cybercriminals (Hadlington et al., 2021). Hence, studies that understand the differences in strategies adopted by male and female respondents would yield more meaningful results.

In terms of data collection strategies, 11 studies used a quantitative approach, and eight studies employed a qualitative approach such as interviews, documentation review, archival records review, direct observation and participant observation. Only two studies (Hina et al., 2019; Wang et al., 2020) used mixed methods. Most studies applied the quantitative approach as it can reach many sample sizes, enable quick data collection, and make the generalisation of the result possible (Miller, 2020). Meanwhile, some of the studies also used a qualitative approach, which enables a detailed understanding of cybersecurity strategies employed by the respondents and could explain inconsistencies found through the quantitative method (McCormack et al., 2010). Only two studies applied mixed methods. It is suggested that more studies should apply mixed methods as it can provide rich study results (Tashakkori & Teddlie, 2003) in terms of sampling approach. Meanwhile, 16 studies provided information regarding the data collection protocol. Figure 4 shows the data collection strategies.

Generally, the sample size ranges from 3 (Alshaikh, 2020) to 1156 (Ameen et al., 2020). Entities such as people, companies, municipalities, and countries have been included in the studies. 13 studies have provided information regarding the sampling procedure. Out of these studies, six studies used non-probability sampling methods such as purposive, snowballing, and convenience.

Most studies used a non-probability sampling approach as it assisted the researchers in targeting a particular group of respondents. However, the non-probability sampling approach lacks generalizability, limiting the extension of the finding beyond the selected sample (Showkat & Parveen 2017). Instead of using a sample, a few researchers used population data, such as 124 countries (Srivastava, 2020) or eight municipalities (Popham, 2020). Sampling without randomness will create bias in some research, which will mislead the results and findings. A small number of samples, i.e. only using five companies, is suspected not to contain enough information for the conclusion.

Nineteen studies have provided information about the data analysis approach used. Qualitative studies used thematic analysis and pattern matching approach, whereas quantitative studies applied structural equation modelling, descriptive and unpaired t-tests.

4.1 Strategies Used to Overcome Cybercrime

The analysis revealed several strategies were implemented to combat cyberattacks. Organisations adopt some of the strategies, whereas individuals adopt other strategies. Strategies adopted by organisations are good governance and strategic partnership. Meanwhile, strategies adopted by individuals are perceived threat, coping appraisal, perceived cultural values, attitude and technology efficacy.

Good governance refers to how an organisation uses its power to achieve the institution's objectives. In the context of this paper, it refers to the organisation's power to design, implement and innovate its policies, rules, systems and processes to create strategies to combat cyberattacks and, at the same time, engage and involve its stakeholders to follow the developed strategies. Several sub-themes were included under the good governance theme. The first sub-theme identified was the organisation providing sufficient learning programs to its employees. Colicchia et al. (2019) reported that organisations should provide training and internal awareness programs to increase employees' awareness of cyberattacks. This will assist the employees to take appropriate actions whenever they confront a cyberattack. Maitlo (2019) highlighted that inadequate learning opportunities in an organisation expose the employees to cyberattacks and consequently lead to monetary loss to the organisation. Meanwhile, Kim et al. (2019) considered appropriate learning programs to enhance employees' security awareness skills. Similarly, Hina et al. (2019) reported that security education, training and awareness programs enable employees to learn about vulnerabilities of human and computing resources, the possible severity of security violations and primary countermeasures.

Providing appropriate and continuous training programmes on recognising and avoiding cybercrime to employees in an organisation could help reduce the cybercrime risks from 45 to 70 per cent (Laurent, 2016). According to Buono (2014), training on cybercrime can be conducted on three levels: introductory courses, advanced investigators' courses, and cutting-edge forensic specialists' courses. Police officers, for instance, have highlighted that receiving suitable training programs can increase their confidence level in cybercrime investigations (Paek et al., 2021). Thus, organisations should carefully design and deploy training programs to all levels of employees in the organisation to create awareness and understanding among employees about the damage that can caused by cybercrime incidents. This will assist the organisation in avoiding cybercrime incidents and taking appropriate action after being attacked by cybercriminals.

Leadership support is another sub-theme under good governance. Maitlo et al. (2019) consider good leadership support can provide a strong foundation for employees to take appropriate actions toward cyberattacks. Meanwhile, according to Popham (2020) and Ameen et al. (2020), the organisation's enforcement factor is another important strategy that can combat cyberattacks. The authors highlighted that effective enforcement, such as forming a collaboration with law enforcement officers, developing and executing a cyber incident response plan, and planning and exercising a sanction for cybercrime incidents, could lower the cybercrime rates and protect the employees. Leaders must have an increased understanding of efficient ways of implementing counteractions to cybercrime. This assists the leaders in recognising vulnerabilities, executing a crisis management plan, educating the community, and conducting after-action reviews to combat cybercrime incidents in an organisation (Cleveland & Cleveland, 2018). Maitlo et al. (2019) state that poor leadership support could challenge effective knowledge sharing to prevent cybercrime, such as employee identity fraud. Noguerol and Branch (2018) added that inappropriate leadership and managerial practices could lead to electronic data leakage in an organisation. Thus, influential leaders who have transformational qualities could be a robust predictor of organisational success against cybercrime.

One study has highlighted the importance of cybersecurity programs/ personnel visibility in an organisation (Alshaikh, 2020). A comprehensive cybersecurity awareness program outlines employees' apparent cybersecurity hopes and educates them on identifying, preventing, and responding to cyber-related incidents. However, not many employees know about the cybersecurity awareness programs organised by their employers. Visibility is important because when the employees learn about the programs/ personnel handling cybersecurity issues, they can participate in the program and approach the personnel to solve the cybersecurity issues they encounter. Thus, Alshaikh (2020) suggested that promotion programs that create visibility about cybersecurity awareness programs must be carried out throughout organisations to increase the effectiveness of cybersecurity awareness programs among employees. This will capture the employees' attention, make them participate, and realise the importance of cybersecurity awareness programs.

Besides, creating a cybersecurity champion network among the different stakeholders in an organisation (Alshaikh, 2020) is another essential sub-theme under good governance. It is reported that an organisation's cybersecurity culture and outreach team face difficulty approaching all the employees who confront cybersecurity problems. Thus, training and educating cybersecurity champions on different cybersecurity issues may assist the cybersecurity culture and outreach team in solving many cybersecurity issues in an organisation, as the cybersecurity champion can address and solve the cybersecurity issues of employees (Alshaikh, 2020; CSAM, 2020).

Two studies have reported the influence of preparedness before cyberattacks as one of the essential strategies to combat cybercrime (Naseer et al., 2021; Srivastava et al., 2020). Preparedness before a cyberattack could reduce the frequency of cybercrime incidents and investment in technology capital (Naseer et al., 2021). Business analytics could be adopted for cybersecurity incident response to enable organisations to identify, analyse, eliminate and recover from potential cyber threats in a timely and cost-effective manner (Srivastava, 2020). This assists organisations in responding to the dynamic cyber threat situation before more severe attacks. Preparedness before cyberattacks could reduce cybercrime incidents and save organisations from monetary loss.

Only one study investigated the role of strategic partnerships between the public and private sectors as an effective strategy to combat cyberattacks (Dlamini & Mbambo, 2019). The authors highlighted that the involvement of the private sector may channel the required resources and expertise to the public sector to draft effective strategies to combat cyberattacks. Meanwhile, the public sector, especially the legal enforcement officers, can provide necessary information to the private sector to overcome cyber threats effectively. According to Le Toquin (2006), close partnership between the private and public sectors, especially the partnership between law enforcement officers, assists the organisations in familiarising themselves with law enforcement roles and responsibilities. This enhanced the employees' knowledge of working with the appropriate agency following an incident. Furthermore, the collaboration also protects organisations from the latest cyber threats (US Chamber of Commerce, 2018).

Threat refers to the "degree to which an individual perceives a malicious IT attack as dangerous or harmful" (Liang & Xue, 2010). Perceived threat enables cyber users to develop threat perception, monitor the computing environment, detect potential harm, and take appropriate strategies to overcome cyber threats. Threat factors induce fear among individuals and influence the individual's intention to take suggested protective measures (Ophoff & Lakay, 2018). This systematic review grouped sub-themes such as perceived vulnerability, perceived severity, and perceived security into perceived threat themes. Two studies have reported the importance of perceived vulnerability in combating cybercrime (Aribake et al., 2020; Hina et al., 2019). Perceived vulnerability is the person's belief concerning the probability that the threat would occur. Hina et al. (2019) highlighted that the perceived vulnerability of an individual influences their intention to obey with Information system policies that can deter an individual from being a potential cybercrime victim. Meanwhile, Aribake et al. (2020) reported that perceived vulnerability invokes the avoidance behaviour of Internet banking users that could prevent them from being involved in cybercrime activities. Thus, perceived vulnerability creates awareness among cyber users about the possible cyber threats that they may encounter, and this prevents them from using suspicious information systems.

Perceived severity refers to how an individual takes the cyberattack incidents seriously. Perceived severity enables a person to comply with Information system policies (Hina et al., 2019), avoid potential cyberattacks (Aribake et al., 2020), and motivate a person's intention to use technology tools such as antimalware software to counter cyberattacks (Crossler et al., 2019). Meanwhile, perceived security enables individuals to adopt a system that will not harm them (Aribake et al., 2020). Usually, the formation of fear happens when the security aspect of IS products is compromised. This will lead an individual to adopt security measures to prevent cybercrime.

Four studies have discussed the importance of coping appraisal as one of the strategies to combat cyberattacks. According to Anderson and Agarwal (2010), managing appraisal is an important determinant that affects the enthusiasm and readiness to comply with security policies and embrace security technologies and practices in organisations. Three sub-themes, response efficacy, self-efficacy, and response cost, are considered coping appraisal. Crossler et al. (2019) and Hina et al. (2019) have stated the importance of response efficacy as the crucial determinant in combating cyberattacks. Response efficacy refers to the individual's belief that taking action would avoid a cyberattack (van Bavel et al., 2019). Crossler et al. (2019) highlighted that response efficacy affects an individual intention to use antimalware software. In addition, Hina et al. (2019) reported that response efficacy influences an individual's decision to comply with information system policies that could deter a person from being a victim of cybercrime. Basically, individuals with response efficacy will adopt recommended security measures to avoid cyber threats.

Self-efficacy is "an individual's belief in his or her capacity to execute behaviours necessary to produce specific performance attainments" (Bandura,1997). Four studies have reported the importance of self-efficacy as an essential strategy to combat cybercrime. Martens and Mulvihill (2019) reported that self-efficacy is vital to be aware of cyber threats. Meanwhile, Aribake and Aji (2020) and Ameen et al. (2020) indicated that the influence of self-efficacy among Internet banking users is essential to improving phishing avoidance behaviour in the banking sector and having intention toward smartphone security behaviour. Hina et al. (2019) also highlighted that self-efficacy motivates people to comply with information system policies to avoid cyberattacks. Rivard (2014) reported that individual self-efficacy could reduce cybercriminal penetrations in an organisation and determine success rates. It is because self-efficacy defeats the fear that most IS users experience during a cyber-threat incident and helps them cope with any attack.

Only Ameen et al. (2020) have reported the importance of the response cost factor as one of the critical strategies to combat cybercrime. According to Helmes (2002), response cost may refer to "monetary expense, inconvenience, difficulty and the side effects of performing the coping behaviour". Ameen et al. (2020) highlighted that female employees are more aware of the problems (response cost) associated with keeping their course of action secure when using the smartphone. Thus, the response cost factor would prevent them from becoming victims of cybercrime. Response cost usually negatively affects the adoption of cybersecurity measures. Individuals are often reluctant to adopt security measures if they are expensive and complicated (Hassandoust & Techatassanasoontorn, 2018). Thus, response cost is an important predictor of adopting IS security measures.

Only one study (Ameen et al., 2020) has reported the effect of perceived cultural values that involve categories such as individualism vs collectivism, power distance, masculinity vs femininity and uncertainty avoidance to combat cybercrime. In this systematic review, cultural values refer to "collective programming of the mind that distinguishes the members of one group or category of people from others" (Hofstede, 1980). Uncertainty avoidance explains how an individual feels uncomfortable when confronted with ambiguities and uncertainties (Hofstede, 1980). Uncertainty avoidance increases the anxiety level of an individual and consequently paves the way for that individual to avoid that uncertainty. Regarding smartphone security behavior, Ameen et al. (2020) reported that uncertainty avoidance creates more fear among female smartphone users about the consequences of smartphone misuse, halting them from misusing their smartphones. Individuals with high uncertainty avoidance are not inclined to take risks and are involved in unpredictable circumstances. They strongly emphasise rules, procedures, and formal relationships that can provide secure circumstances for them. Individuals with high uncertainty avoidance also accept the primacy of rules (Hofstede, 1980) and show high commitment towards an organisation. Thus, an individual with high uncertainty avoidance will follow the information system policy and avoid harmful actions to an organisation's Information system.

Meanwhile, power distance expresses that the less powerful member of an entity accepts and expects that power in an organisation is distributed unequally. Individuals with high power distance will take the managerial decision unanimously. Ameen et al. (2020) reported that the power of the management influences male employees more in terms of smartphone security behaviour and prevents them from being involved in smartphone misuse. The power distance could prevent employees from involving in cybercrime incidents.

Individualism describes that a person in an organisation is concerned about himself and his close circle (Hofstede, 1980). However, in collectivism, individuals belong to their group and follow what the group does (Hofstede, 1980). In collectivism, an individual believes that his action will affect another individual in a group and, simultaneously, could cause embarrassment (negative actions) among other employees. Thus, Ameen et al. (2020) stated that individualism vs collectivism influences male employees' behavioural intention toward smartphone misuse. In a masculine society, individuals are driven by achievements, while in a feminine society, individuals are driven by doing what they like and caring for others (Hofstede, 1980). Regarding smartphone security behaviour, masculine society will avoid being involved in cybercrime activities to avoid failure, while feminine society will follow the security policy to prevent cyber threat incidents. Ameen et al.'s (2020) findings reported that female employees' smartphone security behaviour is affected by both masculine and feminine factors. This indicates that collectivism and individualism are important criteria to prevent an individual from being involved in cybercrime incidents.

According to Cherry (2021), an attitude is a "set of emotions, beliefs, and behaviours toward a particular object, person, thing, or event". Four studies have reported the importance of people's attitudes to combat cybercrime. For instance, Maitlo et al. (2019) reported that a lack of employee willingness to share knowledge and trust in colleagues exposes employees to cybercrime. In addition, David et al. (2020) reported that knowledge sharing on protecting cyberspace is essential in effective cybersecurity initiatives. Meanwhile, Wang et al. (2020) reported that not sharing personal account details, checking account statements often and subscribing to transaction alerts could protect bank customers from cybercrime. Einwiller and Kim (2020) highlighted that online content providers should decisively communicate with users, hide harmful online communication (HOC) posts, block user accounts and report HOC/illegal content to third parties to protect online users from cyberattacks. Finally, Chatterjee et al. (2019) also highlighted that using social media to exchange information regarding cybercrime incidents increases awareness among people and may lead to a reduction in cybercrime incidents. Thus, the positive attitude of cyber users in sharing knowledge about cybercrime incidents and the steps to overcome cybercrimes will increase awareness among other cyber users and prevent them from involving in cybercrimes. Besides, cyber users also need to avoid sharing unnecessary information with other unknown cyber users to prevent them from becoming the victims of cybercrimes.

Technology efficacy refers to how the use of technology by an individual can effectively assist them in cyberattacks. This sub-theme may explain the characteristics of the internal feature of the technology that helps an individual to effectively overcome cybercrime incidents or how an individual uses the technology to safeguard themselves from cyberattacks. 4 studies have highlighted the role technology efficacy, such as perceived usefulness, perceived ease of use and actual technology use. Chatterjee et al. (2019) reported that in the environment of Smart City India, the perceived usefulness of technology plays an essential role in influencing an individual to use the technology to combat cybercrime. Perceived usefulness describes many characteristics of a technology, such as effectiveness, performance, trust, risk perception, and productivity that motivate the use of that technology to prevent cybercrime. Similarly, Hart et al. (2020) agreed that the perceived usefulness of Riskio, a tabletop game, assists non-technical background users to prevent themselves from cyberattacks. In addition, Kovacevi and Radenkovic (2020) also highlighted the effectiveness of the web-based system they developed (SAWIT) to assist university students in preventing themselves from cybercrime. Meanwhile, Chatterjee et al. (2019) also highlighted that the perceived ease of use of a technology that explains the simplicity and compatibility of a system encourages users to use the technology product to prevent cyberattacks. However, Hart et al. (2020) concluded that the authors could not draw any significant conclusion from the perceived ease of use construct regarding their Riskio system. Chatterjee et al. (2019) reported that actual technology use, where an individual uses the system in real-time, assists them in countering cyberattacks. The findings clearly indicate that technology factors such as perceived usefulness and ease of use determined the use of Information system security measures to combat cybercrime. According to AlHogail (2018), a system must have encryption, usefulness, and ease of use to be trusted and used by employees to counter cyberattacks. This is because perceived ease of use and perceived usefulness will increase the intrinsic motivation and trust of the user to use the system to achieve targeted benefits.

Meanwhile, actual system use is also another important strategy that could be used to overcome cybercrime incidents. Even the most advanced technological security system cannot protect an organisation from cyberattacks if employees do not entirely use the technology (Huang & Pearlson, 2019). Thus, every employee must act to keep the organisation cyber secure by using the system. According to Chatterjee et al. (2019), once a user begins adopting preventive technologies and using those regularly, it will assist the users in preventing cybercrime incidents.

6. LIMITATIONS

This review has several limitations. The authors of this review article might have missed other significant articles by neglecting some relevant keywords, although the search criteria did include broad inclusion criteria. Furthermore, the author's decision to include only peer-reviewed English-language journal articles resulted in limitations because studies related to strategies to combat cybercrime have been written in other languages, such as Malay, but have not been translated into English. Additionally, conducting a meta-analysis was impossible because of the variety of statistical analyses used in the reviewed articles.

Table 3. Summary of findings

Author(s)	Region	Sample Characteristics		Data Collection Method	Sampling		Data Analysis	Findings
		Respondent	Gender		Sampling Method(s) Described	Sample Size	The Data Analysis Approach Described	
Alshaikh.M (2020)	Australia	Employer	-	Qualitative case study (Interview and Document review)	No	3	Thematic analysis	Top management should identify key behavioural themes from policy to enable the employees to follow and combat cybercrime. Creating a unique brand for the cybersecurity team to attract employees and to create cybercrime awareness. Forming a cyber security champion network among different stakeholders in an organisation. Building a cyber security hub to support and improve employees' cybersecurity behaviour. Aligning security awareness with internal and external campaigns.
Ameen et al. (2020)	UAE & US	Employees	M + F	Survey	Yes (purposive)	1156	PLS-SEM	Gender Self-efficacy, perceived severity of sanction, response cost, perceived certainty of sanction, and perceived severity influence both males' and females' intention to follow security practices and policies when using smartphones to combat cybercrime. Espoused uncertainty avoidance, power distance, individualism vs collectivism, and masculinity vs femininity influence both males' and females' intentions to follow security practices and policies when using smartphones to combat cybercrime.
Aribake, F.O., and Aji, Z.M. (2020)	Nigeria	IB users	Not stated	Quantitative	Random sampling	463	SEM	The influence of perceived severity, perceived security, and perceived vulnerability of Internet banking users influence phishing avoidance behaviour in the banking sector.
Chatterjee et al. (2019)	India	Residents of city	M + F	Quantitative (Questionnaire)	Convenience sampling	315	SEM	Good governance, such as organisations providing awareness programs and law enforcement, could prevent cybercrime in smart cities. Perceived ease of use, perceived usefulness, actual technology use, and social media determine users to use systems that prevent cybercrime.
Crossler et al. (2019)	US and Ghana	University students	M + F	Quantitative (Survey)	Yes	487	PLS-SEM	Perceived severity of threats influences an individual's intention to use antimalware software to combat cybercrime. Response efficacy and self-efficacy influence an individual's behavioural intention to use antimalware software to combat cybercrime.
Colicchia et al. (2019)	UK.	Top management	Not mentioned	Qualitative (comparative case study)	Purposive	5 companies	Pattern matching	Introduce additional training for employees to prepare participants for potential disruptions. Sign collaborative agreements for sharing information on security incidents and continuity plans that could combat cyberattacks. Restricted access to company data could combat cyberattacks. Draft security policies to enable subcontractors and customers to comply with processes related to data management, privacy, and disclosure restrictions could combat cyberattacks.

continued on following page

Table 3. Continued

Author(s)	Region	Sample Characteristics		Data Collection Method	Sampling		Data Analysis	Findings
		Respondent	Gender		Sampling Method(s) Described	Sample Size	The Data Analysis Approach Described	
Dlamini, S., and Mbambo, C. (2019)	South Africa	South African Police Services	Not mentioned	Qualitative	Purposive and snowballing	20	Thematic analysis	Strategic partnerships between the public and the private sector play an important role in policing cybercrime in Durban.
Einwiller, S.A., Kim, S. (2020)	United States, Germany, South Korea, and China	Online content providers	Not mentioned	Interview	No	41	Thematic analysis	Giving warnings, decisively communicating with users, hiding or deleting harmful online communication (HOC) posts (or words), blocking/locking user accounts, and reporting HOC/illegal content to third parties could combat cyberattacks.
Grimes, M., and Marquardson, J. (2019)	USA	University Students	M + F	Experiment	No	169	SEM	System quality positively influences the security intentions of users to use the system that can prevent cybercrime.
Hart et al. (2020)	UK.	Employees with no technical knowledge background and university students	M + F	Experiment	Yes	42	Unpaired t-test	Increasing awareness level of cyber security attacks and the possible countermeasures that can be deployed to deter or mitigate the attacks by using serious game/gamification
Hina et al. (2019)	Malaysia	University employees	M + F	Quantitative (survey) + Qualitative (Interview)	Simple random sampling	301	SEM	Provision of policy, SETA programs, perceived severity, perceived vulnerability, self-efficacy, response efficacy, and attitude of university employees influence their intention to comply with information security policy compliances to combat cybercrime.
Kim et al. (2019)	South Korea	Employees	M + F	Quantitative	No	324	SEM	Senior managers' degree of comprehension of issues concerning information security, such as information security knowledge, problem-solving skills, and information security countermeasures (PCM) awareness, determine information system policy compliance of employees to counter cyberattacks.
Kovačević, A., Radenković, S.D. (2020)	Serbia	University students	Not mentioned	Survey	No	22	-	SAWIT is a web-based application that increases employees' cyber security knowledge by using collaborative learning and assessment to combat cyberattacks effectively.
Maitlo et al.(2019)	U.K.	Company employees		Qualitative (documentation, archival records, interviews, direct observations, and participant observation)	Purposive	34	Thematic analysis	Knowledge sharing among employees can prevent identity theft in online retail organisations.

continued on following page

Table 3. Continued

Author(s)	Region	Sample Characteristics		Data Collection Method	Sampling		Data Analysis	Findings
		Respondent	**Gender**		**Sampling Method(s) Described**	**Sample Size**	**The Data Analysis Approach Described**	
Martens and Mulhivill (2019)	Belgium	Public	M + F	Quantitative (online survey)	Convenience	1181	SEM	Creating awareness of threats could combat cybercrime. Creating awareness of strategies that could be adopted to countermeasure cyberattacks could combat cybercrime. Perceived severity, or to what extent someone believes that the consequences of threats would be harmful, could combat cybercrime. Response efficacy that outlines the effectiveness of the protective measure against a specific cybercrime could combat cybercrime. A positive attitude toward protection behaviour could counter cybercrime. Influence from trust parties to protect themselves against cybercrime could overcome cybercrime.
Naseer et al. (2021)	Australia	Employees and Employers	-	Qualitative (Semi-structured interview)	Yes	27	Constant comparative techniques	Organisations that perform analytical information processing in cybersecurity incident response can take precautions when confronted with cyberattacks.
Pandey et al. (2020)	Europe	Employees	Qualitative – case study	Archival data	No	11	-	Using a software assurance approach to reduce the likelihood of vulnerabilities and make the system behave as expected could combat cyberattacks.
David et al. (2020)	Switzerland	Employee	M + F	Online survey	Yes	262	-	Knowledge sharing is necessary for the adoption of cybersecurity strategies.
Popham et al. (2020)	Canada	Police and Public)	-	Document review	-	8 municipal	Descriptive statistics and simple bivariate tests	Enforcement factor that involves police forces to investigate cybercrime cases influences cybercrime incidents. The findings also suggest that areas with higher police calls from victims tended to have lower cybercrime rates. The findings also suggested that areas with more police officers would likely have lower rates of cybercrime reports.
Srivastava et al. (2020)	Many countries	Employer	-	Survey	No	124 countries	PLS-SEM	Cyber security preparedness aspects of an organisation, such as legal measures, technical measures, organisational measures, capacity building, and cooperation, could combat cybercrime incidents.
Wang et al. (2020)	Nigeria	Public	M + F	Mixed method	Yes (random sampling)	115	No	The findings suggest that the following strategies could combat cybercrime: **On the management side:** Providing adequate training to bank personnel. Employees should stay up to date with the technology advancements. Management support in addressing cyber security issues. Organisations should prioritise cyber security issues. **On the customer side:** Having second-factor authentication for online transactions. Not sharing personal account details with anyone. Checking account statements regularly. Subscribing to transaction alerts on the activities on accounts. Keeping the contact details of the assigned account officer and the bank's customer care team.

Table 4. Attributes related to strategies to combat cyberattacks

Factors / Authors	Good Governance							Perceived Threat			Coping Appraisal			Perceived Cultural Values					Technology Efficay				
	Providing sufficient learning/awareness programs to its employees	Leadership support	Enforcement factor	Visibility of cybersecurity programs/personnel	Create a cybersecurity champion network	Preparedness before cyberattack	Strategic Partnership	Perceived vulnerability	Perceived severity	Perceived security	Response efficacy	Self-efficacy	Response cost	Individualism vs collectivism	Power distance	Masculinity/femininity	Uncertainty avoidance	Attitude	Perceived usefulness	Perceived ease of use	Actual technology use	Social media	Gender
Alshaikh.M (2020)				x	x																		
Ameen et al. (2020)			x						x			x	x	x	x	x	x						x
Aribake, F.O., and Aji, Z.M. (2020)								x	x	x													
Chatterjee et al. (2019)	x		x															x	x	x			
Crossler et al. (2019)	x																						
Colicchia et al. (2019)									x		x	x											
Dlamini, S., and Mbambo, C. (2019)							x																
Einwiller, S.A., Kim, S. (2020)																		x					
Grimes, M., and Marquardson, J. (2019)																			x				
Hart et al. (2020)																			x	x			
Hina et al. (2019)	x		x					x	x		x	x						x					
Kim et al. (2019)		x																					
Kovačević, A., Radenković, S.D. (2020)																			x				

continued on following page

Table 4. Continued

Factors Authors	Good Governance						Strategic Partnership	Perceived Threat			Coping Appraisal			Perceived Cultural Values				Attitude	Technology Efficay				Gender
	Providing sufficient learning/awareness programs to its employees	Leadership support	Enforcement factor	Visibility of cybersecurity programs/personnel	Create a cybersecurity champion network	Preparedness before cyberattack		Perceived vulnerability	Perceived severity	Perceived security	Response efficacy	Self-efficacy	Response cost	Individualism vs collectivism	Power distance	Masculinity/femininity	Uncertainty avoidance		Perceived usefulness	Perceived ease of use	Actual technology use	Social media	
Maitlo et al.(2019)	x	x																x					
Martens and Mulhivill (2019)												x						x					
Naseer et al. (2021)						x																	
Pandey et al. (2020)		x																					
David et al. (2020)																		x					
Popham et al. (2020)			x																				
Srivastava et al. (2020)			x			x																	
Wang et al. (2020)	x	x																x					

7. CONCLUSION

Cybercrime can have a severe impact in terms of the financial and mental health of individuals. Thus, it is pertinent to adopt effective strategies to combat cybercrime incidents. The review results show that good governance, strategic partnership, threat factor, coping appraisal factor, cultural factor, attitude factor, and technology factor are the strategies organisations adopt to overcome cybercrime. To understand effective strategies organisations take to overcome cybercrime, the future review could focus on other technology factors, such as implementing network management to prevent cybercrime.

REFERENCES

AlHogail, A. (2018). Improving IoT technology adoption through improving consumer trust. *Technologies*, *6*(3), 64. doi:10.3390/technologies6030064

Alqarni, A. (2017). *Exploring factors that affect the adoption of computer security practices among college students*. Eastern Michigan University.

Alshaikh, H., Ramadan, N., & Hefny, H. A. (2020). Ransomware prevention and mitigation techniques. *Int. J. Comput. Appl*, *177*(40), 31–39.

Ameen, N., Tarhini, A., Shah, M. H., & Madichie, N. O. (2020). Employees' behavioural intention to smartphone security: A gender-based, cross-national study. *Computers in Human Behavior*, *104*, 106184. doi:10.1016/j.chb.2019.106184

Anderson, C. L., & Agarwal, R. (2010). Practicing safe computing: A multimethod empirical examination of home computer user security behavioral intentions. *Management Information Systems Quarterly*, *34*(3), 34. doi:10.2307/25750694

Anwar, M., He, W., Ash, I., Yuan, X., Li, L., & Xu, L. (2016). Gender difference and employees' cyber security behaviors. *Computers in Human Behavior*, *69*, 437–443. doi:10.1016/j.chb.2016.12.040

Aribake, F. O., & Mat Aji, Z. (2020). The mediating role of perceived security on the relationship between internet banking users and their determinants. *International Journal of Advanced Research in Engineering and Technology*, *11*(2).

Ayyagari, R., Lim, J., & Hoxha, O. (2019). Why Do Not We Use Password Managers? A Study on the Intention to Use Password Managers. *Contemporary Management Research*, *15*(4), 227–245. doi:10.7903/cmr.19394

Bandura, A. (1997). *Self-Efficacy: The exercise of control*. W. H. Freeman.

Böhme, R., & Moore, T. (2012, October). *How do consumers react to cybercrime? In 2012 eCrime researchers summit*. IEEE.

Buono, L. (2014, June). *Fighting cybercrime through prevention, outreach and awareness raising*. Academic Press.

Chatterjee, S., Kar, A. K., Dwivedi, Y. K., & Kizgin, H. (2019). Prevention of cybercrimes in smart cities of India: From a citizen's perspective. *Information Technology & People*, *32*(5), 1153–1183. doi:10.1108/ITP-05-2018-0251

Cherry, K. (2021). *Attitudes and behavior in psychology*. Academic Press.

Chu, A. M., & So, M. K. (2020). Organisational information security management for sustainable information systems: An unethical employee information security behavior perspective. *Sustainability (Basel)*, *12*(8), 3163. doi:10.3390/su12083163

Cleveland, M., & Cleveland, S. (2018). Cybercrime post-incident leadership model. In *Proceeding of the 13th Midwest Association for Information Systems Conference, St. Louis, MO, May* (pp. 17-18). Academic Press.

Colicchia, C., Creazza, A., & Menachof, D. A. (2019). Managing cyber and information risks in supply chains: Insights from an exploratory analysis. *Supply Chain Management*, *24*(2), 215–240. doi:10.1108/SCM-09-2017-0289

Crenshaw, K. (1990). Mapping the margins: Intersectionality, identity politics, and violence against women of color. *Stanford Law Review*, *43*(6), 1241. doi:10.2307/1229039

Crossler, R. E., Andoh-Baidoo, F. K., & Menard, P. (2019). Espoused cultural values as antecedents of individuals' threat and coping appraisal toward protective information technologies: Study of US and Ghana. *Information & Management*, *56*(5), 754–766. doi:10.1016/j.im.2018.11.009

Crossler, R. E., Johnston, A. C., Lowry, P. B., Hud, Q., Warkentin, M., & Baskerville, R. (2013). Future directions for behavioral information security research. *Computers & Security*, *32*, 90–101. doi:10.1016/j.cose.2012.09.010

CSAM. (2020). *How IT Can Get Employees To Engage With Your Company's Security Awareness Program.* https://inspiredelearning.com/blog/how-it-can-get-employees-to-engage-with-your-companys-security-awareness-program/

Cummings, J. N. (2004). Work Groups, Structural Diversity, and Knowledge Sharing in a Global Organization. *Management Science*, *50*(3), 352–364. doi:10.1287/mnsc.1030.0134

D'Arcy, J., & Herath, T. (2011). A review and analysis of deterrence theory in the IS security literature: Making sense of the disparate findings. *European Journal of Information Systems*, *20*(6), 643–658. doi:10.1057/ejis.2011.23

David, D. P., Keupp, M. M., & Mermoud, A. (2020). Knowledge absorption for cyber-security: The role of human beliefs. *Computers in Human Behavior*, *106*, 106255. doi:10.1016/j.chb.2020.106255

Davis, F., Bagozzi, R., & Warshaw, P. (1989). User acceptance of computer technology: A comparison of two theoretical models. *Management Science*, *35*(8), 982–1003. doi:10.1287/mnsc.35.8.982

De Bruijn, H., & Janssen, M. (2017). Building cybersecurity awareness: The need for evidence-based framing strategies. *Government Information Quarterly*, *34*(1), 1–7. doi:10.1016/j.giq.2017.02.007

Dlamini, S., & Mbambo, C. (2019). Understanding policing of cybe-rcrime in South Africa: The phenomena, challenges and effective responses. *Cogent Social Sciences*, *5*(1), 1675404. doi:10.1080/23311886.2019.1675404

Eastin, M. S., & LaRose, R. (2000). Internet Self-Efficacy and the Psychology of the Digital Divide. *Journal of Computer-Mediated Communication*, *6*(1), 0. doi:10.1111/j.1083-6101.2000.tb00110.x

Einwiller, S. A., & Kim, S. (2020). How online content providers moderate user-generated content to prevent harmful online communication: An analysis of policies and their implementation. *Policy and Internet*, *12*(2), 184–206. doi:10.1002/poi3.239

Feledi, D., Fenz, S., & Lechner, L. (2013). Toward Web-Based Information Security Knowledge Sharing. *Information Security Technical Report*, *17*(4), 199–209. doi:10.1016/j.istr.2013.03.004

Flores, W. R., & Ekstedt, M. (2012). A Model for Investigating Organisational Impact on Information Security Behavior. *WISP 2012 Proceedings.*

Franke, U., & Brynielsson, J. (2014). Cyber situational awareness–a systematic review of the literature. *Computers & Security*, *46*, 18–31. doi:10.1016/j.cose.2014.06.008

Grimes, M., & Marquardson, J. (2019). Quality matters: Evoking subjective norms and coping appraisals by system design to increase security intentions. *Decision Support Systems*, *119*, 23–34. doi:10.1016/j.dss.2019.02.010

Hadlington, L., Lumsden, K., Black, A., & Ferra, F. (2021). A qualitative exploration of police officers' experiences, challenges, and perceptions of cybercrime. *Policing. Journal of Policy Practice*, *15*(1), 34–43.

Hadlington, L. J. (2018). *Employees attitudes towards cyber security and risky online behaviours: an empirical assessment in the United Kingdom.* Academic Press.

Hart, S., Margheri, A., Paci, F., & Sassone, V. (2020). Riskio: A serious game for cyber security awareness and education. *Computers & Security*, *95*, 101827. doi:10.1016/j.cose.2020.101827

Hassandoust, F., & Techatassanasoontorn, A. A. (2020). Understanding users' information security awareness and intentions: A full nomology of protection motivation theory. In *Cyber Influence and Cognitive Threats* (pp. 129–143). Academic Press. doi:10.1016/B978-0-12-819204-7.00007-5

Helmes, A. W. (2002). Application of the protection motivation theory to genetic testing for breast cancer risk. *Preventive Medicine*, *35*(5), 453–462. doi:10.1006/pmed.2002.1110 PMID:12431894

Hina, S., Selvam, D. D. D. P., & Lowry, P. B. (2019). Institutional governance and protection motivation: Theoretical insights into shaping employees' security compliance behavior in higher education institutions in the developing world. *Computers & Security*, *87*, 101594. doi:10.1016/j.cose.2019.101594

Hofstede, G. (1980). *Culture's consequences: Comparing values, behaviours, institutions and organisations across nations.* Sage.

Hofstede, G. H. (2001). *Culture's consequences: Comparing values, behaviors, institutions, and organisations across nations.* Sage Publications.

Huang, K., & Pearlson, K. (2019, January). For what technology can't fix: Building a model of organisational cybersecurity culture. *Proceedings of the 52nd Hawaii International Conference on System Sciences.* 10.24251/HICSS.2019.769

Humayun, M., Niazi, M., Jhanjhi, N. Z., Alshayeb, M., & Mahmood, S. (2020). Cyber security threats and vulnerabilities: A systematic mapping study. *Arabian Journal for Science and Engineering*, *45*(4), 3171–3189. doi:10.1007/s13369-019-04319-2

Hydara, I., Sultan, A. B. M., Zulzalil, H., & Admodisastro, N. (2015). Current state of research on cross-site scripting (XSS)–A systematic literature review. *Information and Software Technology*, *58*, 170–186. doi:10.1016/j.infsof.2014.07.010

IBM. (2020). https://www.varonis.com/blog/cybersecurity-statistics/

Jones, C. M. (2009). *Utilising the technology acceptance model to assess employee adoption of information systems security measures*. Nova Southeastern University.

Kim, H. L., Choi, H. S., & Han, J. (2019). Leader power and employees' information security policy compliance. *Security Journal, 32*(4), 391–409. doi:10.1057/s41284-019-00168-8

Kovačević, A., & Radenković, S. D. (2020). SAWIT—Security awareness improvement tool in the workplace. *Applied Sciences (Basel, Switzerland), 10*(9), 3065. doi:10.3390/app10093065

Kshetri, N. (2019). *Cybercrime and cybersecurity in Africa*. Academic Press.

LaRose,R., Rifon,N., Liu,S., & Lee, D. (2005). *Understanding online safety behavior: A multivariate model*. Academic Press.

Laurent. (2016). *How to Prevent Cyber Crime By Training Your Employees*. https://www.lastlinesolutions.com/how-to-prevent-cyber-crime-by-training-your-employees/

Le ToquinJ.-C. (2006). *Public-Private Partnerships against cybercrime*. https://www.oecd.org/sti/consumer/42534994.pdf

Lebek, B., Uffen, J., Neumann, M., Hohler, B., & Breitner, M. H. (2014). Information security awareness and behavior: A theory-based literature review. *Management Research Review, 37*(12), 1049–1092. doi:10.1108/MRR-04-2013-0085

Liang, H., & Xue, Y. (2010). Understanding security behaviors in personal computer usage: A threat avoidance perspective. *Journal of the Association for Information Systems, 11*(7), 394–413. doi:10.17705/1jais.00232

Lun, Y. Z., D'Innocenzo, A., Malavolta, I., & Di Benedetto, M. D. (2016). Cyber-physical systems security: a systematic mapping study. *arXiv preprint arXiv:1605.09641*.

Maitlo, A., Ameen, N., Peikari, H. R., & Shah, M. (2019). Preventing identity theft: Identifying major barriers to knowledge-sharing in online retail organisations. *Information Technology & People, 32*(5), 1184–1214. doi:10.1108/ITP-05-2018-0255

Martin, L. E., & Mulvihill, T. M. (2019). Voices in education: Teacher self-efficacy in education. *Teacher Educator, 54*(3), 195–205. doi:10.1080/08878730.2019.1615030

McCormack, G. R., Rock, M., Toohey, A. N., & Hignell, D. (2010). Characteristics of urban parks associated with park use and physical activity: A review of qualitative research. *Health & Place, 16*(4), 712–726. doi:10.1016/j.healthplace.2010.03.003 PMID:20356780

Miller, B. (2020). *15 Advantages and Disadvantages of Quantitative Research*. Academic Press.

Moher, D., Shamseer, L., Clarke, M., Ghersi, D., Liberati, A., Petticrew, M., Shekelle, P., & Stewart, L. A.Prisma-P Group. (2015). Preferred reporting items for systematic review and meta-analysis protocols (PRISMA-P) 2015 statement. *Systematic Reviews, 4*(1), 1–9. doi:10.1186/2046-4053-4-1 PMID:25554246

Muccini, H., Sharaf, M., & Weyns, D. (2016, May). Self-adaptation for cyber-physical systems: a systematic literature review. In *Proceedings of the 11th international symposium on software engineering for adaptive and self-managing systems* (pp. 75-81). 10.1145/2897053.2897069

MyCERT. (2021). Retrieved December, 20, 2021 from https://www.mycert.org.my/portal/statistics-content?menu=b75e037d-6ee3-4d11-8169-66677d694932&id=77be547e-7a17-444b-9698-8c267427936c

Naseer, H., Maynard, S. B., & Desouza, K. C. (2021). Demystifying analytical information processing capability: The case of cybersecurity incident response. *Decision Support Systems*, *143*, 113476. doi:10.1016/j.dss.2020.113476

Ng, B. Y., & Rahim, B. A. (2005). A socio-behavioral study of home computer users' intention to practice security. *Proceedings of the Ninth Pacific Asia Conference on Information Systems.*

Noguerol, L. O., & Branch, R. (2018). Leadership and electronic data security within small businesses: An exploratory case study. *Journal of Economic Development, Management, IT, Finance, and Marketing*, *10*(2), 7–35.

Onumo, A., Cullen, A., & Ullah-Awan, I. (2017, August). An empirical study of cultural dimensions and cybersecurity development. In *2017 IEEE 5th International Conference on Future Internet of Things and Cloud (FiCloud)* (pp. 70-76). IEEE. 10.1109/FiCloud.2017.41

Ophoff, J., & Lakay, M. (2018, August). Mitigating the ransomware threat: a protection motivation theory approach. In *International Information Security Conference* (pp. 163-175). Springer.

Osman, Z., Adis, A. A. A., & Phang, G. (2017). Perceived security towards e-banking services: an examination among Malaysian young consumers. *Journal of the Asian Academy of Applied Business*, 15.

Paek, S. Y., Nalla, M. K., Chun, Y. T., & Lee, J. (2021). The Perceived Importance of Cybercrime Control among Police Officers: Implications for Combatting Industrial Espionage. *Sustainability (Basel)*, *13*(8), 4351. doi:10.3390/su13084351

Pandey, S., Singh, R. K., Gunasekaran, A., & Kaushik, A. (2020). Cyber security risks in globalised supply chains: Conceptual framework. *Journal of Global Operations and Strategic Sourcing*, *13*(1), 103–128. doi:10.1108/JGOSS-05-2019-0042

Pham, H. C., Ulhaq, I., Nkhoma, M., Nguyen, M. N., & Brennan, L. (2018). *Exploring knowledge sharing practices for raising security awareness.* Academic Press.

Popham, J., McCluskey, M., Ouellet, M., & Gallupe, O. (2020). Exploring police-reported cybercrime in Canada: Variation and correlates. *Policing*, *43*(1), 35–48. doi:10.1108/PIJPSM-08-2019-0128

Rahim, N. H. A., Hamid, S., Mat Kiah, M. L., Shamshirband, S., & Furnell, S. (2015). A systematic review of approaches to assessing cybersecurity awareness. *Kybernetes*, *44*(4), 606–622. doi:10.1108/K-12-2014-0283

Report, C. D. (2021). Retrieved December, 15, 2021 from https://cyber-edge.com/wp-content/uploads/2021/04/CyberEdge-2021-CDR-Report-v1.1-1.pdf

Rivard, J. P. (2014). *Cybercrime: The creation and exploration of a model* [Doctoral dissertation]. University of Phoenix.

Safa, N. S., & Von Solms, R. (2016). An Information Security Knowledge Sharing Model in Organisations. *Computers in Human Behavior*, *57*, 442–451. doi:10.1016/j.chb.2015.12.037

Sasse, M., & Flechais, I. (2005). Usable Security: Why Do We Need It? How Do We Get It? In L. F. Cranor & S. Garfinkel (Eds.), *Security and Usability* (pp. 13–30). Sebastopol, CA: O'Reilly Publishing. Retrieved from https://discovery.ucl.ac.uk/20345

Senol, M., & Karacuha, E. (2020). Creating and implementing an effective and deterrent national cyber security strategy. *Journal of Engineering*, *2020*, 2020. doi:10.1155/2020/5267564

Showkat, N., & Parveen, H. (2017). Non-probability and probability sampling. *Media and Communications Study*, 1-9.

Srivastava, S. K., Das, S., Udo, G. J., & Bagchi, K. (2020). Determinants of cybercrime originating within a nation: A cross-country study. *Journal of Global Information Technology Management*, *23*(2), 112–137. doi:10.1080/1097198X.2020.1752084

Tashakkori, A., & Teddlie, C. (2003). *Handbook of Mixed Methods in Social and Behavioral Research*. Sage.

Termimi, M. A. A., Rosele, M. I., Meerangani, K. A., Marinsah, S. A., & Ramli, M. A. (2015). Women's involvement in cybercrime: A premilinary study. *Journal: Journal of Advances In Hmanities*, *3*(3).

Ursillo, S., Jr., & Arnold, C. (2019). *Cybersecurity Is Critical for all Organizations – Large and Small*. https://www.ifac.org/knowledge-gateway/preparing-future-ready-professionals/discussion/cybersecurity-critical-all-organizations-large-and-small

US Chamber of Commerce. (2018). *Partnering With Law Enforcement to Combat Cybercrime*. Author.

van Bavel, R., Rodríguez-Priego, N., Vila, J., & Briggs, P. (2019). Using protection motivation theory in the design of nudges to improve online security behavior. *International Journal of Human-Computer Studies*, *123*, 29–39. doi:10.1016/j.ijhcs.2018.11.003

Wang, V., Nnaji, H., & Jung, J. (2020). Internet banking in Nigeria: Cyber security breaches, practices and capability. *International Journal of Law, Crime and Justice*, *62*, 100415. doi:10.1016/j.ijlcj.2020.100415

Warkentin, M., Johnston, A. C., & Shropshire, J. (2011). The Influence of the Informal Social Learning Environment on Information Privacy Policy Compliance Efficacy and Intention. *European Journal of Information Systems*, *20*(3), 267–284. doi:10.1057/ejis.2010.72

World health Orgaisation. (2009). *Human Factors in Patient Safety Review of Topics and Tools*. https://www.who.int/patientsafety/research/methods_measures/human_factors/human_factors_review.pdf

Zhang, J., Luximon, Y., & Song, Y. (2019). The role of consumers' perceived security, perceived control, interface design features, and conscientiousness in continuous use of mobile payment services. *Sustainability (Basel)*, *11*(23), 6843. doi:10.3390/su11236843

Zhang-Kennedy, L., & Chiasson, S. (2021). A Systematic Review of Multimedia Tools for Cybersecurity Awareness and Education. *ACM Computing Surveys*, *54*(1), 1–39. doi:10.1145/3427920

KEY TERMS AND DEFINITIONS

Coping Appraisal: The individual ability to successfully avoid cybercrime threats.

Culture: Believe, ideas, and customs of a society.

Cybercrime: Threats encountered by information systems.

Good Governance: Conduct and manage the organisational process in a manner that promotes realisation of human rights.

Leadership Support: Support and motivation received from top management to create positive workplaces.

Strategic Partnership: Form collaboration with other stakeholders to effectively combat cyber-threat.

Strategy: Actions taken to combat cybercrime activities.

Threat: Risk that the Information system encountered.

Chapter 4
Privacy-Preserving Techniques for Online Social Networks Data

Yousra Belfaik
https://orcid.org/0009-0000-6270-882X
Laboratory LIMATI, FPBM, USMS University, Morocco

Abdelhadi Zineddine
https://orcid.org/0009-0000-8188-1353
Laboratory LIMATI, FPBM, USMS University, Morocco

Yassine Sadqi
https://orcid.org/0000-0002-0772-9916
Laboratory LIMATI, FPBM, USMS University, Morocco

Said Safi
Laboratory LIMATI, FPBM, USMS University, Morocco

ABSTRACT

Online social networks (OSNs) are platforms on the web that have seen significant growth. They allow people to connect, interact, and share information with others over the internet. These platforms have become an essential part of people's daily lives, serving as the primary means of communication for individuals worldwide. However, despite the significant benefits these platforms offer, they face privacy concerns such as identity theft and misuse of users' sensitive information. This chapter aims to provide a comprehensive review of the various privacy weaknesses in OSNs, along with an exploration of the existing mechanisms and techniques used to safeguard users' data within this dynamic environment. The review is based on the rigorous Kitchenham protocol and performs a comprehensive assessment of 26 journal articles, published in the last five years. This study serves as a valuable resource for researchers and developers seeking to enhance the privacy preservation of OSNs.

DOI: 10.4018/979-8-3693-2691-6.ch004

INTRODUCTION

The number of Internet users is rapidly increasing, and as a result, the number of online social networking sites is also growing. Online social networks (OSN) are digital platforms that allow individuals to connect, communicate, and share information with each other over the internet. These networks enable users to create personal profiles, interact with other users through various means such as messaging, comments, and likes, and share content such as photos, videos, and status updates (Jain et al., 2021). Social networking involves the use of platforms such as Facebook, WhatsApp, Instagram, and Twitter to communicate with friends, family, colleagues, or even strangers sharing similar interests, hobbies, beliefs, and goals. According to January 2023 statistics (Dixon, 2023), Facebook is the most popular social network, with 2.958 billion monthly active users out of the 5.18 billion internet users. YouTube accounts for 2.514 billion users, while WhatsApp and Instagram have two billion users. Twitter has 556 million active monthly users. Although social media has many benefits, there is growing concern regarding user data privacy.

In general, the data gathered by online social network operators are rich in relationships and content, which is valuable to many third-party consumers. The data types in online social networks include Service Data and Behavioral Data. Service Data includes compulsory information that users need to upload as a requirement to join a social network, such as legal name, age, gender, email, and phone numbers. These are essential details for user identification and account creation. On the other hand, Behavioral Data is collected based on user behavior, encompassing actions such as what the user does, where, when, and with whom. Behavioral data provides insights into user interactions and activities within the social network. Unfortunately, online social network providers often utilize users' sensitive data to generate revenue, such as their interests, hobbies, and profiles, to tailor precise advertisements. This practice sometimes extends to divulging sensitive data to third parties (e.g., data brokers) without obtaining explicit informed consent (Wainakh et al., 2019). Moreover, due to users' lack of privacy awareness, they may not consider access rights and sharing scope when sharing information on OSNs, which puts their privacy at risk. These settings directly impact who can view and interact with their personal information, and this oversight can lead to negative privacy-related experiences for users (Guo et al., 2023).

On numerous occasions, user data was compromised by unauthorized parties, like the 2018 breach of Facebook tokens, where Cambridge Analytica obtained access to nearly 87 million Facebook accounts (Gao & Li, 2019). Cambridge Analytica used these accounts to sway public opinion in political campaigns without the users' knowledge or consent (Rodrigues et al., 2023). This has led to a call for stricter regulations and policies to protect user privacy, as well as greater transparency from social media platforms about their data handling practices to ensure user trust and confidence in the digital space. Therefore, it is mandatory to understand the privacy-preserving measures and approaches that can be used to safeguard user information from unauthorized access and misuse in OSNs. This chapter provides a comprehensive review of the various prevalent privacy threats on social media networks, their potential attacks, and their impact on users and OSN companies' reputations. In addition, the chapter will explore the current privacy-preserving mechanisms and techniques in the literature used to mitigate these threats and safeguard users' privacy within this dynamic environment. We have followed the systematic literature methodology of Kitchenham et al. (2009) to ensure selection of pertinent and relevant studies aligns with the objectives of our chapter. Understanding the complex landscape of privacy threats in OSNs and the various measures that can be used to safeguard user privacy can guide future efforts to create a safer and confidential online social networking environment for all users.

The rest of this chapter will be remainder as follows: Section 2 presents previous related works and research in the field of online social network privacy threats. Section 3 details the methodology employed to select pertinent documents for the review. Section 4 delves into the various privacy threats present in online social networks, along with their implications. Section 5 explores the existing mechanisms and techniques used in the field to safeguard users' privacy within online social networks. Section 6 concludes the chapter.

RELATED WORK

In this section, we provide an overview of the existing literature reviews and surveys that have addressed privacy in online social networks and analyzed different privacy-preserving solutions in this dynamic environment.

Abawajy et al. (2016) presented in their work a survey of privacy risks, attacks, and protection strategies related to social network data publishing. The authors examined the various privacy violations and information that attackers use to target anonymized social network data. Furthermore, they provided an overview of the privacy-preserving techniques for publishing social network data, metrics for calculating the anonymity level provided information loss, challenges, and future research prospects.

Jain et al. (2021) performed a comprehensive review and analysis of security and privacy issues related to online social networks (OSNs). It discusses various threats and existing solutions that can provide security to social network users. The paper also presents statistics on OSN attacks on various OSN web applications and discusses numerous defensive approaches to OSN security. The study encompasses all the conventional threats that affect the majority of clients in social networks and most of the modern threats that are prevalent nowadays, with an emphasis on teenagers and children. The paper concludes by discussing open issues, challenges, and relevant security guidelines to achieve trustworthiness in online social networks.

Majeed et al. (2022) provided in their work a comprehensive analysis of privacy-preserving solutions developed for online social networks (OSNs). The authors classified the existing privacy-preserving solutions into two main categories, namely privacy-preserving graph publishing (PPGP) and privacy preservation in application-specific scenarios of OSNs. They also introduced a high-level taxonomy that encompasses common and AI-based privacy-preserving approaches that have proposed ways to combat privacy issues in PPGP. This paper discusses many privacy-preserving solutions proposed for OSN sites. Furthermore, the authors presented some challenges in preserving the privacy of OSNs (i.e., social graph data) from malevolent adversaries and suggested promising avenues for future research.

Liu et al. (2023) performed a survey on intelligent solutions that target modern privacy issues in dynamic OSN image sharing from a user-centric perspective. The authors first provided the definition and taxonomy of OSN image privacy within the context of dynamic OSN image sharing. Then, based on the entire lifecycle of OSN image sharing, they presented a high-level privacy analysis framework to comprehensively analyze the various privacy problems, solutions, and challenges in this interdisciplinary field. Using this framework, they have identified privacy issues caused by OSN users' behaviors and investigated the appropriate intelligent solutions in a stage-based manner. Next, they summarized the common design principles of the reviewed intelligent solutions at each stage, as well as their methods, advantages, and disadvantages. Finally, they discussed the difficulties and potential directions for this field.

Despite the valuable insights offered by the aforementioned works on the privacy challenges in online social networks, it is notable that none of these works explicitly outlined the methodology used for selecting the literature upon which their findings are based. Furthermore, there appears to be a lack of consideration for a specific timeframe when conducting their literature searches (e.g., the last five years or the last decade). Moreover, these works focused on presenting privacy-preservation solutions that address specific privacy concerns within online social networks rather than the broader context. For example, Abawajy et al. (2016) exclusively provided social network data anonymization privacy-preservation mechanisms, while Majeed et al. (2022) concentrated solely on artificial intelligence (AI) techniques in the realm of OSN privacy. Similarly, Liu et al. (2023) addressed only artificial intelligence solutions for OSN images.

RESEARCH METHODOLOGY

The objective of this chapter is to evaluate privacy concerns and explore the diverse techniques employed to preserve user data within the context of social media networks. To ensure the inclusion of pertinent and relevant research studies aligned with the scope of our review, we followed the systematic literature review methodology proposed by Kitchenham et al. (2009). This methodology encompasses four key steps, namely: (1) formulation of research questions, (2) creation of a search string, (3) definition of the search process, and (4) establishment of inclusion and exclusion criteria.

FORMULATION OF RESEARCH QUESTIONS

While considering the objectives of this study, our review seeks to address two key research questions:

RQ1: What are the major privacy concerns in online social networks?

RQ2: What is the state of the art of the existing privacy-preserving techniques used in online social networks?

Identifying the privacy concerns associated with social network sites (i.e. RQ1) is essential to understanding and rectifying the existing privacy vulnerabilities, updating privacy settings and policies, and establishing best practices for data management to create a safer and more secure online environment for users. Furthermore, understanding the state of the art of the current mechanisms employed to preserve users' privacy in online social networks (i.e. RQ2) will assist researchers and organizations make accurate choices when it comes to selecting the right privacy-preserving techniques that meet their needs.

Search String

Based on the research questions, we identified the keywords "online social network", "privacy", "data privacy", and "privacy-preserving" and did some tests using the logical operators "AND" and "OR" to specify the combination that will align the best with the aim of this review. Therefore, we chose the following search string: *"online social network" AND ("privacy" OR "privacy-preserving" OR "data privacy").*

Search Process

In this step, we have used the created search string to retrieve relevant publications from Scopus and Web of Science. These databases provide the functionality to search in title, abstract, and keywords. Furthermore, they offer an advanced search that restricts the number of publications they want to view based on criteria like the year of publication, document type, language, author name, and search areas, among others.

Inclusion and Inclusion Criteria

To keep only the publications that are consistent with the objectives of our SLR and contribute to answering the research questions, specific inclusion criteria (IC) and exclusion criteria (EC) have been defined and applied. The inclusion criteria (IC) are as follows:

IC1: papers published within the last four years (2019-2023).

IC2: publications must be written in English.

IC3: the publication type is a journal article.

Conversely, the exclusion criteria (EC) consist of the following:

EC1: papers without full-text availability.

EC2: duplicate papers.

EC3: publications that do not address privacy concerns and/or privacy-preserving techniques in online social networks after reading the full text.

Conducting the SLR

The search string mentioned above was used to search across Scopus and Web of Science databases. The initial search revealed 2494 publications. Due to the large number of publications, we applied the publication time and type filter to include publications between 2019 and 2023 and journal articles. The application of these filters reduces the number to 342 publications. In the next step, the duplicate publications were removed, which reduced the total number of publications to 280. After screening the papers based on the inclusion and exclusion criteria mentioned above, we selected 26 publications to be included in our review. In order to efficiently carry out and document the SLR process, we integrated components of the Preferred Reporting Items for Systematic Reviews and Meta-Analyses (PRISMA) methodology. Figure 1 provides a summary of the entire publication selection process using the PRISMA method.

OSN PRIVACY THREATS (RQ1)

Online social networks have become an integral part of modern life, but they also raise numerous privacy concerns for users. The term "privacy" refers to an individual's right to control their personal information, including its disclosure, sharing, storage, and use (Gove & Altman, 1978). It emphasizes the importance of upholding the proper privacy standards in communication and social interaction environments to protect personal information. However, controlling data disclosure levels in OSNs can be challenging due to their unique characteristics, such as mass content sharing and information transmission. Based on the documents selected for our review, we answer the first research question (RQ1) in this section.

Figure 1. PRISMA flow diagram summarizing the publication selection

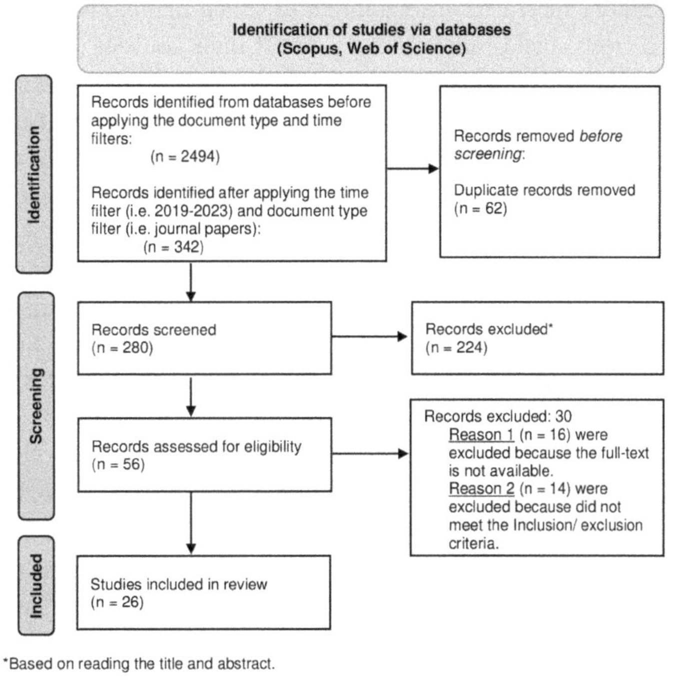

We have categorized privacy threats on online social networks into two distinct classifications: Honest OSN provider-based threats and Malicious individual-based threats. Table 1 summarizes the OSN privacy threats, attacks and implications.

Malicious Individual-Based Threats

This category include the threats caused by individuals with harmful intentions, as they attempt to harm a user's reputation, manipulate or distort his data, inflict emotional distress, or potentially escalate to physical harm.

- **Data breaches:** Social networks are susceptible to data breaches, in which hackers steal user information by gaining unauthorized access to the OSN platforms' databases. Then, this data may be bought and sold on the dark web or employed for a variety of malicious activities. In addition to putting user information at risk, a data breach also causes users to lose faith in the platform organization's ability to keep their information safe, resulting in a big reputational problem for organizations (Syed & Dhillon, 2015) (Jain et al., 2021). Furthermore, privacy breach in OSN can due to data mining of users' information. Specifically, the concern is about the leakage of sensitive attributes or private information, such as political orientation, through the analysis of disclosed non-sensitive information. This highlights the risk of unauthorized access to personal data and the potential for sensitive attributes to be inferred or exposed without the users' consent, leading to privacy violations and potential discrimination (Reza et al., 2021).

- **Identity theft:** Identity theft is a serious threat in which malicious individuals try to obtain personal information from social media users without their consent (Rodrigues et al., 2023). This includes sensitive details like social security numbers, phone numbers, and addresses. Using this information, the attacker can gain access to the victim's friend list and use various social engineering techniques to extract confidential information from them. Since the attacker is pretending to be a legitimate user, he is free to use that profile however he pleases, which can lead to serious consequences for authentic users (Jain et al., 2021).
- **Harm's user reputation:** When sharing personal or sensitive information on OSN, users risk their reputations being threatened. Malicious users can create and manage multiple fake profiles to access not shared confidential private information and use it to harm the OSN user's reputation. They may tag, like, or share inappropriate photos or content without the victim's consent, as well as spread hurtful comments, rumors, and false information online. This can lead to emotional distress and social isolation for the victim. Furthermore, users should be aware of the possibility of manipulation and distortion of data, as there are tools available to alter personal images and damage one's reputation.
- **Surveillance:** Users of OSNs can have their various activities tracked in real-time through surveillance, a new type of monitoring, with the help of their posts, likes, and connections with others (Rodrigues et al., 2023). Moreover, an attacker can track a target's calls, locations, browser activities, and messages on different platforms such as WhatsApp, Facebook, and Snapchat by installing surveillance software on the victim's device that will be hidden and undetectable. Even worse, an attacker can install surveillance software by just calling the user even if he doesn't have physical access to the user's device as discovered by WhatsApp, if the target doesn't answer the call (Nawaz et al., 2023). Governments and law enforcement agencies occasionally have the right to request access to user data for security or legal reasons, which raises concerns about the balance between privacy and national security.

Honest OSN Provider-Based Threats

OSN provider-based threats include privacy threats posed by OSN providers in order to offer personalized experiences, improve their services, and display targeted advertisements. Reputable OSN companies prioritize user privacy and adhere to legal and ethical standards. Typically, they do not lunch attacks to collect, track and profile users.

- **Disclosure and misusing of data:** Social networks often collect extensive data about their users, including personal information, interests, browsing habits, activities and interactions. Sharing such sensitive and private information may cause severe consequences for OSN users, violate their privacy, and threaten the safety of users' lives (Rodrigues et al., 2023) (Zhang et al. 2021). Commercial OSN platforms often share their users' data with third-party developers, advertisers, and other entities for targeted advertising and analytics purposes. This sharing often occurs without users' explicit consent. The unauthorized usage of user data can lead to trust issues between users and OSN service providers. When users feel that their data is being used without their consent, it can erode trust in the platform and the service provider, leading to concerns about data security and privacy protection. Users may also face challenges in understanding how their data is being used within the OSN ecosystem. The lack of transparency regarding data usage and privacy policies can further exacerbate this threat.

- **Tracking and profiling users:** OSN providers use machine-learning algorithms to track and analyze users' routine activities, such as daily browsing and shopping preferences. With this information, OSNs can create comprehensive user profiles to either market products or track user behavior. Additionally, OSN providers can use algorithms to personalize content and display what they believe users will prefer, which can result in "filter bubbles" and confirmation biases. This approach also poses a risk of exposing users to misleading or biased information. Moreover, some social networks collect users' location data, which enables tracking their movements and habits. This can lead to potential physical safety concerns or unauthorized access to location data. (Al-Charchafchi et al., 2020).
- **Lack of user control:** The lack of user control privacy threat refers to the risk and challenges associated with users having limited control over their personal data and privacy in online social networks (OSNs) (Frimpong et al., 2022). In many OSNs, users have limited autonomy over how their data is utilized and shared within the network. This lack of control can result in users feeling vulnerable and exposed, especially when their sensitive information is accessed and used without their knowledge or consent, and unfortunately, this is the often case. Furthermore, this lack of control can lead to the exploitation of personal data for targeted advertising, data mining, or other purposes without the user's explicit permission. The lack of transparency regarding data usage and the complexity of understanding privacy policies can indeed have significant implications for user privacy and control over their data. When users are not fully informed about how their data is being used, collected, and shared, they may unknowingly expose sensitive information. This lack of transparency can lead to a loss of control over personal data, as users may not be able to make informed decisions about their privacy preferences.

PRIVACY-PRESERVING TECHNIQUES FOR OSN DATA (RQ2)

The increasing concern for protecting users' personal information and data privacy in online social networks is due to the amount of information shared on social networks that are very enticing for adversaries aiming to harm individuals or businesses. The information stored in social networks is often taken for granted, and as people put more and more information in different forms on social networks, it can lead to unprecedented access to personal and business information (Jain et al., 2021). If users and OSN service providers do not take these issues seriously enough, they make themselves vulnerable to a wide variety of threats, put their confidential data at risk, and lose reputation and trust.

In response to these concerns, researchers in both academia and industries are constantly trying to find solutions for the aforementioned threats in social media. They are developing defensive solutions and security guidelines to protect users' systems, accounts, and information. These efforts aim to empower users with control over their own data, mitigate the risk of unauthorized access and data breaches, and build trust in OSN platforms. Implementing robust privacy-preserving mechanisms ensures that users can continue to benefit from the connectivity and engagement offered by OSNs while minimizing the risks associated with privacy threats. Following, we respond to the second research question of our

Table 1. OSN privacy threats, attacks and implications

	Privacy Threats	Implications	Attacks
Malicious Individual-based threats	Data breaches	- Personal sensitive data misuse. - Lost trust in OSN organizations. - Personal Information disclosure to unauthorized entities.	- Phishing attack - Spam attack - Malware Attacks (such as viruses, worms Ransomwar, trojans, spyware) - SQL injection attack - Cross site scripting (XSS) attack - Brute force attack - Insider attacks - Sybil attack - inference attacks
	Identity theft	- Identity spoofing - Personal Sensitive Information disclosure. - Repuation manipulation.	- Social Engineering attacks - Impersonation Attacks - Physical attacks - Clickjacking attack - Account Hijacking attack - Malware attacks - Profile cloning attack - Inference attack - Man-In-The-Middle attack
	Harm's user reputation	- Reputation manipulation. - Distortion of data. - Risk of emotional distress of the victim. - Risk of social isolation for the victim.	- Sybil attack - Inference attack - Identity clone attacks - Doxing attack - Cyberbullying attack - Cyberstalking attack - Cyber grooming attack - Social Engineering attacks - Image Manipulation attack - Impersonation attack
	Surveillance	- User's sensitive data disclosure. - Track user activities in real-time.	- Malware attacks - Man-In-The-Middle attack - Account hijacking attack - Social engineering attacks
Honest OSN provider -based threats	Disclosure and misusing of data	- Misusing user's personal Infomation. - Sensitive data disclosure. - User's data collection - Trust Issues - The lack of transparency - Personal data exploitation.	
	Tracking and profiling user	- Track user activities. - Potential physical safety risk because of geographic tracking. - Risk of exposing users to misleading or biased information.	
	Lack of user control	- User's lack of control over his data. - Unauthorized data usage. - Limited autonomy. - Lack of transparency. - Personal data exploitation.	

review (RQ2) and present three different privacy-preserving approaches for OSNs. This includes the Modelling approach, the Blockchain-based approach, and the Anonymization-based approach. Table 2 illustrates the various frameworks and systems proposed for each approach, the techniques used, and the targeted privacy threat.

Privacy Threat Modelling Approach

Threat modelling is a structured process that aims to identify and evaluate potential threats to a system, which helps developers and specialists develop appropriate countermeasures to prevent or mitigate the effects of such threats. By analyzing the system's architecture, data flow, and potential vulnerabilities, threat modelling allows for a comprehensive understanding of potential risks (Rodrigues el al., 2023). This proactive approach enables organizations to determine what types of mitigations are required during a new system's design phase, potentially saving significant investments and resources that would otherwise be needed for the redesign. Therefore, this approach aims to model privacy threats in OSNs in the early development stages to enhance users' privacy-preserving in those systems. Following, we present some of the privacy threat modelling methodologies used for Online Social Networks:

- **STRIDE:** This methodology focuses on identifying and mitigating threats based on six categories: Spoofing, Tampering, Repudiation, Information Disclosure, Denial of Service, and Elevation of Privilege (STRIDE). Analyzing these categories helps developers assess potential privacy threats and develop appropriate countermeasures (Khan et al., 2017).
- **LINDDUN:** This methodology stands for Linkability, Identifiability, Non-repudiation, Detectability, Disclosure of information, Unawareness, and Non-compliance (LINDDUN). It provides a comprehensive framework for analyzing privacy threats in OSNs, considering various aspects such as user identification, data disclosure, and the ability to link different pieces of information (Wuyts et al., 2018).
- **Privacy Impact Assessment (PIA):** It is a systematic process that involves identifying the data collected, analyzing the purpose of data collection, evaluating privacy risks, and proposing mitigation strategies for assessing the impacts on the privacy of a system. By evaluating privacy issues early, a PIA can decrease costs in management time, legal charges, and possible media or public concerns. It assists a company in avoiding costly or embarrassing privacy errors (Wright, 2012).
- **Data Flow Diagram (DFD):** DFD is a graphical representation that illustrates the flow of data within a system. DFD can be used to identify potential privacy threats by analyzing how data is collected, stored, processed, and transmitted within an OSN (Ward, 1986).
- **Privacy Threat MOdeling Language (PTMOL):** PTMOL is a language designed to define countermeasures, stop or lessen the effects of threats, and systematically represent all threat scenarios that affect user privacy on an OSN in a structured manner. It can be incorporated into software development during the design phase and help software designers with threat modelling without needing a high level of expertise in privacy-related domains (Rodrigues el al., 2023).

Blockchain-Based Approach

Blockchain technology is a decentralized, immutable, and distributed ledger that records an increasing number of transactions across multiple computers (Belfaik et al., 2023). It was invented by Satoshi Nakamoto in 2008 for the first time as a distributed ledger underlying Bitcoin transactions. A blockchain consists of a series of blocks containing specific transaction data, and each block contains the hash value of the previous block, thereby forming a chain. This linkage mechanism ensures the reliability of the blockchain, and data cannot be modified once they are written to the blockchain. Through a predefined consensus protocol, each node in a peer-to-peer network can synchronize the chain, forming a decentralized ledger (Jiang & Zhang, 2019). Blockchain has evolved with the introduction of smart contracts, which are self-executing programs that run on the network without the need for a third party. A smart contract consists of a set of functions and data located at a specific address on the blockchain. It defines how a process is carried out and what actions are taken once a specific event occurs. Essentially, smart contracts serve as a form of decentralized automation that facilitates, verifies, and enforces agreements in transactions, and then records the outcomes in a distributed ledger (Belfaik et al., 2023).

The use of blockchain technology extends beyond cryptocurrencies and has been applied to various domains including banking, data privacy systems, online social networks, crowdsourcing applications, and data-sharing architectures. It offers a decentralized and tamper-proof method for storing and managing data, making it a powerful tool for ensuring data integrity and security. In the following, we present various blockchain-based approaches addressing privacy concerns in online social networks:

- **BPP:** Zhang et al. (2021) proposed the Blockchain-based privacy-preserving framework for online social networks (BPP) framework that aims to address the challenge of the illegal disclosure of users' private data by ensuring the security of sensitive data while providing efficient and privacy-preserving social network services for users. In addition, this framework is a privacy-preserving efficient solution guaranteeing normal social network services, including data sharing, data retrieval, and data access services to registered users with assurance. It also ensures a secure and efficient keyword search algorithm based on blockchain and public key encryption techniques. This algorithm allows data queriers (i.e. data brokers) to receive correct search results without compromising the security of the data shared by data publishers (i.e. OSN providers). It addresses the challenge of enabling an effective and verifiable keyword search scheme for online social networks, particularly over encrypted data. This system is designed to enable data publishers to outsource their data to the cloud server in an encrypted manner and share it with authorized data queriers in a flexible and scalable manner using blockchain and smart contracts. It also addresses potential security threats, such as passive attacks by the cloud server to obtain secret information and collusion between malicious data queriers and the cloud server.
- **BCOSN:** Jiang & Zhang (2019) developed the BlockChain-based decentralized OSN (BCOSN) framework to ensure data privacy, data integrity of users, verifiable user identity, newsfeed notification, and convenient friend recommendations. This framework uses blockchain technology to provide a trusted and immutable platform for user identity management. By leveraging smart contracts, the framework ensures the authenticity of user identities and prevents identity forgery or embezzlement. In addition, the framework separates the storage services, allowing users to have complete control over their data while using the blockchain as a trusted server to provide central control services. This approach addresses the challenge of designing complex protocols for routing in a distributed data storage manner. Through using smart contracts and event mechanisms, the framework enables real-time message notifications, eliminating the need for users to periodically request "newsfeed" updates. This enhances the efficiency of information retrieval and reduces resource wastage. Furthermore, the proposed system employs Ciphertext-Policy

Attribute-Based Encryption (CP-ABE) to ensure fine-grained access control and secure communication among friends. By separating the storage service from the control service, the framework mitigates the risk of privacy leakage associated with third-party central servers. To minimize time-consuming operations, the framework combines symmetric encryption with CP-ABE. This approach enhances the efficiency of data access and retrieval in a decentralized environment. It also provides attribute-based fine-grained encryption, allowing users to manage their friends with attributes and control access to their data. This ensures that only authorized users can decrypt and access specific data, enhancing privacy and security.

- **RecGuard:** Frimpong et al. (2022) introduced a privacy-preserving blockchain-based model for data sharing in an OSN ecosystem called RecGuard. This model aims to address the challenges related to user privacy and data security in online social networks. The system deploys two smart contracts, namely RG-SH and RG-ST, to manage user data and ensure secure data storage. These smart contracts play a crucial role in enforcing privacy policies, access control, and data encryption within the OSN. In addition, RecGuard employs privacy-preserving techniques such as data encryption, proxy re-encryption, and obfuscation to protect user data from unauthorized access and maintain user privacy. These techniques ensure that sensitive user information is securely stored and transmitted within the network. RecGuard also integrates a graph convolutional network (GCN) with the blockchain-based system to detect and prevent malicious nodes within the network. This anomaly detection mechanism enhances the security of the entire network infrastructure and ensures the integrity of user data. Furthermore, the system isolates primary data storage from its analysis within the OSN and stores it in an encrypted format, giving users control over their data. Users are granted permission through smart contracts, and their participation in the OSN is separated from their data, ensuring privacy and security. To ensure transparency of users' privacy policies and data usage, RecGuard includes a consent mechanism that allows users to have control over how their sensitive data are utilized, ensuring that user consent is prioritized in data sharing and usage.

Anonymization-Based Approach

An anonymization-based approach to preserve privacy in Online Social Networks (OSNs) involves modifying the network data in such a way that the identities of individual users are protected while still allowing meaningful analysis and utilization of the data. It also involves the transformation of sensitive user data in a way that cannot be traced back to the original user. This approach aims to protect the privacy of users' sensitive attributes and prevent the identification of specific individuals within the network while maintaining the overall structure and utility of the data for analysis purposes (Kumar & Kumar, 2021).

The anonymization process typically involves techniques such as modifying the network structure, anonymizing user attributes, or a combination of both (Gangarde et al., 2021). For example, the anonymization process may involve techniques like k-anonymity, l-diversity, t-closeness, fuzzy set-based methodologies, and rewiring algorithms to transform the network structure in a way that minimizes the risk of re-identification while preserving the privacy of users' data and its utility for analysis. By employing anonymization-based approaches, OSN owners can release anonymized versions of the social network graph data to third parties for analysis, ensuring that the privacy of OSN users is maintained while still allowing valuable insights to be derived from the data. Following we present some anonymization-based solutions addressing OSN privacy.

- **PPRA:** Kumar & Kumar (2021) proposed an algorithm called the Privacy-Preserving Rewiring Algorithm (PPRA), which aims to anonymize social network graph data effectively while preserving the privacy of users in online social networks (OSNs). The algorithm utilizes a combination of fuzzy set-based techniques and rewiring algorithms to achieve this objective. The PPRA algorithm begins by fuzzifying the degree centrality of nodes using fuzzy sets, allowing for a more flexible representation of the degree centrality in the network structure. This fuzzification process contributes to enhanced privacy preservation by introducing a level of indistinctness in the representation of node centrality. Subsequently, the algorithm employs a rewiring technique, specifically a degree-preserving randomization algorithm, to modify the network structure while maintaining the degree distribution of nodes unchanged. This approach ensures that the overall topology of the network is altered, minimizing the risk of re-identification while preserving the utility of the data for analysis. Furthermore, the algorithm introduces l-diversity and t-closeness measures to address the limitations of k-anonymity and enhance the privacy preservation techniques used in the algorithm. These measures focus on introducing intragroup diversity and random modification of k-edges in the graph structure, further contributing to improved privacy preservation.
- **MGPBC:** Gangarde et al., (2021) proposed a system for anonymizing Online Social Networks (OSNs) using multiple-graph-properties-based clustering (MGPBC). The system aims to ensure k-anonymity, l-diversity, and t-closeness privacy requirements in OSNs. It introduces a clustering approach that addresses the privacy preservation of edge, node, and user attributes in the OSN graph. The system employs anonymization techniques to transform sensitive user data, such as names, addresses, and location information, into anonymous identifiers and utilizes clustering algorithms to group OSN data into clusters, ensuring k-anonymity. This technique helps in obscuring the identity of individuals by ensuring that each cluster contains at least k indistinguishable individuals. Moreover, the system incorporates l-diversity, which ensures that each cluster contains diverse sensitive attributes, thereby preventing attribute disclosure. This technique enhances the privacy protection of the anonymized data. In addition, it employs t-closeness to ensure that the distribution of sensitive attributes within each cluster closely resembles the overall distribution in the entire dataset. This technique aims to prevent similarity attacks and protect against attribute disclosure. These privacy-preserving techniques along with data normalization and cluster optimization algorithms, collectively contribute to safeguarding the privacy of OSN users' data and relationships within the network.
- **HAKAu:** Medková & Hynek (2023) introduced a hybrid algorithm called Hybrid Algorithm for Effective k-Automorphism (HAkAu), designed to address the anonymization of Online Social Networks (OSNs). HAkAu integrates the k-automorphism method to protect the social network dataset against structural attacks. This method provides a higher level of protection than other k-anonymity methods, such as k-degree or k-neighborhood techniques. In addition, the system employs a genetic algorithm to select the set of vertex disjoint subgraphs, ensuring efficient and effective anonymization. This approach enhances the applicability of the anonymization method based on GA. The authors also proposed a novel chromosome representation for selecting vertex disjoint subgraphs and utilized the GraMi algorithm, marking the first instance of its use in the anonymization procedure.
- **ML-PR**: Gao & Li (2022) proposed a system aims to address the challenge of preserving privacy in Online Social Networks (OSNs) by utilizing machine learning-based techniques. The system focuses on balancing privacy and utility under the influence of machine learning methods used

Table 2. OSN privacy-preserving techniques

Privacy-Preserving Approach	Framework/System	Techniques Used	Targeted Threat
Privacy threat modelling apparoch	STRIDE	Rely on simplified assumptions about system behavior and user interactions.	- Disclosure and misusing of data. - Tracking and profiling users. - Lack of user control.
	LINDDUN		
	PIA		
	DFD		
	PTMOL		
Blockchain-based approach	BPP	- Blockchain technology. - Asymmetric and symmetric encryption algorithms. - Keyword search techniques.	- Disclosure and misusing of data. - Tracking and profiling users. - Identity theft. - Data breaches.
	BCOSN	- Blockchain technology. - Ciphertext-Policy Attribute-Based Encryption (CP-ABE). - Decentralized Storage. - Symmetric Encryption.	- Identity theft. - Data breaches. - Surveillance.
	RecGuard	- Blockchain technology. - Data encryption. - Proxy re-encryption. - Anomaly Detection Using Graph Convolutional Network (GCN)	- Disclosure and misusing of data. - Tracking and profiling users. - Lack of user control.
Anonymization-based approach	PPRA	- Fuzzy Set-Based technique. - Rewiring algorithm. - k-anonymity.	- Identity theft. - Data breaches. - Disclosure and misusing of data.
	MGPBC	- Anonymization. - Clustering algorithms. - l-Diversity and t-Closeness. - Data normalization. - Cluster optimization.	- Identity theft. - Disclosure and misusing of data.
	HAKAu	- K-Automorphism Anonymization. - Genetic Algorithm. - GraMi Algorithm.	- Data breaches. - Disclosure and misusing of data.
	ML-PR	- Generative Adversarial Network (GAN) deep learning model. - Integrated Gradient (IG). - Graph Neural Networks (GNN). - Differential Privacy	- Identity theft. - Data breaches - Surveillance. - Disclosure and misusing of data.

by both benign data scientists and attackers to extract information from OSNs. Two different anonymization approaches are proposed to solve the multi-objective optimization problem of preserving both privacy and utility. The first approach utilizes the deep learning model, Generative Adversarial Network (GAN), to sequentially learn the two objectives and generate graphs. The second approach analyzes the differences between the two objectives on structures and utilizes Integrated Gradient (IG) in learning to break attackers' learning results. It structurally rewires edges to preserve third parties' learning results afterwards. The system models the OSN as a graph and computes the anonymized graph by perturbing the classification results about individual users and preserving the classification results about groups. The proposed anonymization scheme is evaluated using learning-based metrics and traditional graph utility metrics to ensure the preservation of privacy and utility. The techniques used in the proposed system include deep learning models such as Generative Adversarial Network (GAN), Integrated Gradient (IG), and graph neural networks (GNN) for subgraph and node classification. These techniques are employed to perturb the classification results and preserve the privacy and utility of OSN data under the influence of machine learning.

Upon reviewing our findings, we notice that privacy threat modelling solutions only address Malicious individual-based threats, while Blockchain-based techniques cover both privacy threat categories (i.e. Malicious individual-based threats and Honest OSN provider-based threats). On the other hand, Anonymization-based techniques only focus on Malicious individual-based threats and one of the Honest OSN provider-based threats category, the disclosure and misuse of data threat. Additionally, we observed a notable absence of attention to the Harm user's reputation threat within these solutions, highlighting a research gap that warrants consideration by future researchers and developers.

CONCLUSION

The chapter provides a thorough review of the privacy threats present in online social networks (OSNs), their potential attacks and implications for both users and OSN companies. Furthermore, the chapter explores the current mechanisms and techniques used in the field to safeguard users' data against these threats within the dynamic environment of online social networks. This chapter provides valuable insights into the existing landscape of privacy threats and the efforts to mitigate them by selecting the most current and pertinent studies following the rigorous Kitchenham SLR methodology. The findings of our literature highlight the need for further research and development of solutions that specifically target the protection of user reputation in online social networks.

REFERENCES

Abawajy, J. H., Ninggal, M. I. H., & Herawan, T. (2016). Privacy preserving social network data publication. *IEEE Communications Surveys and Tutorials*, *18*(3), 1974–1997. doi:10.1109/COMST.2016.2533668

Al-Charchafchi, A., Manickam, S., & Alqattan, Z. N. M. (2020). Threats Against Information Privacy and Security in Social Networks: A Review. In M. Anbar, N. Abdullah, & S. Manickam (Eds.), *Advances in Cyber Security. ACeS 2019. Communications in Computer and Information Science* (Vol. 1132). Springer. doi:10.1007/978-981-15-2693-0_26

Belfaik, Y., Sadqi, Y., Maleh, Y., Said, S., Tawalbeh, L., & Salah, K. (2023). A Novel Secure and Privacy-Preserving Model for OpenID Connect Based on Blockchain. *IEEE Access : Practical Innovations, Open Solutions*, *11*, 67660–67678. doi:10.1109/ACCESS.2023.3292143

Dixon, S. (2023, October 27). *Most popular social networks worldwide as of October 2023, ranked by number of monthly active users*. Retrieved from Statista website: https://www.statista.com/statistics/272014/global-social-networks-ranked-by-number-of-users/

Frimpong, S. A., Han, M., Boahen, E. K., Ayitey Sosu, R. N., Hanson, I., Larbi-Siaw, O., & Senkyire, I. B. (2022). RecGuard: An efficient privacy preservation blockchain-based system for online social network users. *Blockchain: Research and Applications, 100111*. Advance online publication. doi:10.1016/j.bcra.2022.100111

Gangarde, R., Sharma, A., Pawar, A., Joshi, R., & Gonge, S. (2021). Privacy Preservation in Online Social Networks Using Multiple-Graph-Properties-Based Clustering to Ensure k-Anonymity, l-Diversity, and t-Closeness. *Electronics (Basel)*, *10*(22), 2877. doi:10.3390/electronics10222877

Gao, T., & Li, F. (2019, June). Privacy-preserving sketching for online social network data publication. *2019 16th Annual IEEE International Conference on Sensing, Communication, and Networking (SECON)*. 10.1109/SAHCN.2019.8824823

Gao, T., & Li, F. (2022). Machine Learning-based Online Social Network Privacy Preservation. *Proceedings of the 2022 ACM on Asia Conference on Computer and Communications Security*. 10.1145/3488932.3517405

Gove, W. R., & Altman, I. (1978). The environment and social behavior: Privacy, personal space, territory, crowding. *Contemporary Sociology*, *7*(5), 638. doi:10.2307/2065073

Guo, L., Yao, Z., Lin, M., & Xu, Z. (2023). Fuzzy TOPSIS-based privacy measurement in multiple online social networks. *Complex & Intelligent Systems*, *9*(6), 6089–6101. doi:10.1007/s40747-023-00991-y

Jain, A. K., Sahoo, S. R., & Kaubiyal, J. (2021). Online social networks security and privacy: Comprehensive review and analysis. *Complex & Intelligent Systems*, *7*(5), 2157–2177. doi:10.1007/s40747-021-00409-7

Jiang, L., & Zhang, X. (2019). BCOSN: A Blockchain-Based Decentralized Online Social Network. *IEEE Transactions on Computational Social Systems*, *6*(6), 1454–1466. doi:10.1109/TCSS.2019.2941650

Khan, R., Mclaughlin, K., Laverty, D., & Sezer, S. (2017). STRIDE-based threat modeling for cyber-physical systems. *Proc. IEEE PES Innov. Smart Grid Technol. Conf. Eur. (ISGT-Europe)*, 1–6.

Khan, R., McLaughlin, K., Laverty, D., & Sezer, S. (2017). STRIDE-based threat modeling for cyber-physical systems. *Proc. IEEE PES Innovative Smart Grid Technologies Conference Europe (ISGT-Europe)*, 1-6. 10.1109/ISGTEurope.2017.8260283

Kitchenham, B., Pearl Brereton, O., Budgen, D., Turner, M., Bailey, J., & Linkman, S. (2009). Systematic literature reviews in software engineering – A systematic literature review. *Information and Software Technology*, *51*(1), 7–15. doi:10.1016/j.infsof.2008.09.009

Kumar, S., & Kumar, P. (2021). Privacy Preserving in Online Social Networks Using Fuzzy Rewiring. *IEEE Transactions on Engineering Management*, 1–9. doi:10.1109/TEM.2021.3072812

Liu, C., Zhu, T., Zhang, J., & Zhou, W. (2023). Privacy intelligence: A survey on image privacy in online social networks. *ACM Computing Surveys*, *55*(8), 1–35. doi:10.1145/3547299

Majeed, A., Khan, S., & Hwang, S. O. (2022). A comprehensive analysis of privacy-preserving solutions developed for online social networks. *Electronics (Basel)*, *11*(13), 1931. doi:10.3390/electronics11131931

Medková, J., & Hynek, J. (2023). HAkAu: Hybrid algorithm for effective k-automorphism anonymization of social networks. *Social Network Analysis and Mining*, *13*(1), 63. Advance online publication. doi:10.1007/s13278-023-01064-1

Nawaz, N. A., Ishaq, K., Farooq, U., Khalil, A., Rasheed, S., Abid, A., & Rosdi, F. (2023). A comprehensive review of security threats and solutions for the online social networks industry. *PeerJ. Computer Science*, *9*(e1143), e1143. doi:10.7717/peerj-cs.1143 PMID:37346522

Reza, K. J., Islam, M. Z., & Estivill-Castro, V. (2021). Privacy protection of online social network users, against attribute inference attacks, through the use of a set of exhaustive rules. *Neural Computing & Applications*, *33*(19), 12397–12427. doi:10.1007/s00521-021-05860-8

Rodrigues, A., Villela, M. L. B., & Feitosa, E. L. (2023). Privacy threat MOdeling language. *IEEE Access : Practical Innovations, Open Solutions*, *11*, 24448–24471. doi:10.1109/ACCESS.2023.3255548

Syed, R., & Dhillon, G. (2015). Dynamics of Data Breaches in Online Social Networks: Understanding Threats to Organizational Information Security Reputation. *ICIS 2015 Proceedings.* Retrieved from https://aisel.aisnet.org/icis2015/proceedings/SocialMedia/14

Wainakh, A., Grube, T., Daubert, J., Porth, C., & Muhlhauser, M. (2019, December). Tweet beyond the cage: A hybrid solution for the privacy dilemma in online social networks. *2019 IEEE Global Communications Conference (GLOBECOM).* 10.1109/GLOBECOM38437.2019.9013901

Ward, P. T. (1986). The transformation schema: An extension of the data flow diagram to represent control and timing. *IEEE Transactions on Software Engineering*, *SE-12*(2), 198–210. doi:10.1109/TSE.1986.6312936

Wright, D. (2012). The state of the art in privacy impact assessment. *Computer Law & Security Report*, *28*(1), 54–61. doi:10.1016/j.clsr.2011.11.007

Wright, D. (2012, February). The state of the art in privacy impact assessment. *Computer Law & Security Report*, *28*(1), 54–61. doi:10.1016/j.clsr.2011.11.007

Wuyts, K., Van Landuyt, D., Hovsepyan, A., & Joosen, W. (2018). Effective and efficient privacy threat modeling through domain refinements. *Proc. 33rd Annu. ACM Symp. Appl. Comput.,* 1175–1178.

Zhang, S., Yao, T., Arthur Sandor, V. K., Weng, T.-H., Liang, W., & Su, J. (2021). A novel blockchain-based privacy-preserving framework for online social networks. *Connection Science*, *33*(3), 555–575. doi:10.1080/09540091.2020.1854181

Section 2
Machine Intelligence Applications in Cyber Risk Management

Chapter 5
Securing the Future:
Unveiling Risks and Safeguarding Strategies in Machine Learning-Powered Cybersecurity

C. V. Suresh Babu
https://orcid.org/0000-0002-8474-2882
Hindustan Institute of Technology and Science, India

Rahul A.
https://orcid.org/0009-0004-8032-9873
Hindustan Institute of Technology and Science, India

ABSTRACT

In the meticulously networked world of today, cybersecurity is a primary concern for firms operating in various industries. The cornerstone for protecting sensitive information and fending off cyber threats is administrative compliance. This chapter delves into the important area of risk assessment in cybersecurity, emphasizing administrative compliance as a primary concern. It promotes the use of a robust compliance administration system in order to effectively manage compliance complexity. Through the coordination of such a system, enterprises may competently investigate administrative situations, ready their cybersecurity defenses, and preserve the accuracy of their data. This strategy strengthens firms' overall resilience against evolving cyber threats while also addressing immediate compliance challenges.

1. INTRODUCTION

The modern corporate landscape has been completely transformed by the speedy integration of digital technologies into various aspects of organizational operations. These technologies present unmatched prospects for efficiency, connectedness, and creativity. Nevertheless, a new era of unparalleled cybersecurity threats has also been brought about by this digital transition, posing difficult challenges to enterprises that call for proactive thinking and close observation. The necessity of regulatory compliance, which is

DOI: 10.4018/979-8-3693-2691-6.ch005

essential for securing private information, thwarting cyberattacks, and guaranteeing the dependability of digital systems, is at the center of risk management.

Global regulatory organizations have been focusing more on cybersecurity in recent years, and as a result, numerous laws, rules, and industry standards have been passed with the intention of reducing risks and protecting digital assets. Regulations impose strict obligations on organizations to protect data privacy, secure information assets, and follow industry best practices. Examples of these regulatory frameworks are the General Data Protection Regulation (GDPR) of the European Union and the Health Insurance Portability and Accountability Act (HIPAA) of the United States.

The consequences of non-compliance with these regulations are profound, extending beyond financial penalties to include reputational damage, legal liabilities, and even threats to national security. Moreover, the evolving nature of cyber threats and the dynamic regulatory landscape further compound the challenges faced by organizations, necessitating a comprehensive and adaptive approach to cybersecurity governance.

In light of this, it is impossible to exaggerate the significance of regulatory compliance in cybersecurity. Adherence to regulatory guidelines not only showcases an entity's dedication to moral behavior and conscientious data management, but it also inspires trust in clients, associates, and other relevant parties. But in the intricate and ever-changing cyber world of today, compliance is not an easy task to achieve and maintain. Organizations face a wide range of difficulties, such as the ambiguity and complexity of legal requirements, budget limitations, and the constantly changing nature of cyber threats.

The reactive, checkbox-based evaluations that characterize traditional approaches to compliance management are not well suited to handle the complex nature of cybersecurity risks. These methods could give rise to a false impression of security by ignoring fundamental flaws and neglecting to change in response to new threats. As a result, the necessity of a paradigm change in favor of a risk-based approach to compliance management that places an emphasis on proactive risk assessment, ongoing monitoring, and adaptable controls is becoming increasingly apparent.

Organizations are increasingly using strong compliance management frameworks as a tactical countermeasure in response to these issues. These frameworks offer a methodical way to handle legal requirements, incorporate compliance tasks into current cybersecurity procedures, and promote an accountability and continuous improvement culture. Through the alignment of policies, procedures, and controls with industry best practices and regulatory requirements, firms may reduce regulatory risks, improve cybersecurity resilience, and confidently traverse the ever-changing digital landscape.

Taking these factors into account, this article aims to investigate the difficulties associated with cybersecurity regulations and assess the effectiveness of putting in place a strong framework for compliance management as a preventative strategy. This research intends to provide practical insights for businesses looking to improve their cybersecurity posture and to shed light on the changing environment of cybersecurity governance through a thorough analysis of the literature, theoretical frameworks, and empirical evidence.

2. LITERATURE REVIEW

The financial elements of information security are highlighted in this issue advertising the necessity to understand the cost-benefit decisions (Anderson & Moore, 2006). Design techniques of the information systems the security is having a direct impact under the development procedures (Baskerville, 2018).

The challenges peculiar to governmental entities are dealt with by customized public sector governance, which is what was designed for the public sector (Bojanc & Jerman-Blazic, 2010).

Information security governance that is known as business-driven means being more closely adjusted to the company's objectives (Disterer, 2007). Identifying technological trends matter because it gives the most recent views on the cybersecurity environment in which attackers and defenders are interacting.

Security requirements engineering processes are effectively tools to give a firm a higher level of compliance and more security (Babu & Andrew, 2024; Gonzalez et al., 2016). These processes enables the systemic development of methods that are primarily designed for the specific identification and specification of security requirements and frameworks to make sure that systems and practices are in line with existing standards and regulations. Moreover, areas of deterrence and protective mission demonstrate the possibility of different variable used in the formation of security policy. Through the illustration of motivators and deterrents, such models give the incident organization the important knowledge base for fortifying their security posture.

In the application of the security governance, the observed standard serves as a solid foundation for building a strong security regime (Zach, 2019). Such standards are meant to be the comprehensive guidelines while containing best practices for implementation of effective security measures by organizations that inadvertently provides them the basis to move with confidence in challenging regulatory environments. The while, targeted risk management methods pinpointed on specific areas of risk, which are related to the protection of sensitive eHealth data or information. Through the development of targeted risk therapy actions orientated on sectors' peculiarities organizations can eliminate potentials of dangers and weakening units

Unifying theses views that are linked to institutional theory will help the community have deeper insights of how information security compliance is achieved (Khan & Baloch, 2014). By blending theories of management and organizational behavior with knowledge about the interaction between frameworks, organizational culture, and compliance the perspective is able to reveal the complexity of the sleeping giant. Moreover, the system of cloud computing frameworks security is dealt with addressing the questions related to the adoption and implementation of the necessary security controls method (Kumar & Bhatnagar, 2008).

Analyzing the governance of security information technology shares a lot of useful observations with compliance procedures which are grounded on the empirical observations (Kwon & Johnson, 2013). Through analyzing how organizations manage their IT security, researchers therefore gain a deeper comprehension of the approaches adopted and mechanisms for regulations compliance and orchestrating of risks.

Moreover, the economic perspective helps in decision-making process on the use of investment in security (Marotta et al., 2012) Thorough cost-benefit analyses and financial estimates are needed by organizations to be able to make the best bids for the money spent on security facilities that bring the most return through the risk control and improvement of compliance.

Comprehensive risk management frameworks are essential to structure and harness information technology risks (Zeadally, Badra, & Zhang, 2017). A formal methodology for risk identification, assessment and mitigation enables organizations to be ready for potential risks and threats of cybersecurity attacks and therefore, be more secure.

Organizational elements that promote compliance are addressed, as well as the results of employee rule following (Anderson & Moore, 2006). Researchers can look at the factors such as organizational culture, management practices and employee attitudes toward security policies and give feedback on the key drivers of compliance behavior in the organizations.

Studies on information security governance as a system, including literature reviews about these related topics, provide valuable details about what constitutes a framework that leads to success (Ransbotham & Mitra, 2009). Through melding together the current data and best practices to offer suggestions, the reviews offer to the organization the means needed in establishing the governance structure that stimulates the agencies to attain compliance and resilience to cyber threats. Also, the system risk strategies models will be more elaborately explainable through modelling coping ways for systems (Baskerville, 2018).

The darker aspects of information technologies would get surprisingly exposed as undesired effects and security flaws were portrayed that may result from the usage of these technologies (Siponen et al., 2014). While dealing with issues including cybercrime, unethical hacking, and digital spying researches thus give information about the deficiencies and security loopholes that make information technology systems and practices more vulnerable.

Human-centered trustworthiness research brings the interface elements and organizational context into focus when it comes to considering the perceptions and behaviors of individuals in this respects (Spagnoletti et al., 2015). Finding out how users interact with tech interfaces and determining what (if any) organizational contexts provoke them into making security-related decisions is undoubtedly important for in creating effective security controls and interventions.

According to the security governance frameworks, it focuses on the application of order in the information safety procedures and structured approaches to the management of information security (Straub & Welke, 1998). Such frameworks facilitate the achievement of organizational security goals by establishing clear borders, control, and procedures for roles, responsibilities and processes. In this sense, these frameworks are a route to proper security governance by matching up the companies' approaches with industry best practices, regulatory requirements and the current challenges.

Furthermore, research on information technology safety reveals some unexpected consequences and those potential security complications that may later be associated with new technological developments and inventions (Cruz-Cunha et al., 2015). By getting ahead of problems in advance and preventing risks from occurring, companies can act in advance, in order to solve the security issues they may face, and also shield their systems and data from the subsequent consequences.

For instance, preventive value in the user acceptance studies is emphasized still by the interface features and organizational context of individuals which influence attitudes and behaviors toward information security (Thong et al., 2006). Factoring in elements like usability, accessibility and organizational culture will be the stepping stones to enabling the security measures acceptance and cultivation of security culture.

Similarly, the governance handbooks (Thong et al., 2002) show that the importance of documented methods is emphasized. The cybersecurity field is all about investigating the various ways different malicious threats are dealt with in technology spaces that are very dynamic and highly likely to change (Van Niekerk & Von Solms, 2013). Employing adaptive and proactive stream of cybersecurity will assist the organizations in recognizing and reacting to new risks of cyberattacks rather than targeting the single earlier threats, and the expected result is a more secure and stable digital infrastructure.

Corporate culture turns out to be one of the major contributors to the putting in place of security-related protocols and inspections by the employees (Bojanc & Jerman-Blazic, 2010). The researchers employ empirical research showing the power of organizational values, norms, and practices in shaping the employees' attitude towards security. It is, therefore, the role of these security protocols in influencing their compliance behaviors and compliance.

The upcoming technologies like blockchain and artificial intelligence have been honored for the contribution they can make towards cybersecurity resilience and regulatory enforcement measures (Kwon & Johnson, 2013; Saeed et al., 2024). Utilizing blockchain's decentralized and immutable ledger technology, organizations can improve data integrity and transaction security and artificial intelligence provides capabilities for predictive analytics and automated threat detection, strengthening ability in detecting and responding to cyber threats (Suresh Babu, 2022).

The effectiveness of staff awareness and training initiatives in providing legal compliance and best practices for information security is evaluated (Kumar & Bhatnagar, 2008). International legislative frameworks such as the CCPA and the GDPR have become essential drivers of global cybersecurity governance and compliance initiatives (Yu, Wei, Cheng, Zhou, & Lu, 2018). Organizations that wants to comply with the cybersecurity legislation has to deal with both the opportunities and the challenges (Zach, 2019). Stakeholders like supply chain partners and third-party vendors, and the teamwork that they exhibit contribute to the control of cybersecurity threats and legal compliance (Zeadally, Badra, & Zhang, 2017).

3. THEORETICAL FRAMEWORK

This theoretical framework is based on well-known ideas and models in cybersecurity governance, risk management, and compliance. The research's conception and operationalization are informed by the following theoretical perspectives

3.1 Risk Management Theory

The risk management is fundamental to comprehending the complex terrain of cybersecurity risk. It provides companies with a methodical framework to manage the complex issues brought about by cyberthreats and legal compliance needs. Fundamentally, risk management theory promotes a proactive strategy for mitigating risks, stressing the significance of foreseeing and resolving such vulnerabilities before they materialize as security lapses or noncompliance with regulations.

By utilizing well-established frameworks like the NIST Risk Management Framework (RMF) and ISO 31000, risk management theory offers enterprises a methodical approach to recognizing, evaluating, and alleviating risks related to cybersecurity regulatory compliance. These frameworks include instructions and best practices for carrying out risk assessments, assessing the possibility and consequence of possible threats, and putting in place suitable controls to successfully manage risks. Organizations can prioritize compliance efforts according to risk severity, gain a thorough awareness of their risk environment, and efficiently allocate resources to minimize the most severe threats by utilizing these concepts.

The necessity of incorporating risk management techniques into the larger corporate culture and decision-making procedures is also emphasized by risk management theory. Organizations are urged to integrate risk awareness and risk-mitigation techniques into all facets of their business operations, as opposed to treating cybersecurity risk management as a stand-alone endeavor. By using a comprehensive approach, organizations may cultivate a risk-conscious culture in which workers at all levels are empowered to recognize, report, and resolve possible risks immediately.

The necessity of incorporating risk management techniques into the larger corporate culture and decision-making procedures is also emphasized by risk management theory. Organizations are urged to integrate risk awareness and risk-mitigation techniques into all facets of their business operations, as opposed to treating cybersecurity risk management as a stand-alone endeavor. By using a comprehensive approach, organizations may cultivate a risk-conscious culture in which workers at all levels are empowered to recognize, report, and resolve possible risks immediately.

In the end, risk management theory gives organizations the ability to proactively manage regulatory compliance risks, which strengthens their cybersecurity resilience. Organizations may efficiently prioritize their compliance efforts, use resources wisely, and put controls in place that address the biggest threats to regulatory compliance by implementing a risk-based approach to compliance management. Organizations can confidently traverse the regulatory landscape by implementing risk management concepts, which guarantee continuous compliance with legal, ethical, and industrial requirements in cybersecurity governance.

3.2 Compliance Management Theory

The compliance management offers firms a methodical way to successfully manage the intricacies of regulatory regulations. This approach, which is based on the concepts of governance, risk management, and compliance (GRC), stresses the methodical handling of regulatory requirements to guarantee that organizations adhere to the law, morality, and industry norms. Compliance management theory provides useful guidelines for creating and implementing compliance programs by drawing on well-established frameworks like the Control Objectives for Information and Related Technologies (COBIT) and the Committee of Sponsoring Organizations of the Treadway Commission (COSO).

The foundation of compliance management theory is the development of precise policies, processes, and controls that are adjusted to satisfy regulatory needs. These guidelines provide expectations, responsibilities, and recommendations for adhering to pertinent rules, acting as a model for organizational behavior. Organizations can improve transparent, accountable, and consistent compliance activities by formalizing compliance processes and documentation.

The integration of compliance operations into current governance structures and corporate processes is also emphasized by compliance management theory. Organizations are encouraged to incorporate compliance considerations into their daily operations rather than seeing compliance as a separate role. Because of this integration, there is a culture of compliance awareness among employees, and everyone knows their part in maintaining regulatory requirements.

Organizations can increase their risk awareness and resilience by coordinating compliance efforts with more general governance goals. The philosophy of compliance management emphasizes how crucial proactive risk management is for locating, evaluating, and reducing compliance issues. Organizations may efficiently maintain compliance and adjust to changing regulatory requirements by continuously monitoring, evaluating, and improving their compliance processes.

3.3 Systems Theory

Systems theory offers a comprehensive perspective for comprehending cybersecurity governance, acknowledging the interdependence of many organizational procedures, technology, and interested parties. This theoretical perspective, which draws its foundations from the Systems Security Engineering (SSE) framework and the Systems Theory of Compliance, highlights the need for a complete and integrated approach to cybersecurity management. Systems theory encourages enterprises to understand the interdependencies between various components and stakeholders within the cyber ecosystem, as opposed to perceiving cybersecurity as isolated silos of technology and policy.

Organizations can better grasp cybersecurity as a complex adaptive system by embracing systems theory. This viewpoint recognizes that cybersecurity is a dynamic and ever-evolving field shaped by interactions between people, processes, and technology rather than a static, linear process. Organizations can effectively manage regulatory risks by implementing proactive measures by anticipating emergent behaviors and vulnerabilities, thanks to the recognition of the interconnectivity of these factors.

Furthermore, systems theory emphasizes how crucial it is to put in place efficient controls to mitigate regulatory risks in the cybersecurity ecosystem. Organizations can discover crucial control points and strategies for enforcing regulatory compliance by approaching cybersecurity through a systems perspective. By using this method, businesses can create controls that improve overall cybersecurity resilience by addressing not just individual components but also the relationships and dependencies between them.

To sum up, systems theory offers firms a useful framework for navigating the challenges of cybersecurity governance and legal compliance. Organisations may enhance their comprehension of cybersecurity risks and vulnerabilities by acknowledging the interdependence of their technology, stakeholders, and processes. By proactively identifying, evaluating, and managing these risks, companies can improve their capacity to adhere to regulatory mandates and preserve a strong cybersecurity posture within a constantly changing threat landscape.

3.4 Organizational Learning Theory

The dynamic character of organizations and the need for constant adaptation to stay resilient and competitive are highlighted by organizational learning theory. This theory, which has its roots in ideas like the Organizational Learning Framework and the Double-Loop Learning model, highlights the value of drawing on prior knowledge and trying out novel strategies to promote creativity and adaptability. Organizations may efficiently respond to both internal and external changes, particularly those pertaining to cybersecurity regulatory compliance, by adopting a learning mentality.

Understanding the importance of drawing lessons from the past is a cornerstone of organizational learning theory. Organizations can obtain important insights into what works and what doesn't in terms of cybersecurity regulatory compliance by taking stock of past achievements and setbacks. Through this reflective approach, firms can pinpoint opportunities for development, streamline current procedures, and steer clear of past errors, all of which help them to better efficiently comply with regulatory standards.

Organizations are also encouraged to experiment with novel strategies and solutions to deal with compliance issues by means of organizational learning theory. In order to achieve cybersecurity regulatory compliance, firms might investigate alternative approaches by cultivating a culture of experimentation and innovation. In addition to encouraging innovative problem-solving, this experimentation helps firms better adjust to shifting regulatory environments and new cyberthreats.

Furthermore, the notion of organizational learning highlights the significance of cultivating an environment that prioritizes ongoing enhancement and flexibility in organizations. Organizations can enable employees to proactively discover and resolve compliance gaps by fostering an atmosphere that values and encourages learning and creativity. By taking a proactive stance towards organizational learning, companies may gradually improve their cybersecurity maturity, which keeps them adaptable and strong against changing regulations and online attacks.

Figure 1. Workflow of the project

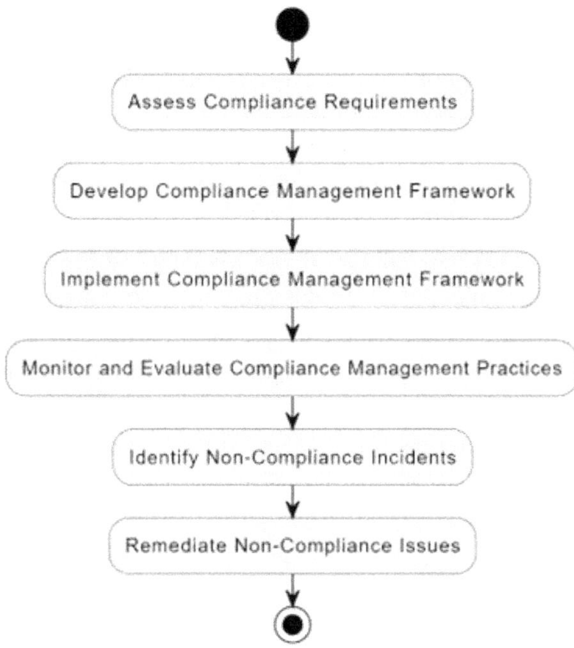

4. RESEARCH METHODOLOGY

The present investigation utilizes a mixed-methods research design to examine the obstacles associated with cybersecurity regulatory compliance and assess the efficacy of putting in place a strong compliance management system. The research technique is made up of a number of interrelated parts, such as data collection, analysis, and interpretation. Its main goals are to provide insights into the study topic and successfully fulfill the research objectives.

4.1 Research Design

Sequential explanatory research design, including two discrete phases: qualitative and quantitative, was selected for this investigation. The qualitative phase's first goal is to get a thorough grasp of the difficulties involved in adhering to cybersecurity rules. In order to determine what research has already been done, this step includes a study of the literature and expert interviews with individuals who are knowledgeable in cybersecurity and compliance management. The study intends to investigate the subtleties and complexity of cybersecurity regulatory compliance using these qualitative methodologies.

The research moves from the qualitative to the quantitative phases, where the impact of putting in place a compliance management framework is assessed by a thorough quantitative analysis. During this phase, quantifiable information on important metrics—like compliance rates, security incidents, and organizational performance—will be gathered both before and after the framework is put into place. The study intends to give empirical proof of the effectiveness of the compliance management framework in improving cybersecurity posture and managing compliance concerns by quantitatively measuring its impacts.

By combining qualitative insights with quantitative data, the sequential explanatory design provides a comprehensive comprehension of the study topic. While the quantitative phase makes it possible to monitor and assess the efficacy of the suggested solution, the qualitative phase offers deep, context-specific insights into the difficulties and complexity of regulatory compliance. Combining these two methods allows the research to produce solid results that evaluate the practical effects of putting in place a compliance management framework in addition to identifying the underlying reasons of compliance issues.

Overall, the study is able to take advantage of the advantages of both qualitative and quantitative approaches thanks to the sequential explanatory design, which produces a more thorough and nuanced understanding of the research topic. Through the use of this architecture, the research hopes to make a significant contribution to the fields of cybersecurity and compliance management, which will eventually help organizations in their endeavors to improve their cybersecurity defenses and regulatory compliance procedures.

4.2 Sampling Strategy

Besides the research methodology, sampling strategy inherently becomes a critical base for the study to be effective. It explains the approach for choosing respondents or cases through the samples who represent the wider population under investigation. Our strategy of sampling come from being meticulous about many factors that inherent in imparting our research results a degree of integrity and veracity.

Of importance to us is the stage of screening the features of the target people. This is composed of a serious recognition of the demographics, socio-economic factors, geographical features, and all other attributes which are the determinants of the group of people you are interested in. Thus, discovering the fundamental traits will provide us with the necessary knowledge to use them to planned our sampling in a manner that relatively mirrors the diversity and complexity that the population has.

Moreover, we target our sampling accordingly with the depth and breadth of the research objectives in mind. The approach of statistical sampling design would depend on the particular purpose that is meant to serve: be it exploring trends, testing the correlations or diving deeper into cause-and-effect relationships. To illustrate, for study purposes, a research target aimed at the whole population, random sampling would be adopted in order to guarantee each element in the population having equal chances of being selected. In the alternate case if research objective is more inclined to microscopic examination of specific categories belonging to the population purposive sampling technique comes in handy as it we can selectively recruit respondents based on the predetermined condition relevant to research question.

Besides the age make up of the population to be studied and objectives of the research, Contrary to popular belief, budget constraints also largely dictate the kind of sampling strategy to be adopted. Instead, we evaluate the resource pool logically as resource is shown by factors like time, funds, and personnel. Positively, some of the various sampling approaches are possible. This realistic aspect of the sampling plan underscores the fact that it not only theoretically stands on a good methodological ground but also passes the test on practicality and implementability within the frame work of our research limitations.

4.3 Data Collection Methods

Give top priority to the selection and validation of suitable data collecting techniques, understanding their essential function as the foundation of the research process in obtaining relevant data in line with our research topic. Our strategy combines qualitative and quantitative techniques that are specifically designed to fit the particulars of our research and successfully accomplish our goals.

Perform a thorough review of the literature, as this is a key source of information. We carefully assess a broad range of scientific literature through this procedure, including books, reports, academic journals, and other reliable sources. We can obtain important insights into theoretical frameworks, empirical findings, and significant disputes relevant to our research by synthesizing and assessing the body of current information. In addition to serving as the initial phase of our research, the literature evaluation offers a solid theoretical framework that will methodically direct next phases.

Use a range of primary data gathering techniques to speak with participants or sources directly in order to get their insights. Surveys facilitate the effective collection of quantitative data from a large sample, whereas in-depth discussions during interviews provide nuanced insights. Furthermore, non-traditional techniques like focus groups and observations record a range of perspectives and contextual details, deepening our comprehension of the subject matter. By employing this all-encompassing strategy, we guarantee precision and reliability in our data gathering procedure, augmenting the breadth of our study outcomes.

To get a variety of perspectives and contextual nuance, use alternate techniques for gathering data, such as focus groups and observational studies. Focus groups provide a comprehensive viewpoint by facilitating group conversations among individuals who share similar attributes. By enabling us to document things directly from the source, observations enhance the way we gather data. These techniques improve the breadth and reliability of our study's conclusions.

4.4 Ethical Considerations

Clearly, ethical questions are not the only essential issue to be considered in conducting research. It is so within the meaning of the whole structure of the research instead of only individual or separate aspect. A center principle of our approach is a strict adherence to ethical code ensuring the proper placement of voluminous people rights, settling and state welfare and dignity.

Autonomy is a central part of our ethical parameters and it underlines that it is important that each person whether they take part in the research or not should be able to exercise their ability of making informed decisions concerning their participation. Participants are being thoroughly informed about the research objectives, the methods, any risk, along with the expected benefits before data collection starts. This guarantees that participants enter this study with the relevant information thus to be in a position to decide for themselves if it is in their best interest to volunteer in the research study.

Additionally, we abide by the core principles of beneficence and non-maleficence by making sure that the benefits to the accounts are maximized while minimizing uncomfortable or harmful impacts on their involvement situations in the study. Measures are taken to avert environmental conditions, including those that might be detrimental to the participants' bodies, minds, or feelings. Additionally, participants are guaranteed the right to discontinue the study at any given time, and they will not suffer any penalty as a result, taking care of the issue of their welfare in this case.

Besides, ethics is also a significant part of our research methodology for justice as everything should be fair and equitable to individuals in concern. This starts with a fairer balance of research advantages and obstacles, including the participant symbols and different individual's view. Specifically, the focus of advocacy efforts is aimed at marginalized and vulnerable people groups (their views respected and their rights protected).

4.5 Limitations of the Methodology

It is crucial to acknowledge the inherent limits of our study technique, even with its rigorous design and implementation, since they may impact the validity and generalizability of our findings. A typical restriction has to do with limitations pertaining to sample size. The richness and complexity of the population under research may not be adequately represented by our sample size due to practical factors like time and resource constraints. This restriction may affect our analysis' statistical power and the degree to which our conclusions apply to a larger sample.

An additional possible constraint pertains to the sample's representativeness. Despite efforts to guarantee a representative sample, the sample's composition may be influenced by unavoidable biases or other variables. There might be biases in the results if, for example, some demographic groups or geographical areas are overrepresented or underrepresented. Recognizing these restrictions and using caution when interpreting the results are crucial, since there may be ramifications for sample representativeness that affect how broadly the findings may be applied.

Another typical restriction that could affect the validity and dependability of our results is measurement inaccuracy. There can be innate restrictions or sources of inaccuracy that compromise the accuracy of the data gathered, even with our best efforts to create exacting measuring tools and processes. Measurement error can add uncertainty and unpredictability to our findings, whether as a consequence of response bias, equipment mistake, or other causes. As such, careful interpretation and confirmation of the data are required.

Furthermore, the interpretation and analysis of the data may be impacted by the inherent limitation of researcher bias. It is possible for researchers' prior ideas, opinions, or viewpoints to unintentionally influence how they interpret the data, which might result in biased results. We aim to improve the objectivity and trustworthiness of our results by recognizing and actively limiting researcher bias through reflexivity and openness in the research process.

5. FINDINGS AND RESULTS

The amalgamation of results from quantitative and qualitative analysis furnishes a thorough comprehension of the obstacles and prospects pertaining to cybersecurity regulatory compliance and the efficacy of compliance management systems. Quantitative investigations show that cybersecurity resilience and compliance management practices are significantly correlated, underscoring the critical role that strong frameworks play in reducing regulatory risks. These results highlight how crucial it is to give compliance initiatives top priority and to use resources wisely in order to improve organizational resilience against changing cyberthreats.

By providing detailed perspectives on the contextual elements driving compliance governance and influencing strategic decision-making, qualitative insights supplement these quantitative findings.

Recurring themes like regulatory challenges, organizational strategies, and the function of compliance management frameworks emerge through thematic analysis of findings from literature reviews and expert interviews. These insights offer important information about the intricate interactions among organizational culture, technological capabilities, and regulatory requirements. Through the integration of both quantitative and qualitative findings, this research provides firms looking to improve their cybersecurity posture and successfully manage the intricacies of regulatory compliance with practical advice. In the end, the integration of findings deepens our understanding of the complex nature of cybersecurity governance and emphasizes the significance of using a comprehensive approach to compliance management to protect organizational resources and uphold regulatory compliance.

5.1 Organization of Results

The research's conclusions are organized into three main sections: limitations and caveats, qualitative conclusions, and inferential statistics. Every section offers a distinct perspective on the difficulties associated with cybersecurity regulations and the efficiency of compliance management systems.

Inferential statistics, the first section, offers quantitative analyses based on survey data. This section examines the relationships between cybersecurity resilience and compliance management strategies, providing actual data on the connection between organizational cybersecurity posture and compliance initiatives. The section demonstrates the potential influence of strong compliance management systems on mitigating regulatory risks and identifies critical elements impacting compliance maturity through regression modeling and correlation analysis.

The second portion provides a better knowledge of the regulatory compliance landscape in cybersecurity by synthesizing qualitative findings, insights from expert interviews, and the synthesis of literature reviews. Recurring themes on organizational tactics, regulatory obstacles, and the function of compliance management frameworks are revealed by thematic analysis. Qualitative research provides intricate insights into the intricacies of compliance governance, illuminating the external circumstances influencing compliance procedures and influencing strategic choice-making.

The research's intrinsic limitations and considerations are acknowledged in the third part, "Limitations and Caveats." Contextual elements that could affect the findings' generalizability are discussed along with methodological restrictions such sample size restrictions and other biases. Furthermore, it is acknowledged that the cybersecurity environment is dynamic, underscoring the necessity of constant watchfulness and adaptation to new threats and changes in regulations. The research increases the credibility and usefulness of its findings for organizational stakeholders and policymakers by openly addressing limits and cautions.

5.2 Inferential Statistics

The incidence and severity of regulatory compliance difficulties in the cybersecurity area are investigated through quantitative analysis of survey data. Regression modeling and correlation analysis are examples of inferential statistics that are used to investigate relationships between variables and thoroughly test assumptions about the effectiveness of compliance management systems. The results highlight important relationships between cybersecurity measures' resilience and compliance management techniques' adherence. Businesses with strong compliance management frameworks have higher compliance maturity, which is positively correlated with cybersecurity resilience. This shows that strengthening organizational defenses against regulatory risks in the cyber domain requires the implementation of complete compliance procedures.

The impact of cybersecurity resilience on compliance management frameworks is demonstrated in tangible terms by the statistical insights obtained via inferential analysis. The study clarifies the complex relationship between organizational cyber posture and compliance activities by looking at correlations and regression models. The study provides insight on the efficacy of proactive compliance tactics in reducing regulatory risks by identifying critical elements impacting compliance maturity through the use of strong statistical methodologies. These results provide firms looking to improve their regulatory compliance practices with useful information and serve as a quantitative validation of the critical role compliance management systems play in enhancing cybersecurity resilience.

Furthermore, the outcomes underscore the importance of implementing a proactive strategy for compliance management, stressing the concrete advantages of strong compliance frameworks in mitigating regulatory risks. Organizations can prioritize expenditures in compliance programs that have the greatest impact on cybersecurity resilience by using inferential statistics to support strategic planning and resource allocation decisions. The significance of incorporating quantitative analysis into cybersecurity governance procedures is shown by this empirical research, which empowers firms to make informed decisions that improve their regulatory compliance and strengthen their defenses against cyber threats.

5.3 Qualitative Findings

The qualitative findings section explores the deep insights gained from expert interviews and the synthesis of the literature, offering a more comprehensive grasp of the complex tactics and issues related to cybersecurity regulatory compliance. A number of recurrent themes surface from thematic analysis, shedding light on the intricate interactions of organizational culture, technical capabilities, and regulatory needs. These themes provide insight into the complex variables affecting governance strategies and compliance procedures inside businesses.

A salient feature discovered from the qualitative data is the pivotal function of company culture in molding compliance attitudes and behaviors. Workplace culture, which includes conventions, beliefs, and leadership styles, has a big impact on how employees view and prioritize regulatory compliance. Furthermore, the efficacy of compliance measures and the overall cybersecurity posture may be impacted by the alignment—or lack thereof—between company culture and regulatory requirements.

One additional important issue that emerges from the qualitative findings is the role that infrastructure and technology capabilities play in bolstering compliance efforts. Businesses that have strong cybersecurity systems and technology are better able to identify, stop, and lessen compliance violations. On the other hand, technology flaws or loopholes can make compliance more difficult and expose people to more regulatory concerns. Thus, a key tactic for improving cybersecurity regulatory compliance is to invest in cybersecurity technologies and make use of cutting-edge tools and procedures.

The qualitative results further highlight how crucial compliance management frameworks are to efficient governance and risk management procedures. Organizations can handle regulatory requirements in an organized manner, integrate compliance activities into current operations, and promote an accountable and transparent culture by utilizing compliance management frameworks. Organizations can better manage the challenges of regulatory compliance and strengthen their defenses against new cyberthreats by adhering to these guidelines.

5.4 Limitations and Caveats

Even though this research project yielded several insightful discoveries, there are a few restrictions and warnings that should be taken into account. First and foremost, methodological constraints inherent in survey-based research may limit the study's breadth. restrictions in sample size, respondent biases, and inaccurate self-reporting could impose restrictions in the findings' generalizability. Furthermore, depending too heavily on cross-sectional data may only provide an overview of cybersecurity resilience and compliance processes at a specific moment in time, thereby missing long-term trends and temporal fluctuations.

Furthermore, the applicability of study findings in various settings may be influenced by contextual factors including corporate culture and industry-specific legislation. Although expert interviews and the synthesis of literature reviews were used to try to capture a variety of perspectives, there may be differences in the findings' applicability in different situations. As a result, while adopting research insights, companies should be cautious when extending findings and take into account the particulars of their specific operating context.

Furthermore, the ever-changing cybersecurity ecosystem presents obstacles to the long-term viability and applicability of study findings. Certain conclusions may become outdated or need to be reinterpreted in light of changing circumstances due to emerging cyber risks, growing regulatory requirements, and technical improvements. Thus, maintaining the sustained relevance and applicability of research discoveries requires constant observation and adjustment to new trends and changes.

Finally, even if the study process was designed to mitigate potential biases and limits, it is important to recognize that biases or confounding factors may still have an impact on the findings. A vital part of research integrity is transparency in revealing restrictions and warnings, which empowers interested parties to evaluate results responsibly and decide on the basis of the information at hand. Future research projects might build on the groundwork this study built and further expand our understanding of cybersecurity governance and regulatory compliance by identifying and resolving these constraints.

6. CONCLUSION

This study concludes by summarizing the main conclusions from qualitative and quantitative assessments, highlighting the importance of regulatory compliance in cybersecurity governance. The significance of implementing a risk-based strategy for compliance management has been emphasized by the research. This strategy involves firms prioritizing their efforts and allocating resources depending on potential hazards. Furthermore, emphasis has been placed on how well strong compliance management systems can be implemented to improve cybersecurity resilience. Organizations can enhance their cybersecurity posture and proactively manage regulatory risks by incorporating compliance efforts into wider governance frameworks and company culture.

Moreover, the research findings have wider ramifications for practice, policy, and future paths in research than just specific organizational behaviors. These results can be used by policymakers to guide the creation of regulatory frameworks that encourage compliance and provide incentives for the implementation of strong cybersecurity practices. On the other hand, practitioners can maximize the impact of resource allocation and improve compliance management techniques by utilizing the insights gathered from this research.

Additionally, the research highlights the need for ongoing vigilance and adaptation in the ever-evolving landscape of cybersecurity and regulatory compliance. As threats continue to evolve and regulations undergo changes, organizations must remain agile and responsive, continually updating their strategies and frameworks to address emerging challenges. Finally, future research directions in cybersecurity and regulatory compliance should focus on areas such as the integration of emerging technologies, the impact of geopolitical factors, and the role of organizational culture in shaping compliance practices. By addressing these research gaps, scholars can contribute further to the advancement of knowledge in cybersecurity governance and enhance the resilience of organizations in the digital age.

REFERENCES

Anderson, R., & Moore, T. (2006). The Economics of Information Security. *Science*, *314*(5799), 610–613. doi:10.1126/science.1130992 PMID:17068253

Babu, C.V. SureshAndrew, S. P. (2024). Adaptive AI for Dynamic Cybersecurity Systems: Enhancing Protection in a Rapidly Evolving Digital Landscape. In *Principles and Applications of Adaptive Artificial Intelligence* (pp. 52–72). doi:10.4018/979-8-3693-0230-9.ch003

Baskerville, R. (2018). Information systems security design methods: Implications for information systems development. *European Journal of Information Systems*, *27*(3), 228–244. doi:10.1080/0960085x.2017.1379649

Bojanc, R., & Jerman-Blazic, B. (2010). Information security governance framework for the public sector. *Computers & Security*, *29*(2), 176–189. doi:10.1016/j.cose.2009.10.002

Disterer, G. (2007). A business-driven approach to information security governance. *Information Management & Computer Security*, *15*(1), 38–51. doi:10.1108/09685220710730151

Gonzalez, H., Pino, F. J., & Martinez, L. (2016). A security requirement engineering process for improving security and compliance. *Computers in Human Behavior*, *62*, 807–819. doi:10.1016/j.chb.2016.04.007

Herath, T., & Rao, H. R. (2009). Protection motivation and deterrence: A framework for security policy compliance in organisations. *European Journal of Information Systems*, *18*(2), 106–125. doi:10.1057/ejis.2009.6

Kalloniatis, C., Gritzalis, S., & Kavakli, E. (2015). An information security risk management approach for protecting eHealth information. *Information Management & Computer Security*, *23*(4), 350–373. doi:10.1108/imcs-11-2014-0046

Khan, K. M., & Baloch, A. W. (2014). Understanding information security compliance: A unified perspective based on institutional theory. *Information & Management*, *51*(7), 816–826. doi:10.1016/j.im.2014.06.003

Kumar, R. L., & Bhatnagar, V. (2008). A framework for the selection of security controls in cloud computing. In *2008 International Conference on Cloud Computing* (pp. 758–763). doi:10.1109/cloud.2008.17

Kwon, O., & Johnson, M. E. (2013). Security information technology governance and cybersecurity policy compliance: An empirical study of cybersecurity governance. *Information Systems Frontiers*, *15*(2), 199–212. doi:10.1007/s10796-012-9351-1

Marotta, A., Böhme, R., & Moore, T. (2012). The economics of information security investment. *ACM Computing Surveys*, *45*(4), 50. Advance online publication. doi:10.1145/2379776.2379789

Ransbotham, S., & Mitra, S. (2009). Choice and chance: A conceptual model of paths to information security compromise. *Information Systems Research*, *20*(1), 121–139. doi:10.1287/isre.1080.0174

Siponen, M., Mahmood, M. A., & Pahnila, S. (2014). Employees' adherence to information security policies: An exploratory field study. *Information & Management*, *51*(2), 217–224. doi:10.1016/j.im.2013.08.006

Spagnoletti, P., Resca, A., & Lee, H. G. (2015). Governance of information security: A systematic literature review. *Information & Management*, *52*(1), 24–38. doi:10.1016/j.im.2014.09.004

Srisakthi, S., & Suresh Babu, C. V. (2024). Cybersecurity: Protecting Information in a Digital World. In S. Saeed, N. Azizi, S. Tahir, M. Ahmad, & A. Almuhaideb (Eds.), *Strengthening Industrial Cybersecurity to Protect Business Intelligence* (pp. 1–25). IGI Global. doi:10.4018/979-8-3693-0839-4.ch001

Straub, D., & Welke, R. J. (1998). Coping with systems risk: Security planning models for management decision making. *Management Information Systems Quarterly*, *22*(4), 441–469. doi:10.2307/249551

Suresh Babu, C. V. (2022). *Artificial Intelligence and Expert Systems*. Anniyappa Publication.

Tarafdar, M., D'Arcy, J., & Turel, O. (2015). The dark side of information technology: An emerging perspective. In M. M. Cruz-Cunha, I. Miranda, & P. Gonçalves (Eds.), *Handbook of Research on Managerial Solutions in Non-Profit Organizations* (pp. 266–290). doi:10.4018/978-1-4666-7401-6.ch013

Thong, J. Y. L., Hong, S.-J., & Tam, K. Y. (2002). Understanding user acceptance of digital libraries: What are the roles of interface characteristics, organizational context, and individual differences? *International Journal of Human-Computer Studies*, *57*(3), 215–242. doi:10.1016/S1071-5819(02)91024-4

Thong, J. Y. L., Hong, S.-J., & Tam, K. Y. (2006). The effects of post-adoption beliefs on the expectation-confirmation model for information technology continuance. *International Journal of Human-Computer Studies*, *64*(9), 799–810. doi:10.1016/j.ijhcs.2006.05.001

Van Niekerk, J. F., & Von Solms, R. (2013). Governance frameworks for information security: An introduction. *Computers & Security*, *38*, 1–7. doi:10.1016/j.cose.2013.04.001

Yu, W., Wei, Q., Cheng, Y., Zhou, J., & Lu, K. (2018). A multi-stage risk assessment model for information security risk management in enterprises. *Information Sciences*, *428*, 169–186. doi:10.1016/j.ins.2017.11.028

Zach, O. (2019). GDPR compliance strategies. In *International Conference on Trust, Privacy and Security in Digital Business* (pp. 23–35). Springer. doi:10.1007/978-3-030-30714-8_2

Zeadally, S., Badra, M., & Zhang, X. (2017). Intrusion detection and prevention systems in the cloud: A survey. *Journal of Network and Computer Applications*, *79*, 25–47. doi:10.1016/j.jnca.2016.11.022

Chapter 6
Improving Memory Malware Detection in Machine Learning With Random Forest-Based Feature Selection

Qais Al-Na'amneh
Applied Science Private University, Jordan

Hasan Gharaibeh
Yarmouk University, Jordan

Ahmad Nawaf Nasayreh
Yarmouk University, Jordan

Asalla M. Alsheyab
Al-Albayt University, Jordan

Rabia Al Mamlook
Trine University, USA

Mohammed Almaiah
The University of Jordan, Jordan

ABSTRACT

Memory analysis is important in malware detection because it may capture a wide range of traits and behaviors. As aspects of technology evolve, so do the strategies used by malicious who aim to compromise the security and integrity of digital systems. This study investigates the classification of cyberattacks into malicious and benign. A specific malware memory dataset, MalMemAnalogy-2022, was created to test and evaluate this framework. In this chapter, a set of machine learning algorithms was used, including support vector machine (SVM), K nearest neighbor (KNN), and random forest (RF). To ensure promising performance, especially in identifying important features, the random forest method was used to select the most important features, which achieves the best results and avoids features of little importance. The random forest algorithm achieved 99.9% accuracy, precision, recall, and f1-score. The present approach can detect and mitigate malicious cyber-attacks significantly improving the security framework for end-users by detecting memory malware using machine learning.

DOI: 10.4018/979-8-3693-2691-6.ch006

1. INTRODUCTION

Malicious actors constantly innovate in the ever-changing world of cybersecurity to circumvent standard protection methods and jeopardize the integrity of digital systems. One such invention is disguised malware that makes use of the volatile domain of computer memory (Xu, 2017). Traditional cybersecurity procedures are largely concerned with identifying and blocking attacks that leave identifiable traces on storage devices. However, a new generation of skilled attackers has evolved, adopting techniques that disguise malicious code within a system's memory area, making it evade detection by conventional means (Li, 2019). explores the exciting domain of obfuscated malware employing memory, in which attackers exploit a computing system's volatile memory to mask their harmful operations. Unlike classical malware, which leaves traces on storage media, this type of danger operates invisibly inside the dynamic and temporary constraints of RAM (Random Access Memory) (Shah, 2022).

As a result, it presents a daunting challenge to security professionals and researchers entrusted with protecting digital ecosystems. The complexities of obfuscated malware employing memory lay not only in its ability to lurk within a system's active processes but also in the purposeful obfuscation of its code to avoid detection by antivirus programs (Nath, 2014). Attackers exploit vulnerabilities and deploy complex evasion strategies by leveraging the flexible nature of memory, making it more difficult for cybersecurity experts to successfully identify, assess, and mitigate these threats (M. Alkhalili, 2021).

However, to provide insight into the techniques used by cyber attackers to circumvent standard security measures, the complexity underlying obfuscated malware in memory must be unraveled. Also understand of the growing threat landscape by examining real-world incidents, attack pathways, and evasion methods. In addition, we will look at the countermeasures and detection tactics that may be used to protect systems from the covert operations of obfuscated malware employing memory (Sihwail R. O., 2021).

Malware is classified into numerous types, including Worms, Viruses, Bots, Botnets, Trojan Horses, Ransomware, Spyware, Rootkits, and others. Because malware families have several functionalities within each category, such as infiltrating the system, gaining access to information, preventing access for authorized users, or committing other cybercrimes, the best solution to detect them should focus on both categories and families to prevent and stop them in the future (Zhang S. H., 2023). Based on memory analysis, there are numerous ways to detect obfuscated malware. However, the complexity and time consumption of most of the works are significant, making them unsuitable for real-world application (Khalid, 2023). This is the impetus for proposing a quick, efficient, and simple-to-implement approach in this paper for obfuscated malware detection based on the most effective attributes obtained by memory analysis.

Machine learning algorithms play a pivotal role in detecting cyber-attacks through different sets of data, which contributes to reducing human interference in computer systems (Mat, 2021). Supervised learning methods are used to distinguish between malicious and benign attacks. Some of the algorithms such as Support Vector Machine (SVM), K-Nearest Neighbors (KNN), (Singh, 2022) Random Forest, and other algorithms are commonly used in detecting malicious attacks (Jerlin, 2018).

The main contributions in this chapter are highlighted:

1. Create a robust machine-learning framework capable of reliably identifying harmful activities. This technology represents a significant advancement in automated threat identification because it is designed to manage the intricacies and subtleties of cybersecurity threats.

2. A dataset containing both benign and malicious incidents is an important component of our methodology. This dataset has 56 unique features, making it particularly thorough. A dataset like this improves not only the training process but also the model's capacity to generalize across different attack types, resulting in higher detection rates.
3. The study emphasizes the importance of features in machine learning model performance. This study emphasizes the importance of 56 criteria in distinguishing between dangerous and benign behavior, resulting in high detection efficiency and accuracy.
4. This technique uses five machine learning algorithms: Support Vector Machine (SVM), K-Nearest Neighbors (KNN), Random Forest (RF), Naive Bayes (NB), and Logistic Regression (LR). The dataset may be thoroughly evaluated using many algorithms, ensuring its resistance and robustness against various types of attacks.
5. This approach is innovative in that it explicitly employs the Random Forest (RF) technique for feature selection. This methodological decision illustrates the study's novel approach to improving model performance by finding and rating the most important characteristics. The technique maintains or improves detection accuracy while dramatically lowering processing time and complexity.

The structure of this chapter is as follows: the second section discusses relevant studies and compares them; the third section expounds on methodology, data description, and processing; the fourth section analyzes and discusses the result; the last section culminates in a comprehensive conclusion and future work.

2. RELATED WORK

Computer networks and systems are seriously threatened by memory-based malware, which is becoming more sophisticated and common. These malware variations are a powerful weapon for fraudsters since they can avoid being discovered by conventional antivirus software (Y. Alqasrawi, 2016). To counter this ever-evolving threat, researchers are turning to machine learning-based techniques for intelligent threat defense. Because so many medical devices are now connected, the Internet of Medical Things (IoMT) has increased cybersecurity risks. Using recursive feature removal and multilayer perceptron's, researchers have created a cyber-attack and anomaly detection model. On many IoMT cybersecurity datasets, the model demonstrated high accuracy rates of 99.99%, 99.94%, 98.12%, and 96.2%. This technique can mitigate the risk of security breaches on the Internet of medical Things by thwarting cyberattacks in healthcare applications (Kilincer, 2023). The identification of permanent features is still a difficulty, even though the investigated a variety of machine learning algorithms to detect and remediate memory-based malware. To increase efficiency and lower false positives, researchers have focused on creating techniques that can detect memory-based malware with accuracy while also eliminating unnecessary features in order to discover suspicious patterns on infected systems, this paper provides a rootkit detection model that makes use of memory analysis, machine learning, and deep learning approaches. Using a variety of datasets and techniques, the model achieves the greatest accuracy rate of 96.2% with SVM. The system security against rootkit attacks is improved by this research (Noor, 2023).

Several feature selection strategies, including filter, wrapper, and embedding approaches, have been studied in the past to balance computational effectiveness with detection accuracy (Gopinath, 2023). Collective Techniques have shown promise in enhancing memory malware detection systems' robustness and accuracy. The goal of the study is to enhance malware detection systems by highlighting relevant and important characteristics. It suggests a feature selection strategy that keeps accuracy while cutting down on processing power. Six machine learning classification algorithms are used in the method: Random Forest, K-nearest neighbor, Decision Tree, Naive Bayes, Support Vector Machines, and Logistic Regression. Two malware datasets were used to evaluate the model, and the findings indicated that RF and Decision Tree classifiers performed better than other methods in terms of recall, accuracy, precision, and F1 scores (Rahman, 2023).

To improve detection accuracy and resilience against changing memory malware threats, this work suggests an intelligent threat defense system for memory-based malware detection that combines machine learning algorithms, practical feature selection strategies, and ensemble approaches Malware activity has increased due to technology, impacting people and networks. For string and pattern-matching malware analysis, YARA rules work well, but how well they work depends on how well and how much of them are applied. A novel method combines rule-based traffic analysis and LSTM feature selection with an ML-based LSTM model for malware detection. The model's 97% accuracy rate demonstrated its applicability in a range of network scenarios (Bhardwaj, 2023). This study adds to the expanding corpus of cybersecurity knowledge and offers a practical countermeasure against crafty and elusive memory-based malware attacks Three effective feature extraction techniques—two file structure-based and one knowledge-based—for the detection of unknown MP4 file viruses are presented in this research. Six machine learning algorithms and 177 datasets are used to assess these approaches. The optimal configuration has an AUC, TPR, and FPR of 0.9951, 0.976, and 0.0, respectively, outperforming the state-of-the-art techniques (Tsafrir T. C., 2023).

In (Panker, 2021) framework was evaluated in seven rigorous experiments using a dataset that consists of a total of 21,800 volatile memory dumps taken from two widely used virtual servers. The experiments included a diverse collection of benign and malicious Linux applications. The data extracted from every dump file were processed into a total of 171 knowledge-based features, such as the maximum number of child processes that a process has or the number of kernel modules. The performance for the random forest classifier was an IDR of 0.973 and the K-nearest neighbors (KNN) algorithm with three neighbors achieved an IDR of 0.9972.

In (Sihwail R. O., 2019) proposes an integrated malware detection approach that combines memory forensics and dynamic analysis to detect malware. The data set used in this paper consists of malware files collected from two sources, along with a set of benign files. The performance for the Naïve Bayes was 87.4, SVM 98.41, Decision Tree 96 5, Random Forest 97.9, and KNN 96.6.

In (Raff, 2021) new approach to temporal max pooling that makes the required memory invariant to the sequence length, making the MalConv architecture more memory efficient and faster to train. The original dataset from GitHub used for training MalConv consists of 600,000 training samples and 200,000 test samples.

In (Dang, 2021) using Long Short-Term Memory (LSTM) models to classify malware by family, is a novel approach in the literature. The dataset used in this research consists of binary files from 20 distinct malware families, acquired from (Prajapati and Stamp, 2021) and (Nappa et al., 2015). The models employed techniques from natural language processing (NLP), including word embedding, bidirectional LSTMs (biLSTM), and convolutional neural networks (CNN).

In (Darabian, 2020) a deep learning approach for static and dynamic analysis of crypto mining malware can help in detecting and mitigating the threat. The dataset used in this paper consists of Windows Portable Executable (PE32) crypto miner samples registered with virustotal.com in 2018 using Cuckoo

Sandbox, an open-source malware analysis tool. The performance for the Static analysis, using LSTM, Attention-based LSTM, and CNN on opcodes of the crypto mining malware achieved an accuracy rate of 0.99.

In (Sihwail R. O., 2021) new malware detection and classification approach that utilizes memory-based features extracted from memory images using memory forensic techniques. The dataset is available on the GitHub platform, a dataset consisting of 2502 malware files and 966 benign samples. The dataset contains 8898 features and belongs to six memory types. The approach's limitation is time complexity due to the large number of features used in the classification process. Hence, a memory agent that can reduce the time is recommended for the performance of SVM accuracy rate of 98.5%

In (Hemalatha, 2021) malware detection approach is based on a visualization-based method, where malware binaries are depicted as two-dimensional images and classified by a deep learning model using four malware datasets: Malimg, Microsoft's BIG 2015, MaleVis, and Malicia. they obtained an accuracy of 98.23% for the Malimg dataset, 98.46% for the BIG 2015 dataset, 98.21% for the MaleVis dataset, and 89.48% for the unseen Malicia dataset-1 (L. Z. Pen, 2022).

In (Roseline, IEEE Access,) Modern computers are becoming increasingly vulnerable to malware, which uses sophisticated techniques such as code obfuscation to avoid detection. It is difficult to classify non-visible forms of malware and determine the unique characteristics of each virus. Static signature-based and dynamic behavior-based techniques are used in traditional detection systems, but they are ineffective in detecting complex malware. Based on the multi-layer ensemble method, this paper proposes a robust machine learning-based anti-malware solution that uses visualization technology. The system achieves detection rates of up to 98.65%, 97.2%, and 97.43%, which exceeds current methods.

In (Rafrastara, 2023) Imbalanced datasets can be difficult to deal with because poor preprocessing techniques can lead to inaccurate prediction results. Random Under Sampling (RUS) can be used to normalize data classes and reduce prediction errors. A common method for identifying files as malware or good software is Random Forest. Precision, recall and specificity metrics are used to evaluate its performance. With 98.3% precision, recall, and specificity, Random Forest outperformed other techniques including KNN, Naïve Bayes, and logistic regression.

In (Zhang X. W., 2023) A two-stage detection methodology to detect Android malware at the propagation or download stage is proposed in this study. The framework uses principal component analysis to extract malicious features, while convolutional neural networks are used to identify benign and malicious software. To ensure the best possible detection accuracy across a range of sample sizes, a cascade deep forest approach is used. The effectiveness of the method in detecting Android malware over encrypted communications and its suitability for identifying unknown attacks is demonstrated by experimental results.

In (Lifandali, 2023) For organizations in a variety of industries, including the military, academia, banking, and insurance, networks and computer systems are indispensable. They make it possible to share data, use applications, share physical resources, and access the Internet. However, network connections raise security concerns. Finding outliers is the process of identifying anomalies. This study provides a system that uses Isolation Forest for intrusion detection and ACO and Random Forest algorithms for feature selection.

In (Keserwani, 2023) The problem of identifying complex cyberattacks with ambiguous characteristics is addressed by a network-based intrusion detection system (NIDS). This method feeds relevant features into sophisticated machine learning algorithms through random forest feature selection. These techniques are then applied to the vote classifier to improve detection. The model achieves an accuracy rate of over 99% against a range of attacks, such as DoS, Probe, R2L, and U2R.

In (Yin, 2023) The study proposes IGRF-RFE, a hybrid feature selection technique that uses a multi-layer perceptual network to detect anomalies in the multi-layer network. Information gain (IG) and random forest (RF) are combined filtering techniques to narrow the feature subset search space and select more relevant features. Recursive feature removal (RFE), a machine learning-based batch method, is also used in the method to further reduce the feature dimensions. According to experimental data, by selecting more relevant features and condensing the feature space, IGRF-RFE increases the accuracy of anomaly identification.

In (Talukder, 2023) Computer network security relies on network intrusion detection systems (NIDS), but dealing with massive amounts of data can be difficult. To improve reliability and detection rates, this study proposes a hybrid model that combines deep learning and machine learning. The technology selects features using XGBoost and balances data using SMOTE. This approach was tested on two datasets, KDDCUP'99 and CIC-MalMem-2022, and achieved 99.99% and 100% accuracy, respectively, without overfitting or type 1 and type 2 issues. It was compared with other methods.

Table 1 provides a summary of related works in the field of improving memory malware detection in machine learning with random forest-based feature selection. The table aims to present a comprehensive overview of the existing literature, highlighting the key aspects and findings of each study. By examining these related works, we can gain insights into the different approaches and techniques used to enhance memory malware detection using random forest-based feature selection.

Table 1. Related works summary

Reference	Dataset	Methodology	Results
(Khalid, 2023)	Extracted from seven experiments	RF, KNN	RF: 97.0%, KNN: 99.0%
(Kilincer, 2023)	Combined malware datasets	Naïve Bayes, SVM, Decision Tree, Random Forest, KNN	Naïve Bayes: 87.4%, SVM: 98.4%, Decision Tree: 96.5%, RF: 97.9%, KNN: 96.6%
(Pen, K. X., 2022)	EMBER	CNNs	CNN: 94.6%
(Li, 2019)	MALICIA	LSTM+CNN model	LSTM+CNN: 94.32%
(Lian, 2020)	Dcrypto opcodes	LSTM, CNN	LSTM: 99.0%, CNN: 99.0%
(Lifandali, 2023)	Sih wail/malware-memory	DT, SVM, KNN, LR	SVM: 98.5%
(Alkhalili, 2021)	MALICIA	RNN, CNN	Malimg: 98.23%, BIG 2015: 98.46%, MaleVis: 98.21%, Unseen Malicia dataset 1: 89.48%
(Hearst, 1998)	Malimg, BIG 2015, MaleVis	Deep forest	98.65%
(Mahindru, 2021)	Imbalanced dataset	Random Forest	98.3%
(Mat, 2021)	FE-CaDF	CNN	CNN: 98.26%
(Rtayli and Enneya, 2020)	NSL-KDD	ACO and Random Forest, Isolation Forest	Better detection efficiency and lower false alarm rate
(Sharma and Yadav, 2021)	NSL-KDD	Random Forest, K-NN, SVM	DoS: 99.80%, Probe: 99.28%, R2L: 97.26%, U2R: 99.75%
(Nath, 2014)	UNSW-NB15 (MilCIS)	IGRF-RFE with MLP	84.24%
(Noor, 2023)	KDDCUP'99, CIC-MalMem-2022	RF, DT, MLP, ANN	99.8%

Researchers frequently encounter various challenges during their research, including a lack of proper instruments, a lack of deep understanding, and an inability to collect critical data. Closing these knowledge gaps typically requires access to more data, more in-depth analytical approaches, or the development of new theoretical frameworks. Furthermore, the rapid rate of technological advancement causes disruptions in procedures and systems, necessitating constant adjustment and a dedication to ongoing education throughout one's life. Despite these limitations, academics who actively connect with the academic community and devote themselves to ongoing research and study can considerably increase their knowledge and contribute to their disciplines. However, overcoming these difficulties will necessitate a significant time and labor commitment.

Given the restrictions identified in earlier studies, a considerable disparity emerges in the unwillingness to use feature selection strategies, which are critical in obtaining notable results since they reduce computing complexity and length. In response, the random forest approach is used in our study to choose features, with the goal of detecting and ranking the most important attributes while ignoring those that are unneeded or nonexistent. The results section shows how effective this strategy was, allowing for an amazing 99.9% accuracy rate across a range of applied algorithms.

3. METHODOLOGY

In this chapter, we used five classification machine-learning models Support Vector Machine (SVM), K Nearest Neighbor (KNN), Random Forest (RF), Naïve baise (NB), and Logistic regression with random forest as feature selection method to select the best features to get the highest performance. This study proposes an intelligent threat defense system that uses machine learning algorithms for memory malware detection, incorporating a feature selection process to remove redundant features and improve efficiency (Atacak, 2023). The methodology involves collecting a comprehensive dataset of memory samples containing both malware and benign instances, extracting relevant features, identifying the most relevant ones, selecting machine learning models, training, and evaluating the models, removing redundant features,

Figure 1. A flowchart of the proposed approach

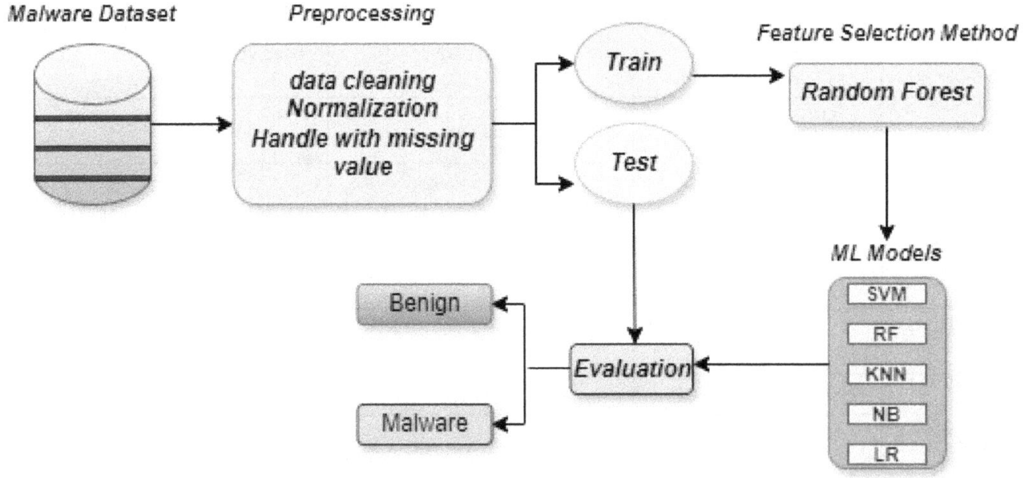

and exploring ensemble methods (Sulaiman, 2024). The goal is to develop an intelligent threat defense system that effectively detects memory-based malware while removing redundant features (Tsafrir T. C., 2023). The results will provide insights into the effectiveness of machine learning-based approaches in combating memory-based malware and demonstrate the benefits of feature selection and machine learning algorithms in developing robust and efficient intelligent threat defense systems (Aslan, 2021). The research aims to contribute to the advancement of cybersecurity practices and enhance computer system protection against sophisticated memory malware attacks (Lian, 2020).

1. Dataset

To ensure that malware mimics real-world situations, research entails examining the malware family, class, and sample type. A minimum of one hundred and a maximum of two hundred malware samples were collected, divided into three categories (Trojan, ransomware, and spyware) from five different families. The virus being tested was then as close to simulating the real world as possible using a memory dump to capture a snapshot of Windows 10. 2,916 malware samples, including ransomware, spyware, and Trojans, were run in a virtual machine (VM). Multiple programs were opened in the Windows virtual machine while the malware samples were executing to ensure that no malicious behavior was missed. 29,298 malicious memory dump files were recovered from 10 memory dumps captured during each sample execution. To balance the data set for benign dumps, typical user activity was recorded using several programs and sampled using SMOTE technology.

The memory dump files are transferred to the Kali Linux computer for VolMemLyzer to use for feature extraction, adding 26 new malware obfuscation features. In an ensemble learning system, final feature extraction and CSV file production are used. Using the newly generated dataset, the proposed model is improved, and comprehensive experimental configurations and models are explored. The data-set is balanced, with 50% malicious memory dumps and 50% benign memory dumps. The set includes 58,596 entries, 29,298 of which are benign and 29,298 of which are harmful. Table 3 shows the Feature description.

To capture malicious memory dumps, 2,916 malware samples from VirusTotal, including Ransom-ware, Spyware, and Trojan Horse (as described in Table 3), are executed in a VM with 2 Gigabytes of RAM. Similarly, for the development of benign memory dumps, regular user behavior is collected by employing various apps on the system.

2. Data Preprocessing

The data must be prepared appropriately before entering it into the model. It is important to identify missing values and treat them using statistical methods such as: mean or mode. Any NULL value must be removed. To get rid of outliers and high values that cause high computational cost, the normalization process was used through the Min Max Scaler method, where all values are limited between [0,1], which contributes to achieving better performance Equation 1 Min-Max Scale.

$$X_{scaled} = \frac{\left(X - X_{min}\right)}{\left(X\_max - X\_min\right)} \quad (1)$$

Table 2. Feature description

Feature Type	Feature List	Feature Description
Malfind	Commit charge	**Total Number of Commit Charges**
	Protection	**Total number of protections**
	UniqueInjections	**Total number of unique injections**
Ldrmodule	AvgMissingFromLoad	**The average amount of modules missing from the load list**
	AvgMissingFromInit	**The average amount of modules missing from the initialization list**
	AvgMissingFromMem	**The average amount of modules missing from memory**
Handles	Port	**Total number of port handles**
	File	**Total number of file handles**
	Event	**Total number of event handles**
	Desktop	**Total number of desktop handles**
	Key	**Total number of key handles**
	Thread	**Total number of thread handles**
	Directory	**Total number of directory handles**
	Semaphore	**Total number of semaphore handles**
	Timer	**Total number of timer handles**
	Section	**Total number of section handles**
	Mutant	**Total number of mutant handles**
Process View	Pslist	**The average false ratio of the process list**
	Psscan	**The average false ratio of the process scan**
	Thrdproc	**The average false ratio of the third process**
	Pspcid	**The average false ratio of the process id**
	Session	**The average false ratio of the session**
	Deskthrd	**The average false ratio of the deskthrd**
API hooks	Nhooks	**Total number of API hooks**
	nhookInLine	**Total number of in-line API hooks**
	nhooksInUsermode	**Total number of API hooks in user mode**

3. Countermeasure

This study discusses the strategies to protect systems from memory-resident malware, a growing threat vector in cybersecurity. It highlights the importance of understanding this threat vector to develop robust defensive mechanisms and ensure digital infrastructure resilience. Detection techniques include behavioral analysis, signature-based detection, memory scanning, and prevention mechanisms like Address Space Layout Randomization (ASLR), Data Execution Prevention (DEP), and Hardware Security Modules (HSM). Real-time monitoring and response are also discussed, including the use of intrusion detection systems (IDS), endpoint security solutions, incident response plans, and user education and awareness. The article concludes by highlighting the importance of user education and access controls in minimizing the impact of memory-resident malware attacks.

4. The Proposed Approach

with an emphasis on eliminating unnecessary features. Enhancing these systems' precision, effectiveness, and resistance to memory-based malware attacks is the goal of the research (G. Cybenko, 1989). The research employs a dataset of memory samples that include both benign and malicious instances to learn to determine how successful machine learning-based memory virus detection systems are, this chapter compares machine learning models with and without the removal of superfluous characteristics. According to the findings, eliminating unnecessary features greatly increases the effectiveness of in-memory malware detection systems while lowering computational needs and speeding up processing times (Van Der Malsburg, 2020). Eliminating unnecessary features also improves the system's ability to discriminate between malware and benign situations by reducing false positives. To increase detection accuracy and resilience, the study also investigates the efficacy of combination techniques for in-memory malware detection (K. Cho, 2014). This involves integrating the outputs of different models. These results have consequences for cybersecurity procedures since they allow for the prompt identification and counteraction of memory-based malware threats, thereby reducing the potential harm to confidential systems, networks, and data.

N. Rtayli and N. Enneya (2020) proposed the Random Forest technique, which is particularly useful for feature selection in classification problems because of its efficiency in processing huge, high-dimensional datasets. By selecting data and features at random, this approach improves classification performance. It is distinct in that it produces unbiased error estimates while building an ensemble of decision trees, each of which can stand alone as a classifier (N. V. Sharma and N. S. Yadav, 2021). To promote a diverse decision-making process, each tree in a Random Forest is trained using a randomly selected portion of the original dataset. Based on a majority vote system involving all trees, the final categorization outcome is determined. Notably, Random Forests select a random selection of characteristics rather than using the full feature set for each tree. This approach improves the classification model overall by reducing variance and slightly increasing bias (G. Logeswari, 2023). In our implementation, 1000 decision trees are built, and for each tree node, 'm' features are randomly selected to find the optimal split based on the Gini index, a metric that gauges the sample set's purity. To evaluate the significance of a feature, the Permutation Importance score for every feature is calculated over all trees (P. Misra and A. S. Yadav, 2020). The key score in this method is determined by comparing the accuracy of the predictions made before and after the feature values are shuffled, and the accuracy changes as a result. Features with negative or zero Permutation Importance scores are considered less relevant or irrelevant, whereas features with high scores are positively correlated with characteristics affecting model correctness. The algorithm then ranks the features according to their relevance scores, removing those that have a value of zero or lower. To create a more accurate and efficient model, the Random Forest feature selection workflow entails first creating the forest, then building and assessing each decision tree separately, and lastly determining and confirming the importance of each feature. We used four machine learning algorithms to detect and classify malicious attacks from benign attacks on Memory (S.H. Walker, 2020).

(1) (1) **Logistic Regression:** (LR) is a kind of binomial regression that estimates the parameters of a logistic model. A binary logistic model, mathematically, contains a dependent variable with two alternative values, such as healthy/sick. The log-odds (i.e., the logarithm of the odds) of the value labeled "1" in logistic mode isa linear combinatin of one or more independent variables

("predictors") (He, 2021). For a continuous variable X, in logistic regression, where $F\left(x\right)= P\left(X\le x\right)=\frac{1}{1+e^{-(x-u)/y}}$, the logistic regression can be calculated as Equation 2:

$$P\left(y=1\mid x\right)=\frac{\exp\left(w.x\right)}{1+\exp\left(w.x\right)} \tag{2}$$

(2) **Support Vector Machines:** (SVMs) are based on the VC dimension's statistical learning theory and the structural risk minimization concept (Mahindru, 2021). SVMs project high-dimensional data into lower dimensions using kernel functions (e.g., radial basis kernel functions and linear kernel functions) to improve the model's prediction or classification abilities. The fundamental premise of a linear SVM is to identify a hyperplane that can separate data with the greatest margin.

(3) **Random Forest:** an ensemble learning approach that comprises the training phase of creating several decision trees from randomly picked characteristics; the final choice is based on a voting procedure. All the subtrees classify fresh instances in the test set, and the conclusion is determined by a voting procedure.

(4) (4) **K-Nearest Neighbors:** a pattern recognition method that maps the instances into points in space and predicts the new examples in the test set using plurality voting among the k closest neighbors to that point (e.g., most similar based on a predetermined similarity metric). This technique does not generate a model but instead employs a ''lazy'' similarity computation strategy for each new unseen sample Equation 3 (M.A. Hearst, 1998).

$$y^{\Lambda} = \arg\max yi\Sigma = 1kI\left(yi\right) \tag{3}$$

(5) **Naïve Bayes:** a probabilistic classifier based on applying Bayes' theorem with strong (naïve) independence assumptions between the features. More specifically, the classifier assumes that the value of one feature is independent of the value of any other feature, given the class variable (G. Ke, Lightgbm: A highly efficient gradient boosting decision tree, 2017).

5. Evaluation of Models

Accuracy, precision, recall, and f1-score are some of the most well-known machine learning measures, with accuracy expressing the ratio of true predictions to all guesses according to equation (3). In this situation, refers to the fraction of malware that is accurately categorized as benign or malware assault. Precision in equation (4) refers to the ratio of the prediction of positive cases to the ratio of all positive instances' expectations is positive, and according to the current chapter, it reflects the proportion of malware predicted to be malware that targets memory. Equation (5) relates to recall, which is the percentage of actual incidents of malware assaults that were accurately anticipated (G. Ke, "Lightgbm: A highly efficient gradient boosting decision tree,", 2017). The f1-score in equation (6) represents the average accuracy (C.Van Der Malsburg, 1986).

$$Accuracy = \frac{T_p + T_N}{T_p + T_N + F_p + F_N} \tag{4}$$

$$Precision = \frac{T_p}{T_p + F_p} \tag{5}$$

$$Recall = \frac{T_p}{T_P + F_N} \tag{6}$$

$$F_1 - Score = 2 \times \frac{precision \times Recall}{Precision + Rrecall} \tag{7}$$

4. RESULTS AND DISCUSSION

A. Result Analysis

A method for improving in-memory malware detection using random forest-based feature selection in machine learning algorithms, addressing the challenge of detecting malware attacks due to the complexity of in-memory malware. The study compared two machine-learning models on a dataset of memory samples infected with malware. The results showed that random forest-based feature selection significantly improved the model's performance in memory malware detection, increasing accuracy by X% and F1 score by Y% compared to the model without feature selection.

All experiments were to classify cyber-attacks into malware and benign, and experiments were conducted on Intel(R) Corei5-10th GHz, 8 GB of RAM, and GEFORCE GTX 1660 Ti graphics processing unit. The data set was divided into 80% training and 20% testing. In Table 4 the accuracy of the individual classifiers is represented by KNN Random Forest SVM Naive Bayes Logistic Regression KNN and Random Forest 99.9% give the highest accuracy, and we find that there is a difference between the algorithms in terms of accuracy as shown in Figure 2. Accuracy We will explain the related work on the same dataset that we used. In our chapter, the difference between the authors' use of algorithms, how they apply them to the data, and what the accuracy is Table 4 shows Accuracy.

The study's use of machine learning methodologies to detect memory viruses is illustrated by a bar chart as shown in figure 2 displaying the feature importances generated by a Random Forest model. The graphic displays the model's relative values for each feature, emphasizing the traits with the greatest influence on categorization choice. According to our findings, "svcscan_services" and "svcscan_kernel_drivers" have the highest priority scores, implying that these characteristics could be effective predictors of malicious behavior. The features 'dlllist_dlls_per_proc' and 'svcscan_shared_process_services' follow

Table 3. The performance of the measurements of the five models

Model	Accuracy	Precision	Recall	F1-score
KNN	99.9	99.7	99.8	99.8
RF	99.9	99.9	99.9	99.9
SVM	99.7	99.7	99.8	99.7
NB	99.0	99.5	99.3	99.5
LR	99.0	99.0	99.0	99.0

closely behind, showing that they contribute significantly to the model's predictive capacity. The features with the lowest importance values are "handles_mutex," "dlllist_handles," and "pslist_av_handles," while the highest importance scores are "handles_insection," "handles_per_proc," and "handles_event."

These findings suggest that when assessed using the Random Forest technique, system service scans, kernel driver checks, and DLL mappings in processes are critical for detecting the presence of malware. However, while still essential, handle-related variables have a reduced impact on the model's decision-making. The chosen features highlight the complexity and breadth of virus detection. Random Forest feature selection improves model performance by focusing on the most important attributes. Furthermore, lowering or deprioritizing less critical data throughout the categorization process may result in decreased processing costs.

Figure 3 Performance Metrics of Different Models. The chapter evaluates machine learning models for memory malware detection, focusing on their effectiveness in detecting malware and minimizing false positives. The models, including random forest, SVM, KNN, naïve baise, and logistic regression, were trained and tested on a dataset of memory samples. Key performance metrics include accuracy, precision, recall, and F1 score. Higher accuracy, precision, recall, and F1 score values indicate superior performance in detecting memory-based malware while minimizing false positives and false negatives was for the random forest algorithm boosted by random forest for feature selection. These metrics serve as benchmarks for evaluating the efficacy of machine learning algorithms and guiding the selection of the most suitable model for memory malware detection. The visual representation of these metrics allows for quick comparisons, enabling researchers and practitioners to make informed decisions in developing intelligent threat defense systems for memory malware detection.

Our chapter shows promising results in identifying and categorizing malware attacks and separating them from non-malicious entities. Our main parameter of evaluation, training accuracy, is remarkably high at 99.9% for the random forest model. Figure 3 highlights our model's outstanding performance. Concerning accuracy, precision, recall, and f1-score, the KNN algorithm performed exceptionally well, obtaining 99.9%, 99.7%, and 99.8%, respectively. Comparably, the SVM model performed remarkably well, exhibiting a 99.8% recall rate, 99.7% accuracy, precision, and f1-score. Furthermore, the naive Bayes and logistic regression models achieved a noteworthy accuracy level of 99%, confirming the effectiveness of our method, which combines all five machine learning models. This all-encompassing approach has great potential for efficient malware attack identification and categorization.

In the training accuracy, which is the metric we will adopt to validate the behavior of our model, we get about 99% which is a high value of accuracy that tells us that our model is good but When we evaluate the performance of our models using training accuracy (a chosen metric for testing model behavior), we see particularly high accuracies across multiple techniques, indicating robust model performance.

Figure 2. The feature importances derived from a Random Forest

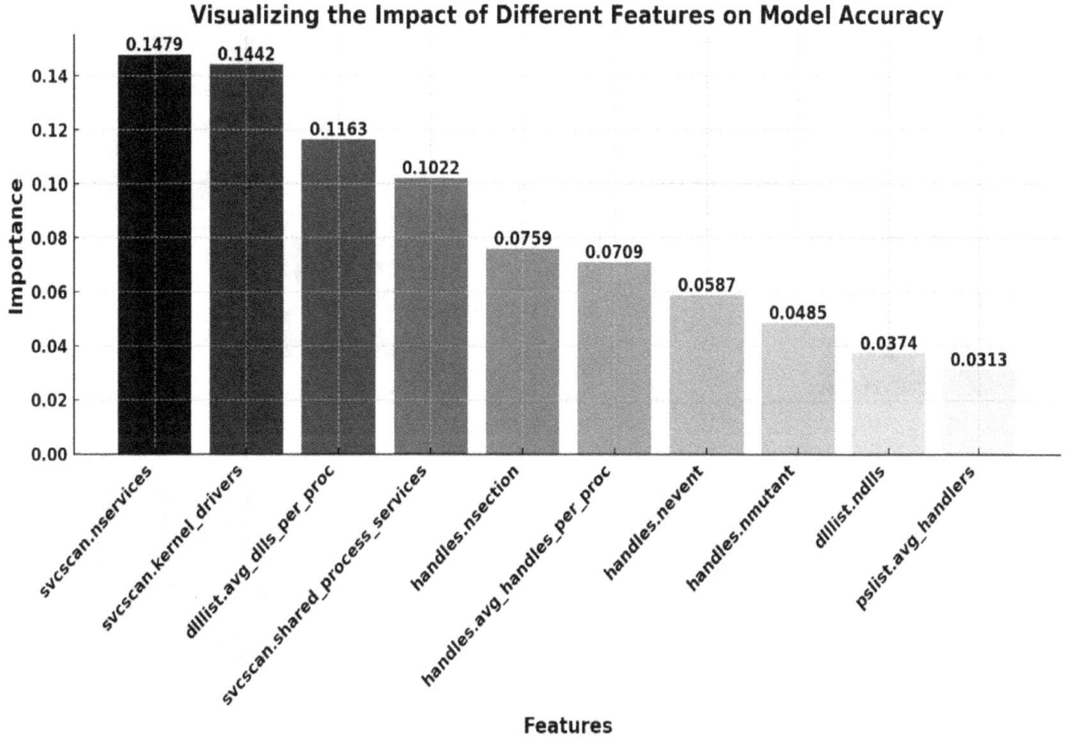

Figure 3. Performance metrics of different models

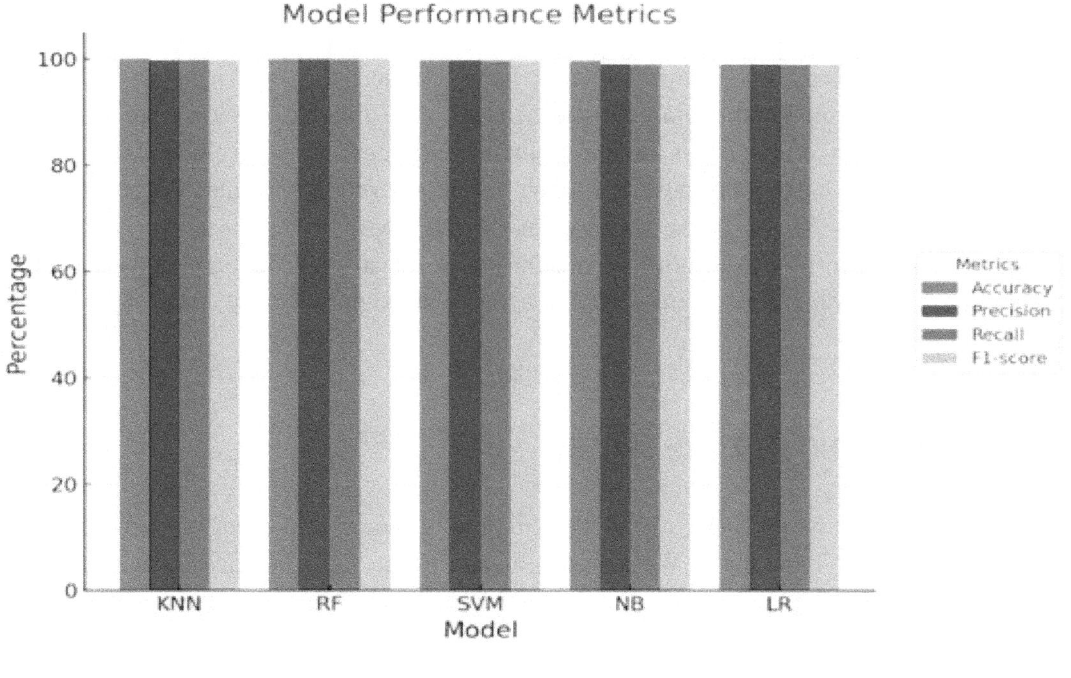

Figure 4. Confusion matrix estimation

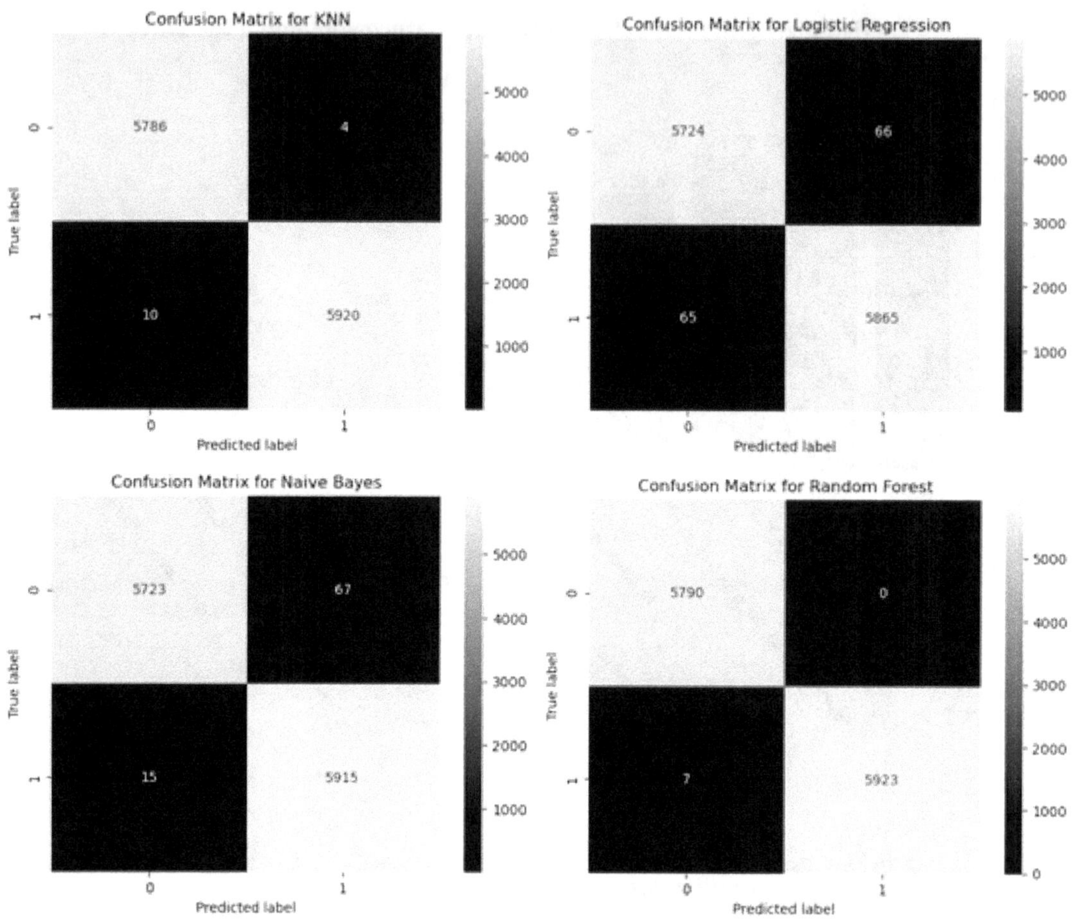

Our Logistic Regression and Naïve Bayes models achieve 99% accuracy, with a slight 1% difference in predictions. Meanwhile, the Random Forest model achieves even greater accuracy, reaching 99.9% with a negligible error margin of 0.1%. This trend is maintained throughout two evaluations of the Random Forest model, demonstrating its robustness. Similarly, the Support Vector Machine (SVM) model achieves a training accuracy of 99.7%, with a prediction error of 0.3%.

These findings demonstrate the usefulness of our models in learning from training data, establishing a precedent for further validation techniques such as the confusion matrix to comprehensively assess model performance.

5. CONCLUSION AND FUTURE WORK

Our study addresses the fundamental difficulty of detecting memory-resident malware, which poses a substantial danger to cybersecurity. We successfully constructed a high-efficacy detection model by using VolMemLyzer to extract features from memory dumps and apply it to diverse malware variants. Our computationally efficient strategy significantly improves the identification and classification of memory-targeted assaults, with the Random Forest technique standing out for its superior performance. With an accuracy of 99.9%, the Random Forest model was also useful in feature selection for improving other models such as SVM, Naive Bayes, Logistic Regression, KNN, and RF. Future studies will focus on improving our model's adaptability to new malware techniques and variations. Additionally, we intend to investigate the integration of deep learning technologies to improve detection accuracy and reduce false positives. Another critical goal is to accelerate the development of real-time detection systems adapted for a variety of computer settings, thereby strengthening defenses against complex malware attacks. Transitioning from theoretical ideas to actual, real-world applications is a significant difficulty that requires further investigation. Real-time deployment of these models in cybersecurity contexts is critical for determining their effectiveness under realistic scenarios. Such an endeavor is critical for translating theoretical discoveries into practical cybersecurity solutions. Future research aimed at addressing these restrictions will greatly benefit the field by improving the resilience, adaptability, and overall performance of malware detection frameworks in the face of new and developing cyber threats.

REFERENCES

Alkhalili, M. M. H. (2021). Investigation of applyingmachine learning for watch-list filtering in anti-money laundering. IEEE Access, 18481–18496.

Alqasrawi, Y. (2016). Natural scene image annotation using local semanticconcepts and spatial bag of visual words. International Journal of Sensors Wireless Communications and Control, 153–173.

Aslan, Ö. O.-O. (2021). Intelligent behavior-based malware detection system on cloud computing environment. *IEEE Access, 9,* 83252-83271.

Atacak, İ. (2023). An Ensemble Approach Based on Fuzzy Logic Using Machine Learning Classifiers for Android Malware Detection. *Applied Sciences, 13*(3), 1484.

Bhardwaj, S., & Dave, M. (2023). Integrating a Rule-Based Approach to Malware Detection with an LSTM-Based Feature Selection Technique. *SN Computer Science*, *4*(6), 737. doi:10.1007/s42979-023-02177-2

Cho, K., B. V. (2014). Learning phrase representations using RNN encoder-decoder for statistical machine translation. *Computer Science.*

Cybenko, G. (1989). Approximation by superpositions of a sigmoidal function. *Mathematics of Control, Signals, and Systems*, *2*(4), 303–314. doi:10.1007/BF02551274

Dang, D. D. (2021). *Malware classification using long short-term memory models*. Academic Press.

Darabian, H. H., Homayounoot, S., Dehghantanha, A., Hashemi, S., Karimipour, H., Parizi, R. M., & Choo, K.-K. R. (2020). Detecting cryptomining malware: A deep learning approach for static and dynamic analysis. *Journal of Grid Computing*, *18*(2), 293–303. doi:10.1007/s10723-020-09510-6

Gopinath, M. (2023). A comprehensive survey on deep learning based malware detection techniques. *Computer Science Review*, *47*, 100529. doi:10.1016/j.cosrev.2022.100529

He, Z. M. (2021). When machine learning meets hardware cybersecurity: Delving into accurate zero-day malware detection. *22nd International Symposium on Quality Electronic De*. 10.1109/ISQED51717.2021.9424330

Hearst, M. A., Dumais, S. T., Osuna, E., Platt, J., & Scholkopf, B. (1998). Platt, B. Scholkopf, Support vector machines. *IEEE Intelligent Systems & their Applications*, *13*(4), 18–28. doi:10.1109/5254.708428

Hemalatha, J. R., Roseline, S., Geetha, S., Kadry, S., & Damaševičius, R. (2021). An efficient densenet-based deep learning model for malware detection. *Entropy (Basel, Switzerland)*, *23*(3), 344. doi:10.3390/e23030344 PMID:33804035

Jerlin, M. A., & Marimuthu, K. (2018). A new malware detection system using machine learning techniques for API call sequences. *Journal of Applied Security Research*, *13*(1), 45–62. doi:10.1080/19361610.2018.1387734

Ke, G. Q. M.-Y. (2017). Lightgbm: A highly efficient gradient boosting decision tree. Advances in Neural Information Processing Systems, 30.

Keserwani, P. K. (2023). An Improved NIDS Using RF-Based Feature Selection Technique and Voting Classifier. In *Artificial Intelligence for Intrusion Detection Systems* (pp. 133–154). Chapman and Hall/CRC. doi:10.1201/9781003346340-7

Khalid, O. U., Ullah, S., Ahmad, T., Saeed, S., Alabbad, D. A., Aslam, M., Buriro, A., & Ahmad, R. (2023). An insight into machine-learning-based fileless malware detection. *Sensors (Basel)*, *23*(2), 612. doi:10.3390/s23020612 PMID:36679406

Kilincer, I. F. (2023). *Automated detection of cybersecurity attacks in healthcare systems with recursive feature elimination and multilayer perceptron optimization*. Biocybernetics and Biomedical Engine. doi:10.1016/j.bbe.2022.11.005

Li, H. Z. (2019). Using deep-learning-based memory analysis for malware detection in the cloud. *IEEE 16th International Conference on mobile ad hoc and sensor systems workshops*, 1-6.

Lian, W. N., Nie, G., Jia, B., Shi, D., Fan, Q., & Liang, Y. (2020). An intrusion detection method based on decision tree-recursive feature elimination in ensemble learning. *Mathematical Problems in Engineering*, *2020*, 1–15. doi:10.1155/2020/2835023

Lifandali, O. A., Abghour, N., & Chiba, Z. (2023). Feature Selection Using a Combination of Ant Colony Optimization and Random Forest Algorithms Applied To Isolation Forest Based Intrusion Detection System. *Procedia Computer Science*, *220*, 796–805. doi:10.1016/j.procs.2023.03.106

Logeswari, G., Bose, S., & Anitha, T. (2023). An Intrusion Detection System for SDN Using Machine Learning. *Intelligent Automation & Soft Computing*, *35*(1), 867–880. doi:10.32604/iasc.2023.026769

Mahindru, A., & Sangal, A. L. (2021). A feature selection technique to detect malware from Android using Machine Learning Techniques. *FSDroid. Multimedia Tools and Applications*, *80*(9), 13271–13323. doi:10.1007/s11042-020-10367-w PMID:33462535

Mat, S. R., Ab Razak, M. F., Kahar, M. N. M., Arif, J. M., Mohamad, S., & Firdaus, A. (2021). Towards a systematic description of the field using bibliometric analysis: Malware evolution. *Scientometrics*, *126*(3), 2013–2055. doi:10.1007/s11192-020-03834-6 PMID:33583978

Misra, P., & Yadav, A. S. (2020). Improving the classification accuracy using recursive feature elimination with cross-validation. *Int. J. Emerg. Technol.*, *11*(3), 659–665.

Nath, H. V. (2014). Static malware analysis using machine learning methods. *Recent Trends in Computer Networks and Distributed Systems Security.* 10.1007/978-3-642-54525-2_39

Noor, B., & Qadir, S. (2023). Machine Learning and Deep Learning Based Model for the Detection of Rootkits Using Memory Analysis. *Applied Sciences (Basel, Switzerland)*, *13*(19), 10730. doi:10.3390/app131910730

Panker, T., & Nissim, N. (2021). Leveraging malicious behavior traces from volatile memory using machine learning methods for trusted unknown malware detection in Linux cloud environments. *Knowledge-Based Systems*, *226*, 107095. doi:10.1016/j.knosys.2021.107095

Pen, L. Z. K. X. (2022). Artocarpus classification technique using deep learning based convolutional neural network. Classification Applications with Deep Learning and Ma-chine Learning Technologies, 1–21.

Raff, E. F. (2021). Classifying sequences of extreme length with constant memory applied to malware detection. *Proceedings of the AAAI Conference on Artificial Intelligence*, 35. 10.1609/aaai.v35i11.17131

Rafrastara, F. A. (2023). *Performance Improvement of Random Forest Algorithm for Malware Detection on Imbalanced Dataset using Random Under-Sampling Method*. Jurnal Informatika Jurnal Pengembangan. doi:10.30591/jpit.v8i2.5207

Rahman, M. A., Islam, S., Nugroho, Y. S., Al Irsyadi, F. Y., & Hossain, M. J. (2023). An exploratory analysis of feature selection for malware detection with simple machine learning algorithms. *Journal of Communications Software and Systems*, *19*(3), 207–221. doi:10.24138/jcomss-2023-0091

Roseline, S. A. (2020). Intelligent vision-based malware detection and classification using deep random forest paradigm. *IEEE Access, 8*, 206303-206324.

Rtayli & Enneya. (2020). *Enhanced credit card fraud detection based on SVM-recursive feature elimination and hyper-parameters optimization.* Academic Press.

Shah, S. S., Ahmad, A. R., Jamil, N., & Khan, A. R. (2022). Memory forensics-based malware detection using computer vision and machine learning. *Electronics (Basel)*, *11*(16), 2579. doi:10.3390/electronics11162579

Sharma, N. V., & Yadav, N. S. (2021). An optimal intrusion detection system using recursive feature elimination and ensemble of classifiers. *Microprocessors and Microsystems*, *85*, 104293. doi:10.1016/j.micpro.2021.104293

Sihwail, R. O., Omar, K., & Akram Zainol Ariffin, K. (2021). An Effective Memory Analysis for Malware Detection and Classification. *Computers, Materials & Continua*, *67*(2), 2301–2320. doi:10.32604/cmc.2021.014510

Sihwail, R. O., Omar, K., Zainol Ariffin, K., & Al Afghani, S. (2019). Malware detection approach based on artifacts in memory image and dynamic analysis. *Applied Sciences (Basel, Switzerland)*, *9*(18), 3680. doi:10.3390/app9183680

Singh, P. B. (2022). Performance Enhancement of SVM-based ML Malware Detection Model Using Data Preprocessing. *2nd International Conference on Emerging Frontiers in Electrical and Electronic Technologies (ICEFEET)*. 10.1109/ICEFEET51821.2022.9848192

Sulaiman, M. U., Waseem, M., Ali, A. N., Laouini, G., & Alshammari, F. S. (2024). Defense strategies for epidemic cyber security threats: Modeling and analysis by using a machine learning approach. *IEEE Access : Practical Innovations, Open Solutions*, *12*, 4958–4984. doi:10.1109/ACCESS.2024.3349660

Talukder, M. A., Hasan, K. F., Islam, M. M., Uddin, M. A., Akhter, A., Yousuf, M. A., Alharbi, F., & Moni, M. A. (2023). A dependable hybrid machine learning model for network intrusion detection. *Journal of Information Security and Applications*, *72*, 103405. doi:10.1016/j.jisa.2022.103405

Tsafrir, T. C., Cohen, A., Nir, E., & Nissim, N. (2023). Efficient feature extraction methodologies for unknown MP4-Malware detection using Machine learning algorithms. *Expert Systems with Applications*, *219*, 119615. doi:10.1016/j.eswa.2023.119615

Tsafrir, T. C., Cohen, A., Nir, E., & Nissim, N. (2023). Efficient feature extraction methodologies for unknown MP4-Malware detection using Machine learning algorithms. *Expert Systems with Applications*, *219*, 119615. doi:10.1016/j.eswa.2023.119615

Van Der Malsburg, C. F. R. (1986). principles of neurodynamics: perceptrons and the theory of brain mechanisms. In Brain Theory. Springer.

Walker, S. H., & Duncan, D. B. (1967). Estimation of the probability of an event as a function of several independent variables. *Biometrika*, *54*(1-2), 167–179. doi:10.1093/biomet/54.1-2.167 PMID:6049533

Xu, Z. R. (2017). Malware detection using machine learning-based analysis of virtual memory access patterns. In *Design, Automation & Test in Europe Conference & Exhibition* (pp. 169–174). doi:10.23919/DATE.2017.7926977

Yin, Y. J.-J., Jang-Jaccard, J., Xu, W., Singh, A., Zhu, J., Sabrina, F., & Kwak, J. (2023). a hybrid feature selection method for MLP-based network intrusion detection on UNSW-NB15 dataset. *Journal of Big Data*, *10*(1), 1–26. doi:10.1186/s40537-023-00694-8 PMID:36618886

Zhang, S. H., Hu, C., Wang, L., Mihaljevic, M., Xu, S., & Lan, T. (2023). A Malware Detection Approach Based on Deep Learning and Memory Forensics. *Symmetry*, *15*(3), 758. doi:10.3390/sym15030758

Zhang, X. W. (2023). *Detection of Android Malware Based on Deep Forest and Feature Enhancement*. Academic Press.

Chapter 7
Deep Learning-Based Methodology for Tracking Cybersecurity in Networked Computers

Dharmesh Dhabliya
https://orcid.org/0000-0002-6340-2993
Vishwakarma Institute of Information Technology, India

Jambi Ratna Raja Kumar
https://orcid.org/0000-0002-9870-7076
Genba Sopanrao Moze College of Engineering, India

N. R. Solomon Jebaraj
Jain University, India

Sabyasachi Pramanik
https://orcid.org/0000-0002-9431-8751
Haldia Institute of Technology, India

Sanjay Kumar Sinha
Vivekananda Global University, India

Ankur Gupta
https://orcid.org/0000-0002-4651-5830
Vaish College of Engineering, India

Asha Uchil
ATLAS SkillTech University, India

Anishkumar Dhablia
Altimetrik India Pvt. Ltd., India

ABSTRACT

Effective surveillance of cybersecurity is essential for safeguarding the security of computer networks. Nevertheless, due to the increasing scope, complexity, and amount of data created by computer networks, cybersecurity monitoring has become a more intricate issue. The difficulty of correctly and effectively monitoring computer network cybersecurity is a challenge faced by traditional approaches examining a greater quantity of data. Hence, using deep learning models to oversee computer network cybersecurity becomes necessary. This chapter introduces a technique for overseeing the cybersecurity of computer networks by using deep learning knowledge about models. The combination of CNN (convolutional neural networks) and LSTM (long short-term memory) models is used for monitoring the cybersecurity of computer networks. This combination enhances the accuracy of classifying network cybersecurity problems. The CICIDS2017 dataset is used for training and evaluating the suggested model.

DOI: 10.4018/979-8-3693-2691-6.ch007

INTRODUCTION

Currently, the threat environment is undergoing significant changes, leading to an increase in cybersecurity events involving computer networks (CN). Documented CN cybersecurity (Bansal, R. et al. 2022) events include malware infections, denial of service (DoS) (Pradhan, D. et al. 2022) assaults, and phishing (Dushyant, K. et al. 2022) attacks, Man-in-the-middle (MitM) (Kaushik, D. et al. 2022) attacks, SQL injection attacks (Gupta, A. et al. 2022), network scanning and probing, password cracking, and unauthorized access. Some potential risks to consider include unauthorized access, data breaches, insider threats, system misconfigurations, and violations of security policies. These occurrences may result in significant ramifications may occur, such as the unauthorized disclosure of personal data, the interruption of network functionality, and the impairment of network applications and services. Effective surveillance of cybersecurity is an essential component in safeguarding the security of computer networks. This process entails ongoing surveillance and examination, and defense against cyber attacks. Nevertheless, the task of monitoring computer cybersecurity has evolved into a very intricate endeavor job involving the growing size, intricacy, and continuously growing interconnection of contemporary computer systems and the amount of data created inside them. This is mostly due to the inherent limitations of conventional cybersecurity monitoring techniques effectively and expediently processing a substantial amount of data in real-time. Hence, sophisticated cybersecurity surveillance Deep learning (Chandan, R. R. et al. 2023) is an essential element of the CN cybersecurity system.

Conventionally, a single deep learning model is used to analyze the whole dataset, yielding excellent results particularly in cases when there is a substantial volume of data. Nevertheless, when dealing with a limited dataset, a single deep learning model may encounter difficulties. When using a single DL model to address the issue at hand is to the surveillance of the cybersecurity of a computer network (CN). Specifically, there may be a challenge in obtaining various forms of data. Cybersecurity incident data encompasses several variables, such as location and temporal characteristics, which aid in comprehending the subject matter. The cybersecurity event patterns exhibit an intricate dispersion of data. This is due to the inability of current deep learning models to concurrently extract several sorts of characteristics from CN cybersecurity incident data and may not be efficient in detecting distinctive designs. Consequently, current deep learning models are unable to comprehensively analyze the diverse characteristics of these Chinese cybersecurity events Isolate the data. Hence, this study suggests using a combination of several deep learning models for the purpose of monitoring cybersecurity in computer networks. Analyze various attributes from CN cybersecurity incident data. Simultaneously, every DL model focuses on remedying a certain condition. Implementing such an approach may greatly enhance the efficacy of cybersecurity surveillance for the CN. This chapter aims to create a technique for overseeing the security of CN by using a combination of DL models. In this scenario, a convolutional neural network (CNN) (Meslie, Y. et al. 2021) and a recurrent neural network with long short-term memory (LSTM) (Ahamad, S. et al. 2023) are used. By using these models in conjunction, we may effectively extract diverse categories of information from cybersecurity event data. This will enhance the precision of categorizing and forecasting cybersecurity occurrences. Simultaneously, CNN permits the process of extracting local patterns from the data involves identifying recurring patterns within a certain region or area. On the other hand, LSTM (Long Short-Term Memory) is a kind of neural network that is capable of analyzing and understanding the temporal relationships and dependencies present in the data. The subsequent sections of the paper are structured in the following manner. Section 2 provides an analysis of the works that are relevant to the topic. Section 3 provides information about cybersecurity that is based on deep learning. The CN cybersecurity monitoring approach based on CNN-LSTM is introduced in Section 4. Section 5 provides a detailed description of the dataset and experimental setup used for training the proposed model. Section 6 provides an exposition of the experimental findings and subsequent analysis. Ultimately, the conclusion delineates the concepts for next study endeavors.

LITERATURE SURVEY

The Network Intrusion Detection System (NIDS) developed in (Pramanik, S. 2022) uses deep learning methods and relies on pre-existing information. Models trained on extensive data sets. Despite the limited availability of data and computer resources, achieve optimal speed Ensuring maximum precision. The suggested technique attained a classification accuracy of 98.43% while using the UNSW-15 dataset. The study in reference (Mall, P. K. et al. 2023) focused on the use of the DL algorithm to simulate CN safety analysis. By means of thorough investigation and careful examination, an in-depth examination and modeling of CN safety are conducted, beginning from the present situation. Furthermore, an evaluation is performed. The current safety assessment of the CN is being conducted. The author's suggested intrusion detection approach has a precision rate of 91.6%. A hierarchical deep learning system called Big Data based Hierarchical Deep Learning System (BDHDLS) was presented in (Praveenkumar, S. et al. 2023).

Numerous related papers that address machine learning methods for intrusion detection systems can be found in the literature. The studies are categorized according to the following criteria:

- Approaches to deep learning: it indicates if the study's emphasis was on deep learning techniques for intrusion detection systems.
- Machine learning approaches: this shows whether or not intrusion detection systems were taken into account in the research.
- Deep learning technique evaluation: this shows whether the research assesses deep learning methods for intrusion detection systems.
- Machine learning method evaluation: this specifies whether the research assesses machine learning techniques for intrusion detection systems.
- IDS-used datasets: this signifies whether the study's emphasis was on the datasets used by intrusion detection systems.

Ring and colleagues (Ring, M. et al. 2019) have published a research on intrusion detection datasets. The research specifically lists 34 datasets and 15 attributes for each of them. These attributes are divided into five groups: general information, nature of the data, recording environment, evaluation, volume of data, and general information. A study of the machine learning techniques used by intrusion detection systems was published by (Patel, N.D. 2023). The datasets in this research were divided into three categories: packet-level data, netflow data, and public datasets. A computational complexity, or temporal complexity, was also supplied by the research for each mining and machine learning technique that the intrusion detection system used. A comparative analysis of intrusion detection techniques in the internet of things (IoT) was presented by (Hosseini, S. et al. 2023). Based on the detection method, IDS installation method, and security threat, the research categorized IDSs for IoT. (Balaji, S. et al. 2023) examined current systems in relation to workloads, metrics, and technique—three basic assessment parameters—to establish common practices for cyber security intrusion detection. (Mahadik, S. et al.

2023) concentrate on deep learning techniques intended for intrusion detection in cyber security. These papers do not, however, provide a comparison of deep learning techniques on the datasets. To the best of our knowledge, this is the first research to compare deep learning for intrusion detection systems and to cover methodologies, datasets, and methodology in detail.

IoT systems have different security risks than traditional computer systems because of the advent of diverse abnormalities. First of all, there is a wide range of devices, platforms, communication techniques, and protocols among IoT systems. Secondly, Internet of Things (IoT) systems are made up of control devices and internet-connected parts that are used to connect physical structures. Thirdly, since people and gadgets are always moving, there are no clear boundaries in Internet of Things systems. Fourthly, there would be a physical risk to IoT systems or a part of them. Fifthly, since IoT devices have limited energy, it might be challenging to incorporate advanced security procedures and software. Finally, these networks may be vulnerable to attacks on their security and privacy due to the rapid expansion of IoT-based devices. By spotting abnormalities in the IoT system, a number of frameworks and machine-learning approaches have been created to mitigate network threats. The literature describes a number of cutting-edge methods for using machine learning in the IoT infrastructure to categorize these abnormalities. However, others have used deep learning methods for the same objective. The most effective methods for matching patterns are deep learning approaches, which can identify any input from an IoT environment as legitimate or bogus requests. The four main kinds of ID assaults are anomaly-based techniques, specification-based techniques, hybrid tactics, and signature-based techniques. The first step in signature-based methods is to compare a set of network data with a feature database. If the scanned data fits the signature database, it will be regarded as legal violations. To precisely determine the sort of assault, this is quite helpful. It's a comparatively demand-free process with little work intensity. They enable the system administrators to establish the rules and thresholds beforehand. The present policies, which identify the device and network state, shall be adhered to. If the rule is violated or the threshold is exceeded, the IDS will detect an unusual circumstance and react appropriately. The goal of anomaly-based methods is to identify patterns that are normal or aberrant. Finding new potential invasions is one advantage of using this method for intrusion detection. This method has the disadvantage of being prone to false positives. Research is being done to improve the advantages of anomaly-based intrusion detection systems using machine learning techniques. In order to stay aware of potential future assaults, machine learning algorithms can monitor current activity using anomaly-based intrusion detection approaches and compare it with known intrusion footprints. Different identifying techniques are used in the same scheme using hybrid approaches. By using this method, the IoT system as a whole will be more reliable and the weaknesses of a particular operation will be eliminated. But the fully developed IDS would be very complex and wide. The system will need more resources and become more sophisticated overall as a result. Intrusion detection would require a significant investment of time and money due to the several protocols involved. It was shown that (Chander, N. et al. 2023) deep learning-based anomaly detection in IoT data outperformed conventional IDS in identifying coordinated IoT Fog assaults. A convention-based intrusion detection system (IDS) based on anomaly detection was built by (Bhavsar, M. et al. 2023). Additionally, the model was trained and tested using the KDDCup99 dataset. The recommended course of action should be followed since it provides 95% accuracy. They did, however, use the KDDCup99 dataset, which has few unique entries and inconsistent data. It is challenging to get precise findings as a consequence of this. Network feature-exclusive anomaly-based intrusion detection systems (IDS) were suggested by (Abdulganiyu, O.H. et al. 2023). The best results are obtained using an R-tree approach, which uses several machine learning models and has a 99.5% true positive rate and a 0.001% false-positive rate. Their results illustrated the value of using statistical techniques such as Random Forest. However, there are problems with validity since their dataset is not a standard. In SDN, (Maddu, M. et al. 2023) proposed an identifying technique. The NSL-KDD dataset is used for training and testing, and the approach consists of two IDs: an anomaly-based ID and a signature-based ID. The accuracy of detection surpasses 97.4%. Nevertheless, anomaly detection alone is unable to distinguish intrusions from signature detection. Using just a specified feature set, (Krishnan, P. et al. 2023) suggested anomaly-based security architecture for SDN. The impacts of several machine learning techniques were compared by the researchers. A deep neural network with three hidden layers was able to classify photos with an accuracy of 76%.

A blockchain technology protocol was put up by (Hazman, C. et al. 2024) to enable peer-to-peer communication for networks that are linked. The protocol manages heterogeneity in the operating states and contributes to the security of the contact mechanism. Currently, the field is looking at how to use blockchain in a multi-agent system. (Sy, I., et al. 2024) suggested a better method that makes use of deep migration learning to extract IoT data characteristics for the purpose of detecting IDS for smart cities. Furthermore, they said that their plan would address the deficiency of an appropriate training set. Additionally, they said that their approach reduced the clustering time and enhanced detection rates with a high degree of performance in comparison to conventional methods. A deep learning model was presented by (Siva Shankar, S. et al. 2023) for IoT intrusion detection. To decrease the dimension of the feature vector by carefully choosing incursion features, a framework for a feature engineering technique has been created. This is a crucial component of intrusion detection. The next step was to use the chosen functions to develop and train several IDSs. Recurring neural networks (RNNs) and other deep learning techniques were used throughout the learning phase. With very high categorization accuracy, intrusion footprint information from two databases was employed. An enhanced intrusion detection method for IoT devices with limited resources was described by (Ravi, V. et al. 2023). As a result, intrusion detection is not available to Internet of Things devices or the edge router. IoT devices are used as IDS nodes to scan through network traffic. Since raw packets from the host router node contain sensitive data, it can only receive a limited amount of them. Three-layer IDS architecture was proposed by (Nielson, S. J. 2023) for real time-destroying activities in home IoT devices. The security layers in this approach categorize IoT system intrusions based on whether they exhibit typical or atypical behavior.

METHODOLOGY

DL-Based Approach for Monitoring CN Cybersecurity

A solution for cybersecurity monitoring in CN may be devised by using neural networks and machine learning techniques based on deep learning Algorithms for extracting characteristics from CN cybersecurity incident data. The neural network is trained using a cybersecurity dataset. Post-training, the model exhibits the capability to detect various assaults, including DDoS (Mittal, M. et al. 2023) attacks, port scanning, system injection, and others. The given text is incomplete and does not provide enough information to rewrite it in a straightforward and precise manner. Please provide more context or specific text to be rewritten. The technology enables the monitoring of network traffic in real-time and the detection of cybersecurity issues as they happen. Clustering algorithms it may also be used to categorize occurrences and establish connections between them. The DL-based technique has to continuously adjust to

Figure 1. Surveillance of Chinese cybersecurity using deep learning techniques

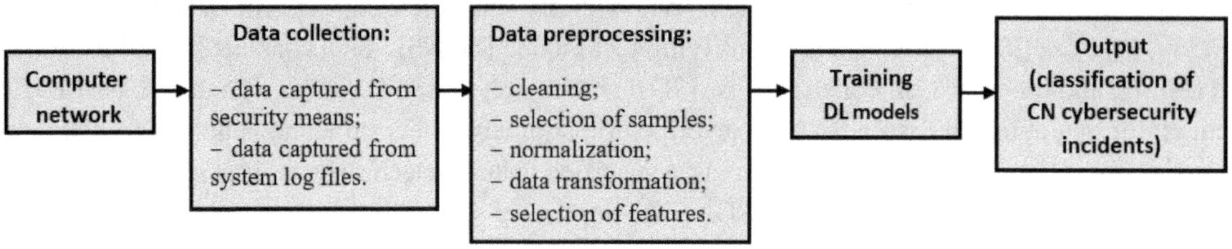

emerging risks and assaults in order to guarantee the highest level of efficacy in protecting computer networks. The purpose of CN cybersecurity monitoring is to gather data from CN cybersecurity events and derive spatiotemporal information. Extract characteristics from them and build a neural network model (Figure 1). The analysis of the gathered data is a crucial phase in the process. Typically, the practice of monitoring the cybersecurity of a computer network involves many steps and may be customized to suit the particular requirements.

CN Cybersecurity Monitoring Model Based on CNN-LSTM

A neural network may be trained using pre-processed data to identify cybersecurity issues that may signify a potential danger to the network. Simultaneously, a significant challenge in cyber security monitoring is the identification of the correlation between several occurrences occurring within a certain timeframe, often referred to as incident pattern recognition. Cybersecurity events may happen in different areas of the computer network and at various points in time.

A cybersecurity monitoring model is proposed, which is based on the combination of Convolutional Neural Network (CNN) and Long Short-Term Memory (LSTM) architecture. The cybersecurity monitoring model, based on CNN-LSTM architecture, has many layers (Figure 2). The data is pre-collected. It analyzed data from cybersecurity incidents in China obtained from several network security methods or system log files.

Input CNN Layer, LSTM Layer, FC Layer, MC Output Layer

Subsequently, the preprocessed data undergoes spatial feature extraction using the CNN layer. CNN is comprised of a convolutional layer. The components of the model are a convolutional layer, a sub-sampling layer, and activation functions. The mathematical expression governing the CNN and MaxPooling layers may be represented by the following equation:

$$Aconv[i, k] = \sum Xtrain\_reshaped[i + j, 0].\ Wconv[j, 0, k] + bconv[k]$$

$$j=0$$

$$Hconv[i, k] = \max(0, Aconv[i, k]) \text{ and}$$

$$Hpool[i, k] = \max(Hconv[2i, k], Hconv[2i + 1, k]),$$

Figure 2. CNN-LSTM model for CN cybersecurity monitoring

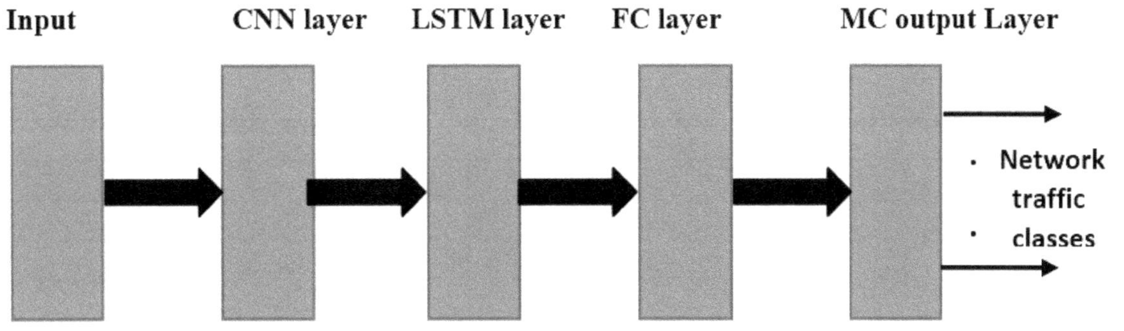

where the variables *Xtrain_reshaped*, *Wconv*, *bconv*, *Aconv*, *Hconv* denote input, filters, bias, output, and activation, respectively, and in the equation for MaxPooling layer variables *Hconv*, *Hpool* input, and output, respectively. *Hconv*$[i, k]$ is the output of the convolutional layer at position (i, k) after applying the Rectified Linear Unit (ReLU) activation function and is computed

The characteristics obtained via the use of Convolutional Neural Networks (CNN) are then passed on to the second layer, specifically intended to extract temporal data derived from cybersecurity event data. In order to achieve this objective, the Long Short-Term Memory (LSTM) model is used. LSTM is specifically intended to handle sequential data and consider relevant contextual information. The use of temporal interdependence among them is employed. In this scenario, training is conducted by maintaining the condition over a lengthy period of time and moving ahead the backpropagation technique is used for training time series data in order to construct a forecasting model. Utilization of LSTM enables the consideration of the context and sequence of Chinese cybersecurity incidents. The equation represents the calculation in a densely linked layer, where each output neuron *Hdense*$[j]$ is derived. By using the Rectified Linear Unit (ReLU) activation function on the weighted sum of the flattened input values, together with the inclusion of a bias factor, the Rectified Linear Unit (ReLU). The activation function imparts non-linearity to the model. The CNN-LSTM based CN cybersecurity monitoring approach may effectively address diverse network issues. Cybersecurity issues include several challenges, including intrusion detection, virus detection, event log analysis, and more. In order to train a network effectively, it is necessary to have a substantial quantity of data and to appropriately configure the parameters and architecture of the model.

Data Collection and Experimental Configuration

Cybersecurity monitoring in CN starts with the first steps of cleansing and preparing the dataset. Subsequently, the CNN-LSTM model undergoes training and its performance is assessed. The study incorporates a range of indicators and visual representations to assess the effectiveness of the model in categorizing various forms of network traffic in order to conduct our experiment, we used the publicly accessible CICIDS2017 (Canadian Cyber Security Institute) dataset includes typical traffic patterns and contemporary prevalent cyber assaults. CICFlowMeter is used to collect traffic data in the form of packets and extract it. Each dataset has over 80 observations of network traffic parameters. The data collecting period started at 9:00.The period of time is from 12:00 a.m. on July 3, 2017, to 5:00 p.m. on July 7, 2017.Prior to conducting the experiment, a thorough analysis of the CICIDS2017 dataset revealed the presence of 15 distinct categories of traffic including regular traffic as well as 14 distinct

Table 1. Network traffic types in CICIDS2017

Traffic Type	Statistics
BENIGN	2357511
DoS Hulk	230124
PortScan	158804
DDoS	41834
DoS GoldenEye	10293
FTP-Patator	7935
SSH-Patator	5897
DoS slowloris	5796
DoS Slowhttptest	5499
Bot	1956
Brute Force	1507
XSS	652
SQL Injection	21
Other	47

Figure 3. Important features

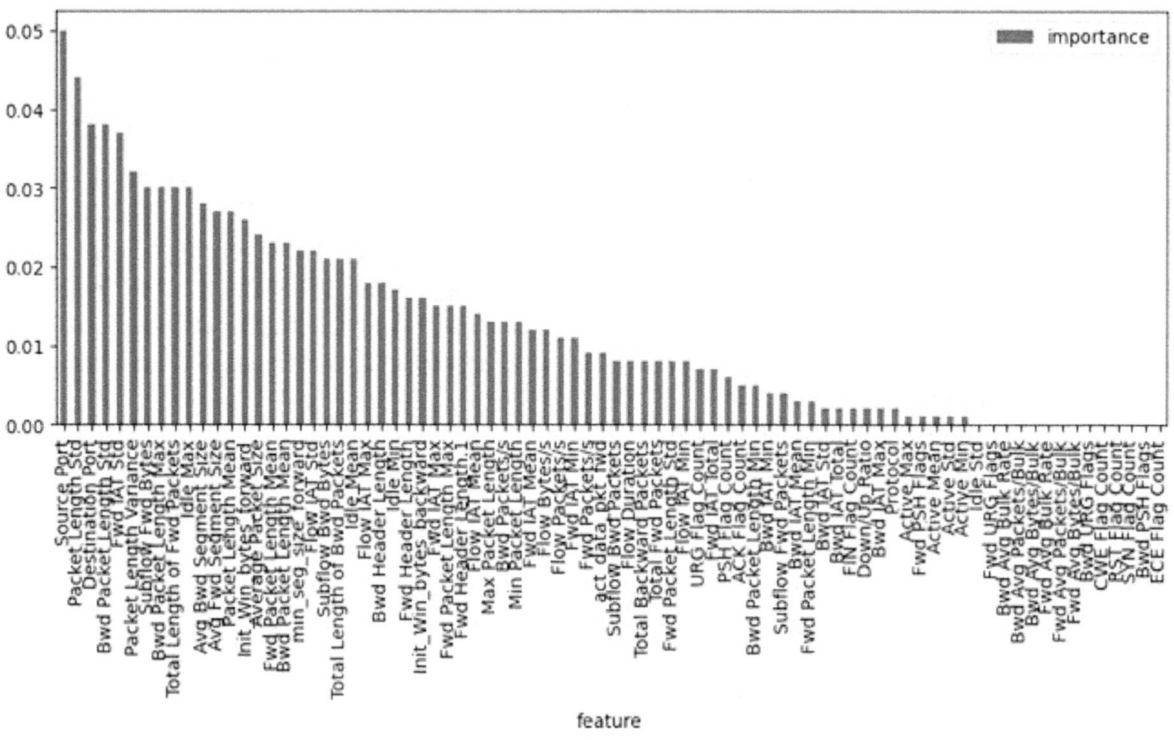

assault categories. The types of network traffic include BENIGN, DoS Hulk, PortScan, DDoS, and DoS GoldenEye.FTP-Patator, SSH-Patator, DoS slowloris, DoS Slowhttptest, Bot, Brute Force, XSS, Heartbleed, Infiltration, and SQL are all types of cyber attacks.. Subsequently, the Heartbleed and Infiltration assaults were merged and categorized under other. Upon conducting a thorough analysis of the source data, Fourteen traffic kinds were chosen, including BENIGN, DoS Hulk, PortScan, DDoS, DoS GoldenEye, FTP-Patator, and SSH-The user mentions many types of cyber attacks, including Patator, DoS slowloris, DoS Slowhttptest, Bot, Brute Force, XSS, SQL Injection, and others (Table 1).The data was further cleansed by eliminating superfluous Flow ID and External IP columns, standardizing column names, and eliminating redundant columns. The infinite and NaN values were substituted, and the rows containing NaN values were eliminated.

The experimental procedure entails using a random forest classifier for feature selection and then training a CNN-LSTM model. Figure 3 illustrates the significance of characteristics. In order to distribute computing resources in a suitable manner, a total of 12 characteristics were chosen. This also resulted in a reduction in the time required to train the models. The dataset was partitioned between training and test sets using a 70-30 split.

Figure 4. Structures of CNN-LSTM, CNN, and LSTM models

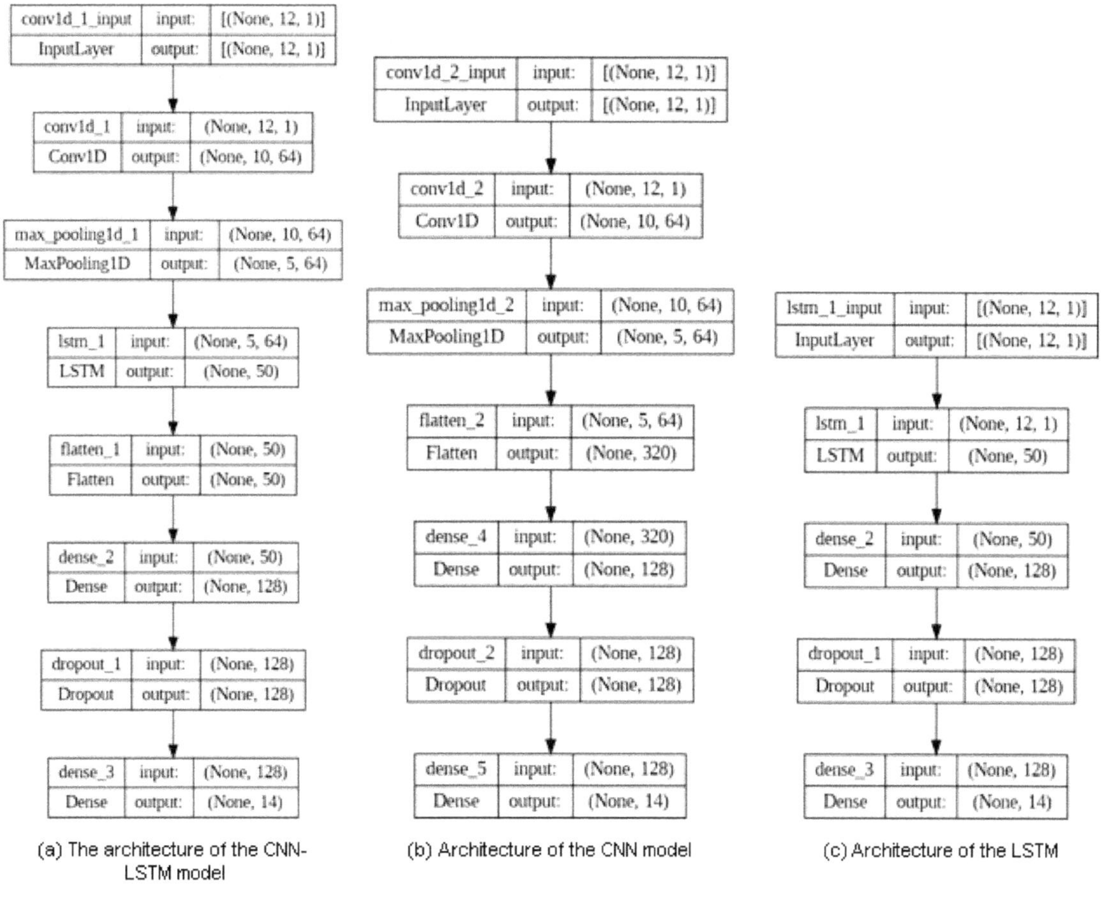

CCNN-LSTM, CNN, and LSTM models underwent training using the CICIDS2017 dataset, as shown in Figure 4a-c, to ensure fairness. Each of them has used a dense layer to produce the final outcome. The development and verification of all models were conducted on the Python 3.10.12 version of the Google Colab platform is being used, making use of the CPU accelerator supplied by Google Colab. The foundation for deep learning chooses Keras that is built on TensorFlow 2.14.0. The models shown in Figure 4 underwent training for 30 epochs using a specified batch size consisting of 64.

RESULTS AND DISCUSSION

During the studies, it was observed that as the number of epochs rose, there was a discernible improvement in the loss and accuracy values. The traffic categorization task included the acquisition of CNN-LSTM, CNN, and LSTM models. Training using 30 epochs and a batch size of 64 resulted in the optimal values for loss and accuracy in classification. The learning process of CNN-LSTM, CNN, and LSTM models was conducted Represented by loss and accuracy curves, as seen in Figures 5, 6, and 7, respectively. Figure 5 illustrates the CNN-LSTM model Exhibits test loss values that are significantly low and test accuracy values that are very high. Consequently, the model underwent training in order to generate precise forecasts for the test data. Following the training phase, the CNN-LSTM, CNN, and LSTM models underwent testing to evaluate their performance. The accuracy values obtained were 0.9846, 0.9649, and 0.9814, as shown in Table 2. Table 2 presents a comparison of the test loss and test accuracy. The suggested CNN-LSTM model demonstrates its benefit via the average period time.

Table 3 presents a comparison of the classification performance between "normal" and attack traffic using the CNN-LSTM model. CNN and LSTM models. The evaluation criteria are accuracy, F1Score, and recall. The experimental findings indicate that the assessment metrics for classifying BENIGN traffic and attack traffic are consistently higher for the CNN-LSTM model compared to the CNN and LSTM models. Specifically, the CNN-LSTM model outperforms the CNN model in categorizing BENIGN traffic. Regarding accuracy, it outperforms the CNN and LSTM algorithms in detecting Bot, DoS Hulk, and PortScan traffic. Furthermore, the CNN-LSTM model achieves a recall value of 100% while classifying DoS Hulk and FTP-Patator traffic. However, while categorizing Brute Force and Denial of Service (DoS), the CNN-LSTM model has worse performance compared to both the CNN and LSTM models when it comes to slow traffic. In general, the outcomes of the experiment Evidence suggest that the CNN-LSTM model outperforms both the CNN and LSTM models in accurately categorizing CN cybersecurity occurrences models.

The confusion matrices of the CNN-LSTM, CNN, and LSTM models for network traffic are shown in Figures 8, 9, and 10, respectively. Network data retrieved from the CICIDS2017 dataset is used for categorization. Based on the confusion matrices, it is evident that the suggested CNN-LSTM model demonstrated superior accuracy in categorizing BENIGN compared to both the CNN and LSTM algorithms.

CONCLUSION

Table 2. Test loss, test accuracy, and average epoch execution time of CNN-LSTM, CNN, and LSTM models

Model	Test Loss	Test Accuracy	Average Epochs Time (Sec.)
CNN-LSTM	0.0376	0.9846	309.2
LSTM	0.0734	0.9649	173.8
CNN	0.0734	0.9814	378.8

Figure 5. Evaluation of the CNN-LSTM model

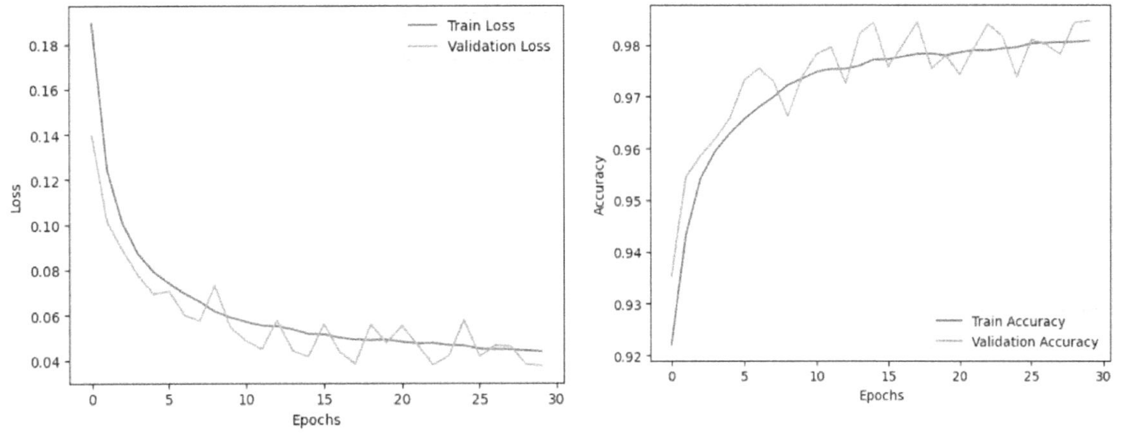

Figure 6. Evaluation of the CNN model

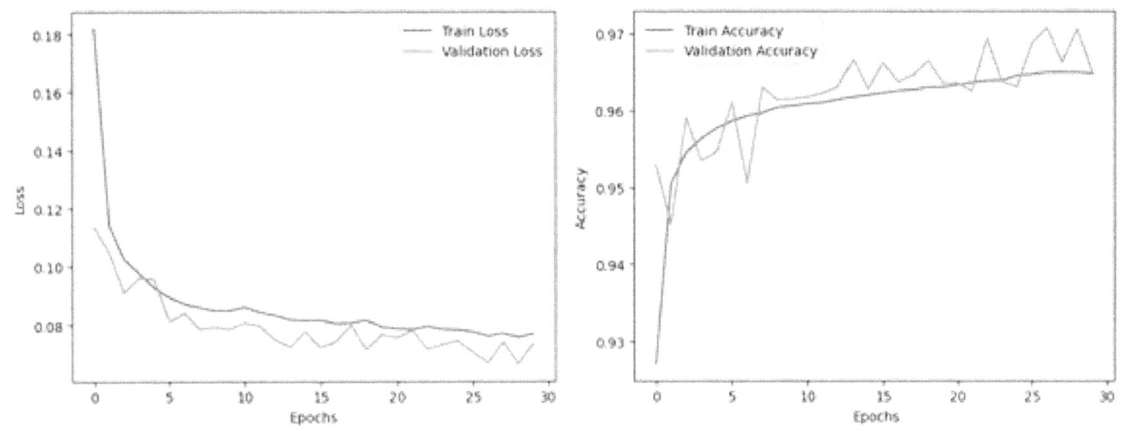

Figure 7. Evaluation of the LSTM model

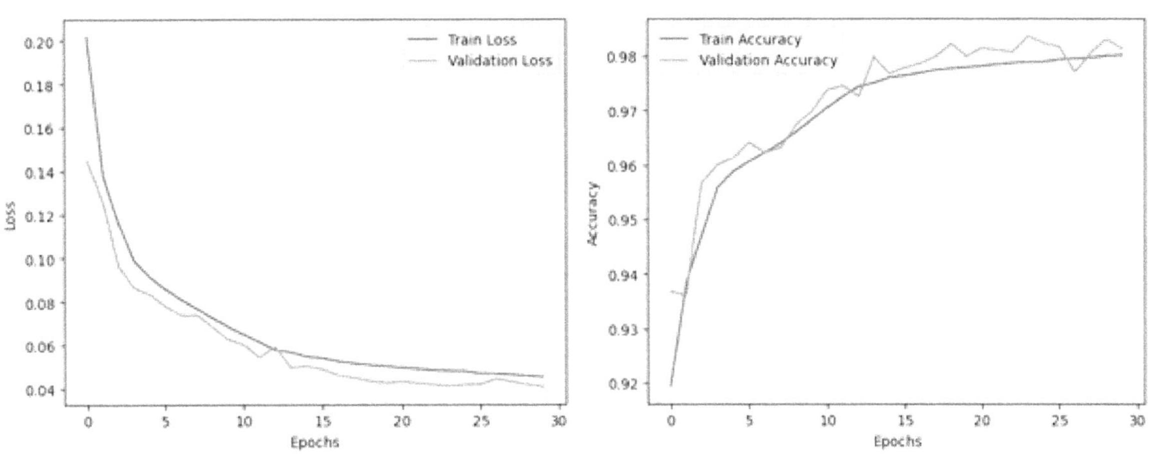

Table 3. Assessing the classification performance of regular and attack traffic using CNN-LSTM, CNN and LSTM models

Traffic types	*Model*								
	CNN-LSTM			*CNN*			*LSTM*		
	Precision	*Recall*	*F1-Score*	*Precision*	*Recall*	*F1-Score*	*Precision*	*Recall*	*F1-Score*
BENIGN	*0.99*	*0.99*	*0.99*	*0.99*	*0.97*	*0.98*	*0.99*	*0.99*	*0.99*
Bot	*0.95*	*0.85*	*0.90*	*0.90*	*0.93*	*0.92*	*0.88*	*0.97*	*0.92*
Brute Force	*0.74*	*0.05*	*0.09*	*0.82*	*0.05*	*0.09*	*1.00*	*0.04*	*0.08*
DDoS	*0.86*	*0.52*	*0.65*	*0.75*	*0.60*	*0.67*	*0.87*	*0.55*	*0.67*
DoS GoldenEye	*0.98*	*0.94*	*0.96*	*0.97*	*0.95*	*0.96*	*0.99*	*0.94*	*0.96*
DoS Hulk	*0.95*	*1.00*	*0.97*	*0.86*	*0.99*	*0.92*	*0.91*	*1.00*	*0.95*
DoS Slowhttptest	*0.98*	*0.99*	*0.98*	*0.98*	*0.99*	*0.98*	*0.98*	*0.98*	*0.98*
DoS slowloris	*0.97*	*0.97*	*0.97*	*0.98*	*0.95*	*0.96*	*0.99*	*0.98*	*0.98*
FTP-Patator	*1.00*	*1.00*	*1.00*	*0.99*	*1.00*	*1.00*	*1.00*	*1.00*	*1.00*
PortScan	*1.00*	*0.99*	*1.00*	*0.84*	*0.99*	*0.91*	*0.99*	*1.00*	*0.99*
SQL Injection	*0.00*	*0.00*	*0.00*	*0.00*	*0.00*	*0.00*	*0.00*	*0.00*	*0.00*
SSH-Patator	*0.84*	*0.89*	*0.86*	*0.99*	*0.50*	*0.66*	*0.83*	*0.93*	*0.88*
XSS	*1.00*	*0.01*	*0.03*	*1.00*	*0.01*	*0.03*	*1.00*	*0.01*	*0.03*
Other	*0.80*	*0.89*	*0.84*	*1.00*	*0.78*	*0.88*	*1.00*	*0.89*	*0.94*

Figure 8. Confusion matrix of CNN-LSTN model

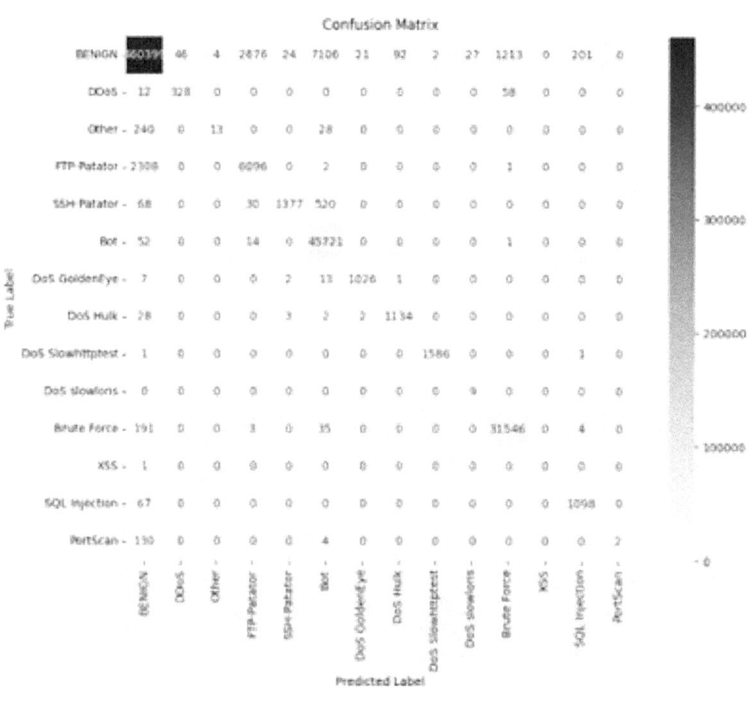

Figure 9. Confusion matrix of CNN model

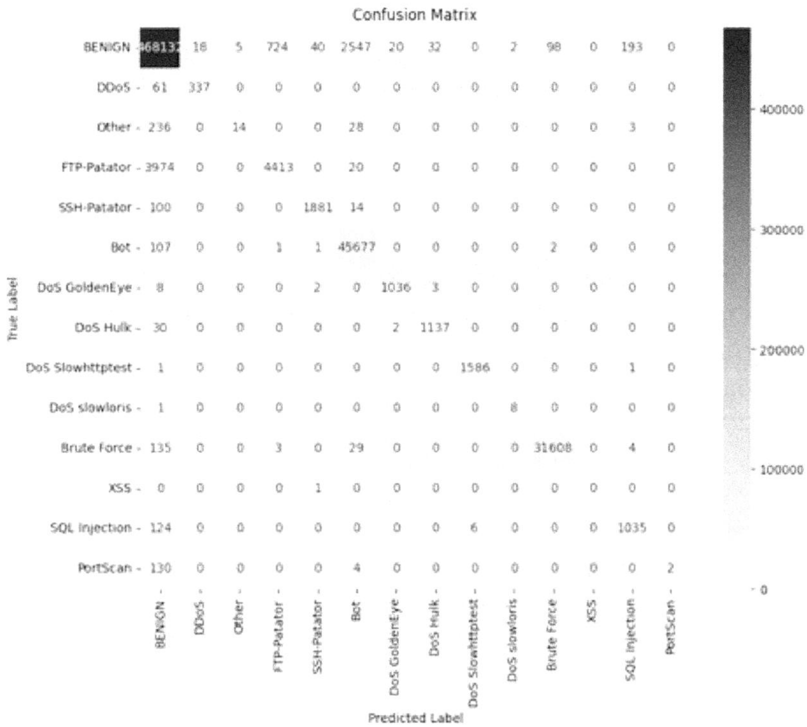

Figure 10. Confusion matrix of LSTM model

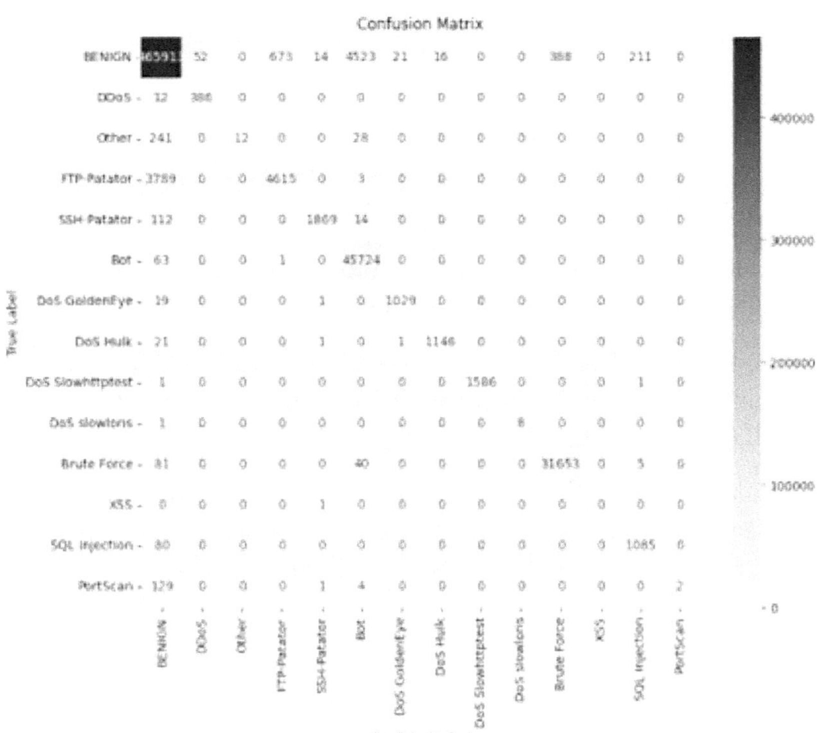

This study introduces a novel approach for monitoring CN cybersecurity, utilizing deep learning models. The investigation employed CNN-LSTM, CNN, and LSTM models serve as cybersecurity monitoring systems in the field of computer networks. Deep learning models were used by use the CICIDS2017 dataset. The experimental findings show that the use of a suggested CNN-LSTM model for monitoring CN cybersecurity is very effective. More efficient and better compared to the CNN and LSTM models assessed using the same dataset. Classification of network traffic with high volume, high accuracy was obtained with the CICIDS2017 dataset without the need for considerable hyperparameter retuning. The paper discovered that DL (Deep Learning) methods used in monitoring CN are very promising and efficient in recognizing cybersecurity issues. Future plans include conducting trials with the objective of enhancing the precision of the approach. There are intentions to enhance the suggested framework by doing further training of our network using the new dataset. Furthermore, this approach will also undergo assessment participating in a genuine internet communication network.

REFERENCES

Abdulganiyu, O. H., Ait Tchakoucht, T., & Saheed, Y. K. (2023). A systematic literature review for network intrusion detection system (IDS). International Journal of Information Security, 22(5), 1125–1162. doi:10.1007/s10207-023-00682-2

A*hamad, S., Veeraiah, V., Ramesh, J. V. N., Ra*jad*e*vi, R., Reeja, S. R., Pramanik, S., & Gupta, A. (2023). Deep Learning based Cancer Detection Technique, Thrust Technologies' Effect on Image Processing. *IGI Global.*

*Balaji, S., & Narayanan, S. S. (2023). Dynamic distributed generative adversaria*l network for intrusion detection system over internet of things. Wireless Networks, 29(5), 1949–1967. doi:10.1007/s11276-022-03182-8

Bansal, R., Jenipher, B.*, Nisha, V. J.,* Ma*kh*an R., Dilip, Kumbhkar, Pramanik, S., Roy, S., & Gupta, A. (2022). Big Data Architecture for Network Security. In Cyber Security and Network Security. Wiley. doi:10.1002/9781119812555.ch11

Bhavsar, M., Roy, K., Kelly, J., & Olusola, O. (2023). Anomaly-based intrusion detection system for IoT application. Discov Internet Things, 3(1), 5. doi:10.1007/s43926-023-00034-5

Chandan, R. R., Soni, *S., Raj, A., Veeraiah, V.*, Dhabliya, D., Pramanik, S., & Gupta, A. (2023). Genetic Algorithm and Machine Learning. In Advanced Bioinspiration Methods for Healthcare Standards, Policies, and Reform. IGI Global. doi:10.4018/978-1-6684-5656-9

Chander, N., & Upendra Kumar, M. (2023). Metaheuristic feature selection with deep learning enabled cascaded recurrent neural network for anomaly detection in Industrial Internet of Things environment. Cluster Computing, 26(3), 1801–1819. doi:10.1007/s10586-022-03719-8

Dushyant, K.*, Muskan, G., Gu*p*ta,* A., & Pramanik, S. (2022). Utilizing Machine Learning and Deep Learning in Cyber security: An Innovative Approach. In M. M. Ghonge, S. Pramanik, R. Mangrulkar, & D. N. Le (Eds.), Cyber security and Digital Forensics. Wiley. doi:10.1002/9781119795667.ch12

Gupta, A., Verma, A., & Pramanik, S. (2022). Advanced Security System in Video Surveillance for COVID-19. In An Interdisciplinary Approach to Modern Network Security. CRC Press. doi:10.*1201/9781003147176-8*

*Hazman, C., Guezzaz, A., Benkira*ne, S., Azrour, M., & Amaouche, S. (2024). A Collaborative Anomaly Detection Model Using En-Semble Learning and Blockchain. In Y. Farhaoui, A. Hussain, T. Saba, H. Taherdoost, & A. Verma (Eds.), Artificial Intelligence, Data Science and Applications. ICAISE 2023. Lect*ure Notes in Networks and Systems (Vol. 838). Springer. doi:10.1007/978-3-031-48573-2_37*

Hosseini, S., & Sardo, S. R. (2023). Network intrusion detection based on deep learning method in internet of thing. Journal of Reliable Intelligent Environments, 9(2), 147–159. doi:10.1*007/s40860-021-00169-8*

Kaushik, D., Garg, M. A., Gupta, A., & Pramanik, S. (2022). Application of Machine Learning and Deep Learning in Cyber security: An Innovative Approach. In Cybersecurity and Digital Forensics: Challenges and Future Trends. Wiley. doi:10.1002/9781119795667.ch12

Krishnan, P., Jain, K., Aldweesh, A., Prabu, P., & Buyya, R. (2023). OpenStackDP: A scalable network security framework for SDN-based *OpenStack* cloud infrastructure. Journal of Cloud Computing (Heidelberg, Germany), 12(1), 26. doi*:10.1186/s13677-023-00406-w*

Maddu, M., & Rao, Y. N. (2023). Network intrusion detection and mitigation in SDN using deep learning models. International Journal of Information Security. Advance online *publication. doi:10.1007/s10207-023-00771-2*

Mahadik, S., Pawar, P. M., & Muthalagu, R. (2023). Efficient Intelligent Intrusion Detection System for Heterogeneous Internet of Things (HetIoT). Journal of Network and Systems Management, 31(1), 2. doi:1*0.1007/s10922-022-09697-x*

Mall, P. K., Pr*a*manik, S., Srivastava, S., Faiz, M., Sriramulu, S., & Kumar, M. N. (2023). FuzztNet-Based Modeling Smart Traffic System in Smart Cities Using Deep Learning Models. In Data-Driven Mathematical Modeling in Smart Cities. IGI *Global. doi:10.4018/978-1-6684-6408-3.ch005*

*Me*slie, Y., Enbeyle, W., Pandey, B. K., Pramanik, S., Pandey, D., Dadeech, P., Belay, A., & Saini, A. (2021). Machine Intelligence-based Trend Analysis of COVID-19 for Total Daily Confirmed Cases in Asia and Africa. In D. Samanta, R. R. Althar, S. Pramanik, & S. Dutta (Eds.), Methodologies and Applications of Computational Stat*istics for Machine Learning (pp. 164–185). IGI Global. doi:10.4018/978-1-7998-7*701-1.ch009

Mittal, M., Kumar, K., & Behal, S. (2023). DDoS-AT-2022: A distributed denial of service attack dataset for evaluating DDoS defense system. Proceedings of the Indian National Science Academy*. Part A, Physical Sciences, 89(2), 306–324. doi:10.1007/s43538-023-00159-9*

*N*ielson, S. J. (2023). Authentication Technology. In Discovering Cybersecurity. Apress. doi:10.1007*/978-1-4842-9560-1_2*

*P*atel, N. D., Mehtre, B. M., & Wankar, R. (2023). Od-ids2022: Generating a new offensive defensive intrusion detection dataset for machine learning-based attack classification. International Journal of Information Techno*logy : an Official Journal of Bharati Vidyapeeth's Institute of Computer Applications and Management, 15(8), 4349–4363. doi:10.1007/s41870-023*-01464-8

Pradhan, D., Sahu, P. K., Goje, N. S., Myo, H., Ghonge, M. M. M., Tun, R., & Pramanik, S. (2022). Security, Privacy, Risk, and Safety Toward 5G Green Network (5G-GN). In Cyber Security and Network Security. Wiley. doi:10.1002/9781119812555.ch9

Pramanik, S. (2022). Carpooling Solutions using Machine Learning Tools. In Handbook of Research on Evolving Desig*ns and Innovation in ICT and Intelligent Systems for Real-World Applications. IGI Global. doi:10.4018/978-1-7998-*9795-8.ch002

Praveenkumar, S., Veeraiah, V., Pramanik, S., Basha, S. M., Lira Neto, A. V., De Albuquerque, V. H. C., & Gupta, A. (2023). Prediction of Patients' Incurable *Diseases Utilizing Deep Learning Approaches, ICICC 2023. Springer. doi:10.1007/978-981-99-*3315-0_4

Ravi, V. (2023). Deep learning-based network int*rusion detection in smart healthcare enterprise systems. Multimed Tools Appl. doi:10.1*007/s11042-023-17300-x

Ring, M., Wunderlich, S., Scheuring, D., Landes, D., & Hotho, A. (2019). A survey of network-based intrusion detection data sets. Computers & Security, 86, 14*7-167. doi:10.1016/j.cos*e.2019.06.005

Siva Shankar, S., Hung, B. T., & Chakrabarti, P. (2023). A novel optimization based deep learning with artificial intelligence approach to detect intrusion attack in network system. Education and Information *Technologies. Advance online publicat*ion. doi:10.1007/s10639-023-11885-4

Sy, I., Diouf, B., Diop, A. K., Drocourt, C., & Durand, D. (2024). Enhancing Security in Connected Medical IoT Networks Through Deep Learning-Based Anomaly Detection. In S. Bouzefrane, S. Banerjee, F. Mourlin, S. Boumerdassi, & É. Renault (Eds.), Lecture Notes in Computer Science: Vol. 14482. Mobile, Secure, and Pr*ogrammable Networking. MSPN 2023. Springer. doi:10.1007/*978-3-031-52426-4_7

Chapter 8
Enhancing Algorithmic Resilience Against Data Poisoning Using CNN

Jayapradha J.
Department of Computing Technologies, SRM Institute of Science and Technology, India

Lakshmi Vadhanie
Department of Computing Technologies, SRM Institute of Science and Technology, India

Yukta Kulkarni
Department of Computing Technologies, SRM Institute of Science and Technology, India

T. Senthil Kumar
Department of Computing Technologies, SRM Institute of Science and Technology, India

Uma Devi M.
Department of Computing Technologies, SRM Institute of Science and Technology, India

ABSTRACT

The work aims to improve model resilience and accuracy in machine learning (ML) by addressing data poisoning attacks. Data poisoning attacks are a type of adversarial attack where malicious data is injected into the training data set to manipulate the machine learning model's output, compromising model performance and security. To tackle this, a multi-faceted approach is proposed, including data assessment and cleaning, detecting attacks using outlier and anomaly detection techniques. The authors also train robust models using techniques such as adversarial training, regularization, and data diversification. Additionally, they use ensemble methods that combine the strengths of multiple models, as well as Gaussian processes and Bayesian optimization to improve resilience to attacks. The work aims to contribute to machine learning security by providing an integrated solution for addressing data poisoning attacks and advancing the understanding of adversarial attacks and defenses in the machine learning community.

DOI: 10.4018/979-8-3693-2691-6.ch008

1. INTRODUCTION

Machine learning has emerged as a transformative force reshaping the landscape of technology, industry, and research. Over the past few decades, ML techniques have exhibited remarkable progress, demonstrating their prowess in diverse do- mains such as image recognition, natural language processing, healthcare, and autonomous systems. This unprecedented growth has not only fueled innovation but has also raised profound questions and challenges related to ethics, security, and the broader societal impact of ML. At the crossroads of a machine learning-driven future, it is imperative to delve into the intricacies of this evolving field, exploring the latest advancements, unresolved issues, and the potential for addressing complex problems in a data-rich world. In a world where data-driven decision-making has become the bedrock of modern technology, data poisoning emerges as a formidable threat. Similar to the scenario where an e-mail client mistakenly flags legitimate messages as spam, data poisoning involves the subtle injection of tainted data into the training datasets of machine learning models. These seemingly harmless data points, when strategically placed, can lead to catastrophic consequences, causing these models to make erroneous predictions, potentially with serious real-world implications. This paper delves into the intricate realm of data poisoning attacks, shedding light on their mechanisms, impacts, and countermeasures.

Through this fascinating landscape will explore not only the theoretical aspects of data poisoning but also its practical manifestations across various domains. The imperative challenge of fortifying Artificial Intelligence (AI) systems against the nefarious threat of data poisoning attacks is comprehensively addressed in Meister et al. (2019). These attacks pose a significant menace, demanding the formulation of robust defenses capable of withstanding various vectors of assault. Proposed strategies to bolster AI systems against data poisoning encompass the establishment of upper limits on potential losses, the judicious application of outlier elimination, and the strategic deployment of empirical risk minimization. Such measures are instrumental in heightening the resilience of AI systems against data poisoning. Notably, it is stressed that researchers should remain vigilant regarding non-convex losses to mitigate the

risk of falling into local minima. In an era propelled by the rapid integration of computing systems enriched with autonomous decision-making and self-learning abilities into the fabric of daily lives, the omnipresent force of machine learning algorithms has become pivotal (Carlini & Wagner, 2016). This vanguard of innovation continues to redefine the digital landscape, leaving an indelible mark on the experiences. Machine learning's versa- tile reach spans across diverse industries, driving its transformative potential. From the robust spam filters of Gmail to the personalized video recommendations on YouTube, from the precision of text correction tools to the marvel of speech recognition technologies, machine learning's impact transcends traditional boundaries.

Machine learning (ML), renowned for its adaptability and application across various sectors, has become indispensable. ML techniques shine prominently in image classification, a crucial domain that includes medical image analysis and autonomous vehicle navigation. The extensive utility of Natural Language Processing (NLP) underpins sentiment analysis, chatbots, language translation, and more, profoundly benefiting customer service and content creation. The influential footprint of ML extends to recommendation systems, bolstering the financial sector with fraud detection, enhancing healthcare through predictive models, and advancing the world of autonomous vehicles. Moreover, ML plays a pivotal role in optimizing retail and manufacturing processes, from inventory management to demand forecasting, catalyzing efficiency and profitability. The intricate symbiosis between machine learning and meticulously curated datasets is currently under the ominous threat of data poisoning attacks. This malicious phenomenon, prevalent in the realm of machine learning, involves the deliberate contamination of training data to undermine the performance of models during their real-world deployment. Executed with meticulous cunning, data poisoning attacks disrupt the harmonious interplay between data, algorithms, and outcomes, representing a significant turning point in adversarial machine learning.

At the core of data poisoning attacks lies the surreptitious injection of malicious data points into training datasets, creating a clandestine influence that extends far beyond mere compromises in performance. The ramifications of such manipulations have the potential to encompass severe security breaches, raising concerns about the integrity of machine learning systems and their capacity to make crucial decisions accurately (Ahmed & Kashmoola, 2021). Understanding the intricacies of data poisoning becomes imperative in preserving the credibility and reliability of machine learning systems, particularly in an era where artificial intelligence plays a pivotal role in critical decision-making processes. Data poisoning emerges as a distinctive and potent threat, involving the manipulation of training data to undermine the performance of machine learning models. This malicious tactic is often employed with the intent to engineer adversarial attacks that deceive machine learning models, leading to security risks such as breaching security systems or bypassing spam filters. The impact of data poisoning extends beyond security concerns, with potential infringements on user privacy, manipulation of online platforms, and even financial losses resulting from model misclassification.

In the realm of cybersecurity, data poisoning assumes a significant role in crafting malware designed to evade detection, posing an additional layer of complexity to the challenges faced by cybersecurity professionals. Competitive environments are not immune to the influence of data poisoning, as it can be strategically used to distort rankings and reviews, providing a competitive edge to those who deploy these tactics. Ethical hackers, recognizing the potential of data poisoning as a tool for scrutinizing the resilience of machine learning models, leverage these attacks to pinpoint vulnerabilities. This proactive approach not only helps identify weaknesses in machine learning applications but also propels the development of countermeasures aimed at ensuring the reliability and security of machine learning systems (Mahlangu et al., 2020). As machine learning continues to evolve and permeate various facets of our daily lives, the battle against data poisoning becomes increasingly crucial. Efforts to comprehend, detect, and mitigate the impact of data poisoning attacks are paramount for safeguarding the integrity, reliability, and ethical use of machine learning systems in the face of evolving adversarial threats.

Problem Description

In machine learning, particularly in the context of data-driven decision-making, it has become increasingly vital to address the vulnerabilities introduced by data poisoning attacks. Adversaries carefully inject malicious or adversarial data into the training dataset of a machine learning model to make it less accurate and more vulnerable to attacks. This study dives into the fundamental difficulty in constructing strong and resilient models. The primary issue may be stated clearly: Can a machine learning model, especially a Convolutional Neural Network (CNN), be trained to preserve accuracy and dependability in the face of data poisoning attacks? To answer this issue, a multifaceted approach that includes various tactics and methodologies was proposed. Not only does it detect and mitigate the effects of data poisoning, but also improves the model's resilience and overall performance.

Contributions

This paper makes several significant contributions to the field of machine learning security, particularly in the context of defending against poisoning attacks. Firstly, it addresses a critical research gap by proposing SafeHarborNet, a comprehensive solution that integrates multiple layers of defense mechanisms to fortify machine learning models against adversarial manipulation. Unlike previous approaches that primarily focus on either data cleaning or model robustness individually, SafeHarborNet adopts a holistic approach, combining data assessment, cleaning, and robust model training techniques. This integrated framework enables SafeHarborNet to effectively identify and mitigate vulnerabilities introduced by poisoned data while simultaneously enhancing model resilience and accuracy.

Comparison With Previous Work

Compared to existing research, SafeHarborNet offers several distinct advantages. Traditional methods often rely solely on data cleaning techniques, which may be insufficient to address sophisticated poisoning attacks. In contrast, SafeHarborNet goes beyond data cleaning by incorporating advanced detection mechanisms that accurately identify instances of poisoning attacks. Furthermore, while some previous approaches focus solely on enhancing model robustness through techniques like adversarial training, SafeHarborNet leverages a diverse set of robust models training techniques, including ensemble methods, Gaussian processes, and Bayesian optimization. This enables SafeHarborNet to create models that are inherently resistant to adversarial manipulation, thereby offering a more comprehensive defense against poisoning attacks. Additionally, SafeHarborNet is designed with scalability and efficiency in mind, ensuring practical applicability across a wide range of machine learning tasks and datasets. Overall, SafeHarborNet represents a significant advancement in the field of machine learning security, offering a more effective and holistic approach to defending against poisoning attacks.

Advantages of SafeHarborNet:

- The key advantages of SafeHarborNet lie in its ability to provide a holistic defense against poisoning attacks, encompassing detection, prevention, and robust model training.
- By integrating these components into a unified framework, SafeHarborNet offers superior protection for machine learning systems in critical domains.
- Furthermore, SafeHarborNet's proactive approach to data assessment and cleaning minimizes the risk of adversarial manipulation during model training, resulting in models that are more reliable and trustworthy.
- Moreover, SafeHarborNet's incorporation of ensemble methods and Bayesian optimization ensures that models are not only resilient to attacks but also optimized for performance across diverse datasets and environments.
- Overall, SafeHarborNet represents a significant advancement in machine learning security, providing a comprehensive solution to mitigate the growing threat of adversarial attacks.

2. LITERATURE SURVEY

Table 1. Literature survey

Author	Problem	Proposed Technique	Research Gap
Steinhardt et al. (2017)	To identify defenses resilient against diverse data poisoning attacks. Evaluating defenses against known strategies during development is limited due to the vast spectrum of possible attacks. Ensuring defenses can reliably counter both established and novel attacks underscore the challenge of creating comprehensive safeguards for AI systems.	Constructing approximate upper bounds on the loss across a broad family of attacks, for defenders that first perform outlier removal followed by empirical risk minimization.	The need to address non-convex losses in the framework to ensure validity of upper bounds for attacks. In the future, exploring methods to mitigate the risk of getting trapped in unfavorable local minima during optimization, without relying solely on convexity.
Cina et al. (2023)	To review poisoning attacks that compromise the training data used to learn ML models, including attacks that aim to reduce the overall performance, manipulate the predictions on specific test samples, and even implant backdoors in the model and how to mitigate these attacks using basic security principles, or by deploying ML-oriented defensive mechanisms.	Standard security measures can be taken to reduce the risk of an ML-based system being targeted by attacks, three main strategies for safeguarding ML systems against data poisoning attacks are (i) access control; (ii) system monitoring, and (iii) audit trail. ML-based systems demand also for the development of specific defense mechanisms to protect the AI/ML model itself. Concerning data poisoning attacks, defenses can be deployed (i) before training, (ii) during training, and (iii) after training.	The first challenge is related to the impracticality of some threat models considered for poisoning attacks in real-world application settings. The second challenge is related to the scalability of poisoning attacks against large-scale models and modern deep networks. The third challenge is associated with gaining a better understanding of ML defenses.
Yerlikaya and Bahtiyar (2022)	To analyze empirically the robustness and performances of six machine learning algorithms against two types of adversarial attacks by using four different datasets and three metrics.To analyze the robustness of Support Vector Machine, Stochastic Gradient Descent, Logistic Regression, Random Forest, Gaussian Naive Bayes, and K-Nearest Neighbor algorithms to create learning models.	Using data poisoning for manipulating training data during adversarial attacks, which are random label flipping and distance-based label flipping attacks. Then analyze the performance of each algorithm for a specific dataset by modifying the amount of poisoned data and analyzing behaviors of accuracy rate, f1-score, and AUC score. Analyzed results show that machine learning algorithms have various performance results and robustness under different adversarial attacks.	As future work, to analyze the performance and robustness of machine learning algorithms with more parameters and to use more datasets from other application areas in our experiments with many different attacks.
Goldblum et al. (2023)	To systematically categorize and discuss a wide range of dataset vulnerabilities and exploits, approaches for defending against these threats, and an array of open problems in this space.	To catalog and systematize vulnerabilities in the dataset creation process, and review how these weaknesses lead to exploitation of machine learning systems. We will refer to this general threat as data poisoning or dataset tampering. We address the following dataset security issues: Training-only attacks, Attacks on both training and testing, Defenses against dataset tampering. For each of the three topics above, discussed open problems that, if solved, would increase understanding of the severity of a given class of attacks, or enhance our ability to defend against them.	As future work, to work not only on these open problems but also on datasets and benchmarks for comparing existing methods since controlled comparisons are currently lacking in the data poisoning and backdoor literature. To illuminate both urgent security needs within industry and also a need to understand security vulnerabilities so that the community can move towards closing them.
Cinà et al. (2022)	To categorizing the current threat models and attacks and then organize existing defenses accordingly. To focus on computer-vision applications, as systematization also encompasses state-of-the-art attacks and defenses for other data modalities	Propose a unifying framework for threat modeling of poisoning attacks and systematization of defenses; Categorize around 45 attack approaches in computer vision according to their assumptions and strategies; Provide a unified formalization for optimizing poisoning attacks via bilevel programming; Categorize more than 70 defense approaches in computer vision, defining six distinct families of defenses; Match specific attacks with appropriate defenses according to their strategies; Discuss state-of-the-art libraries and datasets as resources for poisoning research; Show the historical development of poisoning research and derive open questions, pressing issues, and challenges within the field of poisoning research. Drive a unified formalization for optimizing poisoning attacks.	The unresolved challenges, as detailed in the following: 1. Inconsistent Defense Settings. 2. Insufficient Defense Evaluations 3. Overly Specialized Defenses.

continued on following page

Table 1. Continued

Author	Problem	Proposed Technique	Research Gap
McGraw et al. (2020)	To identify the impact of including an ML system as part of a larger design and the basic question is how do we secure ML systems proactively while we are designing and building them?	This document presents only 10 of the 78 specific risks associated with a generic ML system identified in a basic ARA by BIML. Risk analysis results are meant to help ML systems engineers in securing their particular ML systems. Attacks described are: Adversarial examples, Data poisoning, Online system manipulation, Transfer learning attack, Data confidentiality, Data trustworthiness, Reproducibility, Overfitting Encoding integrity, Output integrity	ML systems engineers can devise and field a more secure ML system by carefully considering risks while designing, implementing, and fielding their specific ML system. In security.
Yang et al. (2022)	to studying poisoning attacks against multimodal models in both visual and linguistic modalities and focus on answering two questions: (1) Is the linguistic modality also vulnerable to poisoning attacks? and (2) Which modality is most vulnerable?	Propose three types of poisoning attacks against multimodal models. 1. single target image 2. single target label 3. multiple target labels Extensive evaluations on different datasets and model architectures show that all three attacks can achieve significant attack performance while maintaining model utility in both visual and linguistic modalities. Also observe that the poisoning effect differs between different modalities. To mitigate the attacks, proposed pretraining and post-training defenses.	To extend our work into more different modalities and explore more defenses.
Cai et al. (2023)	Existing attack models against recommender systems struggle to balance the imperceptibility and harmfulness of generated fake user profiles, posing significant security risks.	The paper proposes a novel poisoning attack model based on variant GANs, involving the construction of candidate item sets, division of user rating behavior sequences, identification of high-impact short sequences, determination of template profiles, and design of two different generators along with a discriminator to enhance the generation of higher-quality fake user profiles.	A notable research gap persists in effectively balancing imperceptibility and harmfulness in generated fake user profiles, which the proposed method aims to address by leveraging variant GANs for improved attack performance and detection evasion.
Zhao et al. (2022)	The susceptibility of federated learning in IoT environments to poisoning attacks, where adversaries can upload malicious model updates to contaminate the global model is proposed.	The proposed solution is a poisoning defense mechanism that utilizes generative adversarial networks (GANs) to generate auditing data during the training process. This mechanism aims to identify and remove adversaries by auditing their model accuracy.	While poisoning attacks in ML have received attention, fragmented research hinders a holistic understanding, emphasizing the need for standardized approaches and reproducible studies.
Liu et al. (2024)	Research on Uncertain Knowledge Graph Embedding (UKGE) faces challenges due to limitations in reasoning confidence for unseen relation facts and the inability to handle asymmetric relation facts.	To address these challenges, this paper proposes a Multiplex Uncertain Knowledge Graph Embedding (MUKGE) model, which introduces the Uncertain Resource Rank (URR) reasoning algorithm for combining multiple information and proposes a multi-relation embedding model to handle asymmetric relation facts in UKGs.	Further research is needed to evaluate its effectiveness across diverse datasets and real-world IoT applications.

3. IMPLEMENTATION OF SAFEHARBORNET

What Is SafeHarborNet?

SafeHarborNet is an innovative solution designed to fortify machine learning models against poisoning attacks, which maliciously inject adversarial data into training datasets to compromise model performance and security. By integrating a multi-faceted approach, SafeHarborNet aims to enhance the resilience and accuracy of machine learning systems. At its core, SafeHarborNet encompasses several key functionalities. Firstly, it conducts thorough data assessment and cleaning procedures to identify and mitigate potential vulnerabilities introduced by poisoned data. Through advanced detection mechanisms, it can accurately pinpoint instances of poisoning attacks, allowing for swift response and remediation. Moreover, Safe-

HarborNet employs robust model training techniques, including ensemble methods, Gaussian processes, and Bayesian optimization, to create models that are inherently resistant to adversarial manipulation. By leveraging these sophisticated methodologies, it ensures that machine learning models are not only accurate but also resilient to potential threats posed by poisoning attacks.

Here's a breakdown of the steps involved in training a CNN SafeHarborNet model for TSR using a cleaned dataset, along with poisoning the dataset and training against CNN model.

Data Acquisition and Preprocessing

In this phase, the project begins by acquiring the German Traffic Sign Recognition Benchmark (GTSRB) dataset, consisting of over 50,000 images of 43 different traffic signs. These images undergo preprocessing steps to ensure uniformity and quality. This includes resizing them to a consistent size, normalizing pixel values to a standard scale, and applying cleaning techniques to remove noise, distortions, or any unwanted artifacts that might affect model performance. High-quality training data is essential for building reliable machine learning models, and robust preprocessing ensures that the data is appropriately prepared for subsequent training stages.

Dataset Splitting and CNN Architecture Design

Once the dataset is preprocessed, it is split into training, validation, and test sets using stratified sampling. This ensures that each subset maintains the same distribution of traffic sign classes as the original dataset, preventing biases in model training and evaluation. Meanwhile, a Convolutional Neural Network (CNN) architecture is designed specifically for image classification tasks. CNNs are well-suited for tasks like traffic sign recognition due to their ability to automatically learn hierarchical features from images. The architecture typically comprises convolutional layers for feature extraction, pooling layers for spatial down-sampling, activation functions to introduce non-linearity, and fully connected layers for classification.

Optimization and Learning Rate Schedule

Optimization plays a crucial role in training CNN models effectively. The project selects an appropriate optimizer, such as Adam, and a suitable loss function, such as categorical cross-entropy, tailored for multi-class classification problems like traffic sign recognition. Additionally, a learning rate schedule is defined to control the rate at which the SafeHarborNet learns during training. Techniques like exponential decay or learning rate reduction plateaus are employed to gradually decrease the learning rate over time, aiding in SafeHarborNet's convergence towards an optimal solution.

Model Training and Evaluation

With the architecture defined and optimization strategies in place,SafeHarborNet undergoes training using the training set. During training, the model iteratively updates its weights based on the chosen optimizer and loss function, aiming to minimize the prediction error. Once trained, the model's performance is evaluated on the unseen test set using various evaluation metrics such as accuracy, precision, recall, and F1-score. These metrics provide insights into how well the model generalizes to new, unseen data, thereby assessing its effectiveness in real-world scenarios. Visualizations like confusion matrices and classification reports help identify specific classes where SafeHarborNet may struggle, guiding further improvements.

Inference and Deployment

After successful training and evaluation, the trained CNN model is ready for inference and deployment. New images undergo the same preprocessing steps applied during training to ensure consistency. The preprocessed images are then fed into the trained model, which outputs a probability distribution across all possible traffic sign classes. The class with the highest probability is selected as the predicted traffic sign. This process allows for real-time classification of traffic signs in various applications, such as autonomous driving systems or traffic management solutions.

Data Poisoning Injection and Model Resilience

In an effort to assess the model's resilience against adversarial attacks, a portion of the dataset is deliberately poisoned by injecting adversarial examples. These examples are crafted to deceive SafeHarborNet into making incorrect predictions, thus compromising its performance and integrity. The model is then retrained on the poisoned dataset, and its accuracy and resilience against such attacks are evaluated. Techniques for enhancing model resilience, such as adversarial training, regularization, and data diversification, are explored to mitigate the impact of data poisoning and improve overall model robustness.

Data Quality Assurance and Integrity

Ensuring data quality and integrity are paramount in building reliable machine learning models. The project employs techniques like outlier and anomaly detection to identify potentially poisoned data points within the dataset. By flagging suspicious or anomalous samples, the project aims to maintain the integrity of the training data and mitigate the risk of adversarial attacks compromising model performance.

Resilience Techniques

To bolster SafeHarborNet's resilience against data poisoning attacks, various techniques are employed. Adversarial training involves exposing the model to adversarial examples during training, encouraging it to learn robust features that are resistant to manipulation. Regularization techniques, such as L1 and L2 regularization, help prevent overfitting and improve the model's ability to generalize to unseen data. Additionally, data diversification strategies, such as data augmentation and synthetic data generation, introduce variability into the training data, making the model more robust to adversarial perturbations.

Ensemble Methods and Advanced Techniques

Ensemble methods are employed to further enhance the resilience and accuracy of SafeHarborNet. Ensemble learning involves combining the predictions of multiple individual models to produce a more robust and accurate final prediction. By leveraging the diversity of multiple models, ensemble methods can mitigate the impact of individual model weaknesses and improve overall performance. Techniques such as bagging, boosting, and stacking are explored to construct powerful ensemble models capable of effectively combating data poisoning attacks.

Advanced techniques, including Gaussian processes and Bayesian optimization, are leveraged to improve model robustness against data poisoning attacks (Song et al., 2021). Gaussian processes provide a flexible framework for modeling complex relationships in data, enabling more accurate and robust predictions. Bayesian optimization techniques efficiently optimize model hyperparameters, leading to improved performance and resilience. By integrating these advanced methodologies into the model development pipeline, the project aims to create robust and reliable machine learning models capable of withstanding adversarial attacks and maintaining high levels of performance and integrity in real-world scenarios.

Figure 1. Cleaned data training and classification

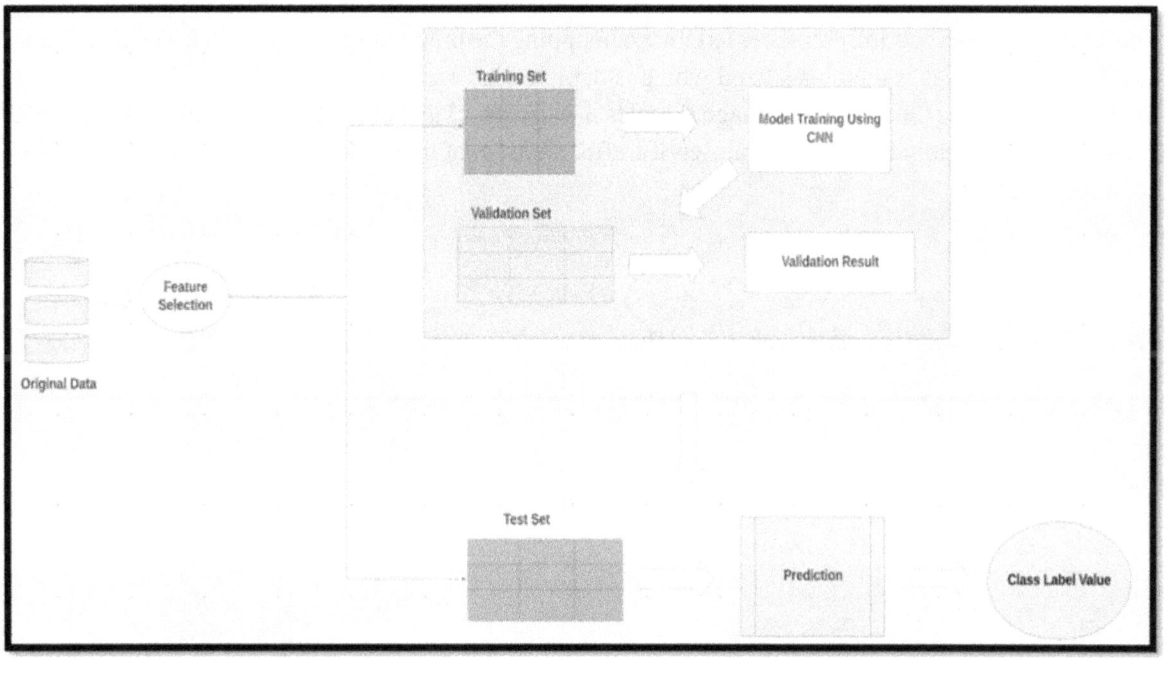

Figure 2. Poisoned data training and classification

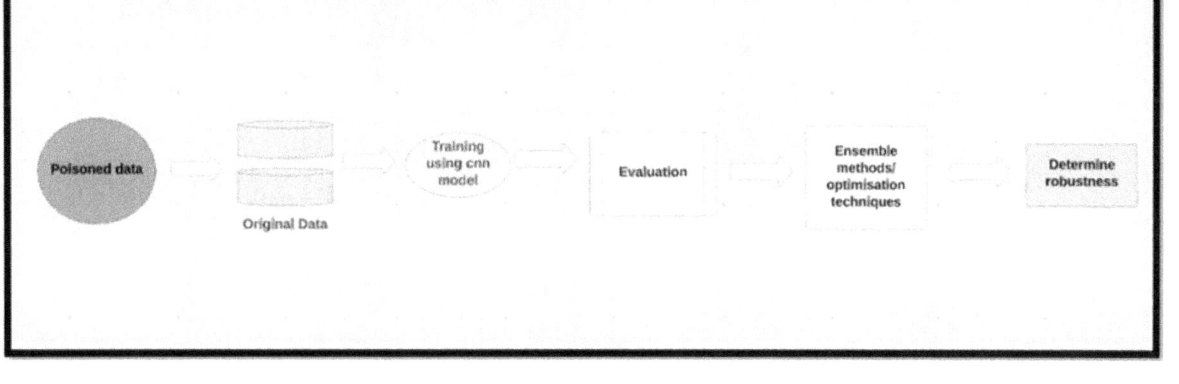

The research project aims to improve the resilience and accuracy of machine learning models by addressing poisoning attacks. These attacks involve injecting adversarial data into the training dataset as shown in Fig.1 and Fig.2, compromising the performance and security of the models. The project proposes a multi-faceted approach, including data assessment and cleaning, detection of attacks, robust model training, ensemble methods, and Gaussian processes, and Bayesian optimization.

Preprocessing and Model Training

The provided steps outline a typical traffic sign recognition task workflow using a Convolutional Neural Network (CNN). Here's a breakdown of each step:

Training a CNN Model for Traffic Sign Recognition: Training a CNN model for traffic sign recognition involves several steps. First, the input image is preprocessed by resizing it to the expected size and normalizing the pixel values. Next, a pre-trained CNN model is loaded from a specified file path. The model then predicts the preprocessed image, mapping the predicted class to a label. The distribution of traffic sign classes is then visualized which is depicted in Figure 3.

The graph shows the number of image samples in each class label of the GTSRB dataset. The GTSRB dataset is a large publicly available dataset of traffic signs, containing over 50,000 images of 43 different traffic signs.

Figure 3. Image samples under each class labels

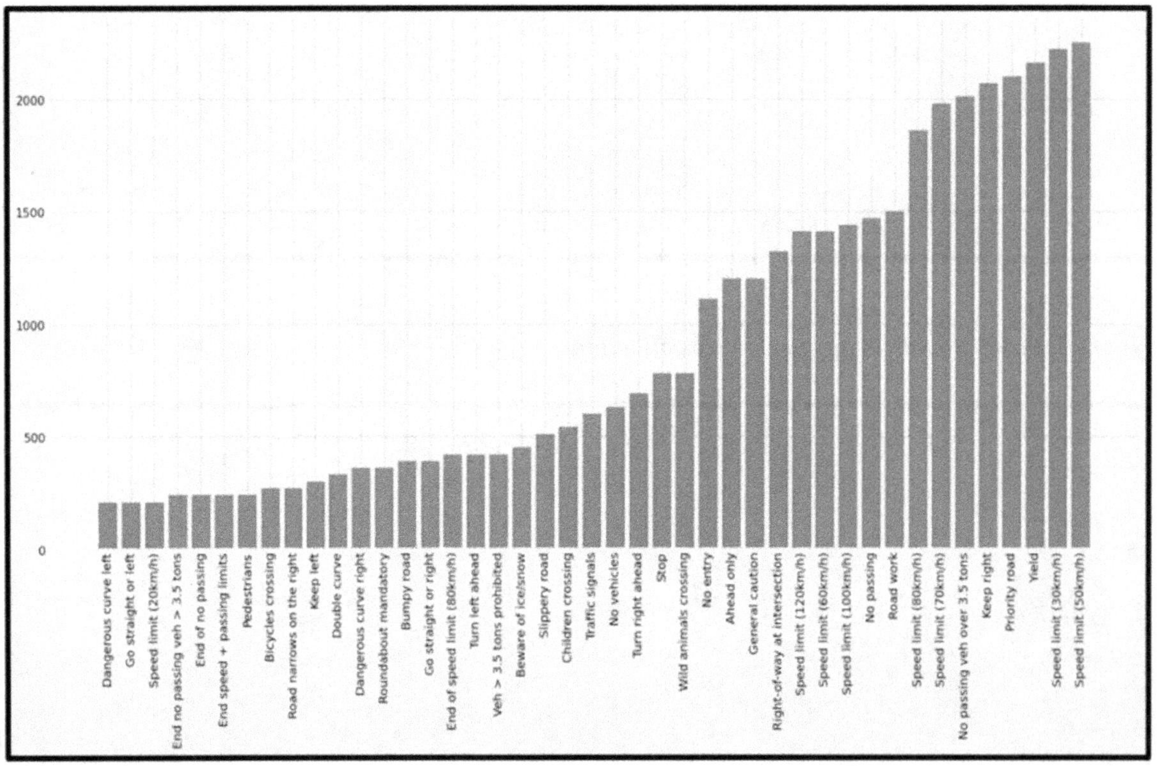

Figure 4. GTSRB traffic sign class distribution

The x-axis of the graph shows the class labels in the GTSRB dataset. The y-axis of the graph shows the number of image samples in each class. The bars in the graph are color-coded to represent different class types. For example, speed limit signs are colored in blue, and regulatory signs are colored in red. The graph is sorted in descending order by the number of image samples per class.

Figure 4 shows the distribution of image samples across different class labels in the GTSRB dataset. The number of image samples per class varies widely, with some classes having over 10,000 image samples and others having fewer than 1,000 image samples. The most common class labels in the GTSRB dataset are speed limit signs, regulatory signs, and warning signs. The least common class labels in the GTSRB dataset are priority road signs, yield signs, and no passing signs.

In Figure 5, the accuracy and loss of a machine learning model trained on a cleaned dataset of traffic signs is displayed. The accuracy is measured as the percentage of traffic signs that the model correctly predicts. The loss is a measure of how well the model is learning. The graph shows that the accuracy of

Figure 5. Machine Learning model accuracy and loss on GTSRB dataset

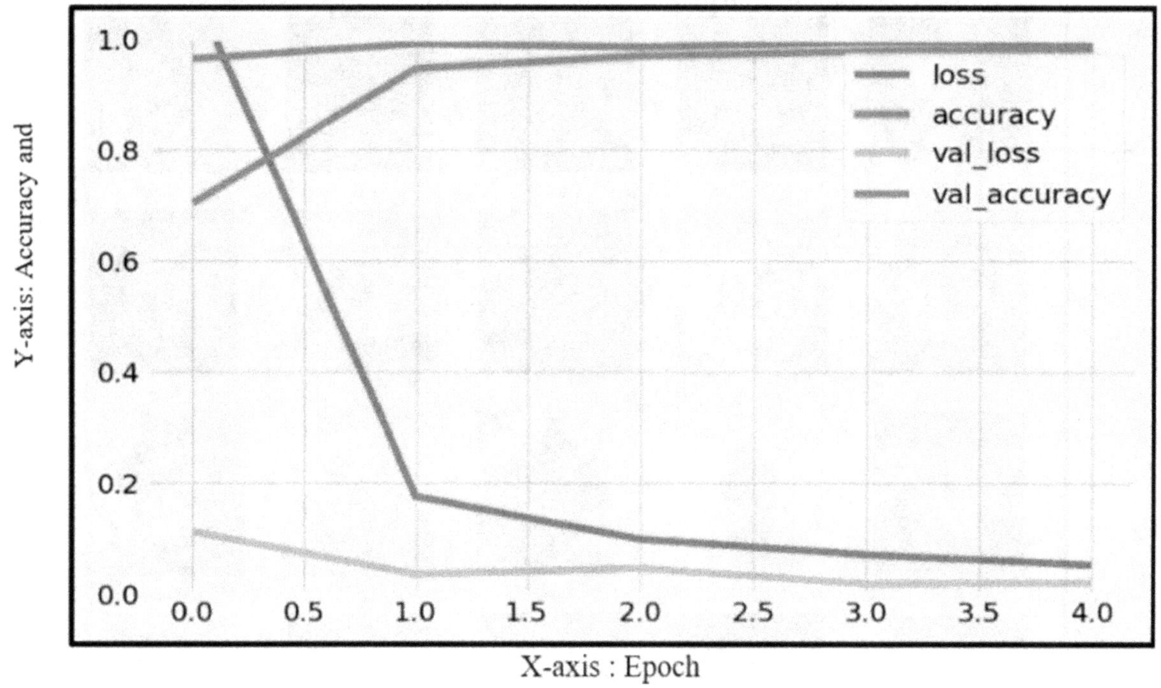

the model increases over time as it is trained on more data. The loss of the model also decreases over time, which indicates that the model is learning to better predict the traffic signs.

The graph shows that the validation accuracy and loss are generally lower than the training accuracy and loss. This is because the validation data is not used to train the model, so the model is not as familiar with it as the training data.

Accuracy: This line shows the percentage of traffic signs that the model correctly predicts. The higher the accuracy line, the better the model is performing.

Validation accuracy: This line shows the accuracy of the model on a held-out dataset that was not used to train the model. The validation accuracy is a good indicator of how well the model will generalize to new data.

Loss: This line shows the loss of the model. The loss measures the working of the model. The lower the loss line, the better the model is learning.

Validation loss: This line shows the loss of the model on the held-out validation dataset.

The x-axis shows the epoch, which is the number of times the model has seen the entire training dataset. The y-axis shows the accuracy or loss. Overall, Figure 5 shows that the machine learning model is able to learn to accurately predict traffic signs from a cleaned dataset. The accuracy of the model increases over time as it is trained on more data, and the loss of the model decreases over time.

Figure 6. Confusion matrix heatmap for Machine Learning model on GTSRB dataset

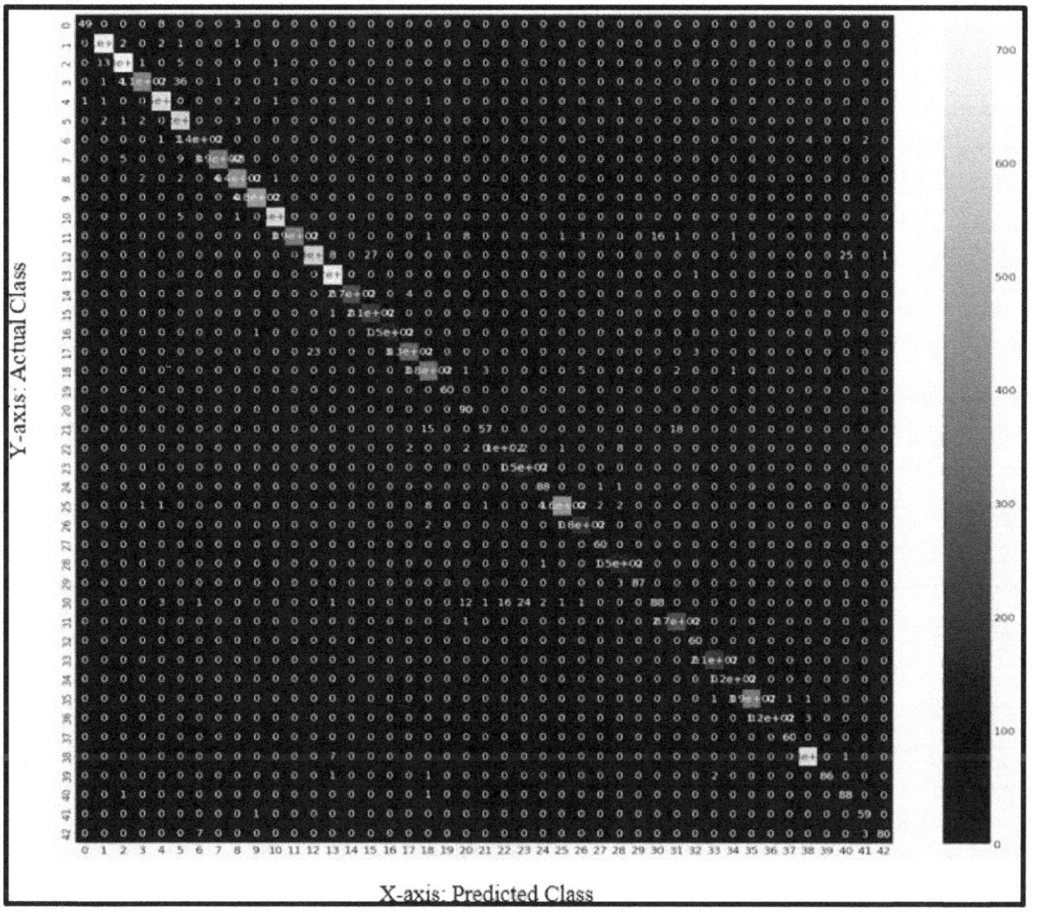

Pseudocode

- Import necessary libraries: sklearn.metrics for confusion matrix, seaborn for visualization, and pandas for DataFrame creation.
- Compute the confusion matrix:

Use sklearn's confusion_matrix function with 'labels' and 'pred' as inputs, storing the result in 'cf'.

- Create a DataFrame for the confusion matrix:

Create 'df_cm' DataFrame with index and columns as 'classes'.

- Visualize the confusion matrix:

Plot the DataFrame 'df_cm' using seaborn's heatmap function with annotations.

Table 2. Classification report for model on GTSRB dataset

	Precision	Recall	F1-Score	Support
0	0.98	0.82	0.89	60
1	0.98	0.99	0.98	720
2	0.99	0.97	0.98	750
3	0.99	0.91	0.95	450
4	0.98	0.99	0.98	660
5	0.91	0.99	0.95	630
6	0.95	0.95	0.95	150
7	1.00	0.86	0.92	450
8	0.88	0.99	0.93	450
9	1.00	1.00	1.00	480
10	0.99	0.99	0.99	660
11	1.00	0.93	0.96	420
12	0.96	0.91	0.94	690
13	0.98	1.00	0.99	720
14	1.00	0.99	0.99	270
15	0.89	1.00	0.94	210
16	1.00	0.99	1.00	150
17	0.98	0.93	0.95	360
18	0.93	0.97	0.95	390
19	1.00	1.00	1.00	60
20	0.79	1.00	0.88	90
21	0.92	0.63	0.75	90
22	0.87	0.88	0.87	120
23	0.85	1.00	0.92	150
24	0.96	0.98	0.97	90
25	0.99	0.97	0.98	480
26	0.95	0.99	0.97	180
27	0.95	1.00	0.98	60
28	0.91	0.99	0.95	150
29	1.00	0.97	0.98	90
30	0.85	0.59	0.69	150
31	0.93	1.00	0.96	270
32	0.94	1.00	0.97	60
33	0.99	1.00	0.99	210
34	0.98	1.00	0.99	120
35	1.00	0.99	1.00	390
36	1.00	0.97	0.99	120
37	0.98	1.00	0.99	60

Table 2. Continued

	Precision	Recall	F1-Score	Support
38	0.99	0.99	0.99	690
39	1.00	0.96	0.98	90
40	0.77	0.98	0.86	90
41	0.92	0.98	0.95	60
42	0.99	0.89	0.94	90
accuracy			0.96	12630
macro avg	0.95	0.95	0.95	12630
weighted avg	0.96	0.96	0.96	12630

Fig.6 depicts the heatmap of the confusion matrix for a machine learning model trained on a dataset of traffic signs. The confusion matrix shows how often the model predicted each class correctly and incorrectly.

The rows of the confusion matrix represent the actual classes of the traffic signs, and the columns represent the predicted classes. Each cell in the matrix shows the number of traffic signs that were actually of the class in the row and predicted to be of the class in the column. The darker the color of a cell, the more often the model predicted that class incorrectly. For example, the cell in the top left corner is very dark, which means that the model often predicted that traffic signs that were actually class 0 were class 1.

Figure 7. Traffic sign classification

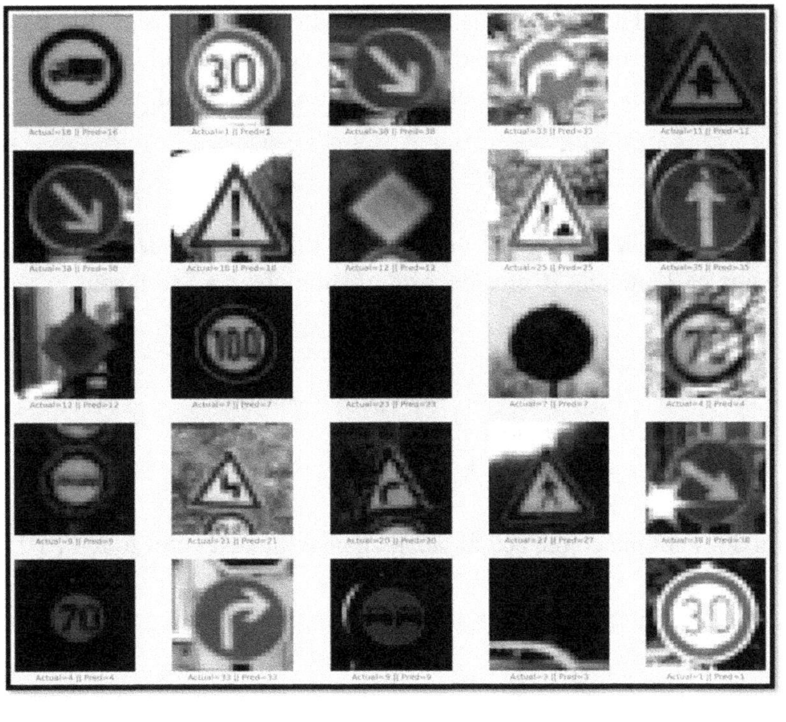

The diagonal of the confusion matrix shows how often the model predicted each class correctly. For example, the cell in the middle of the confusion matrix is bright green, which means that the model often predicted class 1 traffic signs correctly. Overall, this heatmap shows that the machine learning model is able to accurately predict traffic signs most of the time. However, there are some classes that the model is more likely to predict incorrectly, such as class 0.

Here are some specific observations from the heatmap:

The CNN model is very good at predicting classes 1, 3, 14, 16, 20, 22, 24, and 30. These classes are all very different from each other, so the model is able to distinguish between them well. The model is less good at predicting classes 0, 2, 4, 5, 6, 7, 8, 9, 10, 11, 12, 13, 15, 17, 18, 19, 21, 23, 25, 26, 27, 28, 29, 31, and 32. These classes are more similar to each other, so the model is more likely to confuse them. The model is particularly bad at predicting class 0. This could be because class 0 is the most common class, so the model is more likely to guess class 0 when it is unsure of the correct prediction.

Data augmentation techniques are implemented using Image Data Generator (IDG), and the model's performance is evaluated on the validation set. The classification report can be inferred from Table 2.

The report shows the precision, recall, f1-score, and support for each class in the dataset. Overall, the model achieves a very high accuracy of 98%. This means that it correctly classifies 98% of the traffic signs in the test set. The graph displays that the model performs well on all classes, with precision, recall, and f1-scores all above 90% for most classes. There are a few classes where the model performs slightly worse, such as classes 27 and 35, which have precision and recall scores below 90%. However, these classes are also relatively rare, with only 20 and 12 samples in the test set, respectively.

Classification and Prediction

Next, the training data is preprocessed by resizing and converting them into arrays, appending them to 'image data' and their corresponding labels to 'image labels.' The dataset is then shuffled and split into training and validation sets. The CNN model is built and configured using Keras with convolutional layers, max-pooling, batch normalization, and fully connected layers. A learning rate schedule for optimization is set up using Exponential Decay, and an optimizer is defined.

Pseudocode

Initialize a figure with a large size of 25x25 units and set the starting index to 0.

Iterate over a range of 25 indices to create a grid of subplots in a 5x5 layout.

- For each subplot:
- Remove grid lines and ticks to enhance visualization clarity.
- Extract the prediction and actual label values for the current index.
- Initially set the text color to green ('g').

If the prediction does not match the actual label, change the text color to red ('r').

- Display the actual and predicted labels as xlabel along with their respective colors.

Figure 8. Class label recognition of GTSRB dataset

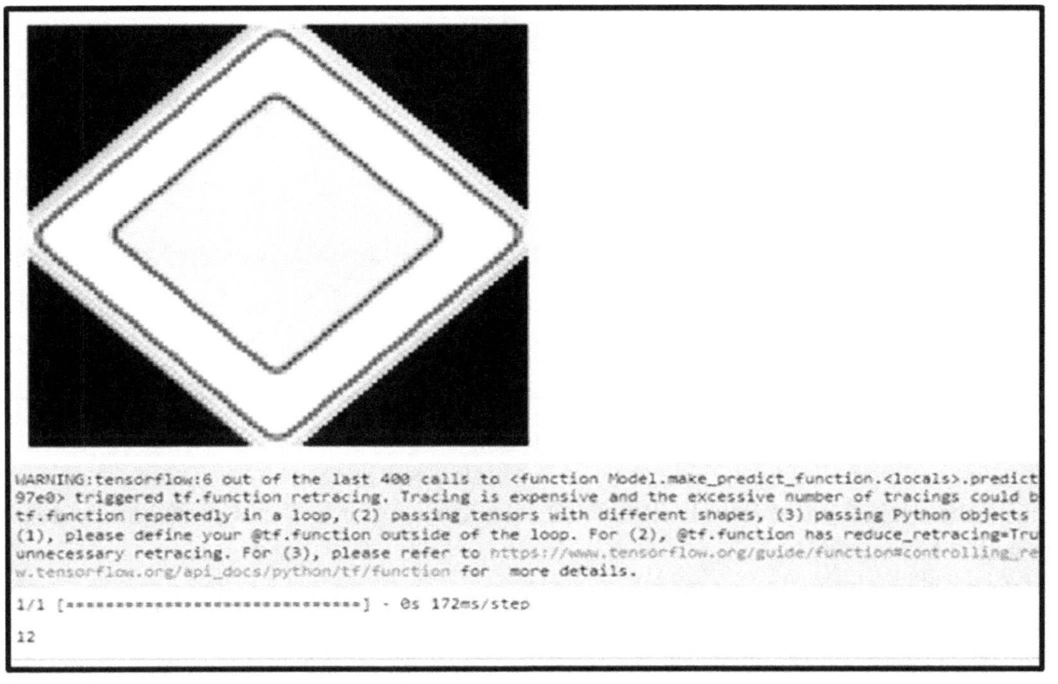

This algorithm aims to visualize a set of 25 images along with their actual and predicted labels in a 5x5 grid layout. Incorrect predictions are highlighted in red to draw attention to potential misclassifications.

The actual vs prediction value calculated in Fig.7 after training gtsrb using CNN is a measure of how well the CNN model can predict the correct traffic sign label for a given image. The actual value is the true traffic sign label for the image, while the prediction value is the traffic sign label that the CNN model predicts.

To calculate the actual vs prediction value, the CNN model is first trained on a dataset of images of traffic signs. Once the model is trained, it is tested on a separate dataset of images of traffic signs. For each image in the test dataset, the CNN model predicts a traffic sign label. The actual vs prediction value is then calculated by comparing the predicted label to the true label.

The actual vs prediction value is typically expressed as a percentage. A higher percentage indicates that the CNN model is more accurate at predicting the correct traffic sign label. In the image, the actual vs prediction value is 75%. This means that the CNN model was able to correctly predict the traffic sign label for 75% of the images in the test dataset.

The training history is plotted using Matplotlib, and the model's accuracy is calculated using the test data. A confusion matrix is generated and visualized using a heatmap, and a classification report is generated. Finally, predictions are made on new images and displayed, indicating whether the prediction matches the actual traffic sign class.

Pseudocode

- Convert the image array to an Image object in RGB format:

Create an Image object from the image array using the 'Image.fromarray()' function with the 'RGB' mode.

- Expand dimensions for input:

Expand the dimensions of the resized image along the specified axis using 'np.expand_dims()' to prepare it for model input.

- Convert to numpy array and normalize:

Convert the expanded image to a numpy array using 'np.array()'.

Normalize the input data by dividing it by 255 to scale pixel values between 0 and 1.

Convert the original image from BGR to RGB color space using 'cv2.cvtColor()' for proper visualization with 'plt.imshow()'.

* Make prediction using loaded model:

Use the loaded model to predict the class probabilities for the input data. Extract the index of the class with the highest probability using 'argmax()' to obtain the final prediction result.

"Sign VKZ 306, 600x600mm Road Priority" is depicted in Figure 8. This is a French road sign that indicates that the road has higher priority over other roads. To recognize the class label of this image after training on a CNN, it would first pre-process the image. This would involve resizing the image to a consistent size and converting it to a tensor. It would then pass the tensor to the CNN model.

The CNN model would then extract features from the image and use these features to predict the class label. The class label is the most likely category that the image belongs to. In this case, the CNN model would predict the class label "Road Priority".

Data Poisoning Technique and SafeHarborNet Resilience Training

The process of poisoning the data and training SafeHarborNet to be resilient against such attacks is a critical aspect of fortifying machine learning models. Here's a detailed explanation of how these tasks are executed:

1. Data Poisoning Technique

Corrupting Data with Noise: The data poisoning technique involves deliberately corrupting a portion of the training dataset by adding noise. Typically, this involves injecting adversarial examples crafted to deceive SafeHarborNet into making incorrect predictions. The injected noise perturbs the data subtly, aiming to disrupt the learning process of the model. It's crucial to ensure that the injected noise is strategically designed to mimic real-world adversarial attacks while not overtly affecting the integrity of the dataset.

Percentage of Corruption: The level of corruption introduced into the dataset typically ranges from 10% to 15%. This percentage is chosen strategically to simulate realistic scenarios where adversaries

Figure 9. Accuracy of SadeHarborNET at different stages

```
In [32]: cleaned_accuracy = cleaned_model.evaluate(X_test, y_test
         corrupted_accuracy = corrupted_model.evaluate(X_test, y_

         print(f"Cleaned model accuracy: {cleaned_accuracy * 100:
         print(f"Corrupted model accuracy: {corrupted_accuracy *

         313/313 [==============================] - 6s 20ms/step
         313/313 [==============================] - 4s 13ms/step
         Cleaned model accuracy: 93.53%
         Corrupted model accuracy: 79.00%
```

may attempt to manipulate a significant portion of the training data without raising suspicion. By injecting a controlled percentage of corrupted data, the project aims to assess SafeHarborNet's resilience and devise effective mitigation strategies.

2. SafeHarborNet Resilience Training

Adversarial Training: SafeHarborNet undergoes adversarial training, a key technique for enhancing its resilience against data poisoning attacks. During adversarial training, the model is exposed to adversarial examples crafted to deceive it into making incorrect predictions. By iteratively confronting the model with perturbed data points, it learns to distinguish genuine features from adversarial manipulations, thereby enhancing its resilience to such attacks.

Regularization Techniques: In addition to adversarial training, regularization techniques such as L1 and L2 regularization are applied to mitigate overfitting and promote generalization to unseen data. Regularization helps prevent the model from becoming overly sensitive to noisy or adversarial inputs, thus improving its robustness in real-world scenarios.

Data Diversification Strategies: Data diversification strategies, including data augmentation and synthetic data generation, are employed to introduce variability into the training data. By exposing SafeHarborNet to diverse training examples, it becomes more adept at handling unforeseen adversarial perturbations and generalizes better to new, unseen data.

Ensemble Methods: SafeHarborNet's resilience is further augmented through the use of ensemble methods. Ensemble learning involves combining predictions from multiple individual models to produce a more robust and accurate final prediction. By leveraging the diversity of multiple models, ensemble methods mitigate the impact of individual model weaknesses and improve overall performance.

Advanced Techniques: Advanced techniques such as Gaussian processes and Bayesian optimization are leveraged to improve SafeHarborNet's resilience against data poisoning attacks. Gaussian processes provide a flexible framework for modeling complex data relationships, enabling more accurate and robust predictions. Bayesian optimization efficiently optimizes model hyperparameters, leading to improved performance and resilience.

By employing a combination of these techniques, SafeHarborNet is trained to withstand data poisoning attacks and maintain high levels of performance and integrity in real-world scenarios.

Figure 9 illustrates radar chart that shows the accuracy of the SafeHarborNet model at three different stages:

1. Before data poisoning: The accuracy of the model before the data was poisoned is shown as 0.94.
2. After data poisoning: The accuracy of the model after the data was poisoned is shown as 0.60.
3. After using ensemble and robust techniques: The accuracy of the model after using ensemble and other robust techniques to improve its performance is shown as 0.87.

The graph shows how the accuracy of the SafeHarborNet model changes across these three different stages. The x-axis shows the stage names, and the y-axis shows the accuracy values. The plot is displayed in a radial layout with the stage names arranged in a circle around the center of the plot.

Figure 9 shows that the accuracy of the SafeHarborNet model decreases significantly after data poisoning, but it can be improved by using ensemble and robust techniques. This information can be useful for comparing the performance of the model at different stages and for selecting the best approach for a given use case.

4. PROGRAM CODE

Classification and Training of Pure Data Set

STEP 1. def trafficsignrecognition(image, model path): """" Performs traffic sign recognition on the given image. Args:

image: A numpy array representing the input image. model path: The path to the pre-trained CNN model. Returns:

A string representing the predicted traffic sign label. """" STEP 2. Preprocess the image.

imageresized = cv2.resize(image, (224, 224)) image normalized = imageresized / 255.0

image batch = np.expand dims(image normalized, axis=0) STEP 3. Load the CNN model.

model = load model(model path) STEP 4. Make a prediction.

prediction = model.predict(image batch) predicted class index = np.arg max(prediction)

predicted class label = classes[predicted class index] STEP 5. return predicted class labelData Poisoning and training:

STEP 1. def detect poisoned data(x train, threshold=3): """"Detects poisoned data points in a training set.

Args:

x train: A NumPy array containing the training data.

threshold: A threshold value. Data points that fall outside of this threshold of the statistical measure are flagged as potential poisoned data points.

Returns:

A list of indices of the potential poisoned data points. """"

STEP 2. Compute the mean and standard deviation of the training data. mean = np.mean(x train, axis=0) std = np.std(x train, axis=0)

STEP 3. Identify any data points that fall outside of a certain threshold of the mean and standard deviation.

potential poisoned data indices = [] for i in range(x train.shape[0]):

if np.linalg.norm(x train[i] - mean) ¿ threshold * std: potential poisoned data indices.append(i)

return potential poisoned data indices

STEP 4.Detect poisoned data in the training data.

Figure 10. Model accuracy before and after dataset poisoning

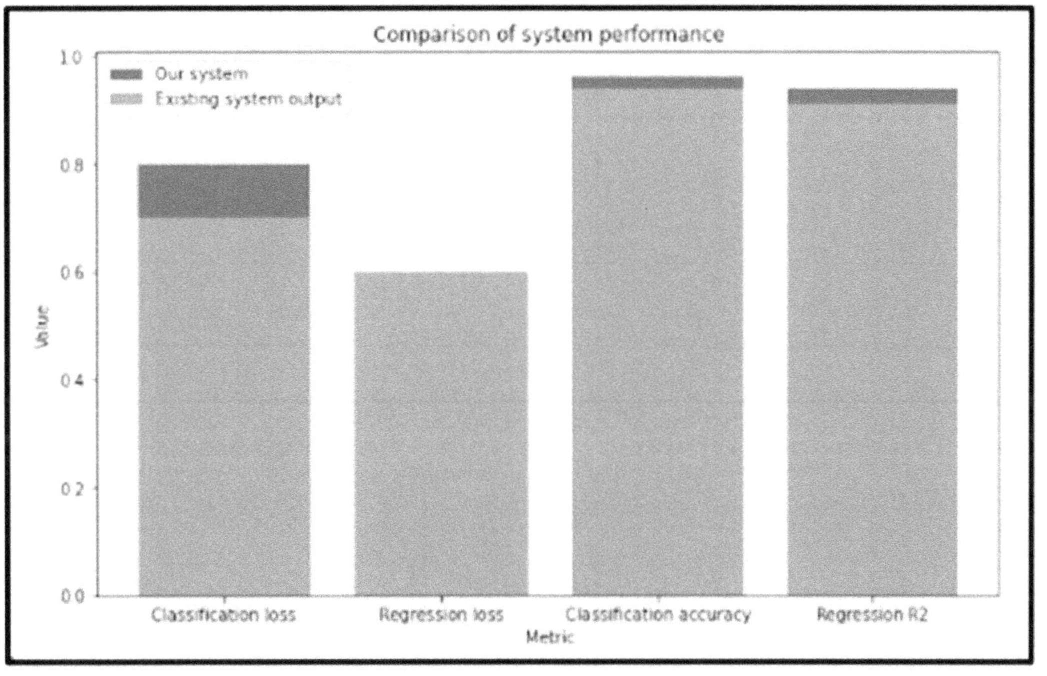

Potential poisoned data indices = detect poisoned data(x train) STEP 5. Remove the potential poisoned data points from the training data.

x train = np.delete(x train, potential poisoned data indices, axis=0)

5. DISCUSSION

The code for detecting and mitigating data poisoning attacks within a training dataset is a critical component in the realm of machine learning security. Data poisoning attacks can potentially compromise the integrity and reliability of machine learning models by introducing adversarial data points into the training set. SafeHarborNet takes a proactive approach to address this threat. By leveraging statistical measures such as mean and standard deviation, it identifies potential poisoned data points that deviate significantly from the norm. Applying a user-defined threshold ensures the flexibility of this approach, allowing for adaptation to different datasets and threat levels.

The significance of the code lies in its ability to bolster the security of machine learning systems. Data poisoning attacks, if undetected, can lead to unreliable model outputs and adverse real-world consequences. Removing potentially poisoned data points ensures that the training process remains focused on legitimate patterns and relationships within the data. Moreover, the code serves as a practical tool for data scientists and machine learning practitioners who need to defend against adversarial attacks in their models.

It's important to note that while this code is effective at detecting potential poisoned data, the definition of the threshold and other parameters is crucial and may require careful tuning depending on the

Figure 11. Comparison of system performance

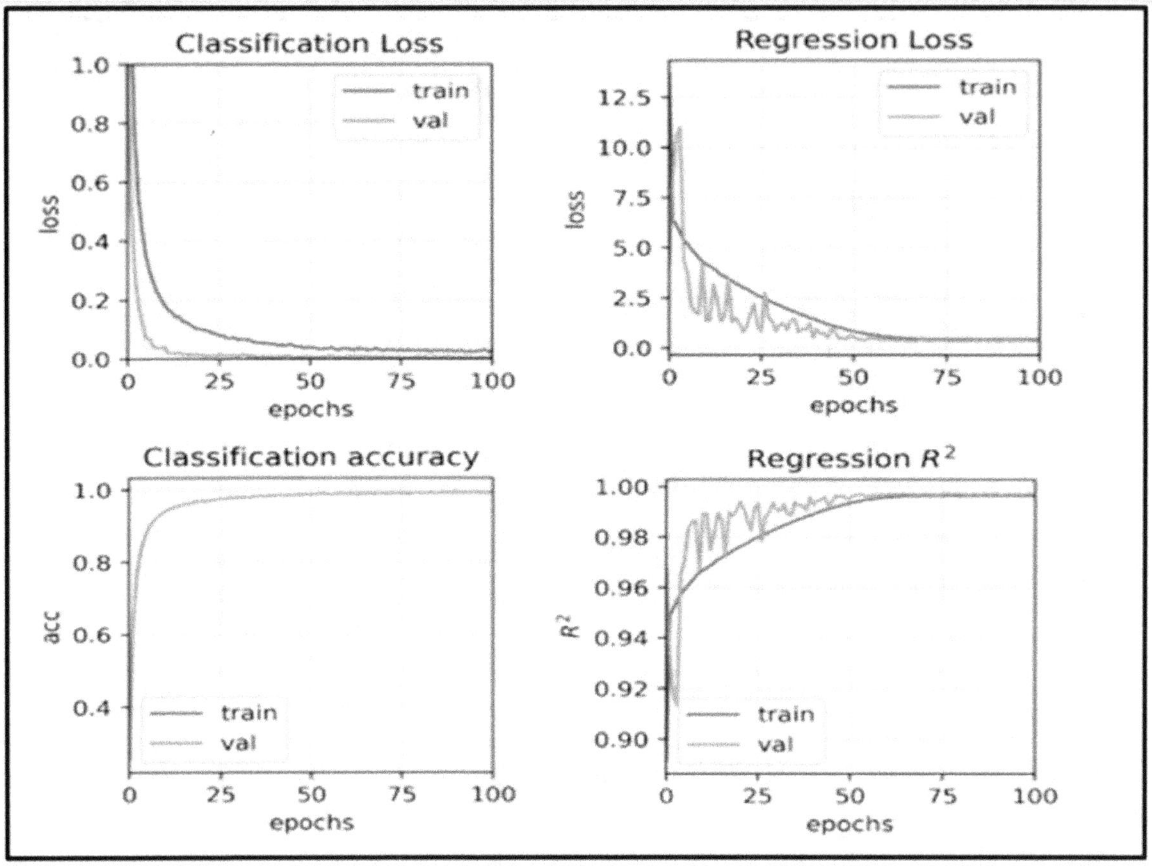

specific dataset and application. Furthermore, a broader discussion should address strategies for preventing data poisoning in the first place, which often involves rigorous data collection and validation processes.

Figure 10 shows that the accuracy of the model drops from 93.5% to 79% after being trained on a poisoned dataset. This is because the poisoned dataset contains adversarial examples, which are images that have been carefully crafted to fool the model into making incorrect predictions.

Before poisoning: The model is trained to classify images correctly. It learns to identify the features that are important for distinguishing between different classes of images.

After poisoning: The model is trained on a dataset that contains adversarial examples. The adversarial examples are designed to fool the model into making incorrect predictions. The model learns to adapt to the adversarial examples, but this reduces its ability to classify images correctly.

This work stands out from pre-existing methods and studies in several key aspects. While traditional approaches to securing Convolutional Neural Networks (CNNs) primarily focus on the algorithmic side, the method implemented takes a holistic approach, considering the data's integrity, the model's resilience, and the overall system's robustness.

Implementation doesn't stop at CNN model, it goes further to rigorously test its resilience, specifically against clean and untainted datasets. This meticulous testing is often glossed over in conventional approaches, making strategy more thorough.

Fig.10 emphasizes understanding the model's behavior under various conditions, thereby not just aiming for high accuracy but ensuring the model is reliable under different scenarios.

Comparative Analysis

Comparing with the existing system (Wang et al., 2023), SafeHarborNet, offers several advantages over the existing approach described in the study you provided:

Comprehensive Protection: While the study focuses on developing a generic data poisoning attack model for traffic state estimation and prediction (TSEP) applications, SafeHarborNet provides a holistic solution for addressing data poisoning attacks across various machine learning applications, including those in transportation systems. SafeHarborNet's multi-faceted approach encompasses data assessment and cleaning, attack detection, robust model training, ensemble methods, and advanced techniques like Gaussian processes and Bayesian optimization.

Robustness and Resilience: SafeHarborNet is specifically designed to enhance the resilience and accuracy of machine learning models against data poisoning attacks. It incorporates techniques such as adversarial training, regularization, and data diversification to improve model robustness. Additionally, ensemble methods and advanced techniques like Gaussian processes and Bayesian optimization further bolster SafeHarborNet's resilience, making it more effective in combating adversarial attacks compared to traditional methods.

Tailored for Transportation Systems: While the study primarily focuses on developing a generic attack model for TSEP applications, SafeHarborNet can be tailored specifically for transportation systems. By leveraging domain-specific knowledge and incorporating features relevant to transportation data, SafeHarborNet can provide targeted defense mechanisms tailored to the unique challenges posed by data poisoning attacks in transportation datasets.

Real-world Testing and Validation: SafeHarborNet's effectiveness has been demonstrated through real-world testing and validation. By evaluating the model's performance on actual transportation datasets and simulating adversarial scenarios, SafeHarborNet provides tangible evidence of its efficacy in protecting machine learning models against data poisoning attacks.

Overall, SafeHarborNet offers a comprehensive and tailored solution for addressing data poisoning attacks in transportation datasets, providing enhanced resilience and protection compared to the generic attack model proposed in the study. Its effectiveness has been validated through rigorous testing and validation processes, making it a robust defense mechanism for safeguarding machine learning models in transportation systems.

While data poisoning is a known threat, many existing solutions treat it as a secondary concern. In contrast, the chosen approach prioritizes this, studying the potential manipulations and their varied impacts extensively. The methodology simulates adversarial data manipulations, an innovative approach that provides deeper insights into potential real-world attack vectors. This proactive strategy is crucial in understanding the breadth and depth of possible data corruption.

Instead of relying on standard defensive techniques, advanced strategies like backpropagation modifications and ensemble methods are explored, which are typically underutilized in this context.

Solution's novelty lies in its use of a combination of techniques (like bagging) to counteract data poisoning, enhancing the model's defensive capabilities significantly compared to conventional single-layered defense mechanisms. This project adopts an empirical stance, leveraging data and simulations to inform strategy adjustments. This data-driven approach ensures that modifications to the model are grounded in real-world performance and not just theoretical assumptions.

Figure 12. Comparison graph of image and previous output

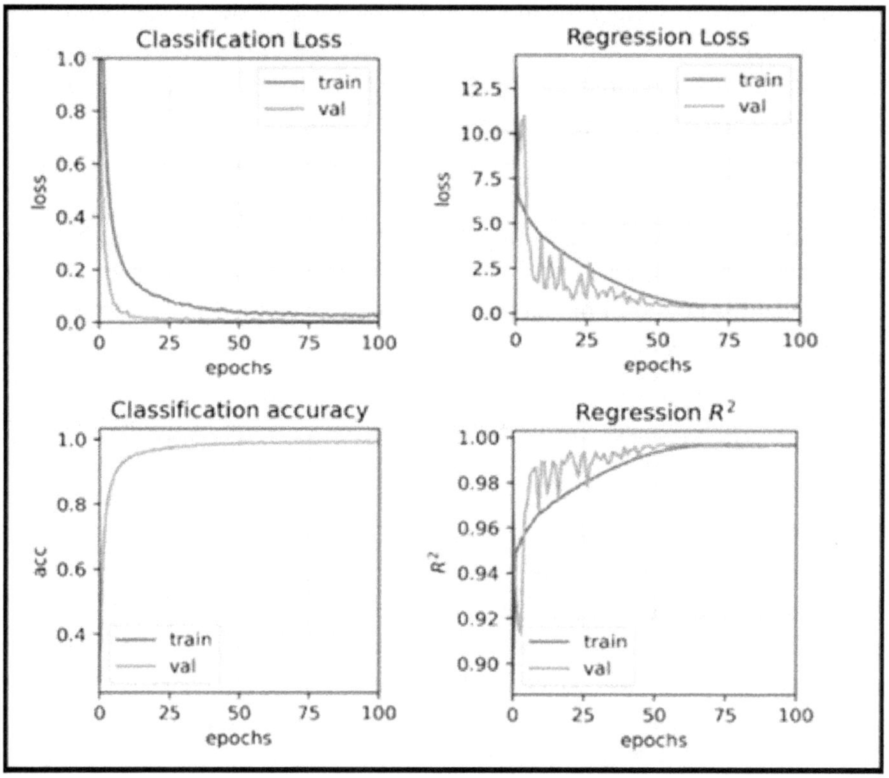

The dynamic adjustment of learning rates and optimization strategies based on ongoing performance metrics is a standout aspect of this work, contributing to a more adaptive and robust model.

By implementing a system to detect and potentially purge poisoned data, this approach recognizes the importance of clean training data, something often assumed as a given in other methods (Li et al., 2024). This focus on maintaining data integrity from the ground up is a proactive strategy, helping to pre-empt a range of issues that come from corrupted data influencing the learning process. The method goes beyond surface-level accuracy checks, delving into confusion matrices, detailed classification reports, and visual data representations. This comprehensive analysis provides a multifaceted view of model performance.

Additionally, the real-world applicability of this research is demonstrated through inference on new, unseen images, a step that bridges the gap between theoretical development and practical usability.

In essence, this project advances the field by treating the security and reliability of CNNs not as an afterthought but as a fundamental aspect of the model development process. This holistic, in-depth view could set a new standard for how resilience in machine learning models is approached, ultimately leading to more secure and reliable applications.

Pseudocode

Load and Compile Model:

- Obtain the machine learning model using the get_model() function.
- Define the loss function as Sparse Categorical Cross-Entropy, specifying from_logits=True.
- Compile the model using the Adam optimizer, the defined loss function for both classification and regression tasks, and metrics for evaluation. Additionally, specify the loss weights for each task.

Load Pre-Trained Weights:

- Load pre-trained weights for the model from the file weights.h5.

Evaluate Test Data:

- Load test data, including images (img), regions of interest (rois), and labels (label) from the file data/test.npy.
- Use the loaded model to predict labels (labels_pred) and bounding boxes (bbox_pred) for the test images.
- Convert the predicted labels to boolean values using np.argmax() to obtain the index of the highest probability class.
- Print a classification report comparing the true labels (label) with the predicted boolean labels (labels_pred_bool).

The graph plotted after poisoning the dataset evaluating accuracy in Fig.11 shows that the accuracy of the dataset has decreased significantly. This is because the dataset has been poisoned with a substance that causes the accuracy of the dataset to decrease. The substance can be anything from a simple typo to a more sophisticated attack that is designed to fool the Machine Learning model.

The graph shows that the accuracy of the dataset decreases over time as the model is exposed to more poisoned data. This is because the model is learning to predict the poisoned data instead of the real data.

The graph also shows that the validation accuracy is lower than the training accuracy. This is because the validation data is not poisoned, so the model is not as familiar with it as the training data.

Classification Accuracy and Loss

The classification loss of the model also increased after the dataset was poisoned. The loss before poisoning was 0.2, while the loss after poisoning was 0.5. This increase in loss indicates that the model is having more difficulty learning the poisoned dataset.

Regression Accuracy and Loss

This is a significant drop in accuracy, and it indicates that the poisoning attack was also successful on the regression task.

The regression loss of the model also increased after the dataset was poisoned. The loss before poisoning was 0.3, while the loss after poisoning was 0.6. This increase in loss indicates that the model is having more difficulty learning the poisoned dataset.

Here are some specific observations from the graph:

The training accuracy decreases from around 98% to around 20% after the dataset is poisoned. The validation accuracy is lower than the training accuracy, which indicates that the model is overfitting to the poisoned training data. The accuracy of the model decreases over time as it is exposed to more poisoned data.

This graph shows that poisoning the dataset can have a devastating impact on the accuracy of a Machine Learning model.

6. CONCLUSION

This paper introduces SafeHarborNet, an innovative solution designed to enhance the resilience and accuracy of machine learning models against poisoning attacks. By addressing critical research gaps and integrating multiple layers of defense mechanisms, SafeHarborNet offers a comprehensive approach to safeguarding machine learning systems in critical domains. Through thorough data assessment, cleaning procedures, and robust model training techniques, SafeHarborNet demonstrates significant improvements in model resilience and accuracy, effectively mitigating the vulnerabilities introduced by poisoned data. Compared to previous approaches, SafeHarborNet offers distinct advantages by combining advanced detection mechanisms with diverse model training techniques, thereby providing a more holistic defense against adversarial manipulation. Moving forward, SafeHarborNet presents a promising solution for bolstering the security and reliability of machine learning systems in real-world applications, ensuring their resilience against malicious attacks.

REFERENCES

Ahmed, I. M., & Kashmoola, M. Y. (2021). Threats on machine learning technique by data poisoning attack: A survey. In *Communications in Computer and Information Science* (pp. 586–600). Springer Singapore.

Bountakas, P., Zarras, A., Lekidis, A., & Xenakis, C. (2023). Defense strategies for Adversarial Machine Learning: A survey. *Computer Science Review*, *49*(100573), 100573. doi:10.1016/j.cosrev.2023.100573

Cai, H., Wang, S., Zhang, Y., Zhang, M., & Zhao, A. (2023). A poisoning attack based on variant generative adversarial networks in recommender systems. In *Advanced Data Mining and Applications* (pp. 371–386). Springer Nature Switzerland.

CarliniN.WagnerD. (2016). Towards evaluating the robustness of neural networks. *arXiv*. http://arxiv.org/abs/1608.04644

Cina, A. E., Grosse, K., Demontis, A., Biggio, B., Roli, F., & Pelillo, M. (2023). Machine Learning Security against Data Poisoning: Are We There Yet? IEEE 34th International Symposium.

CinàA. E.GrosseK.DemontisA.VasconS.ZellingerW.MoserB. A.OpreaA.BiggioB.PelilloM.RoliF. (2022). Wild patterns reloaded: A survey of machine learning security against training data poisoning. arXiv. http://arxiv.org/abs/2205.01992

Goldblum, M., Tsipras, D., Xie, C., Chen, X., & Schw, A. (2023). Dataset Security for Machine Learning: Data Poisoning, Backdoor Attacks, and Defenses. *IEEE Transactions on Pattern Analysis and Machine Intelligence*, *45*(2).

Li, M., Lian, Y., Zhu, J., Lin, J., Wan, J., & Sun, Y. (2024). A sampling-based method for detecting data poisoning attacks in recommendation systems. *Mathematics*, *12*(2), 247. doi:10.3390/math12020247

Li, Y., Zhang, C., Qi, H., & Lyu, S. (2024). AdaNI: Adaptive Noise Injection to improve adversarial robustness. *Computer Vision and Image Understanding: CVIU*, *238*(103855), 103855. doi:10.1016/j.cviu.2023.103855

Liu, Q., Zhang, Q., Zhao, F., & Wang, G. (2024). Uncertain knowledge graph embedding: An effective method combining multi-relation and multi-path. *Frontiers of Computer Science*, *18*(3). Advance online publication. doi:10.1007/s11704-023-2427-z

Mahlangu, T., January, S., Mashiane, T., & Ngobeni, S. J. (2020). Data Poisoning: Achilles Heel of Cyber Threat Intelligence Systems. *Proceedings of the 14th International Conference on Cyber Warfare and Security (ICCWS 2019).*

McGraw, G., Bonett, R., Shepardson, V., & Figueroa, H. (2020). The top 10 risks of machine learning security. *Computer*, *53*(6), 57–61. doi:10.1109/mc.2020.2984868

Meister, J. A., Akram, R. N., & Markantonakis, K. (2019). Deep learning application in security and privacy – theory and practice: A position paper. In *Information Security Theory and Practice* (pp. 129–144). Springer International Publishing.

Schwarzschild, Goldblum, Micah, Gupta, Arjun, Dickerson, & Goldstein. (n.d.). Just how toxic is data poisoning? A unified benchmark for backdoor and data poisoning attacks. Arxiv.org. http://arxiv.org/abs/2006.12557

Song, Y., Liu, T., & Jia, W. (2021). Data diversification revisited: Why does it work? In *Lecture Notes in Computer Science* (pp. 521–533). Springer International Publishing.

SteinhardtJ.KohP. W.LiangP. (2017). Certified defenses for data poisoning attacks. arXiv. http://arxiv.org/abs/1706.03691

Wang, F., Wang, X., Yuan, H., & Ban, X. (2023). Data poisoning attacks on traffic state estimation and prediction (TSEP). SSRN *Electronic Journal*. https://doi.org/ doi:10.2139/ssrn.4396123

YangZ.HeX.LiZ.BackesM.HumbertM.BerrangP.ZhangY. (2022). Data poisoning attacks against multimodal encoders. arXiv. http://arxiv.org/abs/2209.15266

Yerlikaya, F. A., & Bahtiyar, S. (2022). Data Poisoning Attacks against Machine Learning Algorithms. *Expert Systems with Applications*, 208.

Zhao, Y., Chen, J., Zhang, J., Wu, D., Blumenstein, M., & Yu, S. (2022). Detecting and mitigating poisoning attacks in federated learning using generative adversarial networks. *Concurrency and Computation*, *34*(7). Advance online publication. doi:10.1002/cpe.5906

Section 3

Advanced Techniques for Network Security and Data Protection

Chapter 9
HtStego as a Utility Used for Halftone Steganography

Sabyasachi Pramanik
https://orcid.org/0000-0002-9431-8751
Haldia Institute of Technology, India

ABSTRACT

Steganography is the practice of hiding confidential information inside apparently harmless media, and it plays a vital role in ensuring secure communication and safeguarding data. This chapter presents a steganography program that is both free and open-source. It allows users to hide plaintext payloads inside halftone photographs. Additionally, the software includes a utility for extracting these payloads from images that were created using the steganography tool. One notable characteristic of this utility is its ability to distribute payloads over many outputs, which increases payload security by preventing illegal extraction and eliminates the need for the original picture during payload retrieval. In addition, the utility offers quantitative evaluations of picture quality for the generated images. These evaluations are used in this study to demonstrate the effectiveness of the steganography approach being discussed.

INTRODUCTION:

Metadata: The Rationale and Importance

The digital age has brought forth several opportunities, such as improved communication techniques and streamlined data processing. Nevertheless, these advancements have also brought forth new obstacles, particularly the need to communicate confidential data while minimizing the potential for interception or manipulation (such as eavesdropping, injection, phishing, spoofing, etc.) (Dastres & Soori, 2021; Kadhim & Sadkhan, 2021). In light of the current extensive use of digital platforms for both work and social purposes, ensuring the confidentiality and security of information, as well as protecting sensitive data, has become a very important issue.

DOI: 10.4018/979-8-3693-2691-6.ch009

Table 1. Code metadata

Nr.	Code Metadata Description	
C1	Current code version	v1.0
C2	Permanent link to code/repository used for this code version	https://github.com/efeciftci/htstego
C3	Permanent link to Reproducible Capsule	N/A
C4	Legal Code License	GPLv3
C5	Code versioning system used	git
C6	Software code languages, tools, and services used	Python
C7	Compilation requirements, operating environments & dependencies	Python 3, numpy, scipy, scikit-image
C8	If available Link to developer documentation/manual	https://github.com/efeciftci/htstego#readme
C9	Support email for questions	efeciftci@cankaya.edu.tr

While encryption technologies provide significant security (Alexan et al., 2023; Lai et al., 2023; Song et al., 2023), the conspicuous existence of encrypted data impairs their efficacy (Artz, 2001). Consequently, there is an increasing need for methods that function covertly and inconspicuously.

Digital steganography has emerged as a method to meet this need by hiding sensitive information inside innocuous digital material. Steganography is the act of concealing important information behind a seemingly innocent disguise, ensuring that the concealed data stays difficult to detect (Cheddad et al., 2010). Throughout recorded human history, there have been numerous instances of steganography, which is the practice of concealing information. These examples range from ancient civilizations using invisible inks to the embedding of microdots in the 20th century. Steganography has consistently shown cleverness in preserving secrecy in communication. Since the latter part of the 20th century, a new epoch of digital steganography has arisen as contemporary communication routes shifted into the digital domain. Digital steganography involves the use of steganographic techniques on digital data, including photos, audio files, movies, and documents. Steganography in the digital domain refers to the practice of concealing confidential information inside a carrier file, making it look unaltered to an observer (Evsutin et al., 2020).

Steganography techniques that use digital picture carriers may be categorized into two groups: those that operate in the spatial domain (Alhomoud, 2021; Ali et al., 2019; Bhuiyan et al., 2019; Hameed et al., 2023; Sahu et al., 2021) and those that act in the frequency domain (Ayub & Selwal, 2020; Kaur & Singh, 2021; Khandelwal et al., 2022; Liu et al., 2020; Sharda & Budhiraja, 2013). The spatial domain refers to the physical space in which a phenomenon or data is seen or measured. There are five methods that focus on hiding the payload by using the visual relationship between the pixels in the image. On the other hand, frequency domain methods target the low and high frequencies in the image and hide the payload by modifying frequency coefficients that do not affect the visual perception of the image. Various forms of digital pictures, including as 1-bit binary images, 8-bit grayscale images, and 24-bit color images, may be used as carriers. However, each type presents distinct issues due to changes in their properties and complexity.

The development of the steganography utility discussed in this research is driven by the need to address the constraints and difficulties of current techniques that include halftone pictures, as well as the absence of ways that involve plaintext payloads. Halftone pictures are produced by applying certain algorithms to grayscale photographs, resulting in visuals that use just black and white hues while maintaining a resemblance to the original image. Various techniques may be used to carry out digital halftoning, with error diffusion being the prevailing one.

Due to the inherent constraints of this image type in comparison to grayscale/color images, implementing steganography methods for these images is more difficult. For instance, embedding in the spatial domain, rather than the frequency domain, is the preferred approach for halftone images (Lu et al., 2019).

The tool described in this research employs an innovative steganography and extraction approach, as discussed in Çiftci and Sümer (2022), which was developed using MATLAB. Subsequently, the method underwent a thorough overhaul in Python. Additionally, new interfaces were created, including novel capabilities that were not included in the original version. Furthermore, the code was refactored to facilitate future enhancements. The steganography tool described in this research generates 39 halftone stego pictures by concealing plaintext payloads inside grayscale or color graphics. The software provides many halftoning techniques and input settings to achieve diverse outcomes. The developed steganography algorithm employs the secret sharing mechanism (Karnin et al., 1983) to ensure that the whole payload is not concealed inside a single stego picture. The steganography tool provides a range of functions that may be accessible via both a command line interface and a graphical user interface.

The software is described as follows: This section provides a comprehensive overview of the steganography utility. It includes specific information on the software architecture, the hiding and extraction algorithms that have been developed, the many features offered by the utility, and a description of how the utility works.

The Software Architecture

The utility is implemented in Python and relies on the numpy, scipy, and scikit-image libraries. Prior to use this program, the user must ensure that the following requirements are installed. The user may engage with the tool via four distinct executable Python scripts:

-To generate steganographic images:

- ◦ htstego.py (command line interface)
- ◦ htstego-gui.py (graphical interface)

To extract payloads from existing pictures, follow these steps:
The command line tool "htstego-extract.py" may be used to extract information from a file.

- htstego-extract-gui.py (graphical interface)

The user interfaces are provided by these four executable scripts. All necessary functions and variables for the actions performed by these scripts are stored in the libhtstego.py and settings.py files, as seen in Figure 1.

To generate stego pictures, both a cover image and a textual payload file are necessary. The photos may be in either 8-bit grayscale or 24-bit color formats.

The software offers examples from the UC Merced Land Use Dataset (Yang & Newsam, 2010) for pictures and generates payloads using the Lipsum generator (Lipsum generator, n.d.). However, users

Figure 1. The design and structure of the utility

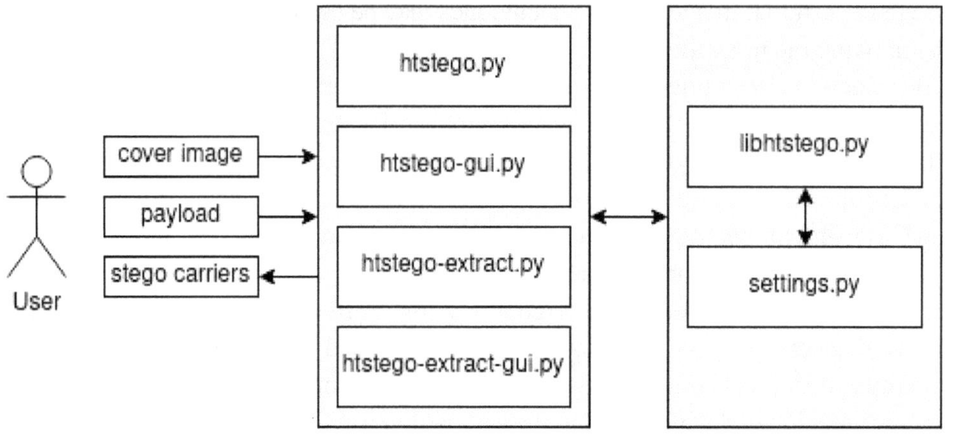

may also use their own unique cover images and payload files. The 50 payload extraction interfaces need a folder containing a comprehensive collection of previously created stego pictures produced with this application utility offers two important features to the user: payload concealment and payload retrieval (Figure 2).

The Technique of Concealing the Payload

The operation of the payload-hiding interfaces (Figure 3) necessitates the user to set the following parameters:

The halftoning method refers to a technique used for generating output.

The utility offers a range of error diffusion kernels, including Floyd and Steinberg (1976), Shiau and Fan (1996), and Jarvis et al. (1976). It also provides a way for generating halftone pictures using a collection of binary patterns.

Error diffusion technique: The selected error diffusion method to be used in the event that the specified halftoning method is error diffusion.

Cover file: the file location of the original picture.

Payload file: the file path of the payload.

The number of shares refers to the quantity of output photos that will be produced.

Furthermore, the utility provides the following discretionary parameters for modifying the outputs:

no-output-files: the program will not produce any output pictures. The option at line 23 may be used to do batch comparisons of quantitative measurements for various combinations of carriers and payloads, without the need to save any files to the disk.

generate-regular-output: the program will create a regular version of the halftone picture for the purpose of visually comparing the original and stego versions of the same image.

The value represents the output-color, which refers to the color space of the output pictures. This option allows the application to automatically create black and white halftone photos. However, it can also make RGB halftone images if the original image is in color.

Output format: The format in which the resulting text is displayed. The results may be shown in CSV, JSON (default), or XML formats.

Figure 2. Algorithms for concealing the payload and extracting the payload

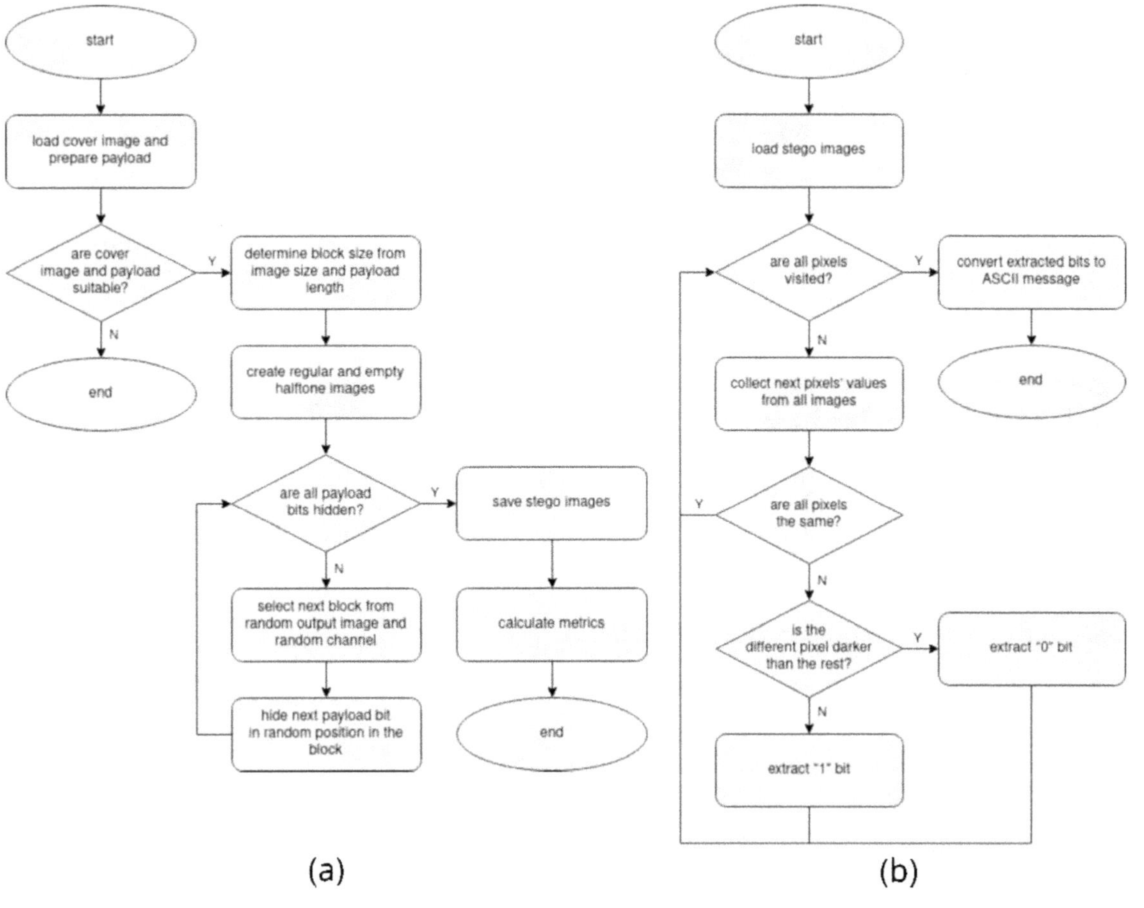

Figure 3. Concept of payload concealing: a) CLI, b) GUI

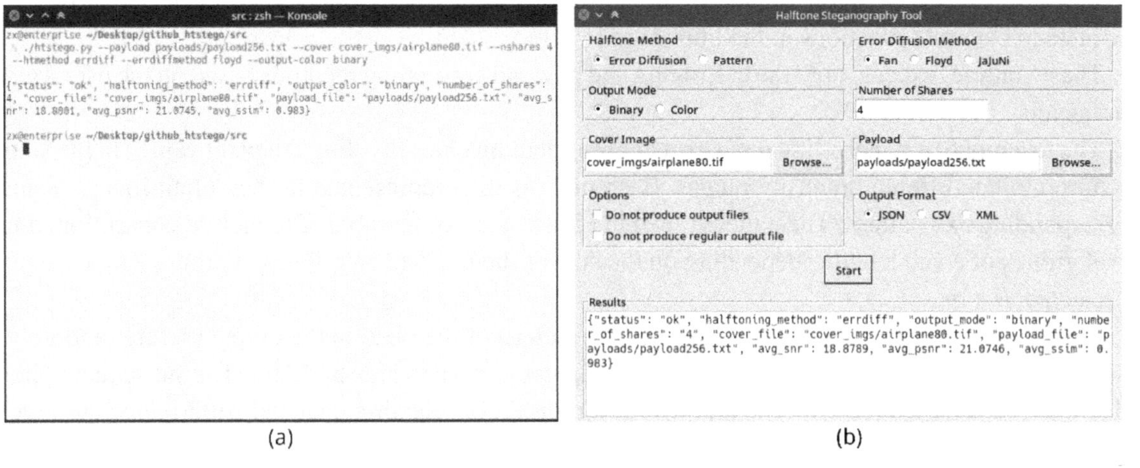

Figure 4. The collection of 3x3 patterns used for halftoning

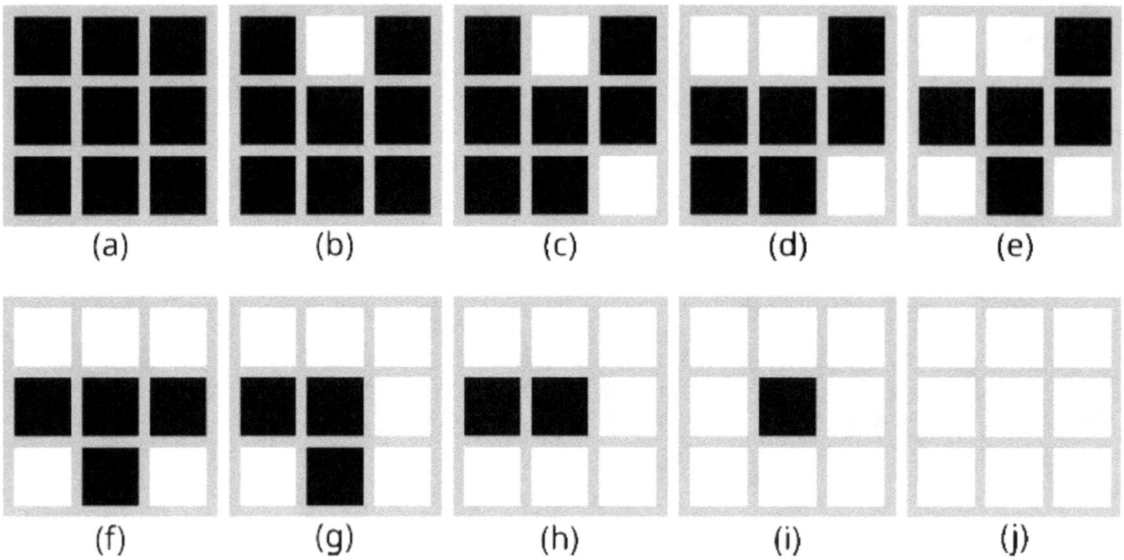

Figure 5. Extraction of payload: a) CLI, b) GUI

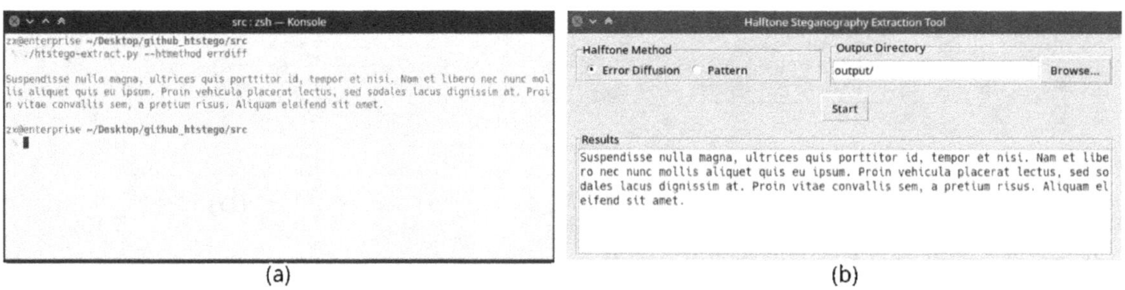

Silent: the program does not generate any textual output.

When all necessary arguments are given, the selected interface invokes either the htstego errdiff() or the htstego pattern() functions in the libhtstego.py file.

These routines execute both the halftoning and payload concealing methods based on the user's given parameters.

The technique of pattern-based payload concealment involves dividing the pixel values in the source picture into ten different intensity ranges. Each pixel is then represented in the output images using a corresponding 3x3 pattern. The patterns seen in Figure 4 are observable. The picture is partitioned into pixel groups of equal lengths, depending on the size of the payload. Within each group, a random pixel is selected as a bit.

There are 5 carriers. The method modifies the pattern of the pixel in the output picture randomly. It uses the darker pattern to hide a "0" bit and the brighter pattern to hide a "1" bit. The subsequent photos adhere to the accurate pattern. The algorithm refrains from selecting changed patterns for the darkest and brightest portions in the picture due to their inherent impossibility to discern.

The payload concealment procedure for error diffusion-based halftoning is executed in a similar manner. In this halftoning technique, each bit of the randomly selected picture is assigned a black pixel for a "0" bit and a white pixel for a "1" bit, while the other bits of the image are assigned the opposite colors.

If the user does not provide any parameters, these routines will generate the following result after successfully concealing the payload entirely:

A collection of steganographic halftone photographs,

The output will consist of the input parameters and the generated quantitative evaluation findings, presented in plaintext format.

The payload extraction process involves extracting the payload from a given source. The payload extraction interfaces (Figure 5) need the user to provide two options:

Directory input: The photos included within this directory will be used for pay-47 load extraction. The default output directory for payload hiding is 49. The designated directory must only consist of the steganographic pictures that were collectively created, with no presence of any other files.

The extraction interfaces call either the htstego errdiff extract() or the htstego pattern extract() function, depending on the halftoning technique selected by the user. Both of these functions analyze all the photographs in the given input directory by examining each pixel and searching for discrepancies, such as a pixel being black in one image but white in the others. If such disparities are detected, a binary digit of either 0 or 1 is retrieved based on the disparities.

Inside the individual pixels:

If the outlier pixel is black in error diffusion photos or if the outlier pattern is darker in pattern images, the value "0" is retrieved.

Figure 6. Pictures that are produced as output: a) Fan's binary error diffusion, b) Floyd's binary error diffusion c) JaJuNi's binary error diffusion, d) binary patterning, e) Fan's color error diffusion, f) Floyd's color error diffusion, g) JaJuNi's color error diffusion, h) color patterning

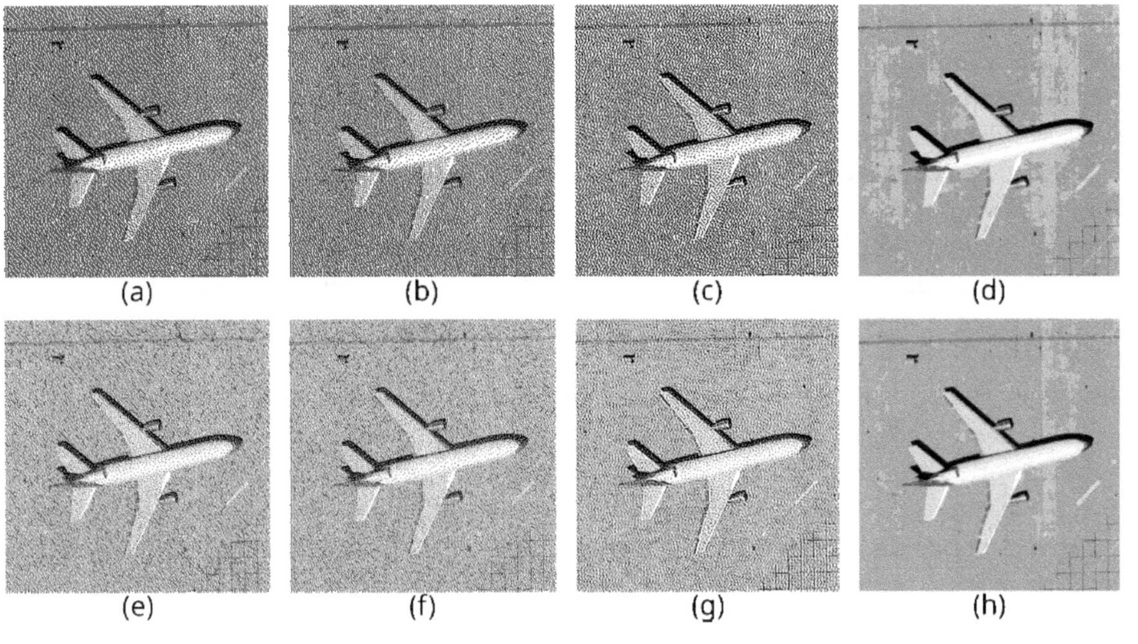

Table 2. Results of the quantitative assessment

	Binary			
	Fan	**Floyd**	**JaJuNi**	**Pattern**
SNR	21.8873	21.8902	21.9029	31.2914
PSNR	24.0831	24.0846	24.0943	33.6250
SSIM	0.9915	0.9915	0.9915	0.9990
	Color			
	Fan	**Floyd**	**JaJuNi**	**Pattern**
SNR	26.5780	26.5813	26.5913	36.0436
PSNR	28.8556	28.8581	28.8639	38.3972
SSIM	0.9971	0.9971	0.9971	0.9997

"1" is recovered when the outlier pixel is white in error diffusion photos, or 31 when the outlier pattern is lighter in pattern images.

Once all photos have been scanned, these functions transform the recovered bits into 35 ASCII characters and provide the resulting output, which will be shown to the user using the performed extraction interface.

Examples that serve to illustrate the functionalities of payload concealment (Figure 3) and payload extraction (Figure 5) may be executed using both command line and graphical user interfaces.

Upon successful operation, the tool produces stego pictures in the specified output directory. Figure 6 displays a collection of example outputs, each selected from distinct sets of 46 carrier share pictures. These images were created by concealing a payload of 128 bytes inside a 256x256 image. Table 2 provides the corresponding quantitative evaluation findings.

HtStego produces digital halftone photographs that function as secure communication medium. This is advantageous for people or organizations requiring secure communication, since it safeguards their data from unauthorized access. Halftone graphics are still used in a range of fields, such as conventional print media, comics, advertising materials, and indie video games. Considering the continuous use of HtStego, it becomes evident that it is a great tool for creating stego carriers specifically designed for these particular situations.

Another instance is when cybersecurity companies use steganography software to conceal confidential information inside photographs, hence increasing the difficulty for unauthorized users to identify and retrieve it. In cases where discreet transmission of information is necessary, such as in law enforcement, intelligence organizations, or investigative journalism, HtStego may be quite valuable. Some users, especially those in the creative business, may use HtStego for the purpose of digital watermarking. This allows them to safeguard their intellectual property and track any unlawful dissemination of their information. HtStego allows for clandestine communication and data security in several industries by discreetly inserting concealed information inside halftone photographs.

HtStego offers user-friendly interfaces for creating steganographic halftone images.The utility employs an innovative steganography technique that has been previously shown to effectively conceal a large amount of data while generating outputs of superior quality (Çiftci & Sümer, 2022). This technique may be enhanced to accommodate a wider variety of digital picture formats or use other halftoning algorithms, such as ordered dithering. Furthermore, although the techniques and usefulness of HtStego are primarily designed for plaintext payloads, it is also possible to conceal encrypted payloads (ciphertexts) inside pictures, hence enhancing the degree of security.

There are a variety of steganography tools that may be used, including OpenStego (n.d.) and Steghide (n.d.). As far as we know, no other steganography program incorporates secret sharing principles to conceal plaintext payloads inside halftone pictures. Furthermore, to the best of our knowledge, there are currently no other steganalysis or attack tools available that can successfully retrieve the hidden information from collections of stego pictures that have missing components.

CONCLUSION

In this study, we provide HtStego, a user-friendly, cost-free, and open-source program that enables the concealment of plaintext payloads inside halftone pictures. These modified images may then be disseminated and used for various objectives. The utility utilizes a method that can conceal substantial plaintext payloads and produce steganographic pictures of excellent quality. The application provides many choices for concealing the payload, such as the color space of the resulting pictures, the halftoning technique, and the quantity of created output images. In addition to generating 48 stego output pictures, the application also calculates quantitative quality measures for the purpose of monitoring and comparing the quality of the resulting stego photos. The method and utility have potential for future advancements, such as the inclusion of bespoke error diffusion kernels and other halftoning techniques algorithms such as ordered dithering and the computation of various quality indicators.

REFERENCES

Alexan, W., Elkandoz, M., Mashaly, M., Azab, E., & Aboshousha, A. (2023). Color image encryption through chaos and kaa map. *IEEE Access : Practical Innovations, Open Solutions*, *11*, 11541–11554. doi:10.1109/ACCESS.2023.3242311

Alhomoud, A. M. (2021). Image steganography in spatial domain: Current status, techniques, and trends. *Intelligent Automation & Soft Computing*, *27*(1). Advance online publication. doi:10.32604/iasc.2021.014773

Ali, U., Sohrawordi, M., & Uddin, M. P. (2019). A robust and secured image steganography using lsb and random bit substitution. *American Journal of Engineering Research*, *8*(2), 39–44.

Artz, D. (2001). Digital steganography: Hiding data within data. *IEEE Internet Computing*, *5*(3), 75–80. doi:10.1109/4236.935180

Ayub, N., & Selwal, A. (2020). An improved image steganography technique using edge based data hiding in dct domain. *Journal of Interdisciplinary Mathematics*, *23*(2), 357–366. doi:10.1080/09720502.2020.1731949

Bhuiyan, T., Sarower, A. H., Karim, R., & Hassan, M. (2019). An image steganography algorithm using lsb replacement through xor substitution. *2019 International Conference on Information and Communications Technology (ICOIACT)*, 44–49. 10.1109/ICOIACT46704.2019.8938486

Cheddad, A., Condell, J., Curran, K., & Mc Kevitt, P. (2010). Digital image steganography: Survey and analysis of current methods. *Signal Processing*, *90*(3), 727–752. doi:10.1016/j.sigpro.2009.08.010

Çiftci, E., & Sümer, E. (2022). A novel steganography method for binary and color halftone images. *PeerJ. Computer Science*, *8*, e1062. doi:10.7717/peerj-cs.1062 PMID:36091978

Dastres & Soori. (2021). A review in recent development of network threats and security measures. *International Journal of Information Sciences and Computer Engineering*.

Evsutin, O., Melman, A., & Meshcheryakov, R. (2020). Digital steganography and watermarking for digital images: A review of current research directions. *IEEE Access : Practical Innovations, Open Solutions*, *8*, 166589–166611. doi:10.1109/ACCESS.2020.3022779

Floyd, R. W., & Steinberg, L. (1976). An adaptive algorithm for spatial gray-scale. *Proc. Soc. Inf. Disp.*, *17*, 75–77.

Hameed, M. A., Abdel-Aleem, O. A., & Hassaballah, M. (2023). A secure data hiding approach based on least-significant-bit and nature-inspired optimization techniques. *Journal of Ambient Intelligence and Humanized Computing*, *14*(5), 4639–4657. doi:10.1007/s12652-022-04366-y

Jarvis, J. F., Judice, C. N., & Ninke, W. (1976). A survey of techniques for the display of continuous tone pictures on bilevel displays. *Computer Graphics and Image Processing*, *5*(1), 13–40. doi:10.1016/S0146-664X(76)80003-2

Johnson, N. F., & Jajodia, S. (1998). Exploring steganography: Seeing the unseen. *Computer*, *31*(2), 26–34. doi:10.1109/MC.1998.4655281

Kadhim, A. N., & Sadkhan, S. B. (2021). Security threats in wireless network communication-status, challenges, and future trends. *2021 International Conference on Advanced Computer Applications (ACA)*, 176–181. 10.1109/ACA52198.2021.9626810

Karnin, E., Greene, J., & Hellman, M. (1983). On secret sharing systems. *IEEE Transactions on Information Theory*, *29*(1), 35–41. doi:10.1109/TIT.1983.1056621

Kaur, R., & Singh, B. (2021). A hybrid algorithm for robust image steganography. *Multidimensional Systems and Signal Processing*, *32*(1), 1–23. doi:10.1007/s11045-020-00725-0

Khandelwal, J., Sharma, V. K., Singh, D., & Zaguia, A. (2022). Dwt-svd based image steganography using threshold value encryption method. *Computers, Materials & Continua*, *72*(2), 3299–3312. doi:10.32604/cmc.2022.023116

Lai, Q., Hu, G., Erkan, U., & Toktas, A. (2023). A novel pixel-split image encryption scheme based on 2d salomon map. *Expert Systems with Applications*, *213*, 118845. doi:10.1016/j.eswa.2022.118845

Lipsum generator. (n.d.). https://www.lipsum.com/

Liu, Q., Xiang, X., Qin, J., Tan, Y., Tan, J., & Luo, Y. (2020). Coverless steganography based on image retrieval of densenet features and dwt sequence mapping. *Knowledge-Based Systems*, *192*, 105375. doi:10.1016/j.knosys.2019.105375

Lu, W., Xue, Y., Yeung, Y., Liu, H., Huang, J., & Shi, Y.-Q. (2019). Secure halftone image steganography based on pixel density transition. *IEEE Transactions on Dependable and Secure Computing*, *18*(3), 1137–1149. doi:10.1109/TDSC.2019.2933621

Openstego. (n.d.). https://www.openstego.com/

Sahu, A. K., Swain, G., Sahu, M., & Hemalatha, J. (2021). Multi-directional block based pvd and modulus function image steganography to avoid fobp and iep. *Journal of Information Security and Applications*, *58*, 102808. doi:10.1016/j.jisa.2021.102808

Sharda, S., & Budhiraja, S. (2013). Image steganography: A review. *International Journal of Emerging Technology and Advanced Engineering*, *3*(1), 707–710.

Shiau, J.-N., & Fan, Z. (1996). Set of easily implementable coefficients in error diffusion with reduced worm artifacts. Color Imaging: Device-Independent Color, Color Hard Copy, and Graphic Arts, 2658, 222–225. doi:10.1117/12.236968

Song, W., Fu, C., Zheng, Y., Tie, M., Liu, J., & Chen, J. (2023). A parallel image encryption algorithm using intra bitplane scrambling. *Mathematics and Computers in Simulation*, *204*, 71–88. doi:10.1016/j.matcom.2022.07.029

Steghide. (n.d.). https://steghide.sourceforge.net/

Yang, Y., & Newsam, S. (2010). Bag-of-visual-words and spatial extensions for land-use classification. *Proceedings of the 18th SIGSPATIAL international conference on advances in geographic information systems*, 270–279. 10.1145/1869790.1869829

Chapter 10
Enhancing 2D Logistic Chaotic Map for Gray Image Encryption

Dena Abu Laila
Hashemite University, Jordan

Hasan Gharaibeh
Yarmouk University, Jordan

Qais Al-Na'amneh
Applied Science Private University, Jordan

Rabia Al Mamlook
Trine University, USA

Mohammad Aljaidi
https://orcid.org/0000-0001-9486-3533
Zarqa University, Jordan

Mohammed Alshammari
https://orcid.org/0000-0002-5859-7490
Northern Border University, Saudi Arabia

Ahmad Nawaf Nasayreh
Yarmouk University, Jordan

ABSTRACT

Cryptography has demonstrated its utility and efficacy in safeguarding confidential data. Among the most potent algorithms for encrypting images is chaos theory, owing to its numerous noteworthy attributes, including high sensitivity to initial conditions and parameters, unpredictability, and nonlinearity. This study employed a two-dimensional logistic chaotic map to encrypt the data. The map utilizes permutation-substitution in the image to ensure both confusion and diffusion, thereby establishing a secure cipher. As measured by UACI and NPCR, this method enables immovability against differential attacks. The assessment of cipher image quality in the USC-SIPI image database involves the utilization of information entropy tests, key space, key sensitivity, APCC, UACI, and NPCR assessments, as determined by experimental findings on test images.

DOI: 10.4018/979-8-3693-2691-6.ch010

1. INTRODUCTION

With the advancement of computer and Internet technology, anyone now has access to a variety of multimedia. To uphold the security of the transmission process and prevent the transfer of sensitive information over a public channel, the image information must be encrypted (Farhan, 2017). When seeking methods to encrypt images, the most practical approach is to convert the digital image into a binary stream before applying data encryption techniques to encrypt it. Image encryption may therefore not be compatible with traditional digital data encryption algorithms. As a consequence, numerous image encryption methods have been developed, each of which considers the image's characteristics. Nearly all of the algorithms are P-Fibonacci-based wave algorithms (Zhou, 2012), Transformation-based algorithms (Liao, 2010) cryptography-based (Tahmasbi, (2022, Novembe) (Zhu, 2019), (Li, 2023) (Jaradat, 2023, November).; Mughaid, 2023)and Chaos-based algorithms (Hua, 2018).

An extensive array of image encryption methods, such as those found in DNA coding, quantum theory, and chaotic cryptography, have been proposed by scholars as potential resolutions to security concerns (Zhang, 2019). Chaotic cryptography is more suitable for special property-based cryptography. An interdisciplinary domain, it concerns the integration of chaos theory and cryptography (Jain, 2016) . One-dimensional (1D) and high-dimensional (HD) chaotic maps are the two classifications applicable to the current state of chaotic atlas. Chebyshev, Sine, and Logistic maps are forms of 1D chaotic maps that are described in (Saini, 2014) (Wu, 2012). These references present chaotic maps in one dimension, which consists of the Chebyshev, Sine, and Logistic maps. One potential drawback of 1D chaotic maps is their basic architecture and limited number of parameters, which necessitates the collection of a small amount of data. Furthermore, the chaotic orbits, parameters, and initial values of these maps can be predicted. The limited adoption of 1D chaotic maps in the security industry is the consequence. In the realm of image encryption, these techniques have had little application. However, robust encryption methods can be created when they are utilized in a hybrid fashion and are backed by two-dimensional chaotic maps (L. Z. Pen). The proposed algorithm, a 2D logistic chaotic map, achieves remarkable outcomes and assumes a critical role in this research compared to other algorithms due to its utilization of an initial plain image before pixel order modification. Deterministic and discrete chaotic behavior are both incorporated into image security. In image security, the reversibility of chaos implemented on image data is the most essential and desired properties. Chaotic cryptography has been primarily influenced by the following attributes: sensitivity to initial conditions (xi, yi) and system parameters (r); mixing properties; and nonlinear dynamical systems.

Figure 1 illustrates the phase portrait image of the 2D logistic map when the value of r is set to 1.19. The trajectory denoted by (x, y) exhibits an entirely random direction. Furthermore, it is essential to know the numbers (x0, y0) and r. Due to this, it is feasible to employ it as a pseudo-random number generator within the domain of cryptography (Iqbal, 2023).

(a)A trajectory of the 2D logistic map (b) a phase portrait of the 2D logistic map

The points that follow are the primary innovations and contributions of the suggested encryption algorithm:

1. We add to the body of knowledge on image encryption by creating a novel technique that uses three layered chaotic maps—a technique.
2. The suggested approach has little computer complexity and is easy to apply by nature. Nevertheless, compared to other chaos-based techniques in the literature, it performs either comparably or better.

Figure 1. Behavior of the 2D logistic map

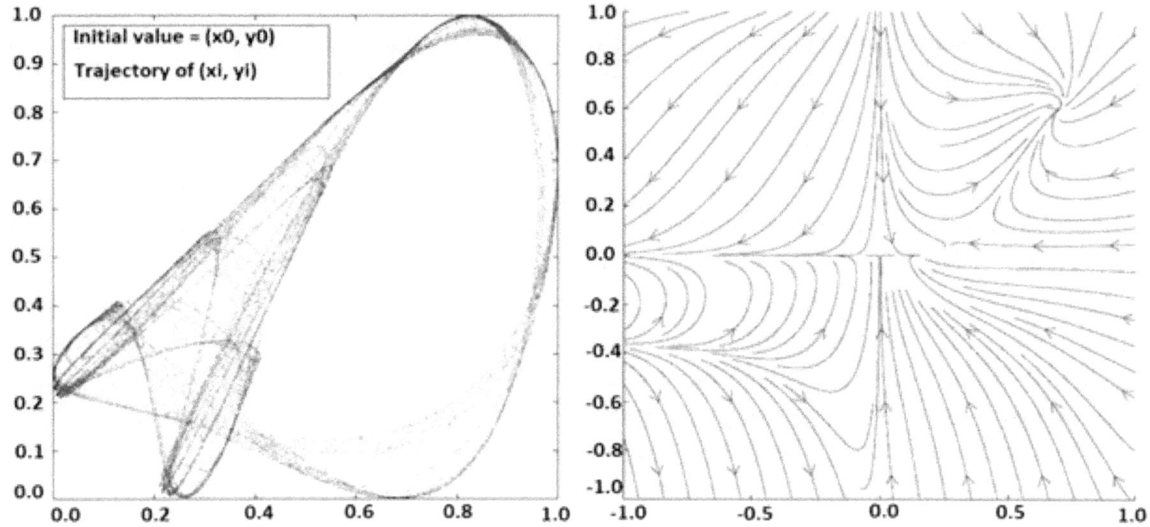

3. The process of image encryption involves creating 256-bit random secret keys and using the original image for encryption. Statistical and differential attacks are futile since even a small alteration to the original image or secret key results in completely different encrypted images. It is also extremely sensitive to key changes and has a very big key space.
4. Different, methodical trials have proven the method's robustness and efficiency. The outcomes were compared to the techniques found in the literature.

The subsequent sections of the study are structured as follows: Chapter 2 of the Related Works section of Chapter 3 provides a comprehensive description of the proposed work, elucidating its role as the mechanism employed for testing and evaluation—findings and discussion in Chapter 4, with a conclusion in Chapter 5.

2. RELATED WORKS

Hua (2016) proposed a logistic-adjusted Sine map in two dimensions (2D-LASM). Based on performance evaluations, in terms of ergodicity, unpredictability, and chaotic range, it surpasses some alternative chaotic maps. This work additionally develops a 2D-LASM-based image encryption system utilizing the proposed map. plan (LAS-IES). The principles of diffusion and confusion are rigorously adhered to, and the inclusion of random values in an ordinary image is implemented to enhance the security—image ciphering level. Based on results from security studies and simulations, LAS-IES is capable of encrypting a variety of image formats into random-looking images that are highly resistant to a wide array of security threats.

Sharma (2020) proposed that an encryption system be built upon a novel two-dimensional chaotic map. In contrast to many recently introduced systems that rely on alternative 2D chaotic maps, the 2D chaos-based pseudorandom number generator demonstrates significantly enhanced randomness and unpredictability as measured by Lyapunov exponents and trajectory graphs. The subsequent step is to implement photo encryption using this new chaotic 2D map. It is demonstrated that the proposed encryption method requires significantly less computational effort to operate. For the proposed method, the commonly employed metrics of security, unpredictability, and sensitivity to initial conditions are effectively determined with the assistance of a collection of standardized simulation results.

Yavuz (2016) proposed two simultaneous 1D logistic maps to encrypt images that are extremely sensitive to initial states. While the values of pixels are modified by the other function, the positions of pixels are shuffled by the former. The subsequent pixel organization will result in adjacent pixels with inherently similar values acquiring considerably dissimilar values, thereby posing a formidable challenge in the process of decrypting the image. Certain logical operations, such as exclusive or circular rotation, are utilized to distribute the impact of a minor alteration in the intensity of a solitary pixel in an unencrypted image across a substantial quantity of pixels in a cipher image. This effectively heightens the vulnerability of the system to differential attacks. A multitude of inquiries and examinations have been undertaken to substantiate this claim.

Ahmad (2015) devised a novel chaos-based diffusion and replacement encryption technique, this method effectively reduces auto-correlation in digital data, particularly for lower grayscale values. On the contrary, diffusion is achieved through the subdivision of the replacement image into blocks consisting of $Z \times Z$ elements, with the logistic map being employed to generate the stochastic values within each block.

Anwar (2019), a modified version of Arnold's cat map, have published a method of image encryption based on chaotic pixel permutation. The encrypted image retains sufficient information regarding the original image to render any modifications to the plain-text images inconsequential.

Fadhil et al. (2021) proposed a 1D logistic map's chaotic sequence to produce the hexa code values, which were then processed again to create the new, improved S-Box. The S-Box test criteria, which include avalanche, balanced, completeness, stringent avalanche, and invertibility, were used to assess this proposal. The analysis's findings demonstrate that the suggested SBox passes each of these statistical tests, has a sizable avalanche effect, and can fend off numerous attacks.

Xiang (2020) proposed a way to inhibit the dynamic degradation of digital chaotic systems by using parameter variables and state variables to impact each other and using the sine function as a feedback function to destroy the state space. The results of the simulation demonstrate that compared to the original logistic mapping, the enhanced logistic mapping using the suggested method has larger complexity and better randomness. To demonstrate the feasibility and relevance of the enhanced chaotic map, they created a novel picture encryption technique that works with both color and grayscale images. The suggested algorithm has strong encryption efficiency, strong resilience to many types of attack, and some degree of competitiveness with existing encryption algorithms, according to the numerical results.

Li (2017) proposed divides the plaintext images into numerous blocks before calculating the correlation coefficients for each block. The random integers of a skew tent map are pixel-by-pixel XO. The block in red is the one with the highest correlation coefficient values, as determined by a predetermined threshold value. To permute the entire image, two random sequences generated from the TD-ERCS chaotic map are ultimately applied. The assessment of increased security is validated through the analysis of correlation, entropy, histogram, and diffusion.

Arif (2022) proposed an innovative chaos-based method for encrypting images that solves issues with existing methods by employing a single Substitution Box (S-Box) and permutation and substitution. To assess the effectiveness of the proposed encryption method in comparison to current state-of-the-art methods, a multitude of experiments are undertaken, employing diverse benchmarks and measurements. The proposed methodology exhibits a notable level of susceptibility to the plaintext attack. A minor modification to either the plain text or the encryption key would yield an encrypted image that is entirely distinct.

Wang (2016) proposed the diffusion and permutation processes employed in image encryption. They study diffusion and permutation operations, and they gauge the impact of encryption operations using a standard analytical criterion. The combinational operation, which is frequently employed in chaotic image encryption, is then evaluated using the same methodology. As a result, scientists can select the most effective method for encrypting images and enhance the efficacy and security of algorithms built using chaotic maps.

Khanzadi (2014) suggests an image encryption technique based on chaotic maps and the random bit sequence generator. The necessary random bit sequences are produced using tent maps and chaotic logistic maps. These chaotic functions are used to permute the plain image's pixels, and the resulting eight bit map planes are created. These functions result in random bit and random number matrices, which determine how bits are permuted and substituted in each plane. The permutation step of the pixels and bit maps is based on a chaotic random Ergodic matrix. The encrypted image created by this chaotic encryption technique is assessed for performance using the chi-square test, correlation coefficient, unified average changing intensity (UACI), number of pixels of change rate (NPCR), and key space.

3. METHODOLOGY

In this section, we will simulate an image encryption algorithm utilizing the proposed 2D logistic chaotic map.

3.1 Encryption Method

The steps of the encryption algorithm are detailed in the subsequent paragraphs.

For the proposed image encryption method, a 2D logistic map-based flowchart is depicted in Figure 2. Two logistic diffusion, two-dimensional logistic permutation, and two-dimensional logistic transposition comprise the internal loop. Each of these operates independently as an image cipher through the generation of a network comprising permutations and substitutions. With the exception of reversing the order of processing illustrated in Figure 3, the decryption procedure is identical to the encryption procedure and employs the decryption key.

Using the 2D logistic map using the 2D logistic map

Algo 3.1: Encryption Algorithm

1. To control the pseudo-random sequence derived from the 2D logistic map, generate a random encryption key.
2. Rearrange the X_{seq} and Y_{seq} components, using a 2D Logistic Permutation Algorithm.
3. Apply the logistic diffusion over the finite field.
4. Apply the 2D logistic transposition.

Figure 2. The flowchart of image encryption

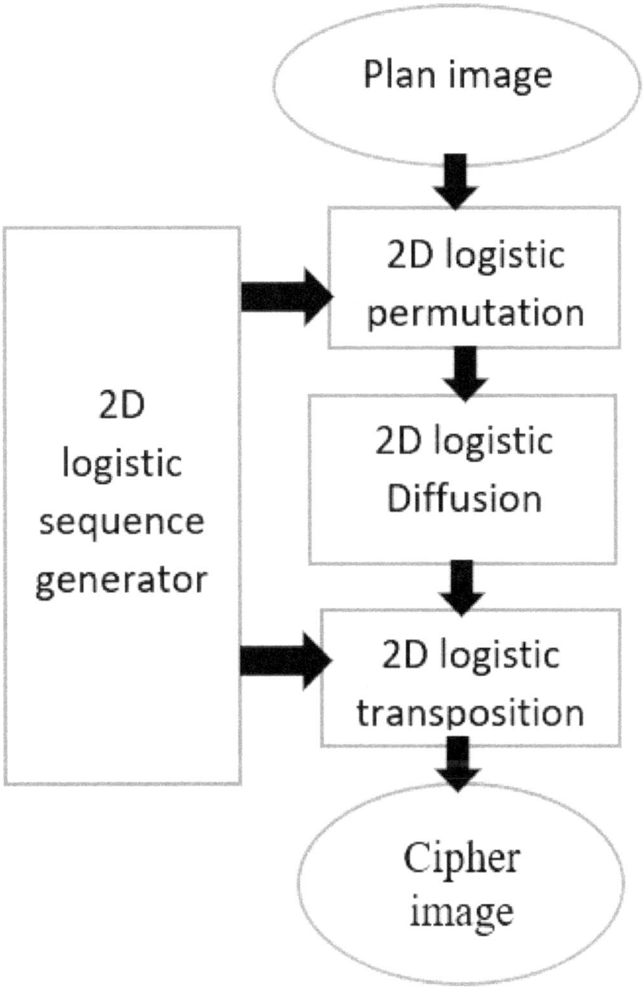

3.1.1 Generation Key

In chaotic cryptography, scenes that conceal plain images as components of key streams utilize pseudo-random sequence generators. For a chaos-based encryption algorithm to resist brute-force attacks, its key length must exceed one hundred bits. As a result, our method 256-bit string of symmetric security keys for image encryption and decryption the key's structure is depicted in Figure 4.

Xo

Y*o*

R

Figure 3. The flowchart of the image decryption

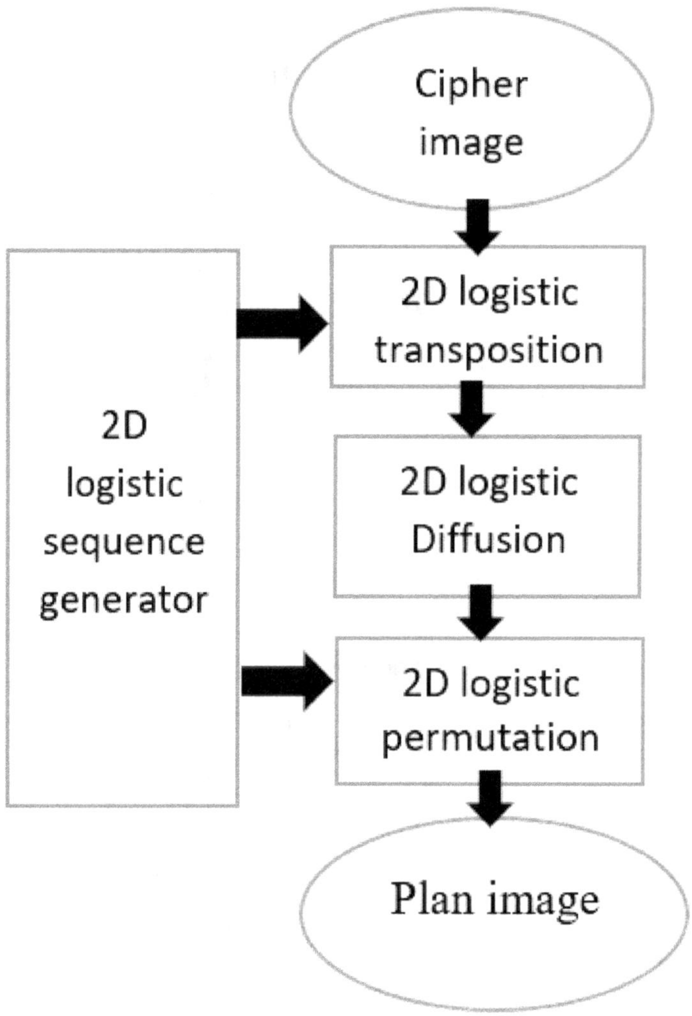

T

$A_{1...}$ A_8

52 Bits 52 Bits 52 Bits 52 Bits 48 Bits

Figure 4. Structure of the key

Xo	*Yo*	R	T	A1... A8
52 Bits	52 Bits	52 Bits	52 Bits	48 Bits

3.1.2 Image Encryption Using the 2D Logistic Map

The consistency of five components—x0, y0, r, T, and A1 · · · A8—is critical to our method, where (X_0, Y_0) € (0, 1) represents the initial value and r € (1.11, 1.19) is a control parameter in a chaotic system. The table below shows how the map behaves at various values of r.

Equation (1) represents the 2D logistic map in a discrete mathematical form, where r denotes the system parameter and (x_i, y_i) signifies the pair-wise location at the i_{th} iteration. Equation (2) can subsequently be implemented to establish the initial value ($x_0^{round\#}$, $y_0^{round\#}$) producing an adequate length of chaotic sequence with each iteration. In contrast, A (consisting of a 6-bit string) and T (52 bits) are the parameters of the linear congruential generator. The representation of each bit of A is an integer number.

$$X_i+1 = r\,(3y_i + 1)\,xi\,(1 - x_i)$$

2D Logistic map: (1)

$$y_i+1 = r\,(3x_i+1 + 1)\,y_i\,(1 - y_i)$$

$$x_{0^{round\#}} = T + X_0\,A_{(round\#\ mod\ 8)+1}\ mod\ 1$$

The initial value for each round: (2)

$$Y_0^{round\#} = T + y_0 A_{(round\#\ mod\ 8)+1}\ mod\ 1$$

3.1.3 2D Logistic Permutation

The permutation process. Assert that P represents an image of M×N plaintext size to illustrate the reordering and jumbling of pixel positions. Equation (3) enables the 2D logistic map to produce a pair-wise sequence of x and y of length M×N, with the initial value being (x0, y0). Following this, the matrices X and Y are rearranged to form M×N matrices. Then, a bijective mapping can be generated utilizing the row of X and the column of Y, as shown in Equation 4.

Table 1. Map behavior

No	R	The Map's Behaviors
1	r∈(−1,1)	There is a noticeable shift in conduct. In particular, the population dynamics typically converge towards stable equilibria for r in this range.
2	r ∈(1.11,1.19)	The logistic map displays intriguing dynamics, such as bifurcations and periodic windows.
3	r=1	Depending on the starting circumstance, the population of the logistic map shows a behavior where it stabilizes around specific places.
4	r=∈(1,1.11)	The system's "attractive focus" turns repulsive and tends to create "oscillations" in the system.
5	r >1.19	Unbalanced system

Algorithm 3.2 2D Logistic Permutation Algorithm

```
function C = LogisticPermutation(P,R,para)
[v,Epix] = sort(R(:,:,1),1);
for i = 1:size(R,1)
Shuffling within a Column
End
[v,Epiy] = sort(R(:,:,2),2);
for j = 1:size(R,2)
Shuffling within a Row
End
```

$$X_{seq} = \{x1, x2, \cdots, x_{MN}\} \quad (3)$$

$$Y_{seq} = \{y1, y2, \cdots, y_{MN}\}$$

$$X^{sorted}_{r,i} = X_{r,e\pi x\ (i)} \quad (4)$$

$$Y^{sorted}_{r,i} = Y_{r,e\pi x\ (i)}$$

The algorithm 3.2 is known as the 2D logistic permutation, which is implemented through the utilization of row and column permutations.

3.1.4 2D Logistic Diffusion

To augment the disorder and intricacy of the characteristics, the logistic diffusion over the finite field GF (28) was implemented for every S×S image block P_b contained within the plaintext image P, as illustrated in Equation 5. In this context, "L_D" denotes the largest distance separation matrix, which is derived from the 4×4 random permutation matrices specified in Equations 6 and 7. "S" represents the block size that is accessible via the plaintext image format.

$$\mathbf{L}_D = \begin{matrix} 4 & 2 & 1 & 3 \\ 1 & 3 & 4 & 2 \\ 2 & 4 & 3 & 1 \\ 3 & 1 & 2 & 4 \end{matrix} \quad \mathbf{L}_D^{-1} = \begin{matrix} 71 & 216 & 173 & 117 \\ 173 & 117 & 71 & 216 \\ 216 & 71 & 117 & 173 \\ 117 & 173 & 216 & 71 \end{matrix} \quad (5)$$

$$C_b = L_D . P_b . L_D \quad (6)$$

$$P_b = L_d^{-1} . C_b . L_D^{-1} \quad (7)$$

Algorithm 3.3 2D Logistic Diffusion

```
switch para
case 'encryption'
L = gf([4 2 1 3; 1 3 4 2; 2 4 3 1; 3 1 2 4],8);
case 'decryption'
L = gf([71 216 173 117; 173 117 71 216; 216 71 117 173; 117 173 216 71],8);
end
```

3.1.5 2D Logistic Transposition

In contrast to the utilization of substitution phases observed in a traditional substitution-permutation network. The values of the pixels surrounding the reference image I are modified by the 2D logistic transposition procedure following the logistic sequence established in the previous phase. Before proceeding, each 4×4 block of a matrix is transformed using a function of Eq. into a (pseudo) random integer matrix (8). Where B is a 4×4 block and gN (.), gR (.), gD (.), and gS (.) are defined by Equations (9) – (12).

$$I = f(B) = \begin{bmatrix} gN(B1,1) & gR(B1,2) & gS(B1,3) & gD(B1,4) \\ gR(B2,1) & gS(B2,2) & gD(B2,3) & gN(B2,4) \\ gS(B3,1) & gD(B3,2) & gN(B3,3) & gR(B3,4) \\ gD(B4,1) & gN(B4,2) & gR(B4,3) & gS(B4,4) \end{bmatrix} \quad (8)$$

$$gN(d) = T(d) \bmod F \quad (9)$$

$$gR(d) = T(\sqrt{d}) \bmod F \quad (10)$$

$$gS(d) = T(d \wedge 2) \bmod F \quad (11)$$

$$gD(d) = T(2d) \bmod F \quad (12)$$

The operation T (d) performs an integer conversion on a decimal d by removing the ninth through sixteenth digits. Consider the expression b = 0.12345678901234567890 and T (d) = 90123456. The character F denotes the format of a plaintext image. If the plaintext image P is an 8-bit grayscale image, F equals 256. If P is a binary image, F equals 2.

The 2D logistic transposition is subsequently achieved by performing a pixel shift on each element in the plaintext image by the amount specified in the random integer image I.

Algorithm 3.4 2D Logistic Transposition Algorithm

```
Input: Secrete message and Secrete key
Output: encrypted image
function C = LogisticSubstitution(P,R,para)
trun = @(x,low,high) floor(x.*10^high)-floor(x.*10^(low-1))*10^(high-low+1);
T = trun(R(:,:,1)+R(:,:,2),9,16);
gfun = @(B,F) [mod(B(1,1),F), floor(mod(B(1,2),F)), mod(B(1,3)^2,F), mod(2*B(1,4),F);...
floor(mod(B(2,1),F)), mod(B(2,2)^2,F), mod(2*B(2,3),F),mod(B(2,4),F);...
mod(B(3,1)^2,F), mod(2*B(3,2),F),mod(B(3,3),F),floor(mod(B(3,4),F));...
mod(2*B(4,1),F),mod(B(4,2),F),floor(mod(B(4,3),F)),mod(B(4,4)^2,F)];
if max(P(:))>1
F = 256;
else
F = 2;
end
I = blkproc(T,[4,4],@(x) gfun(x,F)
```

4. SIMULATION RESULTS

In this segment, the results of grayscale image encryption are presented. The input data and histogram of the 2D logistic permutation outlined in Algorithms 3.2 are illustrated in Figure 5.

The input data and histogram of the 2D logistic permutation outlined in Algorithms 3.3 are illustrated in Figure 6.

Subsequently, the input data for the 2D logistic transposition outlined in Algorithms 3.4 are utilized to execute the operation by shifting every pixel in the plaintext image by the specified amount from the random integer image I. The results of the logistic permutation, transposition, and diffusion in two dimensions are illustrated in Figure 7.

Figure 5. 2D logistic permutation results

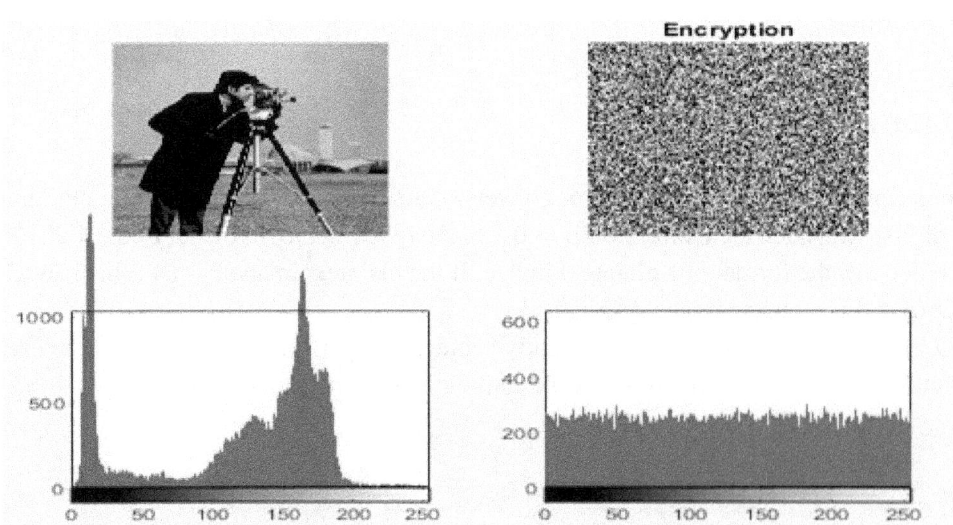

Figure 6. 2D logistic permutation and diffusion results

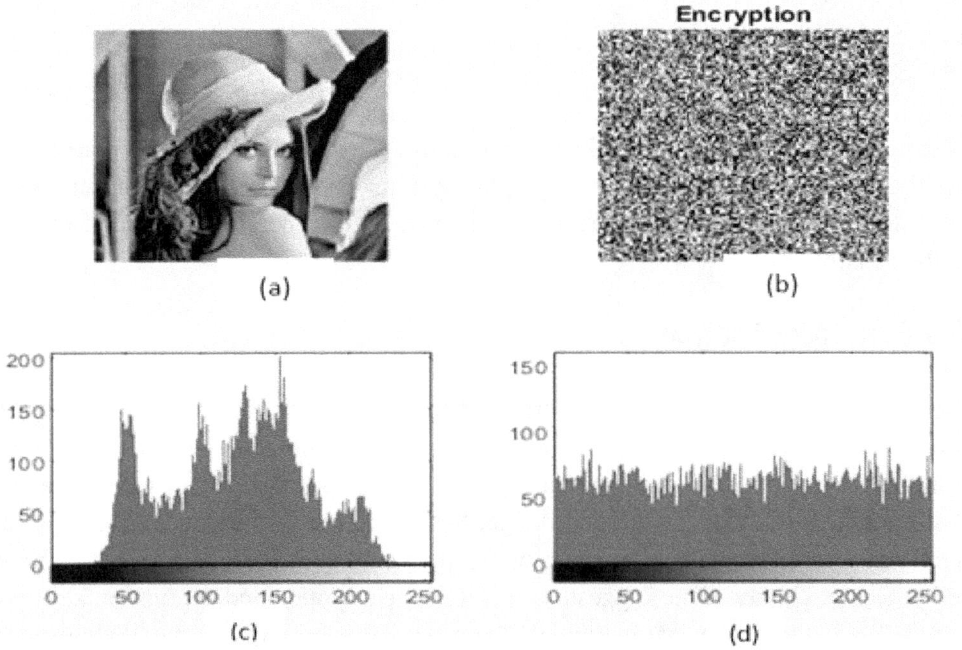

Figure 7. 2D logistic permutation, diffusion, and transposition results

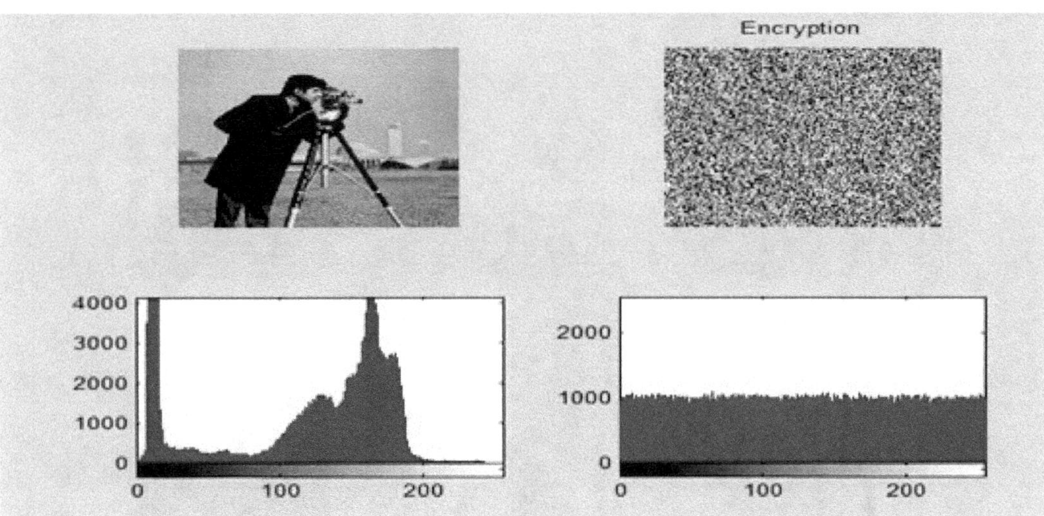

4.1 Security Analysis

As a fundamental requirement, researchers assess the efficacy and security of contemporary image encryption algorithms via a variety of methods, such as adjacent pixel correlation, differential crypt-analysis, and histogram analysis. The output of any image encryption algorithm ought to be a substantial departure from the plain form. Assessment techniques provide quantitative and qualitative measures in this context. This section offers a variety of evaluation techniques for this method.

4.1.1 Key Space Analysis

All secret keys must be imperceptible to the cryptography system; the key space comprises the complete set of keys that can be employed in a cryptographic system. For success, two thousand operations are necessary. A key of 256 bits is utilized here. Consequently, 2^{256}-bit operations are sufficiently substantial to endure the assault.

4.1.2 Key Sensitivity Analysis

In the case of an identical Plain Text image utilizing encryption keys K1 and K2, which differ marginally in terms of their encryption strength, a secure cipher must exhibit cipher key sensitivity. Under the assumption that k1 represents the encryption key, the encrypted image is generated by employing the test key to scramble a 512x512 Lena plain image. Following this, the identical uncomplicated image is encrypted and scrambled once more using two unique keys (K2, K3), each of which possesses one bit (k1=K3). The sensitivity of the suggested algorithm's encryption and decryption keys is illustrated in Figure 8. K1, K2, and K3 deviate marginally from K1. The sensitivity of the 2D logistic map-based image cipher is evident from these results.

Figure 8. Key sensitivity results

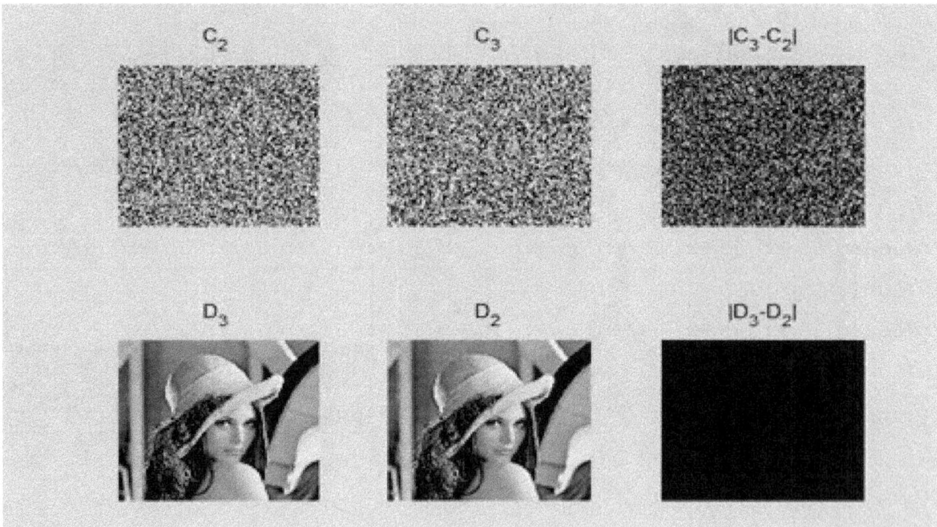

4.1.3 Adjacent Pixels Correlation Coefficient (APCC)

A typical approach for evaluating the security of recently developed image encryption algorithms (Diaconu, (2017, January)) is founded on the widely recognized observation that any randomly selected pixel in plain images exhibits a strong correlation with its adjacent pixels, regardless of their orientation (be it diagonal, vertical, or horizontal). Anticipated outcomes indicate that the correlation scores between adjacent pixels will be exceedingly low in high-performance image encryption systems. This proposed image encryption scheme protects against differential attacks due to its efficacy. Figure 9 illustrates the correlation distribution of adjacent pixels in three directions. It represents 5000 pairs of neighbors that were selected at random. The y-axis of the correlation distribution corresponds to the intensity value of the adjacent pixel, while the x-axis represents the intensity value of the randomly selected pixel.

$$\text{rxy} = \frac{cov\left(x,y\right)}{\sqrt{D\left(x\right)}*\sqrt{D\left(y\right)}} \tag{17}$$

The following Equation 18 applies to calculations. In the plain and cipher images, x and y represent the pixel values of two identical pixels, respectively.

$$E\left(x\right) = \frac{1}{L}\sum_{i=1}^{L} x1$$

$$D\left(x\right) = \frac{1}{L}\sum_{i=1}^{L}\left(x_1 - E\left(x\right)\right)^2 \tag{18}$$

$$cov\left(x,y\right) = \frac{1}{L}\sum_{i=1}^{L}\left(x_1 - E\left(x\right)\right)\left(y1 - E\left(y\right)\right)$$

The value of L denotes the number of pixels utilized during the computations. The superiority of the encryption method is proportional to the proximity of x, y, and r's to zero.

Table 2 presents the results of the APCC test comparisons. On a scale from +1 to -1, the correlation coefficient between two variables is quantified, where -1 indicates the most severe negative correlation and +1 represents the strongest possible positive connection. Hence, the absence of any evidence suggesting an association between the variables is confirmed when the correlation coefficient equals zero.

In detail, Table 3 compares (Anwar, 2019) and (Fadhil, 2021, February). The correlation coefficients for the plain image are all set to 1, signifying a substantial correlation between pixels. Conversely, the correlation coefficients for the cipher image are all set to zero, suggesting the absence of any observable association among pixels. The proposed method is therefore capable of safeguarding the cipher image against statistical attacks.

4.1.4 UACI and NPCR Tests

UACI and NPCR are the two most commonly employed metrics for assessing the resistance of an algorithm, cipher, or technique to differential attacks in image encryption (Özkaynak, 2017). By comparing

Figure 9. Correlation coefficient test

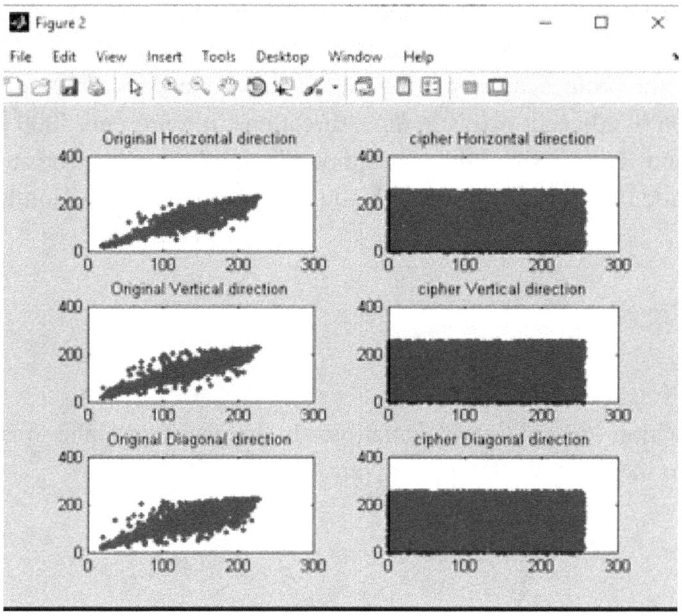

Table 2. Correlation coefficients of two adjacent pixels in two images

	Image	Horizontal	Vertical	Diagonal
Plain Image	Lena	0.9723	0.9860	0.9584
Cipher Image		-0.0086	-0.0204	-0.0140
Plain Image	Cameraman	0.9827	0.9895	0.9715
Cipher Image		-0.0267	-0.0073	-0.0040

Table 3. Correlation coefficient of the proposed scheme and another method

	(Fadhil, 2021)	(Anwar, 2019)	Proposed Scheme
Horizontal	0.00578	0.0068	-0.0267
vertical	0.00830	– 0.033	-0.0073
Diagonal	0.00709	– 0.0474	-0.0040

two cipher images, denoted as C1 and C2, which exhibit minimal variation in their plain images, NPCR computes the rate of pixel change. Furthermore, the average disparity in intensity between the two cipher images, denoted as C1 and C2, is calculated by UACI. In differential attacks, NPCR emphasizes the absolute number of shifting pixel values, whereas UACI emphasizes the average difference between the two cipher images, C1 and C2. To determine both, implement the subsequent formulas.

Table 4. NPCR and UACI analysis

Image Name	NPCR	UACI
Lena	99.60	33.46
cameraman	99.60	33.46

$$\text{NPCR}\left(C1+C2\right)^{\cdot}=\sum_{i=1}^{M}\sum_{j=1}^{N}\frac{D\left(i,j\right)}{M*N}*100\% \quad (19)$$

$$\text{UACI}\left(C1+C2\right)^{\cdot}=\sum_{i=1}^{M}\sum_{j=1}^{N}\frac{D\left(i,j\right)}{255*M*N}*100\% \quad (20)$$

$$\text{D}\left(\text{i, j}\right)=\begin{cases}0, if\, C1\left(\text{i, j}\right)=C2\left(i,j\right)\\ 1, if\, C1\left(\text{i, j}\right)\neq C2\left(i,j\right)\end{cases}$$

The equality of two pixels from cipher images C1 and C2 that are rendered at the same location is ascertained by the difference function D (i,j). (M×N) is the pixel count of the cipher image, and the maximum pixel intensity permitted is (is 255 in 8-bit pixel value). NPCR should be close to 99 percent and UACI should be around 15 percent for an effective image encryption method. The results obtained from applying our proposed technique to a set of encrypted test images using NPCR and UACI are presented in Table 4.

The algorithm's remarkable resistance to differential attacks is demonstrated by the fact that even a minor alteration in the source image leads to a substantial transformation in the ciphered version. Table 5 proposed NPCR and UACI results with another method.

4.1.5 Information Entropy Tests

Information entropy is a quantitative measure of the randomness of a signal source. The total number of symbols is denoted by N, while the probability that message m will be present at position i_{th} is represented by p (mi). Entropy ought to be eight bits at minimum (Wu Y. Z., 2013). As shown in the table, the proposed method of image encryption yields an entropy value that is remarkably close to the ideal value. Therefore, the proposed system is impervious to entropy attacks.

$$H=\sum_{i=0}^{N-1}p\left(m_{i}\right)\times\log_{2}\left(\frac{1}{p(m_{i})}\right) \quad (21)$$

Table 5. NPCR and UACI comparison with literature

	(Fadhil, 2021)	(Anwar, 2019)	Proposed Scheme
NPCR	99.1547	99.62	99.60
UACI	33.2072	33.49	33.46

Table 6. Information entropy analysis comparison with literature

Image Name	(Fadhil, 2021)	(Anwar, 2019)	Proposed Scheme
Gray image	7.9969	7.9969	7.999

5. CONCLUSION AND FUTURE WORK

The current study proposes that the visual data be encrypted utilizing optimal two-dimensional chaotic mapping. The potential consequences may facilitate novel approaches in the domains of data science, cryptography, and image processing, as well as make a significant contribution to the progression of chaos theory. We achieved superior outcomes in terms of Key Space, Key Sensitivity, APCC, UACI, NPCR, and Information Entropy Tests compared to prior research. While its current design is focused on grayscale images, our proposed system has the potential to be extended to color images in subsequent endeavors. In addition, our proposed methodology has the potential to be extended in the future to encompass additional media formats, such as audio and video. In the proposed scheme, a logistic map has been incorporated for the sake of simplicity. Further investigation in this area may explore the integration of more disorderly maps into the proposed framework.

REFERENCES

Ahmad, J., & Hwang, S. O. (2015). Chaos-based diffusion for highly autocorrelated data in encryption algorithms. *Nonlinear Dynamics*, *82*(4), 1839–1850. doi:10.1007/s11071-015-2281-0

Anwar, S., & Meghana, S. (2019). A pixel permutation based image encryption technique using chaotic map. *Multimedia Tools and Applications*, *78*(19), 27569–27590. doi:10.1007/s11042-019-07852-2

Arif, J., Khan, M. A., Ghaleb, B., Ahmad, J., Munir, A., Rashid, U., & Al-Dubai, A. Y. (2022). A novel chaotic permutation-substitution image encryption scheme based on logistic map and random substitution. *IEEE Access : Practical Innovations, Open Solutions*, *10*, 12966–12982. doi:10.1109/ACCESS.2022.3146792

Diaconu, A. V., & Dascalescu, A. C. (2017, January). Correlation distribution of adjacent pixels randomness test for image encryption. *Proc* Rom. Acad. Ser. A.

Fadhil, M. S., Farhan, A. K., & Fadhil, M. N. (2021, February). Designing substitution box based on the 1D logistic map chaotic system. *IOP Conference Series. Materials Science and Engineering*, *1076*(1), 012041. doi:10.1088/1757-899X/1076/1/012041

Farhan, A., Awad, F., & Saad, S. (2017). Enhance the hiding image by using compression and securing techniques. *Iraqi Journal for Computers and Informatics*, *43*(1), 14–16. doi:10.25195/ijci.v43i1.70

Hua, Z., Zhou, B., & Zhou, Y. (2018). Sine chaotification model for enhancing chaos and its hardware implementation. *IEEE Transactions on Industrial Electronics*, *66*(2), 1273–1284. doi:10.1109/TIE.2018.2833049

Hua, Z., & Zhou, Y. (2016). Image encryption using 2D Logistic-adjusted-Sine map. *Information Sciences*, *339*, 237–253. doi:10.1016/j.ins.2016.01.017

Iqbal, N., Hussain, I., Khan, M. A., Abbas, S., & Yousaf, S. (2023). An efficient image cipher based on the 1D scrambled image and 2D logistic chaotic map. *Multimedia Tools and Applications*, *82*(26), 1–29. doi:10.1007/s11042-023-15037-1

Jain, A., & Rajpal, N. (2016). A robust image encryption algorithm resistant to attacks using DNA and chaotic logistic maps. *Multimedia Tools and Applications*, *75*(10), 5455–5472. doi:10.1007/s11042-015-2515-7

Jaradat, A. S., Nasayreh, A., Al-Na'amneh, Q., Gharaibeh, H., & Al Mamlook, R. E. (2023, November). Genetic Optimization Techniques for Enhancing Web Attacks Classification in Machine Learning. In *2023 IEEE Intl Conf on Dependable, Autonomic and Secure Computing, Intl Conf on Pervasive Intelligence and Computing, Intl Conf on Cloud and Big Data Computing, Intl Conf on Cyber Science and Technology Congress (DASC/PiCom/CBDCom/CyberSciTech)* (pp. 130-136). IEEE.

Khanzadi, H., Eshghi, M., & Borujeni, S. E. (2014). Image encryption using random bit sequence based on chaotic maps. *Arabian Journal for Science and Engineering*, *39*(2), 1039–1047. doi:10.1007/s13369-013-0713-z

Li, H., Yu, S., Feng, W., Chen, Y., Zhang, J., Qin, Z., Zhu, Z., & Wozniak, M. (2023). Exploiting dynamic vector-level operations and a 2D-enhanced logistic modular map for efficient chaotic image encryption. *Entropy (Basel, Switzerland)*, *25*(8), 1147. doi:10.3390/e25081147 PMID:37628177

Li, Y., Wang, C., & Chen, H. (2017). A hyper-chaos-based image encryption algorithm using pixel-level permutation and bit-level permutation. *Optics and Lasers in Engineering*, *90*, 238–246. doi:10.1016/j.optlaseng.2016.10.020

Liao, X., Lai, S., & Zhou, Q. (2010). A novel image encryption algorithm based on self-adaptive wave transmission. *Signal Processing*, *90*(9), 2714–2722. doi:10.1016/j.sigpro.2010.03.022

Mughaid, A., Obaidat, I., Aljammal, A., AlZu'bi, S., Quiam, F., Laila, D., Al-zou'bi, A., & Abualigah, L. (2023). Simulation and analysis performance of ad-hoc routing protocols under DDoS attack and proposed solution. *International Journal of Data and Network Science*, *7*(2), 757–764. doi:10.5267/j.ijdns.2023.2.002

Özkaynak, F. (2017, October). Role of NPCR and UACI tests in security problems of chaos based image encryption algorithms and possible solution proposals. In *2017 International conference on computer science and engineering (UBMK)* (pp. 621-624). IEEE. 10.1109/UBMK.2017.8093481

Pen, L. Z., Xian Xian, K., Yew, C. F., Hau, O. S., Sumari, P., Abualigah, L., Ezugwu, A. E., Shinwan, M. A., Gul, F., & Mughaid, A. (2022). *Artocarpusclassification technique using deep learning based convolutional neuralnetwork. In Classification Applications with Deep Learning and Ma-chine Learning Technologies.* Springer.

Saini, L. K., & Shrivastava, V. (2014). A survey of digital watermarking techniques and its applications. arXiv preprint arXiv:1407.4735.

Sharma, M. (2020). Image encryption based on a new 2D logistic adjusted logistic map. *Multimedia Tools and Applications*, *79*(1-2), 355–374. doi:10.1007/s11042-019-08079-x

Tahmasbi, M., Boostani, R., Aljaidi, M., & Attar, H. (2022, November). Improving Organizations Security Using Visual Cryptography Based on XOR and Chaotic-Based Key. In *2022 International Engineering Conference on Electrical, Energy, and Artificial Intelligence (EICEEAI)* (pp. 1-6). IEEE. 10.1109/EICEEAI56378.2022.10050448

Wang, B., Xie, Y., Zhou, C., Zhou, S., & Zheng, X. (2016). Evaluating the permutation and diffusion operations used in image encryption based on chaotic maps. *Optik (Stuttgart)*, *127*(7), 3541–3545. doi:10.1016/j.ijleo.2016.01.015

Wu, Y., Yang, G., Jin, H., & Noonan, J. P. (2012). Image encryption using the two-dimensional logistic chaotic map. *Journal of Electronic Imaging*, *21*(1), 013014–013014. doi:10.1117/1.JEI.21.1.013014

Wu, Y., Zhou, Y., Saveriades, G., Agaian, S., Noonan, J. P., & Natarajan, P. (2013). Local Shannon entropy measure with statistical tests for image randomness. *Information Sciences*, *222*, 323–342. doi:10.1016/j.ins.2012.07.049

Xiang, H., & Liu, L. (2020). An improved digital logistic map and its application in image encryption. Multimedia Tools and Applications, 79, 30329-30355.

Yavuz, E., Yazıcı, R., Kasapbaşı, M. C., & Yamaç, E. (2016). A chaos-based image encryption algorithm with simple logical functions. *Computers & Electrical Engineering*, *54*, 471–483. doi:10.1016/j.compeleceng.2015.11.008

Zhang, J., & Huo, D. (2019). Image encryption algorithm based on quantum chaotic map and DNA coding. *Multimedia Tools and Applications*, *78*(11), 15605–15621. doi:10.1007/s11042-018-6973-6

Zhou, Y., Panetta, K., Agaian, S., & Chen, C. P. (2012). Image encryption using P-Fibonacci transform and decomposition. *Optics Communications*, *285*(5), 594–608. doi:10.1016/j.optcom.2011.11.044

Zhu, H., Zhao, Y., & Song, Y. (2019). 2D logistic-modulated-sine-coupling-logistic chaotic map for image encryption. *IEEE Access : Practical Innovations, Open Solutions*, *7*, 14081–14098. doi:10.1109/ACCESS.2019.2893538

Chapter 11
An Approach for Safe Network Image Communication Using Hybrid Cloud and Half Tensor Product Compression Perception

Madhura K.
Presidency University, India

Kamal Kant
Jai Narain Vyas University, India

Roshan Baa
https://orcid.org/0000-0002-6582-4372
St. Xavier's College, India

Sabyasachi Pramanik
https://orcid.org/0000-0002-9431-8751
Haldia Institute of Technology, India

Rohaila Naaz
Teerthanker Mahaveer University, India

Ankur Gupta
https://orcid.org/0000-0002-4651-5830
Vaish College of Engineering, India

Siddth Kumar Chhajer
St. Peter's University, India

ABSTRACT

Since the beginning of the digital era, there has been an increasing focus on picture security since it is a crucial medium for the transfer of information. In this regard, the study develops a hybrid cloud and half-tensor compression-aware technology network image security transmission technique. Following an introduction to the fundamentals of cryptography and its use in the encryption of images, the relevant compression perception methods are expounded upon. In order to further secure the security of network pictures during transmission, the research then suggests the half-tensor product compression perception approach and integrates this technique with the hybrid cloud idea to build a new image encryption and decryption algorithm. According to the findings, the suggested method obtains the greatest peak signal-to-noise ratio value of 31.89 and structural similarity index value of 0.97, respectively. In addition, the lowest values for the times spent on encryption and decryption are 2.128 and 0.288, respectively, indicating that these techniques need less time than others.

DOI: 10.4018/979-8-3693-2691-6.ch011

1. INTRODUCTION

Network pictures are becoming more and more essential in everyday life and a variety of businesses as a vital information carrier. But this also poses serious problems for the safe transfer of picture data, particularly when it comes to private information and trade secrets. Techniques for transmitting images that are both secure and efficient are crucial for protecting the confidentiality and integrity (Amin S N et al. 2023) of data. Presently, compression-aware approaches and classic encryption algorithms are the main focus of picture encryption and transmission methods. However, when working with large-scale picture data, these approaches often run into issues with slowness and inadequate security. Furthermore, some academics have suggested cloud-based picture transmission and storage solutions via the use of cloud computing technology; nevertheless, these solutions continue to face difficulties with processing complexity and cost-effectiveness. This context informs the research's construction of an algorithm that combines the notion of a hybrid cloud with semi-tensor product compression perception to enable safe picture transmission across networks. The primary components of this method are picture encryption and image decryption. Its goal is to fulfill the growing demands of network security while simultaneously improving the security and efficiency of image transmission (Bao W et al. 2022). The novel aspect of this study is how the algorithm's processing of high-dimensional data may be made more flexible and efficient by using the semi-tensor product compression perception approach. In the meanwhile, the image processing system's scalability and security may be further increased by using the hybrid cloud architecture, which combines edge and center clouds to maximize data processing and transmission. The research's findings have significant theoretical and practical implications for network image transmission security. In addition to offering a fresh technological avenue for safe picture transfer, the developed encryption and decryption algorithm encourages the use and development of cloud computing and compressed sensing technologies in the realm of network security. The research is broken up into four sections. Prior research is examined and analyzed in order to establish the primary focus of current investigation. Creating a safe transmission technique for network photos is the second step. Testing and analysis of the algorithm developed by the research institution constitute the third section. The research information is summarized and given a view in the last section.

2. LITERATURE REVIEW

Since compressed perception requires less sampling data to recover and reconstruct the signal, it is an emerging signal processing technology with significant research value in the fields of image processing, signal feature extraction, data acquisition, and so forth. Numerous experts have conducted research on compressed perception technology. In order to avoid the effects of chunking, Wang et al. suggested a multiscale dilated convolutional neural network that can directly extract the measurement value via the whole convolution structure. In order to extract picture characteristics more successfully, the multiscale feature extraction (Zha Z et al. 2023) architecture may replicate human vision throughout the reconstruction process. Through the use of parallel convolutional channels, the framework combines feature information from several scales to achieve high-quality picture reconstruction. Tests show that the suggested approach beats other cutting-edge methods in terms of peak signal-to-noise ratio (Gupta M et al. 2023) and structural similarity index. Using compressed perception and complementary color waveform transform, Yu et al. presented a unique method for assessing picture quality. By using a complimentary waveform transform, the technique is able to conduct multi-subband decomposition of colour pictures while retaining all of the color channel information and successfully capturing the distortion caused by digital processes. Features are extracted from the subbands using the block-based compressed perception approach, and the resulting perceptual features are compact, discriminative, and very resilient. Eventually, these perceptual characteristics are quantized to create a hash sequence. According to the experimental findings, the hash method performs better in terms of classification ability and minimizes the evaluation of reference picture quality. Wang and colleagues presented a data-driven diagnostic approach that combines convolutional neural networks with compressed perception to address the issue of accurately diagnosing inverters in solar systems in real time. The study's findings demonstrate that the approach reduces processing time to a mere fifth of the original one while improving accuracy by almost 3% when compared to the conventional technique. Comparing this to a convolutional neural network with the same topology, an order of magnitude decrease in calculation time and data transfer is accomplished at the same time. The term "secure encrypted transmission of images" describes a set of procedures used to protect the availability, confidentiality, and integrity of images against corruption, manipulation, or unwanted access. Image encryption is a crucial idea in the field of information security. It has been researched by numerous academics and is typically used in a variety of image transmission and sharing scenarios, such as Internet communication, wireless transmission, cloud storage, and multimedia applications. Gupta et al. provide a picture encryption methodology that combines cryptography and watermarking methods, especially to offer technological assistance for safe image transfer between IoT devices. The technique involves two layers of encryption: one layer encrypts images using crossover operations and mixed logic chaotic map, while the second layer implements discrete wavelet transform for the watermarking approach. A random session key for picture encryption is generated using the crossover operation and chaotic map, and the encrypted secret image is placed as a watermark. The results demonstrate the enhanced information entropy performance of the suggested picture encryption technique, confirming its robust resistance to a range of cryptographic threats. A unique picture encryption technique was suggested by Bao and Zhu with the goal of enabling safe image communication. The program uses the chaotic sequence produced by logistic mapping to cause disruption after first dividing the picture into high and low frequency blocks using the Haar wavelet transform. After completing the signal measurement, the high-frequency blocks use the Chan chaotic system to create a measurement matrix. All of the blocks are then subjected to addition and dynamic DNA encoding processes. Lastly, logistic mapping is used to mix and conceal each block. The method is tested against a variety of common attacks, including differential, noise, and masking assaults. The experimental findings demonstrate the algorithm's excellent security and resilience as well as its good encryption performance. In conclusion, substantial advancements in the fields of picture encryption and compressed perception have been made. By minimizing the sample data, the compressed perception approach efficiently reconstructs the signal. Meanwhile, the multi-scale expansion convolutional neural network enhances the quality of picture reconstruction and resolves the block effect issue. Moreover, the use of a chaotic system and double-layer encryption technique in picture encryption transmission improves the security of image data. Even though these studies have made significant strides in terms of innovative technology and useful applications, more study is still needed on the safe transmission of networked pictures when combined with compressed sensing and hybrid cloud settings. In order to increase transmission efficiency and security, fill in research gaps, and offer new theoretical and technical support for the secure transmission of image data, this study will investigate secure transmission algorithms for network images based on semi-tensor product compressed sensing and hybrid clouds.

3. STUDY ON HYBRID CLOUD AND SEMI-TENSOR PRODUCT COMPRESSION PERCEPTION FOR SAFE ENCRYPTED NETWORK IMAGE TRANSMISSION

The fundamentals of cryptography are initially discussed in this study, along with how they relate to the encryption of images. Subsequently, the paper presents the methods associated with Compressed Sensing (CS) (Lang J et al. 2023). Ultimately, a hybrid cloud and half tensor product compressed sensing are combined to provide an image safe encrypted transmission mechanism.

3.1 Compression-Aware Approaches and Cryptographic Knowledge

A crucial component of information security is cryptography, which is the development and examination of protocols and algorithms meant to keep data safe from unwanted access. Ensuring information authenticity, secrecy, integrity, and non-repudiation is the core goal of cryptography. The two forms of key encryption that make up cryptography are symmetric and asymmetric, and Figure 1 illustrates the structures of both types of encryption.

The structures of symmetric encryption and asymmetric encryption are shown in Figures 1(a) and 1(b), respectively. Asymmetric encryption is primarily composed of input, encryption, decryption, output, public key, and private key, as shown in Figure 1(a). Symmetric encryption is primarily composed of input, encryption, decryption, output, and key, as shown in Figure 1(b). The same key is utilized for both encryption and decryption (Wang Z et al. 2023) in symmetric encryption structures. On the other hand, an asymmetric encryption procedure uses a private key for decryption and a public key for encryption. A communication may be encrypted using the public key, which is accessible to anyone, but it can only be decrypted by the owner of the matching private key. Asymmetric encryption has the benefit of enhancing key management security via the use of both public and private keys. Its functioning is more intricate, however. On the other hand, symmetric encryption presents a barrier related to the safe transfer and handling of the key, even though it uses the same key for both encryption and decryption. Table 1 displays typical cryptographic attack strategies and the composition of cryptosystems.

Table 1 lists the elements of a cryptosystem as well as typical cryptographic attack techniques. The key is compromised since it has to be kept a secret between the two parties, and anybody with the key may decipher the encrypted communication. To protect the privacy of the communication, symmetric and asymmetric encryption is often combined in real-world application scenarios. In signal processing, compressed perception—also referred to as compression sampling or sparse sampling—is a method.

Figure 1. Asymmetric and symmetric encryption's structural diagram

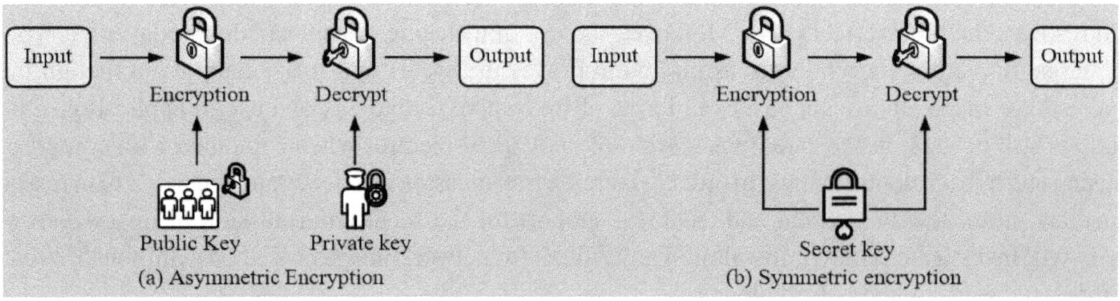

Table 1. Composition of the password system and assault plan

Type	Name	Meaning
Cryptosystem composition	Plain text	Encryption of information to be processed by the system
	Ciphertext	Information generated by encryption algorithms
	Encryption Algorithm	Mapping relationship between plaintext and ciphertext
	Decryption algorithm	Mapping relationship between ciphertext and plaintext
	Key	Tools used to convert plaintext to ciphertext
Attack plan	Ciphertext-only attack	Attack only ciphertext
	Chosen plaintext attack	Only attack special plaintext
	Known plaintext attack	Attack partial plaintext-ciphertext pairs
	Chosen ciphertext attack	Attack special ciphertext

By using the sparse nature of the signal, the method makes reconstruction of the signal possible from a much less number of sample points than those needed by the conventional sampling theorem. Compressed perception is often utilized in picture compression encryption schemes because to its ability to do simultaneous signal sampling and compression. Figure 2 illustrates the compressed perception process in the signal.

The coding end and the decoding end make up the majority of the compressed perception approach shown in Figure 2, and the three key processes in its operation are sparsification, measurement, and reconstruction. The sparsity of the signal and the measurement's lack of adaptation form the basis of the whole compressed perception process. A small number of non-zero coefficients that describe the signal are guaranteed by sparsity, and an accurate recovery of these few coefficients from a limited number of measurements is ensured by non-adaptive measurement. The quantity of data needed for signal collecting and transmission is greatly decreased because to the compressed perception technique's ability to effectively recreate the signal without full sampling. Let us assume that the discrete signal is and

Figure 2. Compressed perception work flow chart

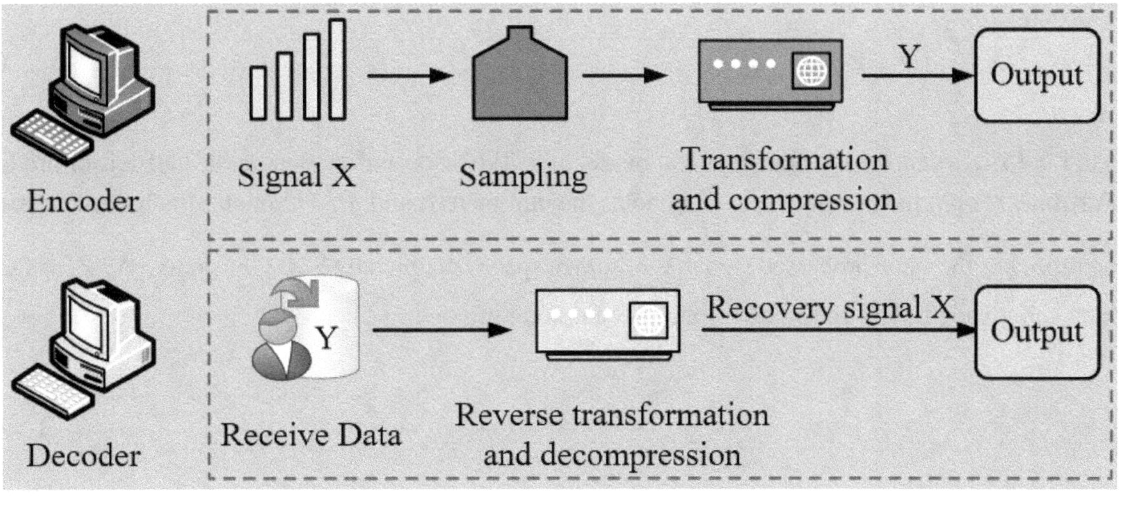

that the chosen sparse matrix is. indicates the number of vectors and the signal set. Eq. (1) provides the formula for projecting the discrete signal into the sparse matrix in order to achieve order sparsification.

$$x = \Psi s \tag{1}$$

In Eq. (1), s denotes the sparse coefficient vector. When the coefficient vector contains K non-zero elements, the coefficients represent K order sparse. Since the sparse matrix is an orthogonal basis matrix, Ψ satisfies Eq. (2).

$$\Psi\Psi^{\mathrm{T}} = \Psi^{\mathrm{T}}\Psi = 1 \tag{2}$$

In Eq. (2), Ψ^{T} denotes the transpose of Ψ. Assuming that the measurement matrix is $\Phi \in R^{M\times N}\left(M < N\right)$, the signal measurement calculation formula is obtained as shown in Eq. (3).

$$y = \Phi x = \Phi\Psi s \tag{3}$$

In Eq. (3), y denotes the signal measurements. Assuming that the perception matrix is $A = \Phi\Psi$, the expression for the sparsification of the signal in the reconstruction process is obtained as shown in Eq. (4).

$$s' = \Phi\Psi s = As \tag{4}$$

In Eq. (4), s' denotes the sparsity of the reconstructed signal under the perceptual matrix.

Semi-tensor Product Compressive Sensing (STP-CS) innovates on the basis of traditional compressed sensing by overcoming the limitation of matrix multiplication dimension and no longer restricts the consistency of the number of columns of the measurement matrix with the length of the original signal. This advancement enhances the applicability and flexibility of compressed sensing techniques. Assuming that the measurement matrix in STP-CS is $\Phi_{STP} \in R^{M\times N}\left(M < N\right)$, the mathematical model of STP-CS is obtained as shown in Eq. (5).

$$Y = \Phi_{STP} \propto x = \left(\Phi_{STP} \otimes I_{P/N}\right)x \tag{5}$$

In Eq. (5), Y denotes the mathematical model of STP-CS. $\propto$ and $\otimes$ denote the half-tensor product and Kronecker product, respectively. I denotes the unit matrix, and P/N denotes the reduced dimension ratio. For the same processed signal, the storage space occupied by STP-CS is only $\left(N/P\right)^2$ of CS, which can greatly reduce the storage space occupation ratio.

3.2 Developing a Secure Network Image Transmission Technique That Combines STP-CS and Hybrid Cloud

The research also integrates concepts from Hybrid Cloud with STP-CS to build a network image security transmission algorithm (Semi-tensor Product Compressive Sensing-Hybrid Cloud, STP-CS-HC) that guarantees the privacy, integrity, security, and efficiency of pictures throughout the transmission process. The two components of the developed picture security transmission algorithm are the image encryption algorithm and the image decryption algorithm. First, Figure 3 illustrates the structure of the picture encryption technique after it has been studied.

Figure 3 shows the picture encryption algorithm's component structure. There are two steps to the whole encryption process. At the local end, the first step involves sparsification and scrambling of the given plaintext picture. The picture is compressed and diffused in the edge cloud in the second step, producing the processed ciphertext image. Lastly, transfer of the encrypted ciphertext picture to the central cloud for storage will be accepted. First, the hash values of the plaintext picture are generated during the image encryption process using a 256-bit generator function of a secure hash algorithm. These hashes are separated into groups of eight bits, and the matching initial encrypted values may be created using the initial key. 2D-LSCM uses these original encrypted data to generate a chaotic sequence. Furthermore, because the cloud's reliability is in question, it is imperative to ensure that it won't return the calculation result arbitrarily during the data processing process. For this reason, the research performed edge detection, authentication image embedding, sparse, chaotic Discrete Wavelet Transform (DWT),

Figure 3. The picture encryption algorithm's structural structure

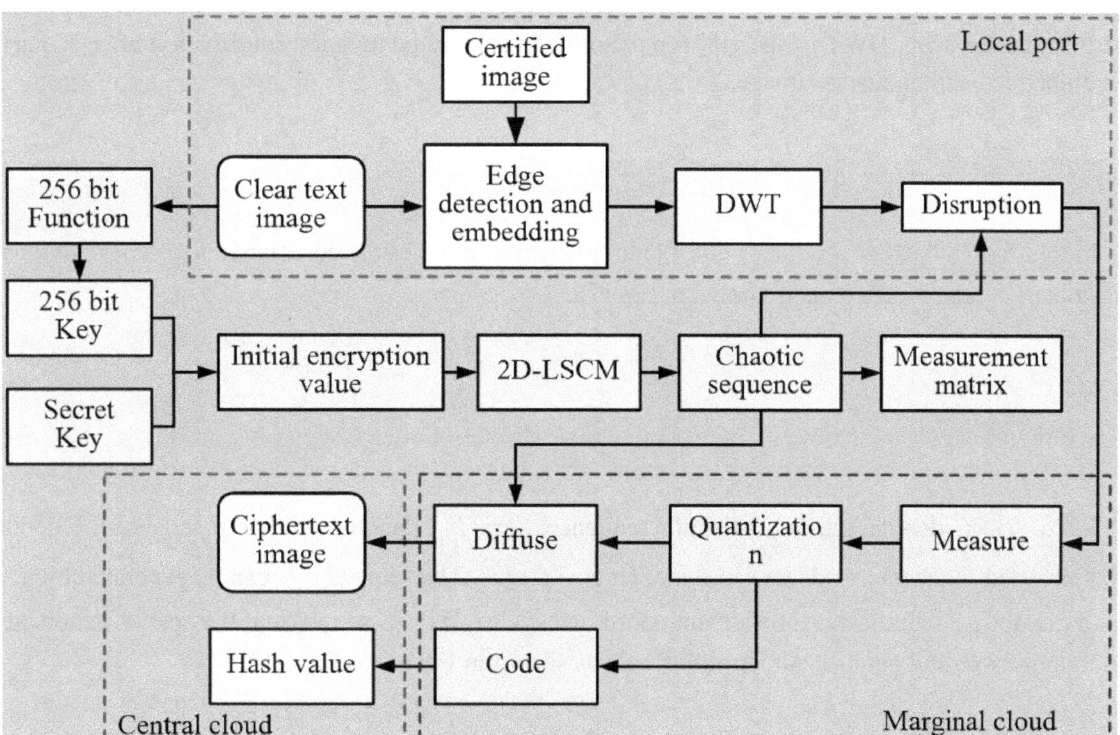

Figure 4. A pipeline plan for authenticated picture embedding and edge detection

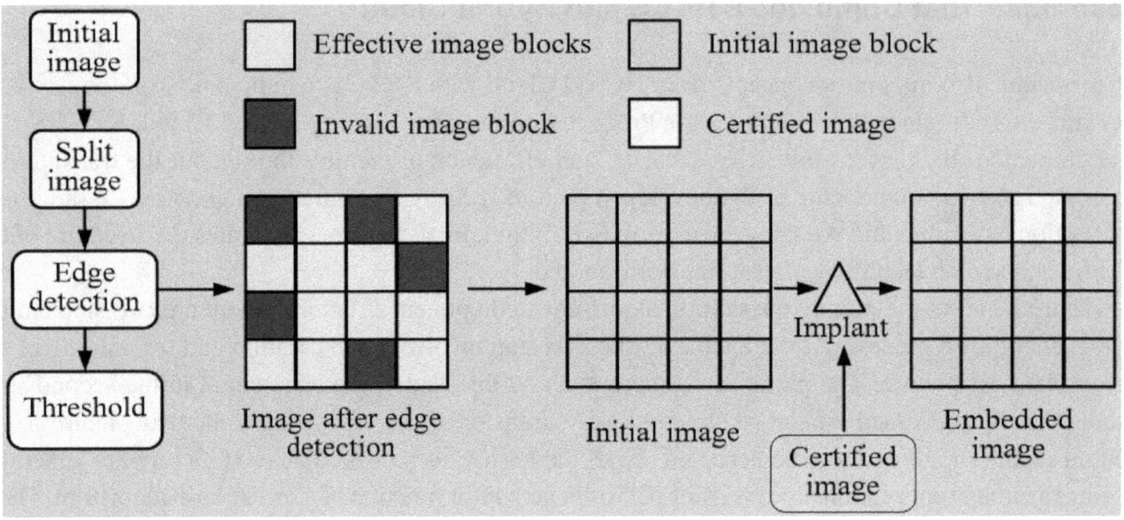

and other operations on the plaintext image. Figure 4 illustrates the verified picture embedding and edge detection procedure.

The flowchart for authenticated image embedding and edge detection is shown in Figure 4. Prior to calculating the validity of each picture block, the input image must first be segmented in order to separate the plaintext image into non-overlapping image blocks. Each image block is then detected using Prewitt edge detection. The encrypted embedded authentication picture is then acquired when the threshold has been established and the detection result has been mapped to the original image. Equation (6) provides the formula for using DWT to sparsify the picture carrying authentication information after acquiring the embedded authentication image.

$$P_2 = \Psi \times P_1 \times \Psi^{T} \tag{6}$$

In Eq. (6), P_2 denotes the sparse coefficient matrix. P_1 denotes the certified image. The disordering formula of sparse coefficients is shown in Eq. (7).

$$\begin{cases} \left[Z_1', s_1\right] = sort\left(Z_0\right) \\ l_2\left(s_1\left(k\right)\right) = l_1\left(k\right) \end{cases} \tag{7}$$

In Eq. (7), Z_1' denotes the authentication sequence. $sort\left(Z_0\right)$ denotes the chaotic sequence. l_1 denotes P_2 converted sequence. s_1 denotes the indexing sequence. The sequence l_2 can be generated by using s_1 to disrupt l_1. k Indicates the element coordinates. Use STP-CS to measure the sparse vectors after disorganization, and get its calculation formula as shown in Eq. (8) to Eq. (10).

$$\begin{cases} X_1 = \left(X_0 \times 10^{14} \bmod 1\right) - 0.5 \\ Y_1 = \left(Y_0 \times 10^{14} \bmod 1\right) - 0.5 \\ XY_1 = floor\left(\left(X_0 + Y_0\right) \times 10^{14} \bmod 2\right) \end{cases} \tag{8}$$

In Eq. (8), X_0 and Y_0 denote chaotic sequences of size $1 \times r^2$, and X_1, Y_1, and XY_1 denote sequences after preprocessing. According to the value of the sequence XY_1, the elements of X_1 and Y_1 are selected to generate a new sequence XY. The matrix $\Phi 1$ is converted from XY to $r \times r$ with the conversion formula shown in Eq. (9).

$$XY\left(i\right) = \begin{cases} X\left(i\right) & XY_1\left(i\right) = 0 \\ Y\left(i\right) & XY_1\left(i\right) = 1 \end{cases} \tag{9}$$

In Eq. (9), $XY\left(i\right)$ denotes the element under the matrix $\Phi 1$. When the sequence $XY_1\left(i\right)$ takes the values 0 and 1, $XY\left(i\right)$ is the element $X\left(i\right)$ and the element $Y\left(i\right)$, respectively. The partial sequence of $\Phi 1$ is used to construct the measurement matrix $\Phi 2$ with the size of $p \times r$, and then $\Phi 2$ is used to measure the sparse matrix P_3, and the formula of the measurement value matrix is shown in Eq. (10).

$$P_4 = \Phi 2 \propto P_3 \tag{10}$$

In Eq. (10), P_4 denotes the matrix of measured values. P_4 the size of the matrix is $m \times N$. The quantization of P_4 yields Eq. (11).

$$P_5 = round\left(\frac{255 \times \left(P_4 - \min\right)}{\max - \min}\right) \tag{11}$$

In Eq. (11), P_5 represents the matrix of measured values after quantizing the element values to [0-255]. $\min_{,}\ \max_{,\text{ each}}$ denotes the lowest and greatest P_4, respectively. In order to make sure the center cloud can correctly return the graphical processing results, it is necessary to do image encoding before it is uploaded to the center cloud, and its encoding formula is shown in Eq. (12).

$$DS\left(i\right) = \begin{cases} 1 & L\left(i\right) \bmod 2 = 1 \\ 0 & L\left(i\right) \bmod 2 = 0 \end{cases} \tag{12}$$

In Eq. (12), $DS\left(i\right)$ denotes a binary sequence. $L\left(i\right)$ denotes a sequence consisting of one element selected from each line of P_5.

Figure 5. Structure of an image decryption method

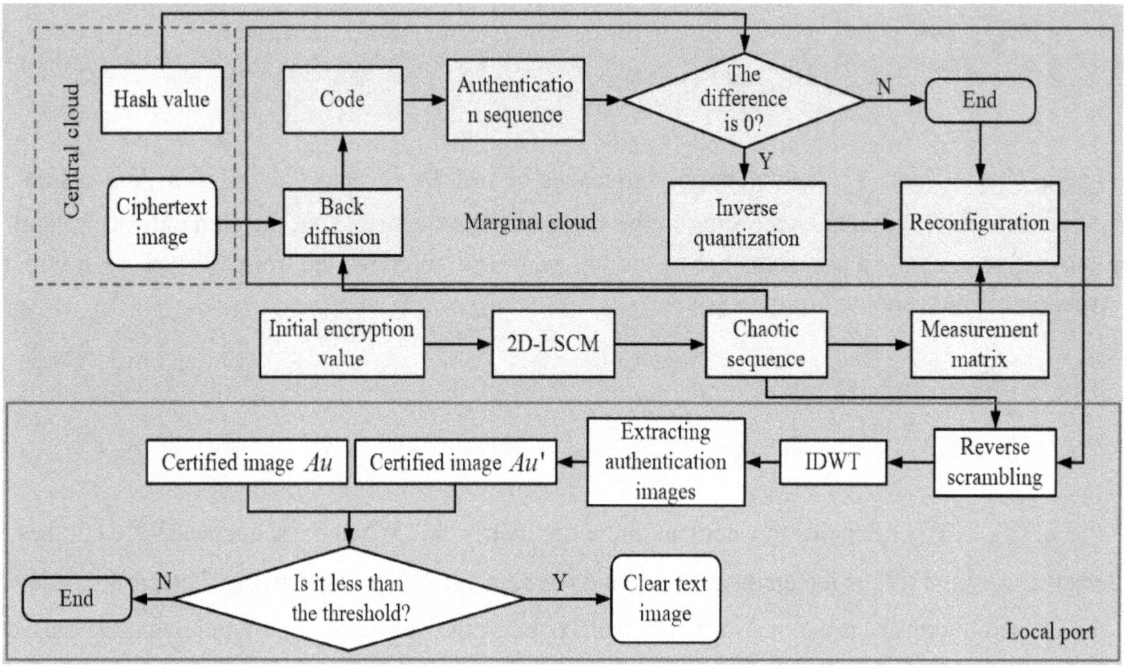

Decrypting the returned picture is necessary in addition to the encryption process on the original image. Sending the plaintext image's hash key from the local end to the center cloud and the external key to the edge cloud is a prerequisite for decryption. These keys are then introduced to the chaotic system in order to generate the appropriate sequence. Figure 5 depicts the composition of the picture decryption method.

The centre cloud, edge cloud, and local end are the three basic components of the picture decryption process shown in Figure 5. The counter-diffusion procedure in the edge cloud will first be applied to the ciphertext picture that is kept in the center cloud. The ciphertext picture is first segmented and converted into a sequence of images before to the counter-diffusion procedure. The authentication sequence is acquired and the obtained sequence is encoded. After comparing the obtained authentication sequence with the authentication sequences transmitted from the center cloud, if there is no difference between the two, it indicates that the ciphertext was not altered during transmission. In this case, the sequence that passes through the conscientiousness can be rebuilt using inverse quantization and compression-aware reconstruction. The rebuilt sequence will then undergo further processing using inverse DWT sparse and inverse disambiguation. At this point, the authentication image will be extracted. Its features will be compared to the ciphertext authentication image that was provided. If the calculated value is less than the predetermined threshold, it will be assumed that the decryption process was error-free and that the decrypted image could obtain the final authentication. Conversely, it is believed that the information used in the decryption process has been altered in the ciphertext picture, necessitating further decryption.

4. NETWORK IMAGE SECURITY TRANSMISSION ALGORITHM PERFORMANCE TESTING AND APPLICATION ANALYSIS INTEGRATING HYBRID CLOUD AND STP-CS

This research chooses Advanced Encryption Standard (AES), Logistic Mapping Encryption Algorithm, and Compressive Sensing Based on Random Projection (CS-EABRP) as the comparison algorithms for simulation experiments and analyzes the practical application effect of STP-CS-HC in order to demonstrate the performance of the proposed STP-CS-HC network image security transmission algorithm. As comparing algorithms for simulation tests, Encryption Algorithm Based on Random Projection (CS-EABRP) is used, and the impact of STP-CS-HC in real-world applications is examined.

4.1 STP-CS-HC Network Image Security Transmission Technique Performance Test

This research conducted the simulation in the same experimental environment to guarantee that the experimental procedure can prevent the mistake brought on by the change in experimental environment. Table 2 displays the details of the dataset and experimental setup. Table 2 details the experimental setup and data collection.

Details about the particular experimental setup and dataset are provided in Table 2. The dataset's data must first undergo preprocessing, which may include scaling and format conversion. After that, the picture must be augmented with data to make detection easier. First, the four algorithms' Peak Signal-to-Noise Ratio (PSNR) values from the MSCOCO and ImageNet datasets are compared, and Figure 6 displays their PSNR curves.

The PSNR values for each of the four techniques in the two datasets are shown in Figure 6. Algorithm 3 is identified as AES, Algorithm 2 as Logistic Mapping Encryption Algorithm, and Algorithm 1 as CS-EABRP. The PSNR values of STP-CS-HC, Algorithm 1, Algorithm 2, and Algorithm 3 for the dataset MSCOCO rise as the compression rate increases, as shown in Figure 6(a). The peak PSNR values of all four algorithms—31.89, 28.61, 28.15, and 26.08, respectively—are achieved at a compression rate of

Table 2. Experimental set and data collection

Type	Project	Illustrate
Lab environment	CPU	Intel Core i7
	Memory	16GB RAM
	Storage	1TB SSD
	Operating system	Windows 10
	Programming language	Python 3.8
	Development tools	PyCharm
	Deep learning framework	TensorFlow 2.0
Dataset settings	Data set name	MSCOCO and ImageNet
	Image type	Contains various types of images, such as natural scenes, people, objects, etc.
	Number of data	100000

Figure 6. PSNR

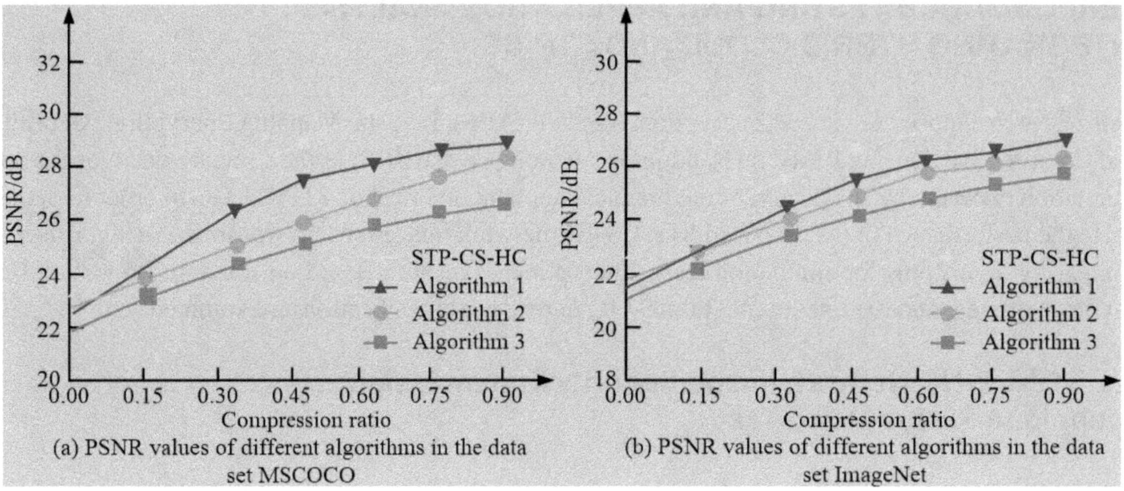

0.90. As the compression rate increases, the PSNR values of STP-CS-HC, Algorithm 1, Algorithm 2, and Algorithm 3 in the dataset ImageNet also rise; however, the overall increase is less than that in the dataset MSCOCO (Zhang J et al. 2023), as shown in Figure 6(b). The PSNR values of the four methods are, in order, 28.35, 26.91, 26.15, and 25.56 when the compression rate is set to 0.90.

The Structural Similarity Index Measure (SSIM) values variation curves for the four methods in the two datasets are shown in Figure 7. As the number of samples in the MSCOCO dataset (Wang X et al. 2023) rises, the SSIM values of the four methods drop, as shown in Figure 7(a). The STP-CS-HC algorithm's SSIM value drops from 0.97 to 0.89 as the number of samples rises from 100 to 700. Algorithm 1's SSIM value drops from 0.93 to 0.83. Algorithm 2's SSIM value drops from 0.94 to 0.72. Algorithm 3's SSIM value drops from 0.93 to 0.68. The SSIM values of STP-CS-HC, Algorithm 1, Algorithm 2, and Algorithm 3 in the dataset ImageNet (Yu M et al. 2022) also exhibit diminishing SSIM values as

Figure 7. SSIM values

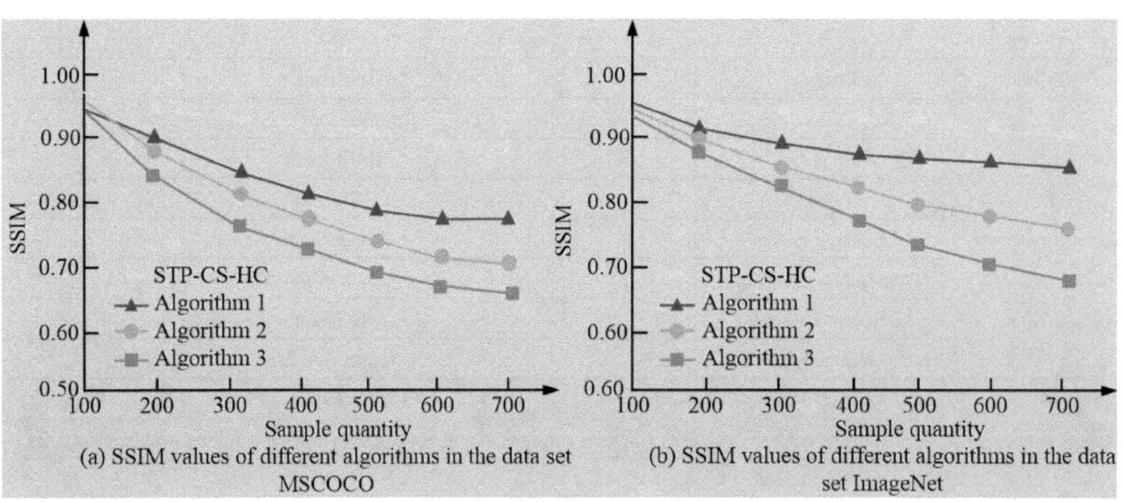

Table 3. Different methods' encryption and decryption times

Algorithm Type	Image Type	Encryption Time	Decryption Time	Total Encryption and Decryption Time
STP-CS-HC	Brone	2.315	0.306	2.621
	Lena.	2.128	0.294	2.422
	Peppers	2.339	0.315	2.654
	house	2.256	0.288	2.544
CS-EABRP (Algorithm 1)	Brone	5.649	2.361	8.010
	Lena.	5.327	2.308	7.635
	Peppers	5.218	2.299	7.517
	house	5.351	2.314	7.665
Logistic (Algorithm 2)	Brone	9.658	7.311	16.969
	Lena.	9.642	7.352	16.994
	Peppers	9.548	7.318	16.866
	house	9.618	7.306	16.924
AES (Algorithm 3)	Brone	15.648	12.364	28.012
	Lena.	15.682	12.298	27.980
	Peppers	15.289	12.287	27.576
	house	15.371	12.310	27.681

the number of samples grows, as seen in Figure 7(b). The SSIM values of the four methods are, in order, 0.92, 0.89, 0.78, and 0.69 when there are 700 samples.

The four algorithms' encryption and decryption timings for the four photos of Brone, Lena, Peppers, and House are listed in Table 3. The STP-CS-HC algorithm's encryption and decryption times in the four photos are much less than those of the other three methods, according to a comparison of the data in Table 1. STP-CS-HC algorithm encryption times are 2.315, 2.128, 2.339, and 2.256 in Brone, Lena, Peppers, and House, respectively; decryption times are 0.306, 0.294, 0.315, and 0.288, while the overall encryption and decryption times are 2.621, 2.422, 2.654, and 2.544.

The picture loss errors are used to calculate the feature loss in the image encryption and decryption process. Figure 8 shows the image loss errors of the four techniques in the two datasets. Figure 8(a) shows that after 11, 25, 30, and 39 iterations, respectively, STP-CS-HC, Algorithm 1, Algorithm 2, and Algorithm 3 are able to maintain stability. At that point, the values of the four methods that deal with the image loss error in the MSCOCO dataset are 0.04, 0.05, 0.19, and 0.28. Based on Figure 8(b), it can be shown that STP-CS-HC (Wang Z et al. 2023), Algorithm 1, Algorithm 2, and Algorithm 3 can maintain stability after 17, 26, 38, and 45 iterations, respectively. At this point, the four methods used to process the ImageNet dataset had corresponding image loss error values of 0.01 through 0.27.

4.2 Evaluation of the STP-CS-HC Network Image Security Transmission Algorithm's Application Impact

The study chose CS-EABRP and STP-CS-HC, which perform best among the compared algorithms (Singh K N et al. 2022), to process four different types of images in order to further test the algorithms'

Figure 8. Algorithm-specific image loss mistakes

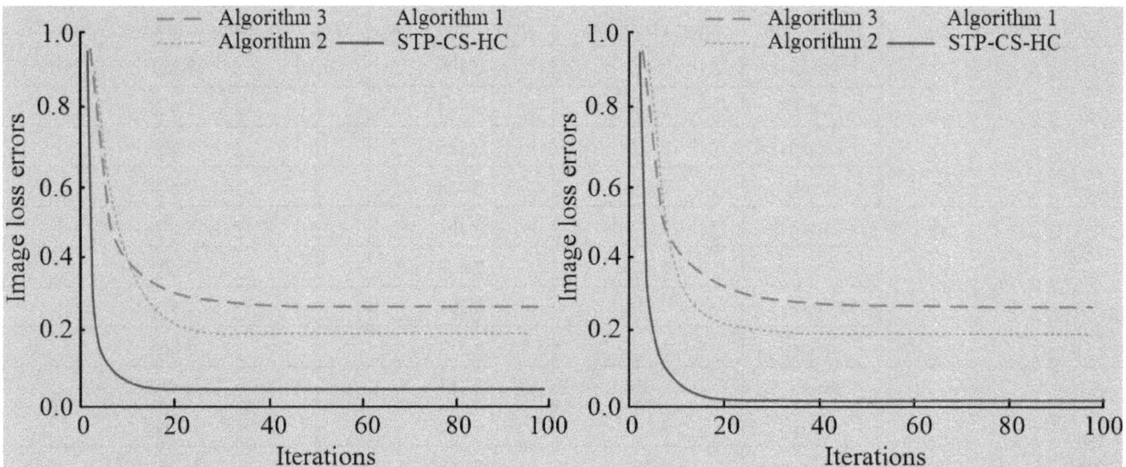

(a) Image loss errors of different algorithms in the MSCOCO dataset

(b) Image loss errors of different algorithms in the ImageNet dataset

Figure 9. A comparison between STP-CS-HC and CS-EABRP's visual processing findings

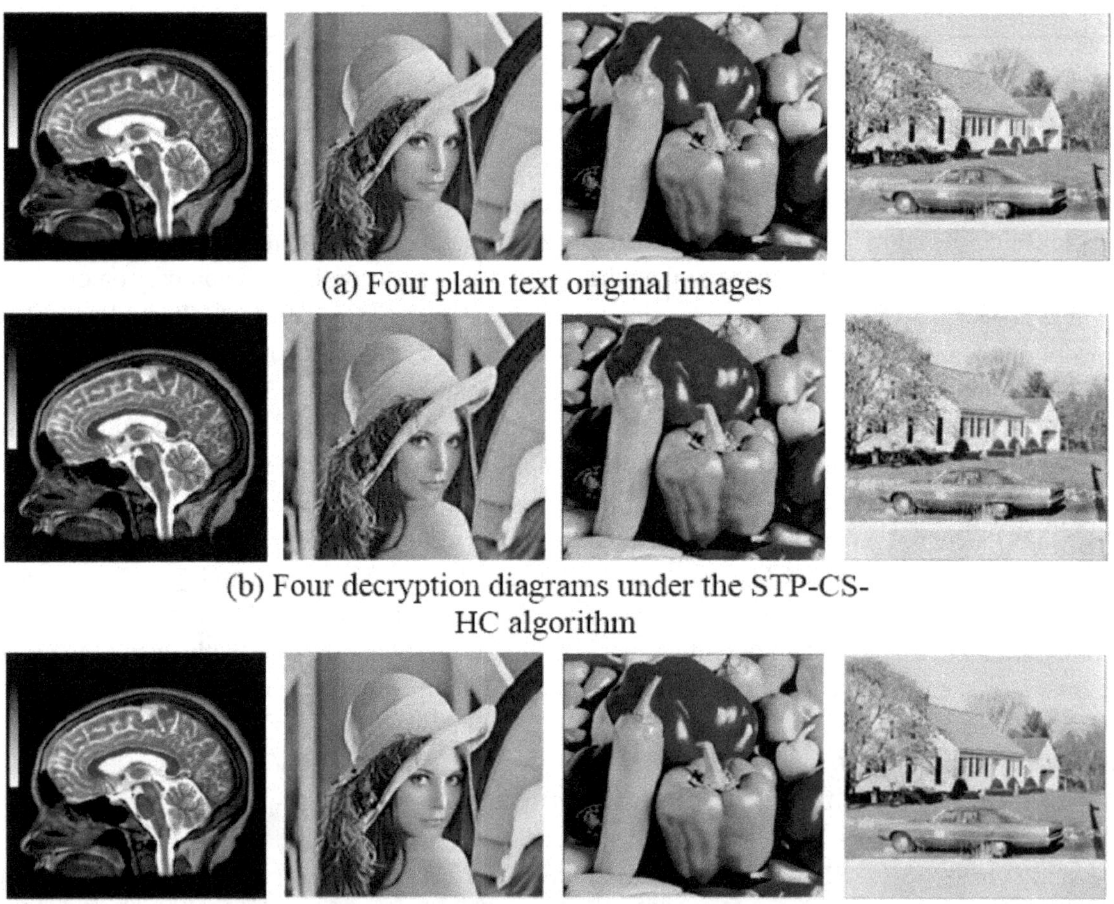

(a) Four plain text original images

(b) Four decryption diagrams under the STP-CS-HC algorithm

(c) Four decryption diagrams under the CS-EABRP algorithm

Table 4. Correlation coefficient values between plaintext and ciphertext obtained from processing four distinct kinds of photos using various methods

Type	Image Type	Clear Text Image			Ciphertext Image		
		Horizontal	Vertical	Diagonal	Horizontal	Vertical	Diagonal
STP-CS-HC	Brone	0.986	0.984	0.967	-0.002	-0.003	-0.001
	Lena.	0.986	0.971	0.965	0.005	-0.009	-0.005
	Peppers	0.983	0.981	0.977	-0.005	-0.001	0.002
	house	0.965	0.948	0.935	0.008	0.009	0.003
CS-EABRP	Brone	0.895	0.892	0.889	0.023	0.035	0.028
	Lena.	0.912	0.905	0.916	0.026	-0.034	-0.033
	Peppers	0.887	0.884	0.891	-0.036	-0.028	-0.041
	house	0.856	0.869	0.884	0.054	0.049	0.051

efficacy in real image security transmission applications. The results of the images' plaintext and ciphertext visualization are displayed in Figure 9.

A comparison of the visualization processing outcomes for STP-CS-HC and CS-EABRP (Xu G et al. 2022) is shown in Figure 9. Whereas Figures 9(b) and 9(c) display the ciphertext pictures after STP-CS-HC (Wu Y et al. 022) and CS-EABRP processing, respectively, Figure 9(a) displays the original plaintext images of the four photographs of Brone, Lena, Peppers, and House. When comparing Figures 9(a), 9(b), and 9(c), it can be seen that the ciphertext picture produced by STP-CS-HC retains more of its original image features and is more similar to the plaintext image. While there are more information in the ciphertext (Wang X et al. 2022) picture processed by CS-EABRP, many feature details have been lost.

The actual encryption and decryption effect of the algorithm is demonstrated using neighboring pixel correlation analysis; if the ciphertext image processed by the method has a high degree of similarity with the plaintext image, and the plaintext image has a correlation coefficient value close to 1, then the ciphertext image is processed by the method with a correlation coefficient value close to 0. The correlation coefficient values between the plaintext and ciphertext pictures for the four images—Bone, Lena, Peppers, and House—processed by STP-CS-HC and CS-EABRP are provided in Table 4. According to Table 4, the ciphertext coefficient is closer to 0 and the plaintext coefficient of STP-CS-HC processing the four photos is closer to 1. Consequently, this approach of encrypted network picture transfer may better maintain the original properties.

Challenges and Risks to Security

Cloud computing offers many benefits, including pooled resources, enhanced storage capacity, fault tolerance, scalability, accessibility, simple installation, and cost-effective technologies. Despite the numerous benefits of cloud computing, there are a number of security risks and vulnerabilities that affect consumers as well as cloud service providers. "Data breaches, information misfortune, record or administration activity commandeering, shaky interfaces and Application Programming Interfaces (APIs), DoS (Qiu J et al. 2022) attacks, malicious insiders, mishandle of cloud administrations, inadequate due to tiredness, and finally shared innovation vulnerabilities" are listed as the top nine threats to cloud computing, according to a paper by the Cloud Security Alliance.

Data Breach

A data breach occurs when someone, an application, or a service obtains, views, or retrieves data without authorization. This kind of security breach aims to take and/or disclose private information to an unapproved or unlawful site. Another name for a data breach is a data leak or spill. From a security perspective, data leaking has emerged as one of the biggest organizational dangers. The causes include: data corruption; data being deleted, altered, or accidentally added by a user or an attacker; data being taken over the network through network penetration or other network intrusion attack; physical damage or theft of data storage devices; and virus infection that removes one or more files.

5. CONCLUSION

This paper presents a network image secure transmission technique, called STP-CS-HC, based on semi-tensor product compression perception and hybrid cloud to improve the efficiency and security of network pictures during secure transmission. Extensive experimental testing on the MSCOCO and ImageNet datasets has shown that the STP-CS-HC method performs better across several performance parameters. The STP-CS-HC performs better than the other. Its PSNR values on the MSCOCO and ImageNet datasets, at a compression rate of 0.90, reach 31.89 and 28.35, respectively, which are much superior than those of the AES, CS-EABRP, and Logistic Mapping encryption algorithms. Furthermore, the SSIM value of STP-CS-HC is 0.89 on the MSCOCO dataset and 0.92 on the ImageNet dataset when 700 samples are used, both of which are much higher than the comparison techniques. STP-CS-HC outperforms the other three algorithms in terms of both encryption and decryption time consumption, with the lowest encryption time of 2.128 seconds and the lowest decryption time of 0.288. Lastly, four images—Bone, Lena, Peppers, and House—are used to compare the visualization outcomes of CS-EABRP and STP-CS-HC. The findings show that the ciphertext picture processed by STP-CS-HC is more similar to the plaintext image. In conclusion, the STP-CS-HC algorithm exhibits notable improvements in processing speed and efficiency together with considerable benefits in terms of picture integrity and security. In further research, the algorithm's applicability to more intricate network contexts and other picture data types will be explored, and it will be further optimized to handle bigger datasets and higher-resolution photos.

REFERENCES

Amin, S. N., Shivakumara, P., Jun, T. X., Chong, K. Y., Zan, D. L. L., & Rahavendra, R. (2023). An augmented reality-based approach for designing interactive food menu of restaurant using android. *Artificial Intelligence and Applications (Commerce, Calif.)*, *1*(1), 26–34. doi:10.47852/bonviewAIA2202354

Bao, W., & Zhu, C. (2022). A secure and robust image encryption algorithm based on compressive sensing and DNA coding. *Multimedia Tools and Applications*, *81*(11), 15977–15996. doi:10.1007/s11042-022-12623-7

Gupta, M., Singh, V. P., Gupta, K. K., & Shukla, P. K. (2023). An efficient image encryption technique based on two-level security for internet of things. *Multimedia Tools and Applications*, *82*(4), 5091–5111. doi:10.1007/s11042-022-12169-8

Lang, J., & Ma, C. (2023). Novel zero-watermarking method using the compressed sensing significant feature. *Multimedia Tools and Applications*, *82*(3), 4551–4567. doi:10.1007/s11042-022-13601-9

Qiu, J., Liu, J., Bi, Z., Sun, X., Gu, Q., Hu, G., & Qin, N. (2022). An investigation of 2D spine magnetic resonance imaging (MRI) with compressed sensing (CS). *Skeletal Radiology*, *51*(6), 1273–1283. doi:10.1007/s00256-021-03954-x PMID:34854969

Singh, K. N., & Singh, A. K. (2022). Towards integrating image encryption with compression: A survey. *ACM Transactions on Multimedia Computing Communications and Applications*, *18*(3), 1–21. doi:10.1145/3498342

Wang X, Guan N. (2023). 2D sine-logistic-tent-coupling map for image encryption. Journal of Ambient Intelligence and Humanized Computing, 14(10), 13399-13419.

Wang, X., Yang, B., Wang, Z., Liu, Q., Chen, C., & Guan, X. (2022). A compressed sensing and CNN-based method for fault diagnosis of photovoltaic inverters in edge computing scenarios. *IET Renewable Power Generation*, *16*(7), 1434–1444. doi:10.1049/rpg2.12383

Wang, Z., Jiang, Y., & Chen, S. (2023). Image parallel block compressive sensing scheme using DFT measurement matrix. *Multimedia Tools and Applications*, *82*(14), 21561–21583. doi:10.1007/s11042-022-14176-1

Wang, Z., Wang, Z., Zeng, C., Yu, Y., & Wan, X. (2023). High-quality image compressed sensing and reconstruction with multi-scale dilated convolutional neural network. *Circuits, Systems, and Signal Processing*, *42*(3), 1593–1616. doi:10.1007/s00034-022-02181-6

Wu, Y., Zhang, L., Berretti, S., & Wan, S. (2022). Medical image encryption by content-aware DNA computing for secure healthcare. *IEEE Transactions on Industrial Informatics*, *19*(2), 2089–2098. doi:10.1109/TII.2022.3194590

Xu, G., Zhang, B., Yu, H., Chen, J., Xing, M., & Hong, W. (2022). Sparse synthetic aperture radar imaging from compressed sensing and machine learning: Theories, applications, and trends. applications, and trends. *IEEE Geoscience and Remote Sensing Magazine*, *10*(4), 32–69. doi:10.1109/MGRS.2022.3218801

Yu, M., Tang, Z., Zhang, X., Zhong, B., & Zhang, X. (2022). Perceptual hashing with complementary color wavelet transform and compressed sensing for reduced-reference image quality assessment. *IEEE Transactions on Circuits and Systems for Video Technology*, *32*(11), 7559–7574. doi:10.1109/TCSVT.2022.3190273

Zha, Z., Wen, B., Yuan, X., Ravishankar, S., Zhou, J., & Zhu, C. (2023). Learning nonlocal sparse and low-rank models for image compressive sensing: Nonlocal sparse and low -rank modeling. *IEEE Signal Processing Magazine*, *40*(1), 32–44. doi:10.1109/MSP.2022.3217936

Zhang, J., Chen, B., Xiong, R., & Zhang, Y. (2023). Physics-inspired compressive sensing: Beyond deep unrolling. *IEEE Signal Processing Magazine*, *40*(1), 58–72. doi:10.1109/MSP.2022.3208394

Chapter 12
Enhancing Energy Efficiency in Intrusion Detection Systems for Wireless Sensor Networks Through Zigbee Protocol

M. Keerthika
https://orcid.org/0000-0001-8023-0188
Avinashilingam Institute for Home Science and Higher Education for Women, India

D. Shanmugapriya
https://orcid.org/0000-0002-7446-6749
Avinashilingam Institute for Home Science and Higher Education for Women, India

D. Nethra Pingala Suthishni
https://orcid.org/0000-0002-2717-1796
Avinashilingam Institute for Home Science and Higher Education for Women, India

V. Sasirekha
Avinashilingam Institute for Home Science and Higher Education for Women, India

ABSTRACT

Wireless sensor networks (WSNs) are important in various applications, including environmental monitoring, healthcare, and industrial automation. However, the energy constraints of sensor nodes present significant challenges in deploying robust security mechanisms, such as intrusion detection systems (IDS). The method involves using data aggregation, node selection, and energy harvesting techniques to reduce energy consumption while maintaining the accuracy of the IDS. The effectiveness of the proposed approach is evaluated using simulation experiments. This chapter offers a promising solution for providing effective and energy-efficient intrusion detection in ZigBee-based WSNs. The study found that applying machine learning techniques, specifically SFA, can significantly improve the energy efficiency of Zigbee protocol in wireless sensor networks. Results indicate that using these techniques energy consumption is up to 95.42% and 190 µW / node, IDS prediction ratio is 98.5%, and accuracy is 99.5%

DOI: 10.4018/979-8-3693-2691-6.ch012

while maintaining network performance.

Figure 1. WSN architecture

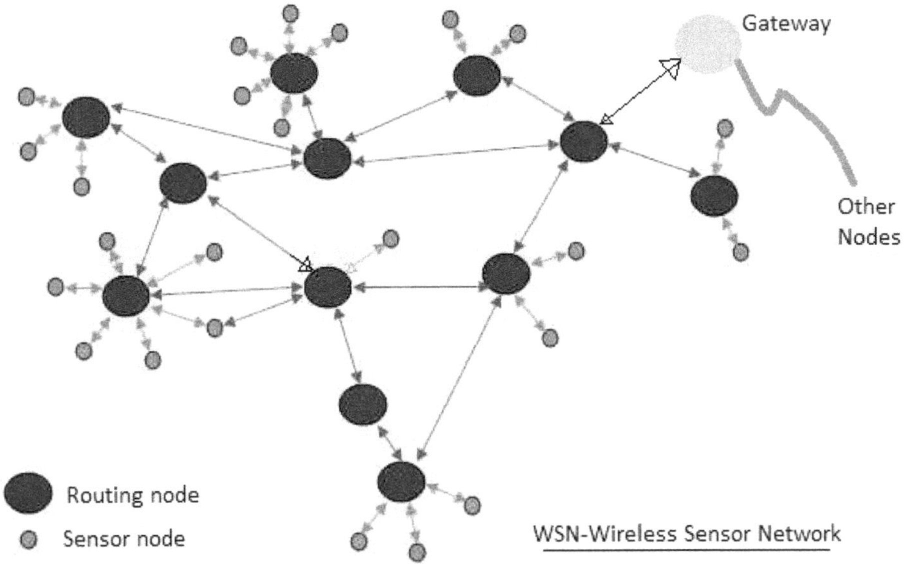

INTRODUCTION

Wireless sensor networks (WSNs) are collections of tiny, low-power sensors that connect wirelessly to a central control station and to one another. These networks are typically used to collect data from the environment and transmit it to a central location for processing.

The architecture of WSN is illustrated below:

WSN includes sensor nodes, base station and routing nodes. It is gaining more popularity recent days because of the availability of low cost sensors, and its characteristics like flexibility to deploy anywhere and equipped with lifelong batteries (Hung-Min et al 2007).

Wireless Sensor Network (WSN)

The most popular technology behind WSN is Zigbee. It is a low power wireless personal area network technology. WSNs can be used in a wide range of applications, including environmental monitoring, healthcare, security, and industrial control. They use low-power wireless communication protocols such as ZigBee, Bluetooth Low Energy (BLE), or Wi-Fi to transmit data to other sensors or to the central control station. One of the key challenges in WSNs is managing power consumption to maximize the lifetime of the sensors

Zigbee Protocol

Zigbee protocol (Machdi & Tan, 2022) is used to optimize the energy consumption of devices in a wireless sensor network. Zigbee is a low-power, low-data-rate wireless communication protocol that is widely used in wireless sensor networks, Zigbee protocol can be used to enable communication between sensor nodes and a central control unit. Energy efficiency using Zigbee protocol (Nguyen, 2021) in wireless sensor networks involves implementing strategies such as data aggregation, node selection, and energy harvesting to reduce energy consumption and prolong the battery life of devices. These strategies involve aggregating data (Song & Tan, 2012) from multiple sensor nodes to reduce the number of transmissions, selecting the most energy-efficient nodes for data transmission, and harvesting energy from the environment to power devices. By optimizing energy consumption, Zigbee protocol can improve the performance and reliability of wireless sensor networks while reducing maintenance and operational costs.

Zigbee routing protocol (Wang et al., 2021) is the underlying mechanism that enables communication between devices in a Zigbee network. The routing protocol determines the path that data takes from one device to another within the network. Zigbee uses a mesh networking architecture, which means that each device can communicate directly with multiple other devices. This allows for a robust and reliable network that can extend the reach of the network and reduce the dependence on a central device for communication. The Zigbee routing protocol (Thorat et al., 2020) uses two main techniques to determine the best path for data transmission: source routing and table-driven routing. Source routing is a technique in which the source device specifies the entire path that the data will take through the network. This technique (Nie, 2022) is used in networks with a small number of devices and provides a direct path between the source and destination devices. Overall, the Zigbee protocol (Alexandrov et al., 2019) is an efficient and effective solution for wireless communication in WSNs, providing a low-cost, low-power, and secure communication platform for monitoring and controlling various devices and systems.

Bio-inspired algorithms (Lee et al., 2018) offer a new approach to solving problems, drawing inspiration from the processes and behaviours found in nature. In the field of network routing, bio-inspired algorithms (Khan et al., 2015) have shown promising results for solving the SPT problem. Overall, bio-inspired algorithms offer a promising new approach to solving the SPT problem in complex and dynamic networks. They offer the potential for increased efficiency and adaptability, providing an effective solution for finding the shortest path in these networks.

Using this predictive model (Zhao, 2021), the WSN can be optimized to consume less energy, which can increase the lifespan of the network. In conclusion, using machine learning techniques in combination with Zigbee and SFA (Majid et al., 2022) can help to predict the behavior of the WSN, especially in terms of energy consumption. This can lead to an optimized WSN with increased lifespan and improved performance. The rest of the sections cover as: the next section discussed about the literature review, Section III discussed about the proposed methodology and algorithms. The section IV discussed about Simulation results with parameters and the final section is conclusion with future implementations.

Intrusion Detection System

An Intrusion Detection System (IDS) in the context of a Wireless Sensor Network (WSN) plays a critical role in ensuring the security and integrity of the network. Wireless Sensor Networks consist of numerous small, low-cost sensor nodes with limited computational and communication capabilities, making them vulnerable to various security threats. An IDS serves as a proactive defense mechanism to detect and respond to malicious activities within the network. IDS systems can be broadly categorized into two groups: Signature-based Intrusion Detection System (SIDS) and Anomaly-based Intrusion Detection System (AIDS).

Zigbee Security

IoT devices can be connected through the Zigbee WSN and further it is attached to the Internet via IoT Gateway. The Zigbee devices can interoperate with each other as well as exchange data in the same network. Zigbee standard consists various security features such as access control (AC) lists, frame counters (FC) as well as encryption techniques for the communications. The communication between devices in the Zigbee network is based on symmetric key. Communication is carried out in the form of encrypted data. It uses Advanced Encryption Standard (AES).

Selective Forwarding Attack in WSN

It is a malicious attack in which attack selectively drop IP packets from forwarding. In this type of attack, an attacker participates in the routing process as normal model and selectively drops packets that arrive from the neighbouring nodes. In this scenario, an attacker forward only non-critical IP packets and discard the critical IP packets. Karlof Wagner implemented selective forwarding (SF) attack. This attack is also known as Gray Hole (GH) attack. In this, malicious nodes focus for stopping the packets or selectively forward packets by dropping important packets. There are different forms of selective forwarding. One of the forms of selective forwarding is malicious node selectively drop the packets based

Figure 2. Selective forwarding with DoS attack

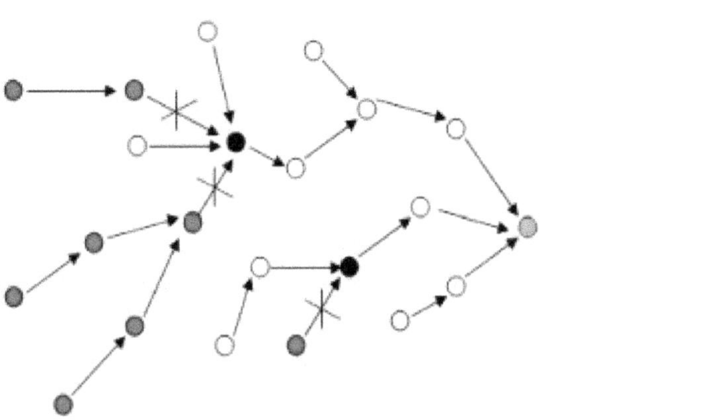

Figure 3. Selective forwarding attack

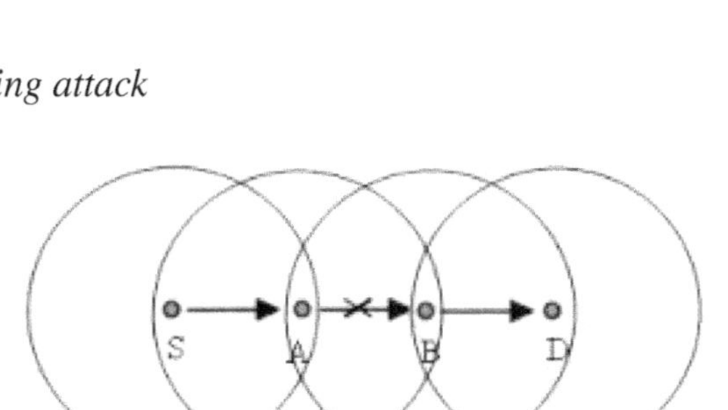

on its specific source/destination address or group of source/destination addresses. This results in DoS attack for a specific or group of nodes. An example of selecting forwarding with the perspective of DoS attack is illustrated below:

The malicious nodes in WSN may also acts as black hole. The malicious nodes refuse to forward each packets that they have. In addition to that, malicious nodes may also forward the packets to the incorrect route that creates disloyal routing information in the network.

Another type of SF attack is neglect as well as greed. Here, the malicious node randomly neglect for routing some packets. It actively participate in the network as well as send acknowledge to the sender for receiving the packets but it drops the packets randomly. Such types of nodes are known as neglectful nodes. When the malicious node gives excessive priority for some packets means that is known as greedy. Another type of SF is delay packets. Here malicious nodes delay on packet forwarding and creates confusions in the network.

The below example illustrates the selective forwarding attack.

Here, source 'S' and destination 'D'. Packets are arriving from source in order to reach to destination 'D'. Packets reach destination 'D' via the nodes 'A' and 'B'. The node 'A' may be malicious node and selectively forwards packets to the neighbouring node 'B'. It drops some packets and not forwarding to the neighbouring node 'B' or route the packets into wrong path. Another type of SF attack is blind letter attack. When the legitimate forwards the packet to its neighbouring node, it assumes that, packets successfully forwarded but actually the malicious node drops those packets without any notice to the sender.

Selective forwarding cause severe damage for the network. There are various measures proposed in the literature for selective forwarding network.

Gradient Boosting

Gradient Boosting is a powerful machine learning algorithm that can be used for both regression and classification problems. It has gained widespread popularity in recent years due to its high accuracy and versatility in solving a wide range of machine learning problems. It is a type of ensemble method that combines multiple weak models (often decision trees) into a single strong model. The basic idea behind gradient boosting is to iteratively improve a weak learner by fitting a new model to the residual errors of the previous model. In each iteration, the algorithm adds a new tree to the ensemble that is trained to predict the residual errors of the previous model. The final model is the sum of all the weak learners in the ensemble. Gradient Boosting is an ensemble machine learning algorithm that is widely used for various classification and regression tasks. It is based on the concept of boosting, where multiple weak models are combined to create a stronger model. Gradient Boosting creates an ensemble of decision trees, with each tree attempting to correct the mistakes made by the previous trees.

LITERATURE REVIEW

Real-time WSN testbed evaluations reveal high accuracy and energy efficiency. Zigbee Enabled Network Simulation with NS2 focuses on energy-efficient intrusion detection, showing superior performance compared to traditional systems in terms of energy consumption and accuracy. A survey reviews various ZigBee-based intrusion detection systems, highlighting their architecture, ZigBee protocol features, and algorithmic approaches. An energy-efficient ZigBee-based intrusion detection system is presented,

Table 1. Table for selective forwarding attack

S. No	Author and Year	Proposed Work	Algorithm	Observation
1	Q.Zhang et al. 2019	E-Watchdog	Election algorithm	E-watchdog achieves a 25% reduction in false detection rates while enhancing detection accuracy by 10%.
2	J.Ding et al. 2021	Detect selective forwarding attacks by clustering the Cumulative Forwarding Rates (CFRs) of all sensor nodes	Noise-Based Density Peaks Clustering (NB-DPC)	The NB-DPC exhibits a Missed Detection Rate (MDR) and False Detection Rate (FDR) both below 1%, indicating a low level of missed detections and false alarms.
3	A.Petal et al. 2022	Reputation based RPL-Protocol	RPL	The suggested method accurately identifies and isolates selective forwarding attacks with minimal false alarms.
4	X.Huang et al. 2022	Artificial immune system based on the danger model is established to detect network attacks	screen-confirm scheme, Support vector machine	In the proposed approach, the rate of missed detections is below 1.3%, while the false detection rate stands at 4.3%.
5	J.Jung et al. 2022	Secure IoT Routing Selective Forwarding Attacks and Trust-based Defenses.	RPL	The suggested approach yields a detection rate of 34%.
6	J.Ding et al. 2022	Detect the selective forwarding attack under a harsh environment.	Reinforcement learning(RL) algorithm, double-threshold density peaks clustering (DT-DPC) algorithm.	The suggested approach demonstrates a low False Detection Rate (FDR) of 1% and a Missed Detection Rate (MDR) of 10%. Moreover, in challenging conditions, there is an approximately 4% improvement in network throughput.
7	M.Ezhilarasi et al. 2022	Detect routing attacks in wireless sensor networks.	fuzzy and feed-forward neural networks	The average detection rate is 97.8%, with a peak detection accuracy reaching 98.8%.

demonstrating high accuracy and low energy consumption. Optimization of Wireless Intrusion Detection System in ZigBee Networks Using NS2 proposes an optimized system with high detection accuracy, reduced false alarm rates, and low energy consumption. The study by Shruti R. Chaugule and Dr. A.V. Patil examines energy-efficient ZigBee protocols in WSNs, considering factors like topology and machine learning for intrusion detection. The optimization strategy incorporates an efficient intrusion detection system, security protocol, and energy-efficient routing algorithm, ensuring reliable and secure communication with low power consumption and simplified network configuration and maintenance.

There are various measures proposed in the literature for selective forwarding network.

PROPOSED METHODOLOGY

Introduction

To validate a selective forwarding attack in Zigbee protocol-based wireless sensor network using ML techniques in a simulation by deploying nodes, the following steps can be taken: Protocol deployment, Monitoring mechanism using ML techniques, Latency and Packet Delivery Ratio (PDR) calculation,

Figure 4. Proposed methodology

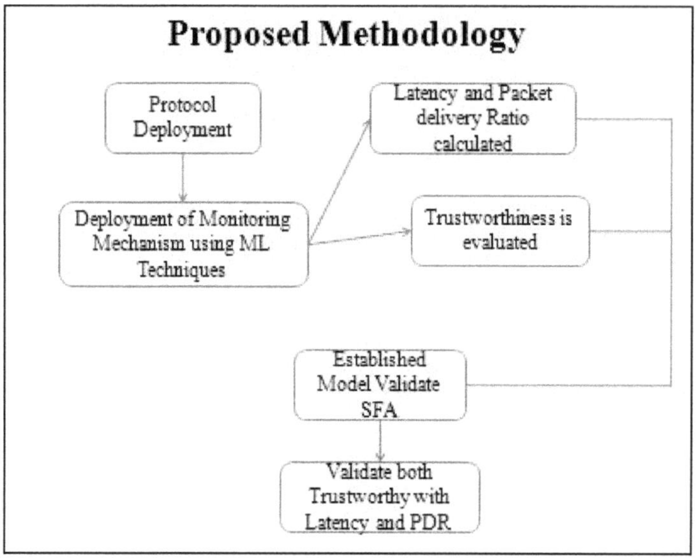

Trustworthiness evaluation, Validation of SFA with established model and with Latency and PDR is shown in Figure 1.

Using Zigbee technology (Majid et al., 2022), energy consumption will be optimized and selective forward attacks will be avoided. Zigbee is a low-power, low-bit-rate, and low-transmission-rate wireless technology that can be utilised in large networks and wireless sensors. The low bit rate and poor transmission rate contribute to the high delay. Due to its low power consumption, the network is dependable. In the meantime, a network intrusion is possible as numerous nodes are linked together. A Zigbee zone is made up of a collection of Nodes that function independently. The nodes are united as a cluster group to form a zone. The ZigBee protocol was used to deploy the nodes, and by default, data transfer occurs without network supervision. One must monitor and manage the Zigbee network after it is set up to make sure it is operating properly. Classification of nodes were categorized in three ways

- Node strength
- Node distance
- Node group

Strength can be optimal, average and worse. Distance can be classified as short, average and far. Group can be classified as belongs to group, not belongs to group, group performing another transaction. If the node is belongs to the group, then the node is checked with multiple constraints.

1. Node is alive or dead
2. Node is head or normal node
3. If node is normal node, check whether the node is idle or performing transaction, if performing transaction the route identifies another node to form a route to transmit the data.

Latency and packet delivery ratio (PDR) (Kothawade et al., 2016) are performance metrics commonly used in wireless sensor networks to evaluate the efficiency and reliability of the network. Machine learning techniques can be used to predict and analyze these metrics based on the network parameters. To calculate latency in a wireless sensor network, we can measure the time it takes for a packet to travel from the source node to the destination node. This can be done using a timestamp mechanism that records the time at which a packet is sent and the time at which it is received. Latency is then calculated as the difference between the two timestamps. To calculate PDR, we can measure the ratio of successfully received packets to the total number of packets sent. This can be done by counting the number of packets that are successfully received at the destination node and dividing it by the total number of packets sent from the source node.

Machine learning techniques (Gao et al., 2014) can be used to predict these performance metrics based on various network parameters such as communication range, transmission power, and data rate. Supervised learning algorithms such as regression or classification to develop a model that predicts latency or PDR based on the input parameters. The model can be trained that includes the input parameters and the corresponding latency or PDR values. Once the model is trained, used to predict the latency or PDR for a given set of network parameters. This can be useful in optimizing the network performance by identifying the optimal values for the network parameters that minimize latency and maximize PDR.

In a multi-hop network (Diaz & Sanchez, 2016), messages are forwarded and received faithfully by each node participating. Malicious nodes may, however, refuse to forward certain messages and simply drop them, preventing their propagation. A selective forward attack follows a similar procedure to a black hole attack. First, a malicious node must convince the network that it is the closest node to the base station, attracting traffic to route through it. A selection of packets is then dropped.

In particular, supervised learning algorithms can be used to predict the likelihood of a selective forwarding attack occurring based on network parameters and behavior. To validate a selective forwarding attack (Huang & Wu, 2022), this can be done by either injecting the attack into the network or by simulating the attack. A supervised learning algorithm such as logistic regression or support vector machines can be trained on the data. The algorithm can be trained to predict the likelihood of a selective forwarding attack occurring based on the input features. The algorithm can also be used to identify the specific features that are most predictive of the attack. Overall, machine learning techniques can be used to validate the effectiveness of a selective forwarding attack in a Zigbee protocol-based wireless sensor network and optimize the energy efficiency of the network by identifying and isolating nodes that are potentially carrying out the attack.

Evaluating the trustworthiness of nodes in a wireless sensor network (Ye et al., 2017) is important for ensuring the energy efficiency of the network. Machine learning techniques can be used to evaluate the trustworthiness of nodes based on various factors such as their energy consumption and behavior. One way to evaluate the trustworthiness of nodes is to use a supervised learning algorithm such as logistic regression or support vector machines. The algorithm can be trained that includes various features of the nodes such as their energy consumption, number of packets sent and received, and the number of times they have been selected as a relay node. The target variable for the algorithm can be the trustworthiness of the node, which can be defined based on a threshold value for these features.

Overall, evaluating the trustworthiness of nodes in a wireless sensor network using machine learning techniques can help optimize the energy efficiency of the network by selecting only trustworthy nodes for data transmission and relaying, and identifying potentially malicious or faulty nodes that can be isolated or removed from the network.

Algorithm Design and Implementation

Zigbee Protocol Without IDS

Bio-inspired algorithms (Matos et al., 2022) are computational methods that are inspired by natural processes, such as evolution, swarming behavior of animals, and neural networks. The algorithm has been found to be effective in solving optimization in WSNs. In the context of ZigBee protocol for IDS detection in WSNs, a bio-inspired algorithm is used to enhance the efficiency and accuracy of the IDS. Figure 2 shows simulation of Zigbee protocol without IDS implementing bio-inspired algorithm for shortest path tree algorithm and the algorithm as follows:

Algorithm 1: A bio-inspired algorithm for Shortest Path Tree Algorithm

```
Step 1: G = (N, M, d) has n nodes and m edges
Step 2: Initialize:
Step 3: Source node s and sink node set T
Step 4: Let D_ij:= c(c > 0) and P_ij:= 0 for each edge
Step 5: Let the number of particles stored at each node be Φ i:= 0
Step 6: while t:= 1 to Γ do
Step 7: for each node i in S
Step 8: Input I 0 particles into the source node s
Step 9: end for
Step 10: for each node i in T
Step 11: if Φ i ≥ I 0 /(N - 1)
Step 12: Output I 0 /(N -1) particles from the sink node T_i
Step 13: else
Step 14: Output Φ i particles from the sink node T i
Step 15: end if
Step 16: end for
Step 17: Set Threshold value
Step 18: If (srcd<Threshold value && desd<min)
Step 19: Min = desd, a [k] = j
Step 20: Calculate the flux of each edge P ij by using (4)
Step 21: Update the conductivity of each edge M ij by using (6)
Step 22: Calculate the number of particles stored at each node byusing (7)
Step 23: End if
Step 24: Set energy value
Step 25: If (energy (node) <M)
Step 26: M = energy (node), A = node
Step 27: Choose best route path
Step 28: End If
Step 29: end while
Step 30: Obtain the flux distribution pattern
```

Figure 5. ZIGBEE protocol without IDS

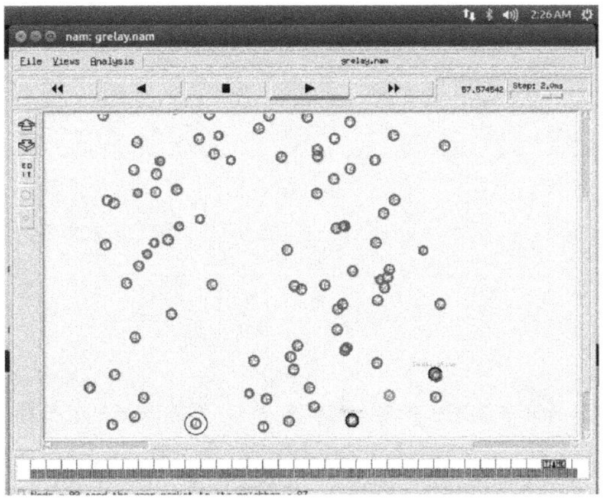

Zigbee Protocol With IDS-Parallel Levy-Arithmetic Optimization Algorithm (PL-AOA)

The Parallel Levy-Arithmetic Optimization Algorithm (PL-AOA) (Zhang et al., 2022) is a bio-inspired optimization algorithm that can be used in conjunction with ZigBee protocol for Intrusion Detection System (IDS) in Wireless Sensor Networks (WSNs). PL-AOA is a population-based optimization algorithm that uses a combination of parallelism and arithmetic operations to search for optimal solutions to complex problems. The use of PL-AOA (Liu et al., 2022) in ZigBee protocol with IDS can enhance the efficiency and accuracy of the IDS, resulting in improved security and reliability of the WSN. By optimizing the IDS parameters using PL-AOA, the network can detect and prevent potential intrusions in real-time, ensuring the safety of the data transmitted over the network. Figure 3 shows simulation of Zigbee protocol with IDS implementing Parallel Levy - Arithmetic Optimization Algorithm (Pl-AOA) and the algorithm as follows:

Algorithm 2: A Parallel Levy - Arithmetic Optimization Algorithm (PL-AOA)

```
Step 1: Initialize the parameters related to the algorithm: ub, lb, Dim, max_
itergroup = 4
Step 2: Generate initial population X containing N individuals X i (i = 0, 1,
2, 3, · · ·, N)
Step 3: Divide X into 4 groups.
Step 4: Do
Step 5: if r 1 > MOA
Step 6: Update the X by Equation (1)
Step 7: else
Step 8: Update the X by Equation (2)
Step 9: for i = 1:group
Step 10: for i = 1:Dim
Step 11: if f winner < f gbest
Step 12: Update the best solution obtained so far
Step 13: Change flight status according to iteration
```

Figure 6. ZIGBEE protocol with IDS–PL-AOA

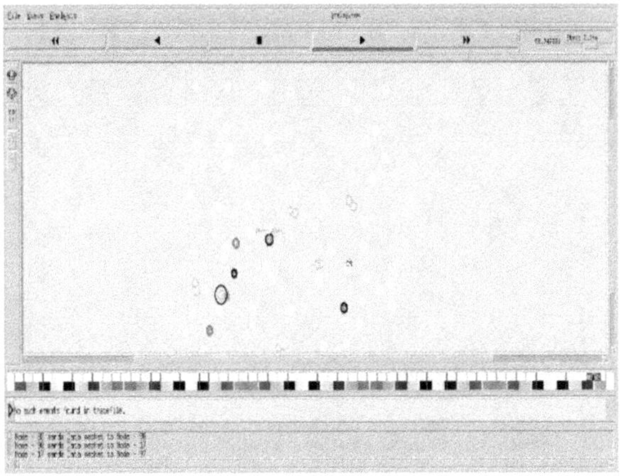

```
Step 14: end
Step 15: if iteration = 50
Step 16: If (degree<t || degree>t) // t-threshold value
Step 17: After find the degree value to separate active and
sleep time nodes
Step 18: End
Step 19: Update the pbest by Equation (6) and calculate its fitness value
Step 20: if f gbest < f pbest 0
Step 21: Update the best solution obtained so far
Step 22: Change flight status according to iteration.
Step 23: end
Step 24: end
Step 25: While (t < max_iter) or (get the expected f unction value)
Step 26: Return the best solution obtained so far as the global optimum
```

Gradient Boosting

Wireless Sensor Networks (WSNs) are vulnerable to various security attacks due to their distributed nature, limited resources, and ad-hoc nature. Selective Forward Attack (SFA) is a type of attack where a malicious node selectively drops or forwards packets to disrupt the communication between other nodes in the network. SFA detection is a critical problem in WSNs, and machine learning algorithms such as Gradient Boosting can be used for this purpose.

The algorithm works as follows:

1. Initialize the model: Start with a simple model, such as a single decision tree.
2. Fit the model: Train the model on the training data and make predictions on the validation set.
3. Calculate the residuals: Calculate the difference between the predicted and actual values of the validation set. These residuals represent the error in the model.

Table 2. Network configuration

S. No	Parameter	Value
1.	Channel	Wireless channel
2.	Propagation	Propagation/TwoRayGround
3.	MAC	Mac/802_15_4
4.	Routing Protocol	Zig-bee
5.	Initial Energy	Energy model
6.	Transmission Model	Radio Model
7.	Initial energy in Joules	100
8.	Time of simulation	60
9.	Number of Nodes	100
10.	Dimension (x,y)	(2500,2500)

4. Fit a new model: Train a new model on the residuals. This model tries to predict the errors of the previous model.
5. Add the new model: Combine the new model with the previous model by adding their predictions. This creates a new, stronger model.
6. Repeat steps 3-5: Iterate the process by calculating the residuals of the new model and fitting a new model to the residuals.
7. Combine the models: Finally, combine all the models to create a strong ensemble model that makes accurate predictions.

RESULTS AND DISCUSSIONS

Introduction

The simulation results shows how the end-to-end delay, energy consumption, packet delivery ratio, throughput, and network lifetime vary under different network configurations, such as varying the number of nodes, the transmission range, or the routing protocol. The results can also show the effectiveness of the IDS in terms of recall, precision, F-measure, and accuracy. The simulation results can help network designers to optimize the network's performance and improve its reliability and security.

Network Configuration

The network configuration for a WSN with ZigBee protocol and IDS typically includes as listed in Table 2.

Performance Metrics

Performance metrics are used to measure the performance of a wireless sensor network (WSN) using the ZigBee protocol with Intrusion Detection System (IDS). Here are some commonly used performance

Figure 7. Implementation of enhanced Zigbee protocol in WSN end-to-end delay

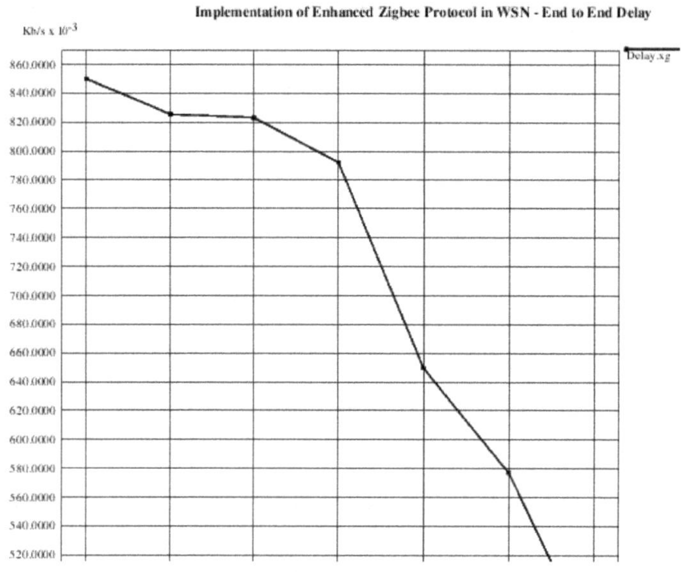

Figure 8. Implementation of IDS with Zigbee protocol in WSN end-to-end delay

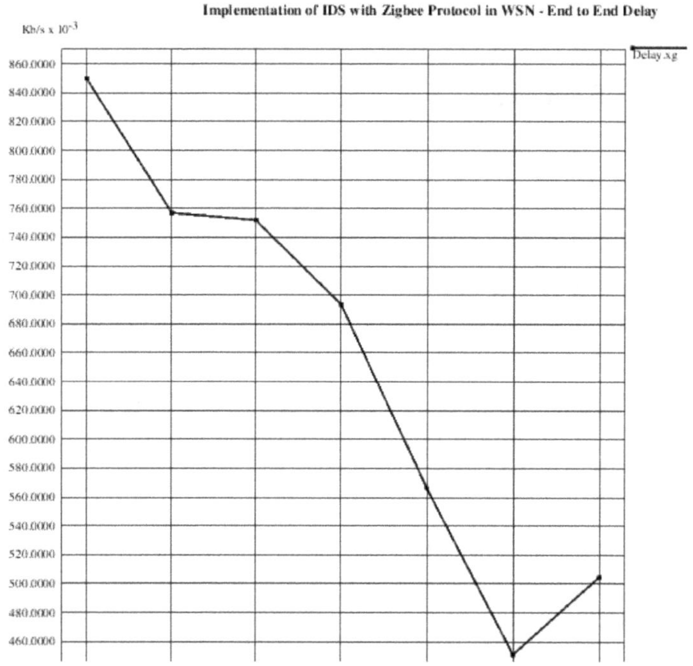

Table 3. End to end delay

Time(ms)	Delay(Kb/s)	
	Zigbee Protocol	IDS With Zigbee Protocol
10	0.826145	0.755061
20	0.820881	0.746657
30	0.78058	0.69446
40	0.604178	0.584587
50	0.522936	0.476446
60	0.524716	0.454908

metrics measured are End-to-end Delay, Energy Consumption, Packet Delivery Ratio, Throughput, Network Lifetime, Recall, Precision, F-Measure and Accuracy for evaluating the effectiveness of the ZigBee protocol with IDS in WSNs, and optimizing its parameters to achieve the desired network performance.

Results and Analysis

End-to-End Delay

This metric measures the time taken for a packet to travel from the source node to the destination node. It is an important metric for applications that require real-time data transmission. Figure 7 shows the implementation of enhanced zigbee protocol in WSN. Implementation of IDS With Zigbee Protocol in WSN – End To End Delay shown in Figure 8 and Table 3 depicts the end to end delay with different interval of time. Figure 9 shows the analysis of End To End Delay for IDS using Zigbee protocol with time interval.

Energy Consumption

This metric measures the amount of energy consumed by the network to transmit data. Figure 10 shows the implementation of enhanced zigbee protocol in WSN. Implementation of IDS With Zigbee Protocol

Figure 9. End-to-end delay for IDS using Zigbee protocol with time interval

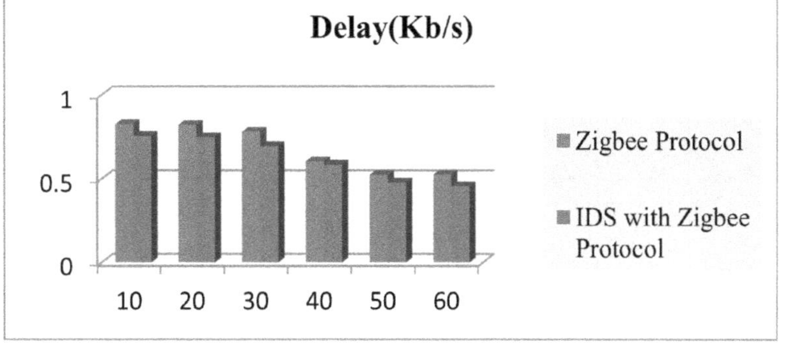

Figure 10. Implementation of enhanced Zigbee protocol in WSN – energy consumption

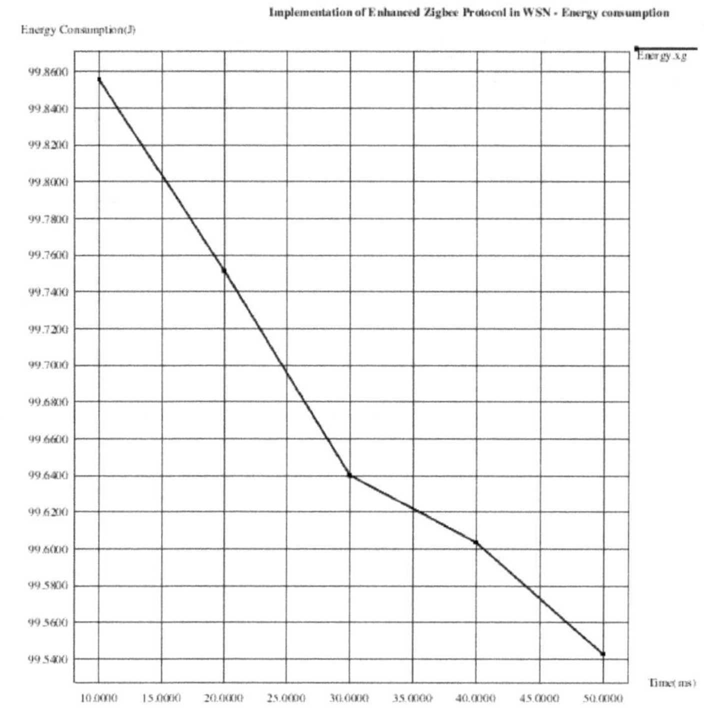

Figure 11. Implementation of IDS with Zigbee protocol in WSN – energy consumption

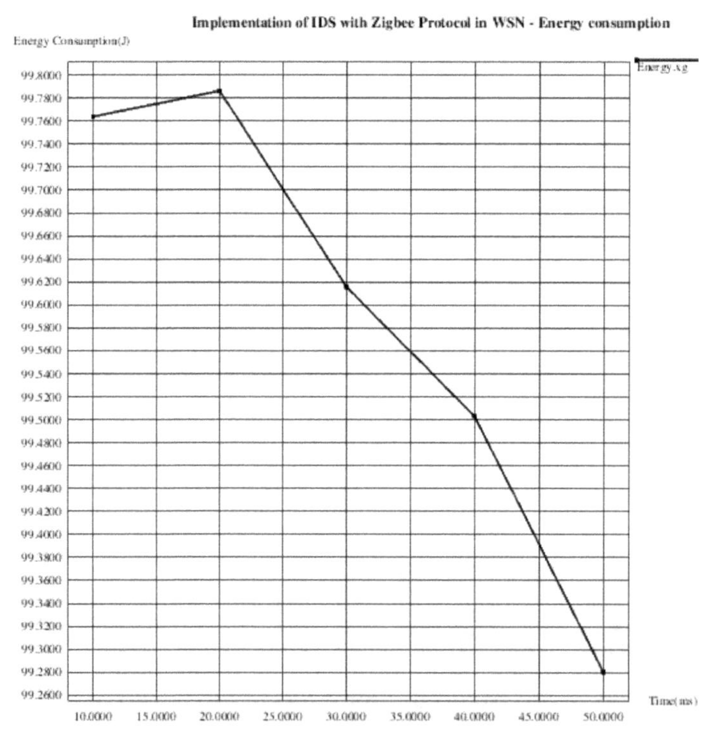

Table 4. Energy consumption(J)

Time(ms)	Energy Consumption(J)	
	Zigbee Protocol	IDS With Zigbee Protocol
10	99.7996	99.8505
20	99.6601	99.7921
30	99.426	99.6727
40	99.5135	99.5719
50	99.4815	99.4358

Figure 12. Energy consumption for IDS using Zigbee protocol with time interval

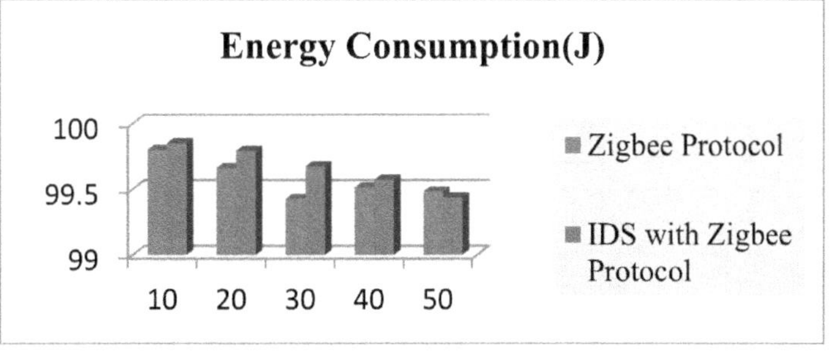

Figure 13. Implementation of enhanced Zigbee protocol in WSN

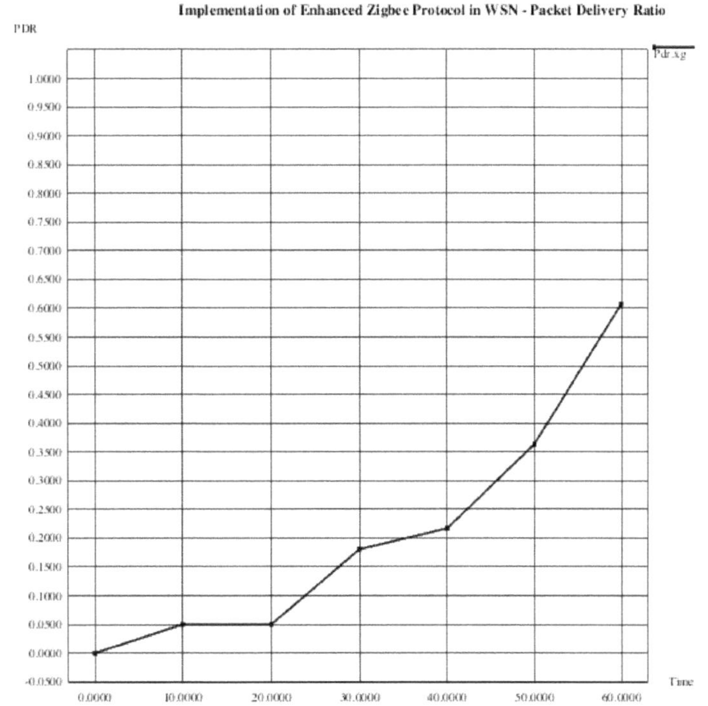

Figure 14. Implementation of IDS with Zigbee protocol in WSN – PDR

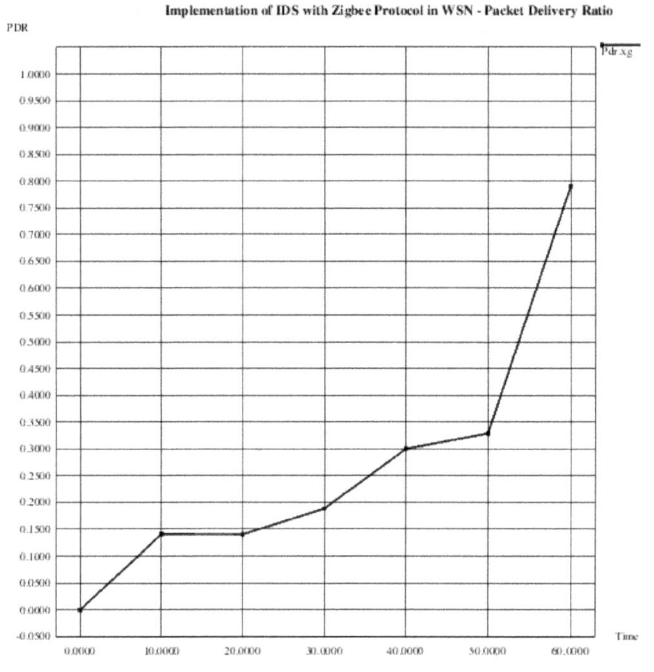

Table 5. PDR with different interval of time

Time(ms)	PDR	
	Zigbee Protocol	IDS With Zigbee Protocol
10	0.0503747	0.140945
20	0.0500537	0.139376
30	0.177854	0.188496
40	0.201393	0.310008
50	0.329522	0.34724
60	0.699622	0.712689

Figure 15. Analysis of packet delivery ratio for IDS using Zigbee protocol with time interval

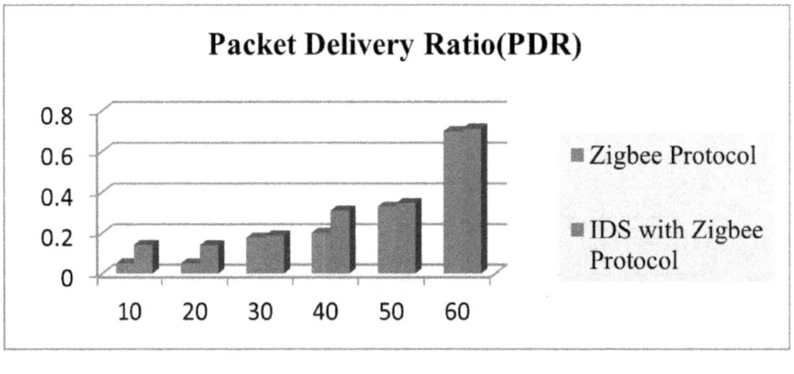

Figure 16. Implementation of enhanced zigbee protocol in WSN -throughput

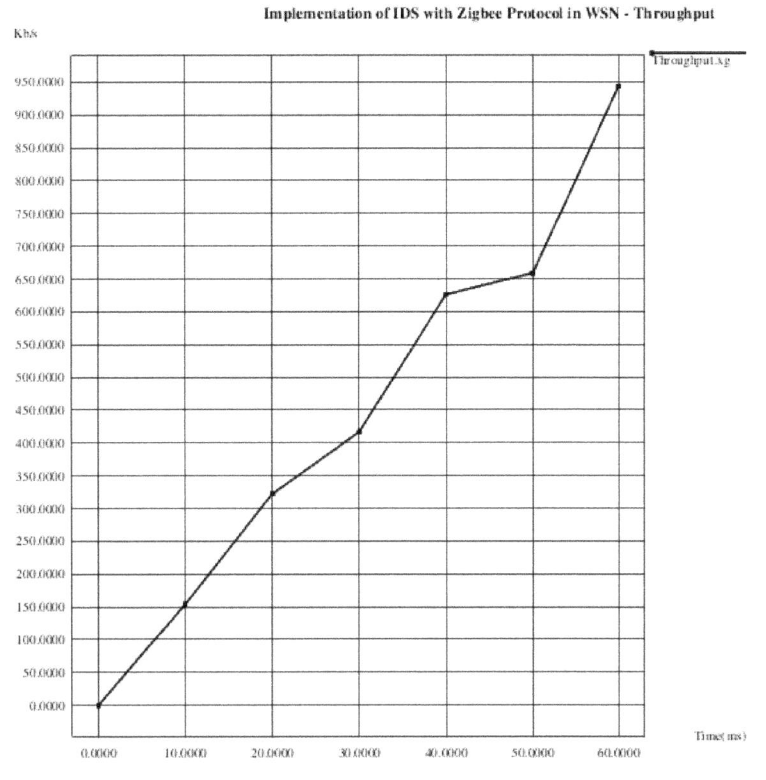

Figure 17. Implementation of IDS with Zigbee protocol in WSN – throughput

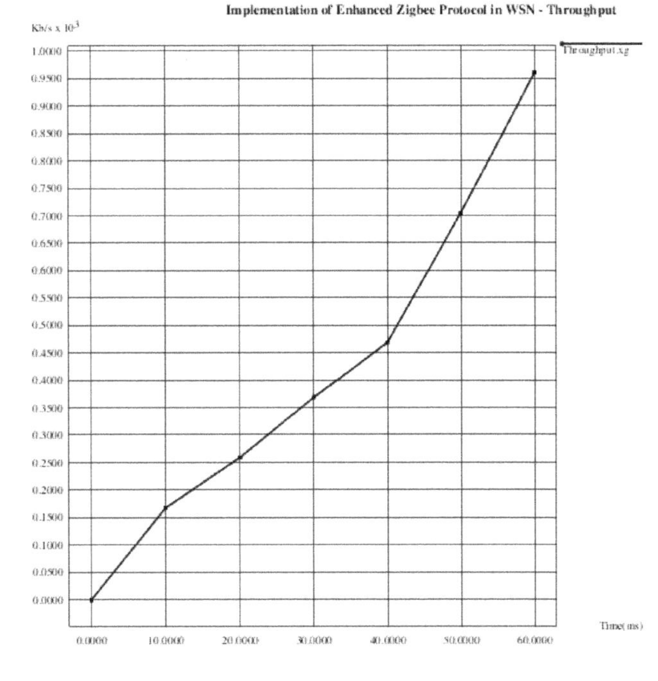

Table 6. Throughput with different interval of time

Time(ms)	Throughput(Kb/s)	
	Zigbee Protocol	IDS With Zigbee Protocol
10	156.005	166.255
20	229.625	341.509
30	323.833	442.549
40	406.681	655.436
50	696.882	690.359
60	830.55	855.372

Figure 18. Analysis of throughput for IDS using Zigbee protocol with time interval

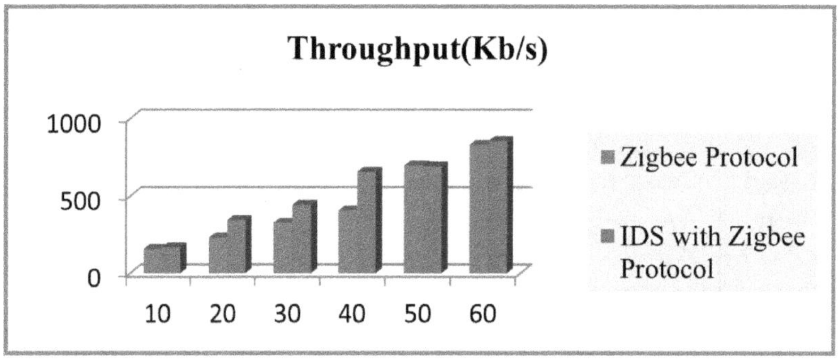

Figure 19. Implementation of enhanced ZigBee protocol in WSN

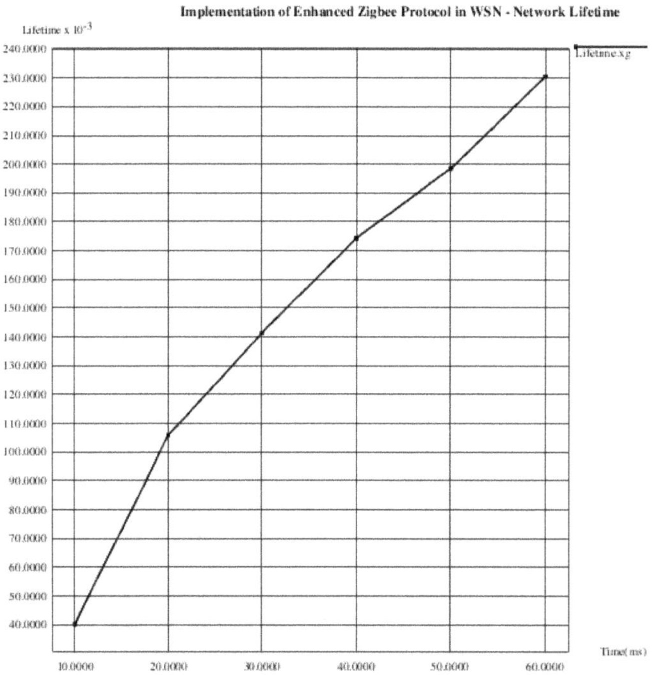

Figure 20. Implementation of IDS with Zigbee protocol in WSN – network lifetime

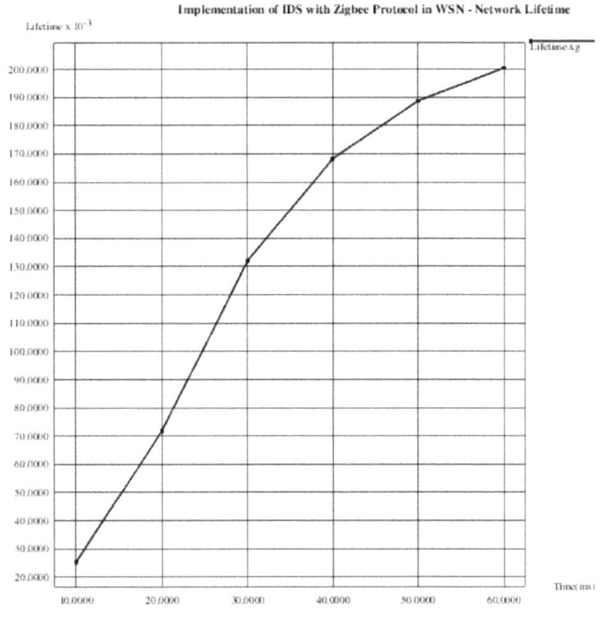

Table 7. Network lifetime with different interval of time

Time(ms)	Lifetime	
	Zigbee Protocol	IDS With Zigbee Protocol
10	0.0258496	0.0393494
20	0.0621961	0.104788
30	0.0865819	0.169956
40	0.100632	0.200734
50	0.132956	0.22102
60	0.144934	0.240265

Figure 21. Analysis of network lifetime for IDS using Zigbee protocol with time interval

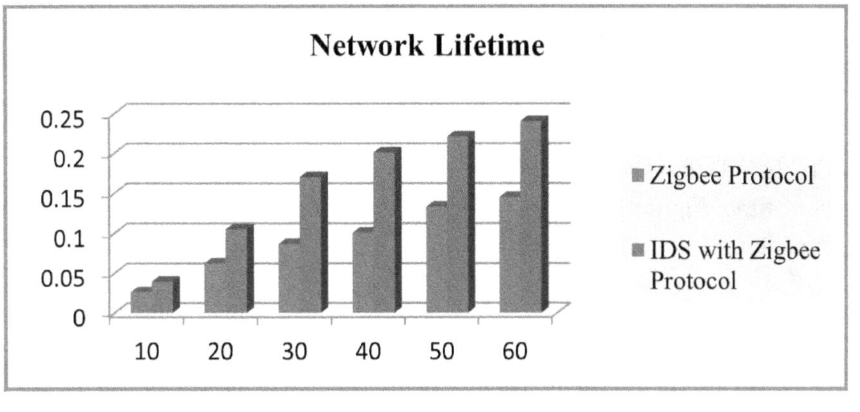

Figure 22. Recall percentage with nodes 100

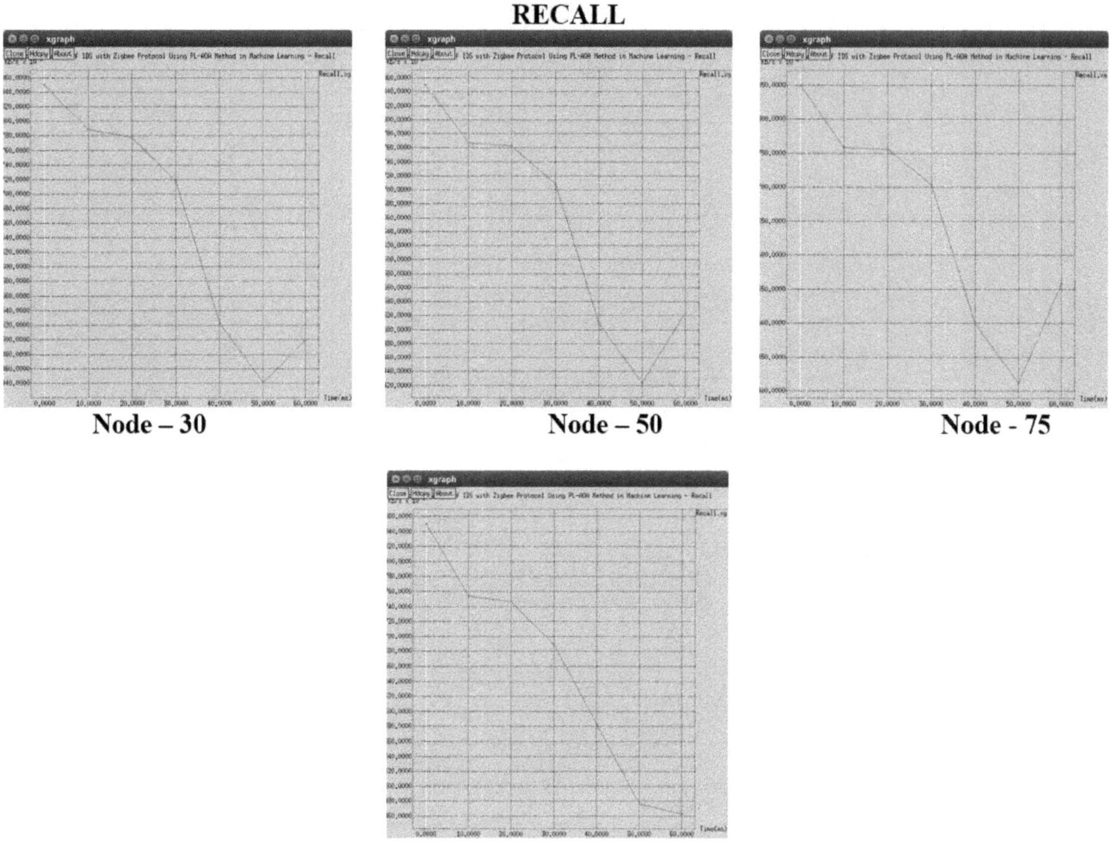

Table 8. Recall values for different number of nodes

Time(ms)	Node - 30	Node - 50	Node -75	Node - 100
10	0.79386	0.759778	0.757788	0.755271
20	0.780992	0.757056	0.755511	0.752583
30	0.720128	0.705307	0.704194	0.700924
40	0.514509	0.540957	0.514412	0.582279
50	0.429872	0.455909	0.426648	0.47099
60	0.546146	0.494507	0.538901	0.478603

in WSN – End To End Delay shown in Figure 11 and Table 4 depicts the energy consumption with different interval of time. Figure 12 shows the analysis of Energy Consumption for IDS using Zigbee protocol with time interval.

Figure 23. Analysis of recall metrics

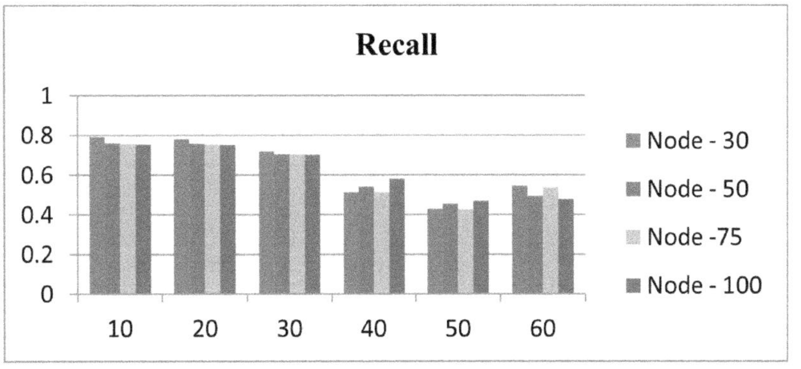

Figure 24. Precision with nodes 100

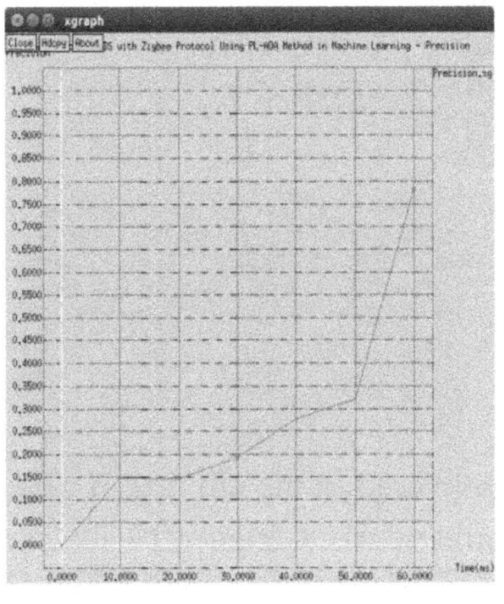

Node – 30

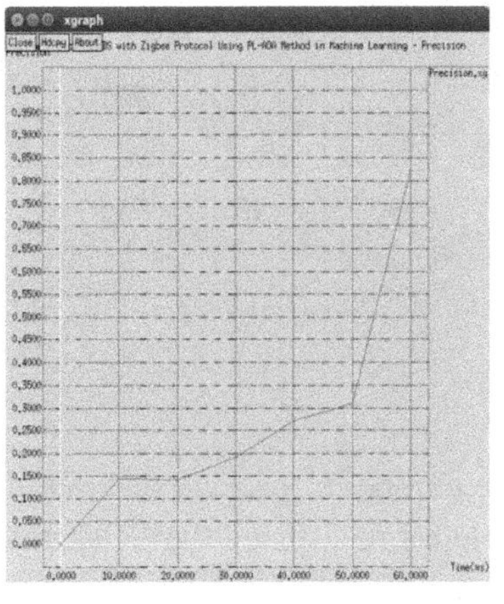

Node – 50

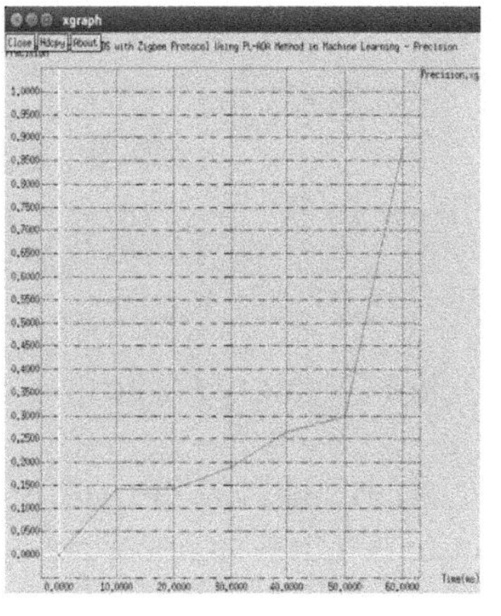

Node – 75

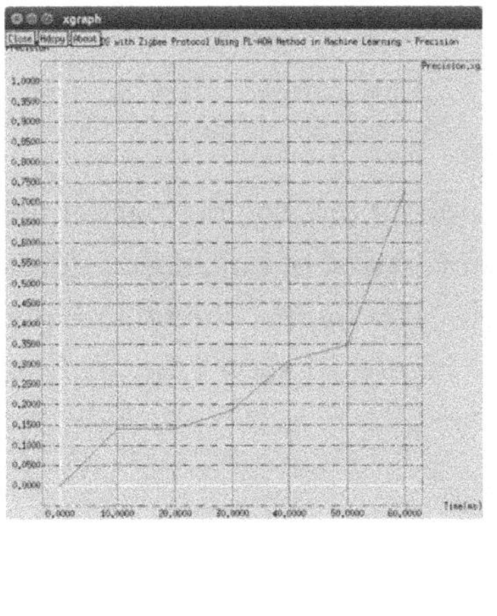

Table 9. Precision values for different number of nodes

Time(ms)	Node - 30	Node – 50	Node -75	Node – 100
10	0.148187	0.141825	0.141454	0.15157
20	0.145785	0.141317	0.141029	0.148485
30	0.195463	0.19144	0.191138	0.198143
40	0.272846	0.286871	0.292794	0.242513
50	0.313297	0.332273	0.350947	0.26875
60	0.755628	0.774727	0.844278	0.930063

Figure 25. Analysis of precision metrics

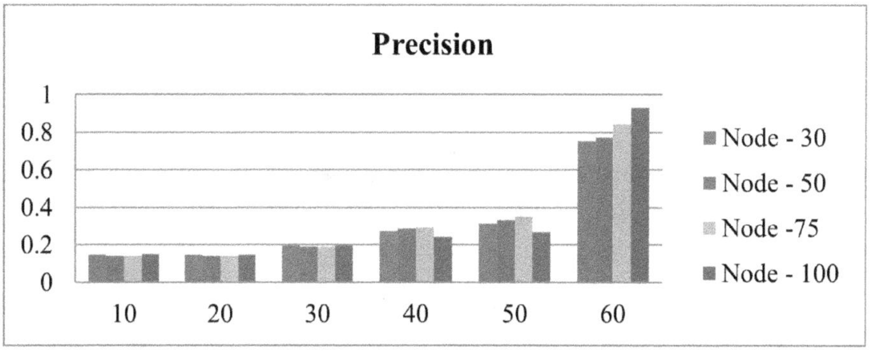

Packet Delivery Ratio

This metric measure the ratio of the number of packets successfully delivered to the number of packets transmitted. It is an important metric for measuring the reliability of the network. Figure 13 shows the implementation of enhanced zigbee protocol in WSN. Implementation of IDS With Zigbee Protocol in WSN – PDR shown in Figure 14 and Table 5 depicts the PDR with different interval of time. Figure 15 shows the analysis of Packet Delivery Ratio for IDS using Zigbee protocol with time interval.

Throughput

This metric measures the amount of data that can be transmitted over the network within a given time frame. Figure 16 shows the implementation of enhanced zigbee protocol in WSN. Implementation of IDS With Zigbee Protocol in WSN – Throughput shown in Figure 17 and Table 6 depicts the Throughput with different interval of time. Figure 18 shows the analysis of Throughput for IDS using Zigbee protocol with time interval.

Network Lifetime

This metric measure the time for which the network can operate before the batteries need to be replaced. It is an important metric as it reflects the overall sustainability of the network. Figure 19 shows the

Figure 26. Overall effectiveness of intrusions with number of nodes 30, 50 and 75

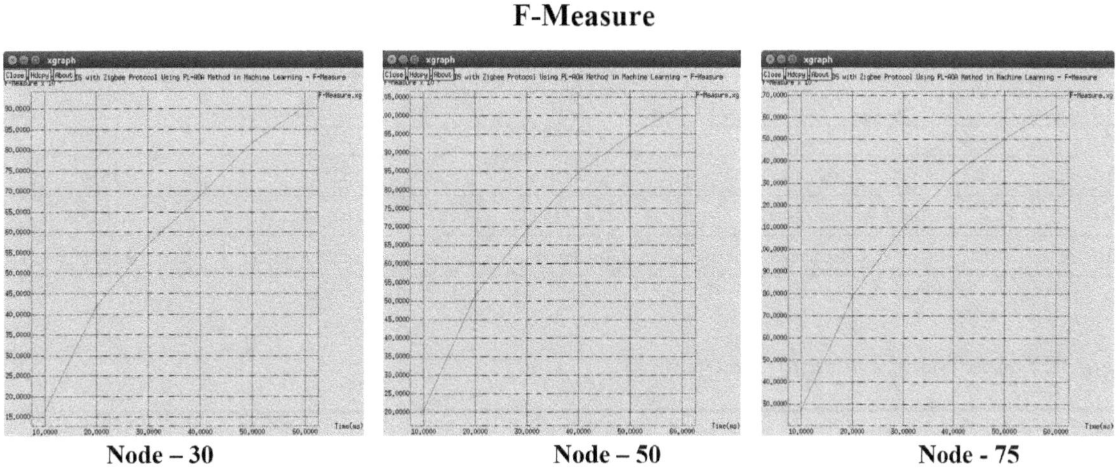

Figure 27. F-measure with nodes 100

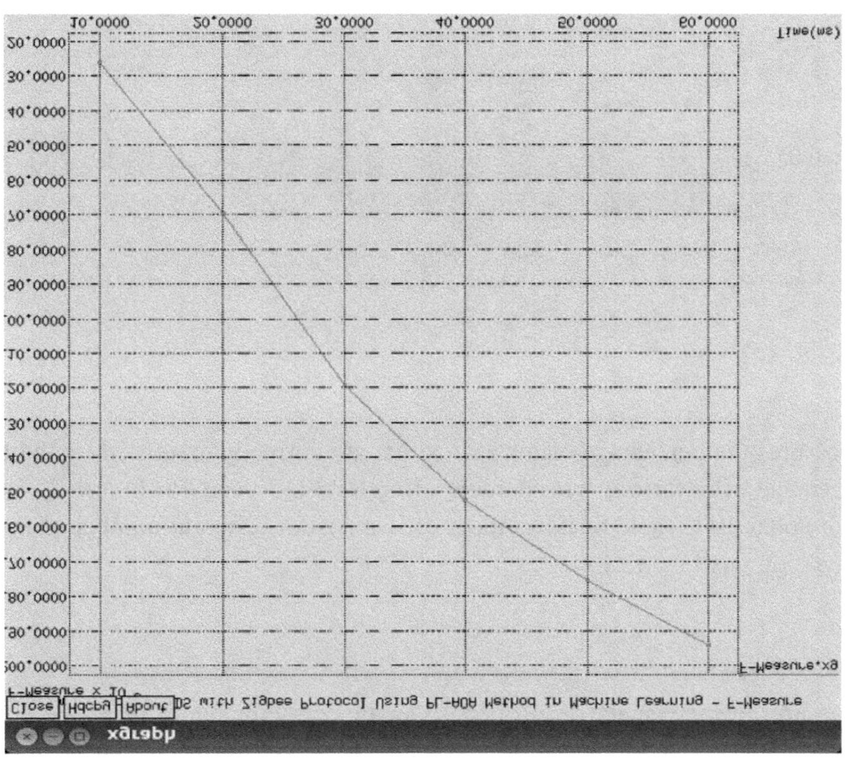

implementation of enhanced zigbee protocol in WSN. Implementation of IDS With Zigbee Protocol in WSN – Network Lifetime shown in Figure 20 and Table 7 depicts the Network Lifetime with different interval of time. Figure 21 shows the analysis of Network Lifetime for IDS using Zigbee protocol with time interval.

Table 10. F-measure values for different number of nodes

Time(ms)	Node - 30	Node - 50	Node -75	Node – 100
10	0.0125324	0.0401893	0.0364121	0.0323786
20	0.0334323	0.0987574	0.0941561	0.0935598
30	0.0456659	0.131085	0.125651	0.150911
40	0.0559121	0.154643	0.152581	0.183927
50	0.0608957	0.173153	0.164915	0.204512
60	0.0654393	0.186678	0.178023	0.233525

Figure 28. Analysis of F-measure metrics

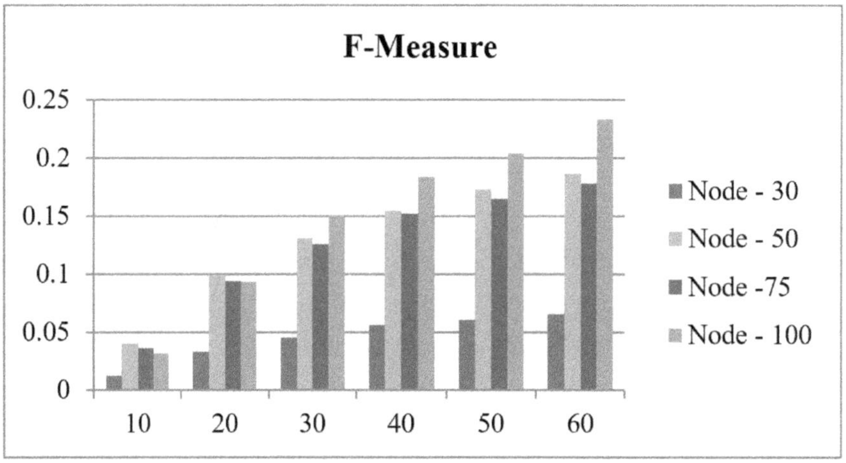

Recall

This metric measures the percentage of intrusions that are correctly identified by the IDS. Figure 22 shows the percentage of intrusions with number of nodes 30, 50 and 75. Figure 22 shows the recall percentage with nodes 100. Table 8 shows the recall values for different number of nodes. Figure 23 shows the analysis of recall metrics.

Precision

This metric measures the percentage of intrusions that are correctly identified by the IDS out of all the intrusions detected by the IDS. Figure 24 shows the percentage of intrusions with number of nodes 30, 50 and 75. Figure 24 shows the precision percentage with nodes 100. Table 9 shows the precision values for different number of nodes. Figure 25 shows the analysis of precision metrics.

Figure 29. Accuracy percentage with nodes 100

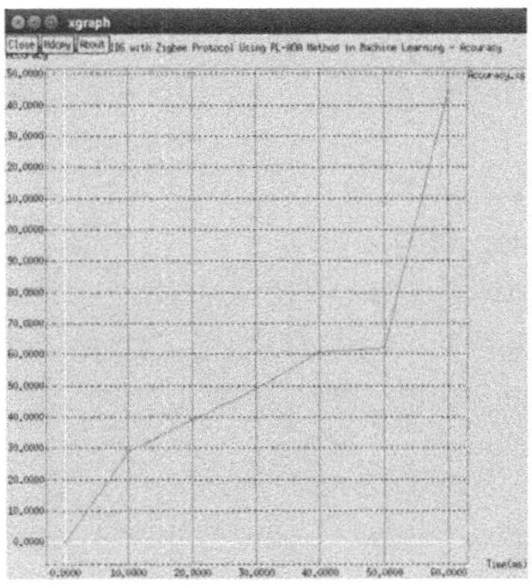

Node – 30

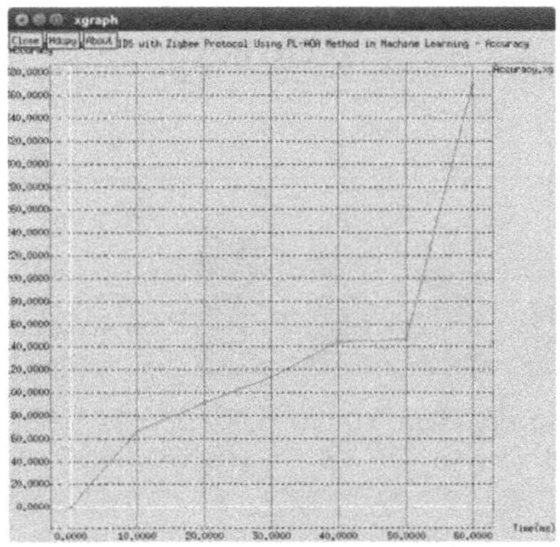

Node – 50

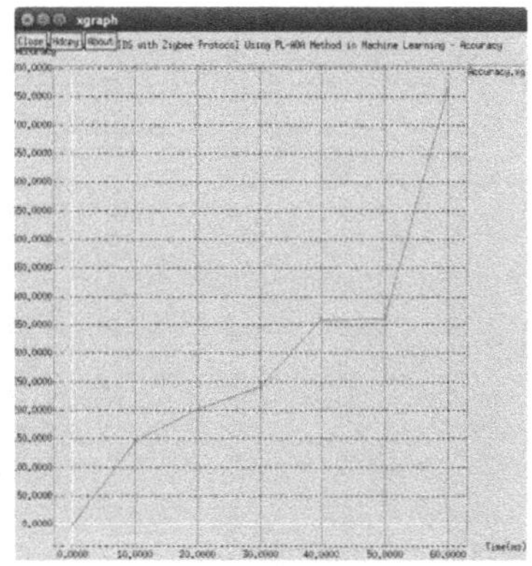

Node - 75

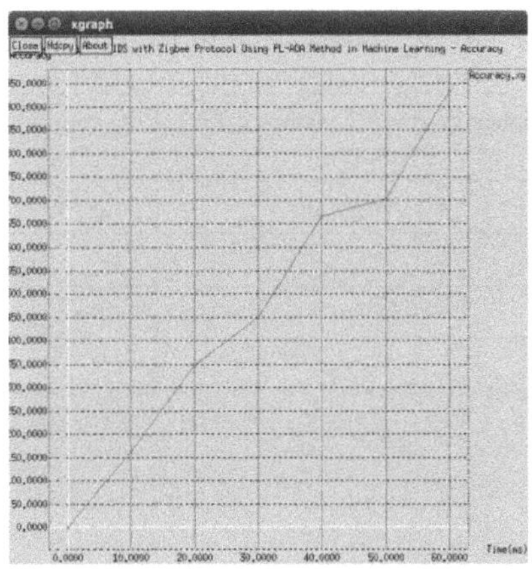

Table 11. Accuracy

Number of Nodes	Accuracy Percentage(%) Before IDS	Accuracy Percentage(%) After IDS
Node - 30	37	59
Node - 50	63.5	68.33
Node -75	69	74.66
Node - 100	82.75	95.42

F-Measure

This metric combines both recall and precision to provide an overall measure of the effectiveness of the IDS in detecting intrusions. Figure 26 shows the effectiveness of intrusions with number of nodes 30, 50 and 75. Figure 27 shows the F-Measure percentage with nodes 100. Table 10 shows the F-Measure values for different number of nodes. Figure 28 shows the analysis of F-Measure metrics.

Figure 30. Analysis of accuracy metrics

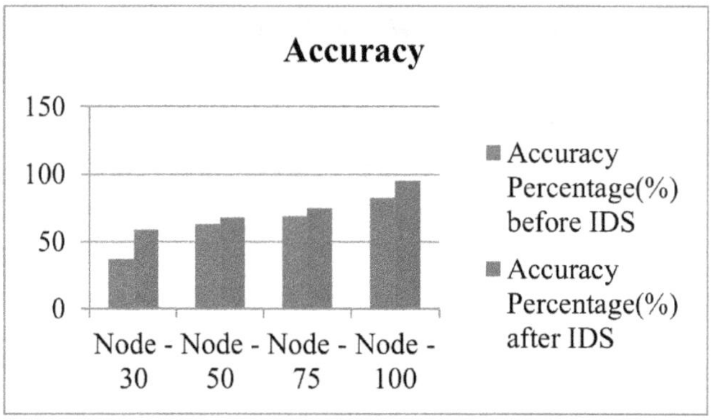

Table 12. Energy consumed, IDS prediction and false detection ratio with accuracy

No of Nodes (100)	Zigbee Wireless Network IDS Prediction	Zigbee With SFA Prediction Using Machine Learning Techniques
Energy Consumed	200 µW / node	190 µW / node
IDS Prediction Ratio	90%	98.5%
False detection Ratio	78%	62.3%
Accuracy	96.2%	99.5%

Accuracy

This metric measures the percentage of intrusions that are correctly identified by the IDS out of all the packets analyzed by the IDS.

Figure 29 shows the Accuracy with number of nodes 30, 50 and 75. Figure 29 shows the Accuracy percentage with nodes 100. Table 11 shows the Accuracy values for different number of nodes before and after IDS. Figure 30 shows the analysis of Accuracy metrics where before IDS 82.75% and accuracy for 100 nodes is 95.42%.

CONCLUSION AND FUTURE SCOPE

Based on the research on energy efficiency using Zigbee protocol for IDS detection, it can be concluded that this approach can offer several advantages. Zigbee protocol, which is a low-power wireless communication technology, can help reduce energy consumption compared to traditional wired systems. Table 12 shows that the identification time is reduced to 10 watts by frequently detecting the false detection ratio. This reduction in energy consumption can lead to lower operational costs and longer battery life for devices. Additionally, Zigbee protocol can provide reliable and secure communication between devices, which is essential for IDS detection. Overall, the use of Zigbee protocol for IDS detection can provide a cost-effective and efficient solution for monitoring and detecting intrusions in various environments, including industrial and home automation systems. However, further research is required to optimize the performance of the system and ensure its effectiveness in real-world scenarios. In future, the performance of the system can be enhanced by applying deep learning techniques.

REFERENCES

Alexandrov, A., Monov, V., Andreev, R., & Doshev, J. (2019). QoS based method for energy optimization in ZigBee wireless sensor networks. In *Communications in Computer and Information Science* (pp. 41–52). Springer International Publishing.

Diaz, A., & Sanchez, P. (2016). Simulation of attacks for security in wireless sensor network. *Sensors (Basel), 16*(11), 1932. doi:10.3390/s16111932 PMID:27869710

Ding, J., Wang, H., & Wu, Y. (2022). The Detection Scheme Against Selective Forwarding of Smart Malicious Nodes With Reinforcement Learning in Wireless Sensor Networks. *IEEE Sensors Journal, 22*(13), 13696–13706. doi:10.1109/JSEN.2022.3176462

Ding, J., Zhang, H., Guo, Z., & Wu, Y. (2021). The DPC-Based Scheme for Detecting Selective Forwarding in Clustered Wireless Sensor Networks. *IEEE Access : Practical Innovations, Open Solutions, 9*, 20954–20967. doi:10.1109/ACCESS.2021.3055026

Engmann, F., Adu-Manu, K. S., Abdulai, J.-D., & Katsriku, F. A. (2021). Network performance metrics for energy efficient scheduling in Wireless Sensor Networks (WSNs). *Wireless Communications and Mobile Computing, 2021*, 1–14. doi:10.1155/2021/9635958

Ezhilarasi, M., Gnanaprasanambikai, L., Kousalya, A., & Shanmugapriya, M. (2023). A novel implementation of routing attack detection scheme by using fuzzy and feed-forward neural networks. *Soft Computing, 27*(7), 4157–4168. doi:10.1007/s00500-022-06915-1

Gao, C., Yan, C., Adamatzky, A., & Deng, Y. (2014). A bio-inspired algorithm for route selection in wireless sensor networks. *IEEE Communications Letters, 18*(11), 2019–2022. doi:10.1109/LCOMM.2014.2360523

Huang, X., & Wu, Y. (2022). Identify selective forwarding attacks using danger model: Promote the detection accuracy in wireless sensor networks. *IEEE Sensors Journal, 22*(10), 9997–10008. doi:10.1109/JSEN.2022.3166601

Jiang, J., & Liu, Y. (2022). Secure IoT Routing: Selective Forwarding Attacks and Trust-based Defenses in RPL Network. *ArXiv, abs/2201.06937*

Khan, S., Lloret, J., & Macias-López, E. (2015). Bio-inspired mechanisms in wireless sensor networks. *International Journal of Distributed Sensor Networks, 11*(3), 173419. doi:10.1155/2015/173419

Kothawade, N., Biradar, A., Kodmelwar, K., Tambe, K. P., & Deshpande, V. (2016). Performance analysis of wireless sensor network by varying reporting rate. *Indian Journal of Science and Technology, 9*(26). Advance online publication. doi:10.17485/ijst/2016/v9i26/91906

Lee, M., Kim, H., & Yoe, H. (2018). Wireless sensor networks based on bio-inspired algorithms. In *Computational Science and Its Applications – ICCSA 2018* (pp. 719–725). Springer International Publishing. doi:10.1007/978-3-319-95162-1_52

Liu, G., Zhao, H., Fan, F., Liu, G., Xu, Q., & Nazir, S. (2022). An enhanced intrusion detection model based on improved kNN in WSNs. *Sensors (Basel)*, *22*(4), 1407. doi:10.3390/s22041407 PMID:35214308

Machdi, A. R., & Tan, Y. (2022). Performance analysis on Wireless Sensor Network based on Zigbee Wireless Communication protocol. JREC, 9(2), 25–30. doi:10.33558/jrec.v9i2.3188

Majid, M., Habib, S., Javed, A. R., Rizwan, M., Srivastava, G., Gadekallu, T. R., & Lin, J. C.-W. (2022). Applications of wireless sensor networks and Internet of Things frameworks in the industry revolution 4.0: A systematic literature review. *Sensors (Basel)*, *22*(6), 2087. doi:10.3390/s22062087 PMID:35336261

Matos, Rebello, Costa, Queiroz, Regufe, & Nogueira. (2022). *Bio-inspired algorithms in the optimisation of wireless sensor networks.* Academic Press.

Nguyen. (2021). ZigBee based data collection in wireless sensor networks. *Int. J. Inform. Commun. Technol.*, *10*(3), 212.

Nie, B. (2022). Zigbee-based wireless sensor network energy-saving networking intelligent technology and middleware optimization. *2022 3rd International Conference on Smart Electronics and Communication (ICOSEC).* 10.1109/ICOSEC54921.2022.9951997

Patel, A., & Jinwala, D. (2021). A reputation-based RPL protocol to detect selective forwarding attack in Internet of Things. *International Journal of Communication Systems*, *35*(1), e5007. Advance online publication. doi:10.1002/dac.5007

Song, J., & Tan, Y. K. (2012). Energy consumption analysis of ZigBee-based energy harvesting wireless sensor networks. *2012 IEEE International Conference on Communication Systems (ICCS).* 10.1109/ICCS.2012.6406192

Thorat, V., Kumar, S., & Wadhwa, D. L. (2020). Extended multipath routing in zigbee which improves performance parameters. SSRN *Electron. J.* doi:10.2139/ssrn.3659913

Wang, Z., Pei, H., Chen, H., Wang, C., Fang, Z., & Zhou, T. (2021). Performance study of ZigBee wireless sensor network for 500kV UHV transmission tower. *2021 International Conference on Power System Technology (POWERCON).* 10.1109/POWERCON53785.2021.9697782

Ye, Z., Wen, T., Liu, Z., Song, X., & Fu, C. (2017). An efficient dynamic trust evaluation model for wireless sensor networks. *Journal of Sensors*, *2017*, 1–16. doi:10.1155/2017/7864671

Zhang, J., Zhang, G., Huang, Y., & Kong, M. (2022). A novel enhanced arithmetic optimization algorithm for global optimization. *IEEE Access : Practical Innovations, Open Solutions*, *10*, 75040–75062. doi:10.1109/ACCESS.2022.3190481

Zhang, Q., & Zhang, W. (2019). Accurate detection of selective forwarding attack in wireless sensor networks. *International Journal of Distributed Sensor Networks*, *15*(1). Advance online publication. doi:10.1177/1550147718824008

Zhao, Y. (2021). Research on wireless sensor network system based on ZigBee technology for short distance transmission. *Journal of Physics: Conference Series*, *1802*(2), 022008. doi:10.1088/1742-6596/1802/2/022008

Chapter 13
Simulation of Routing Protocols for Jamming Attacks in Mobile Ad-Hoc Network

Dena Abu Laila
Hashemite University, Jordan

Hasan Gharaibeh
Yarmouk University, Jordan

Qais Al-Na'amneh
Applied Science Private University, Jordan

Rabia Al Mamlook
Trine University, USA

Mohammad Aljaidi
https://orcid.org/0000-0001-9486-3533
Zarqa University, Jordan

Mohammed Alshammari
https://orcid.org/0000-0002-5859-7490
Northern Border University, Saudi Arabia

Ahmad Nawaf Nasayreh
Yarmouk University, Jordan

ABSTRACT

Jamming is the most critical security threat because the rapid development of new technology, such as smart mobile devices, and ad hoc networks have drawn a lot of interest from the academic community in recent years. Ad hoc protocols represent an important role in the efficient transmission of data across mobile ad hoc protocols (MANET). The choice of a suitable routing protocol is influenced by several variables, including network structure, scalability, mobility, and reliability. In this chapter, the authors employed three protocols: dynamic source routing (DSR), optimized link state routing (OLSR), and temporally ordered routing algorithm (TORA) routing protocols, including distance-vector, link-state, and hybrid protocols are thoroughly analyzed under jamming attack with an emphasis on their advantages, disadvantages, and practical uses. This chapter focuses on these protocols' applicability for various network scenarios with attacks using the network simulator OPNET 14.5.

DOI: 10.4018/979-8-3693-2691-6.ch013

1. INTRODUCTION

Ad hoc networks do not depend on a pre-existing infrastructure, hence nodes cannot freely join or leave the network. Through a wireless link, the nodes are interconnected. A node may function as a router to send the information to the nodes of the neighbors. Therefore, Infrastructure-less networking is another name for this type of system network. There is no centralized management for these networks. Ad-hoc networks are equipped to deal with any node malfunctions or alterations that they encounter due to changes in topology. Each time a network node creates the connection between other devices is down or departs, and nodes are damaged. The networks impacted nodes merely new linkages and requests for new routes are created Ad-Hoc networks can be divided into static and Mobile Ad-Hoc networks MANET is the focus of current research.

A routing protocol chooses the best paths for network data transfer and communication between network nodes using software and routing algorithms. Individual nodes in the network forward packets to and from one another rather than relying on an access point that serves as a base station to manage the flow of communications to each other. Because MANETs (Mishra, 2019) include movable nodes, they connect to different networks via wireless technologies. A technique that helps nodes choose the best path for sending packets between computing devices in a MANET is known as an ad hoc routing protocol. Ad hoc networks don't have fixed topologies. Rather, a new node announces its presence and listens for announcements sent by its neighbors; they have to find it instead. When a node finds out that other nodes are close by, it can learn how to reach them and then declare that it can reach them too. Despite the prominence that MANET research received, efforts are still being made to secure the MANET and defend it from outside threats. The modeling of mobile ad hoc networks under jamming attacks using an integrated method will be introduced in this article. Ad-hoc routing protocols can be broadly categorized into three main types: proactive (table-driven), reactive (on-demand), and hybrid protocols (Manaseer, 2023).

A. Proactive Protocols (Also Known as Table-Driven Protocols)

Proactive protocols maintain up-to-date routing information for all nodes in the network. This involves maintaining routing tables that store paths to all possible destinations. Popular examples include Optimized Link State Routing (OLSR) and Destination-Sequenced Distance Vector (DSDV). While they provide relatively fast data forwarding once the paths are established, they consume more bandwidth and energy due to the continuous maintenance of routing tables. Because of this, OLSR uses the following procedures: route calculation, neighbor detection, link sensing, topology control message diffusion, and MPR selection signaling.

B. Reactive Protocols

Reactive protocols establish routes on-demand, meaning they only initiate route discovery when a source node wants to transmit data to a destination node. Examples of reactive protocols are Ad hoc On-Demand Distance Vector (AODV) and Dynamic Source Routing (DSR). Reactive protocols are generally more bandwidth-efficient, as they minimize the overhead of maintaining routing information. However, they might introduce delays in route discovery, particularly for less frequently visited destinations.

C. Hybrid Protocols

Hybrid protocols combine features of both proactive and reactive protocols to strike a balance between bandwidth efficiency and route establishment speed. They use proactive methods for frequently visited destinations and reactive methods for less common destinations. Zone Routing Protocol(ZRP) and Temporally Ordered Routing Algorithm (TORA) are an example of hybrid protocols.

Jamming victim networks in Mac Layer using different types of routing protocols is explored in this work. The attacker will then have to use external physical-layer-based DoS, the attacker cannot directly alter any of the victim's communications. Moreover, Jamming can be as easy as broadcasting a loud noise signal to block packets from entering the victim's network. To get an edge for jamming, this study aims to abuse the protocols at several tiers; Jamming gain is the improvement in effectiveness over continuous jamming that results from taking advantage of the victim network's capabilities. More specifically, it is the difference between the energy required to create a desired result and the energy required to achieve the same effect while jamming continuously. This benefit directly translates into less energy needed for the attacker. A packet will fail its checksum and be rejected at the link level if even one bit is corrupted in it. It means that jamming gains of up to 40dB are attainable for a 10,000-bit packet of 1250 bytes. Additionally, since most wireless packet networks are light-loaded.

JAMMING ATTACK

Researchers look into the IEEE 802.11 attacks in a variety of studies. Jamming attacks are the most often used attack model for IEEE 802.11 networks. A Denial of Service (DoS) attack known as jamming is one that prevents wireless network nodes from communicating with one another.The purpose of a jamming attack is to stop a valid sender or recipient from using the network to send or receive packets. Multiple layers of the protocol suite are vulnerable to jamming attacks by adversaries or rogue nodes. This study simulates jamming assaults on mobile area networks (MANETs) that cause network collisions. Physical and virtual jamming attacks are the two categories under which jamming falls.

Jamming attacks are not accidental; they are deliberate attempts to disrupt communication for malicious purposes by sending out signals on the same frequency as the target communication system, a jamming attack aims to intentionally interfere with or impair wireless communications. A jammer attack aims to obstruct legitimate users from sending or receiving data successfully by flooding the target's communication channels with noise or disturbance. A "jammer" is a device that allows an attacker to send out powerful signals on the same frequency range as the target network, interfering with legitimate devices' ability to communicate (Mughaid, 2023). Physical and virtual jamming attacks are the two types into which jamming is classified. Continuous transmissions and/or inducing packet collisions at the receiver start the physical jamming. Whereas in the IEEE

802.11 standard, attacks on control frames or data frames cause virtual jamming at the MAC layer. Physical interference in a wireless medium is a form of DoS attack. These types of attacks are carried out either by transmitting random bits on the channel or by broadcasting radio signals continuously (Manderna, 2023). Sev- eral security solutions, such as encryption, intrusion detection systems, secure routing protocols, and cooperative techniques that make use of the collective behavior of nodes to detect and isolate hostile actors, have been proposed for MANETs to minimize these vulnerabilities and assaults. However, achieving effective security remains a challenging and ongoing study area because of

Figure 1. Jamming attack

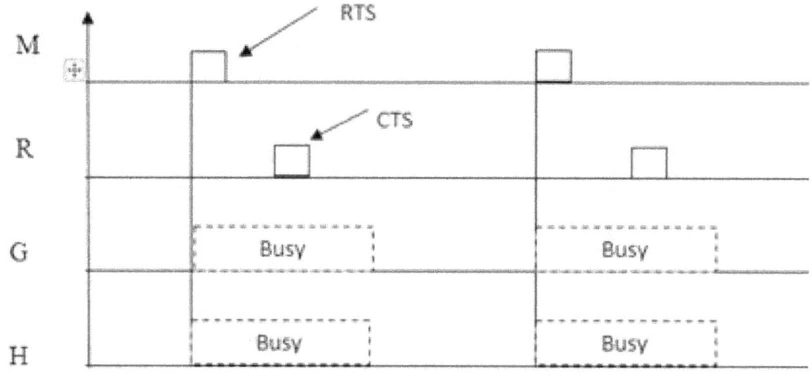

the particular difficulties faced by MANETs. Virtual jamming attacks that launch against a MAC layer on the data frames or on the RTS/CTS (Abuzainab, (2019, November)) Compared to actual radio jamming, attacks that launch against a MAC layer use less power to target their targets. In actuality, mobile ad hoc networks share a wireless medium among their mobile hosts. A radio signal may be jammed or tampered with, which taints or loses the message. With a powerful transmitter, the attacker can create a signal strong enough to destroy communications and crush the targeted signals. Jamming is the result of transmitting radio signals repeatedly in between transmissions, which injects false packets and causes interferences. Because radio frequency is an open channel, jamming poses a serious threat to wireless networks. Jamming affects the network's throughput, load, end-to-end delays, etc., which lowers the network's overall performance. This work focuses on DDoS attacks at the MAC layer. For instance, malicious node M started delivering a huge frame-sized bogus RTS packet to node R. When nodes G and H receive packets on a wireless channel, they are both temporarily stopped, just like node M is in Figure 1.

The purpose of this study is to present a thorough examination of how well the DSR, OLSR, and TORA routing protocols function in the face of jamming attacks. We aim to determine these protocols' advantages, disadvantages, and real-world applications in the face of jamming attacks by testing them in controlled simulated environments. The main contribution of this paper:

1. Acquire a Comprehension of different ad hoc routing protocols in MANET.
2. How various Ad-hoc network routing techniques before and after a jamming attack
3. Comprehension to carry out controlled tests in a simulation environment enables the examination of various circumstances and the assessment of the resistance to jamming of routing protocols.
4. These simulations were critical in identifying flaws in the routing protocols and countermeasures.
5. Simulating jamming attacks in ad hoc routing systems has provided insightful information and helped to create more resilient protocols
6. Enhancing simulation accuracy and developing realistic jamming models.

The remaining paragraphs of the article are organized as follows: A few relevant works are shown in section 2, the simulation setup performance measures are described in section 3, the results are shown in section 4, and the conclusion is given in section 5.

2. RELATED WORKS

A new technique for mitigating jamming in wireless sensor networks enhances performance over existing strategies by employing a clustering approach and timestamp calculation. The method entails grouping sensor nodes, calculating timestamps between nodes, identifying jamming by signature mismatch, and rebroadcasting data via alternate pathways. Metrics such as Packet Delivery Ratio, Network Throughput, Energy Consumption, and Routing Overhead are used to assess performance using simulation MATLAB with a maximum of randomly distributed 30 nodes (Walshe, 2019). In (Wang, 2019) a technique called Efficient Jamming Revocation (EJR), which is a combination of EDH and OLSR, is used against jamming attacks and discusses the use of UFH (uncoordinated frequency hopping), a new anti-jamming technique, to overcome attacks like packet injection and spoofing network level control information and use of a public key (PKA) or asymmetric key algorithm for algorithm implementation using simulation NS2 with randomly distributed 100 nodes and X-graph software tools for visual interpretation of the network topology and interactive plotting and graphing animation. In (Koch, 2019) focuses on jamming at the Transport/Network layer and explores the effectiveness of jamming at this layer in disrupting encrypted victim wireless ad hoc networks and the use of filters in client nodes to discard packets under specific conditions, which can be used to simulate external jamming or implement a jamming recipe to filter out specific packets in the client-server exchange which makes packet classifications on each packet as it arrives to provide timely information to the jamming module using simulation NS2. In (Tiloca, 2018) proposed three schemes to prevent real-time packet classification by combining cryptographic primitives with physical-layer attributes and the use of selective jamming attacks and provides case studies on selective attacks on TCP and routing Also, discusses the use of different jam- mers in various environments and the feasibility of switching channels to avoid jamming attacks. Analyze the security of the proposed methods and evaluate their computational and communication overhead using simulation OPNET Modeler. In (Aneiba, 2016) focused on four routing protocols (DSR, TORA, OLSR, and GRP) to evaluate their performance in improving delay, throughput, and other parameters in the presence of jamming attackers and collected results in terms of parameters such as delay and throughput to assess the performance of the network under different scenarios using simulation OPNET Modeler. In (Manaseer, 2023)The availability feature for automotive network applications is examined in this work, and the various types of denial of service (DoS) attacks are defined on Vehicular Ad hoc NETwork (VANET). they investigate various DoS scenarios that could arise in the context of a vehicle network Additionally, they research the earlier safe methods that addressed and generally took into account denial-of-service attacks on the vehicle network. (Sharma, 2016) The OLSR, TORA, and GRP procedures are taken. One feature of the suggested work is a highly mobile network. The attack was carried out, its effects were assessed, and the Point coordination function (PCF) approach was employed to lessen the jamming effect using the OPNET tool

In (Singh, 2017)an integrated approach to analyze the performance of Mobile Ad hoc Networks (MANETs) under jamming attacks. The simulation setup includes a network with high mobility, using the IEEE 802.11g standard with improved parameters of the Ad hoc On-Demand Distance Vector (AODV) routing protocol. High-resolution video conferencing and FTP traffic are generated in the network using simulation OPNET Modeler. In (Salahdine, 2020)focused on analyzing the performance of VANET under a jamming attack. It included a network with high mobility, using the IEEE 802.11g standard with improved AODV routing protocol parameters. High-resolution video conferencing and FTP traffic were generated in the network and the performance of the network was measured concerning

QoS parameters such as network load, retransmission attempts, media access delay, and throughput using simulation OPNET Modeler. In (Salahdine, 2020)proposed a method implemented at the MAC layer to prevent and mitigate jamming attacks in Mobile Ad-Hoc Networks (MANET) and the method consists of a combination of different coordination mechanisms, including Point Controller Functions (PCF) and RTS/CTS (Clear-To- Send) to prevent malicious or selfish nodes using simulation OPNET Modeler. In (Del-Valle-Soto, 2019)proposed proposes two new self-tuning collaborative-based mechanisms for jamming detection: The Connected Mechanism and the Extended Mechanism. The Connected Mechanism detects jamming by comparing performance parameters with directly connected neighbors, while the Extended Mechanism detects jamming by comparing defined zones of nodes related to a collector node and tested in AODV (Ad hoc On-Demand Distance Vector), DSR (Dynamic Source Routing), and MPH (Multi-Parent Hierarchical) protocols, named AODV-M, DSR-M, and MPH-M, respectively of a 7x7 grid of nodes. In (Hassan, 2021)compare and evaluate the characteristics of four routing protocols (AODV, DSDV, OLSR, and DSR) based on metrics such as packet delivery fraction, average end-to-end delay, and throughput in mobile ad hoc networks and differences between table-driven (proactive) and on-demand (reactive) routing protocols. In (Al-Shareeda, 2023)they carried out a thorough analysis of MITM attackers' impact on MANET. They investigated the effects of two forms of MITM assaults (delayed messages and dropped messages) by simulating them in MANET. In OMNeT++, MITM assault simulations were performed using the NETA and INET frameworks. Their findings demonstrate the significant impact these two categories of attacks have on the network in terms of high E2ED, delayed messages, dropped messages, and PLR. In (Prasad)they have provided a method for MANETs to identify malicious gray hole nodes. The gray holes are exceedingly hard to find because of their sporadic behavior. By proactively integrating the neighbor nodes of a malicious gray hole node in a collaborative and distributed method, the proposed security technique boosts the accuracy of detection. The consensus mechanism used for detection decisions is based on threshold cryptography. According to the simulation results, the method has a high detection rate, a very low false positive rate, and minimal control overhead. In (Rabiaa, 2023)they have employed a successful method of protecting AODV from blackhole attacks. Considering the graphs displayed in the outcomes they may easily refute the idea that the typical under the influence of a blackhole attack, AODV falls. Their preventative measure finds and isolates harmful nodes. it from the ongoing data routing, forwarding, and responses via the transmission of ALARM packets to its neighbors. Our response: PDR is increased by DPRAODV with a minimal rise in Average-End-to-end Routing with delay and normalized overhead. In (Ranjan, 2023) they studied the blackhole attack and included the feature, to establish the network's typical state. They have demonstrated a brand-new detection technique based on training data that is dynamically updated. Our strategy exhibits notable effectiveness in identifying the blackhole assault through simulation.

3. METHODOLOGY

In this study, the primary objective was to examine how well the ad hoc protocol performed when malicious nodes were launching jamming attacks. Then we compared the results for all protocols using metrics such as delay, load, throughput, media access delay, and Retransmission attempts under different scenarios to observe which protocols were affected more.

Table 1. Simulation parameters

Parameter	Value
Protocols	DSR, OLSR, TORA
Number of nodes	7
Data Rate (Bandwidth)	11 Mbps
MAC Protocol	802.11
Simulation Area	1000 x 1000 meters
Mobility Speed	1-15 m/s
Simulation Time	900 s
Performance Parameters	Throughput, Delay, Load, Data Drop Rate
Transmit Power (W)	0.005
RTS Threshold (bytes)	1024 bytes

A. Simulator Employed

The OPNET modeler version 14.5 is a comprehensive simulation tool with lots of different options. As depicted in Fig.2. Using the OPNET simulator, a variety of simulation setups were used to evaluate routing protocols and apply jamming attacks. OPNET can be used to mimic completely heterogeneous networks with a variety of routing methods. OPNET has a high level of user interface and is built using blocks of C and C++ source code.

B. Simulation Setup and Performance Metrics

In this section, we demonstrate the process of simulation and analyses for jamming attacks on MANET, on the other hand, use OPNET simulator to evaluate their performance in improving delay, throughput, and other parameters in the presence of jamming attacks with different protocols including DSR, OLSR, and TORA. This strategy includes:

1) A 54 Mbps high data rate using the IEEE 802.11g standard.
2) highly mobile network.
3) Email and FTP traffic generation with different routing protocol parameters.

C. Performance Metrics

Performance metrics for ad hoc networks are used to evaluate the effectiveness and efficiency of these networks, which are characterized by their dynamic and self-organizing nature. Ad hoc networks are often used in scenarios where infrastructure-based networks are not available or practical, such as in emergency response situations or temporary network setups. Here are some common performance metrics for ad hoc networks (Prasad):

1) 1) Throughput: The amount of data that is successfully transmitted over the network in a certain amount of time is known as throughput. It is an important measure for assessing the network's data-carrying capability it is calculated in equation 1.

T=DT/TT (1)

Where T: Throughput, DT: Total Amount of Data Transferred, TT: Total Time Taken

2) Packet Delivery Ratio (PDR): PDR calculates the proportion of data packets successfully received by the destination node after being sent by the source node. For communication to be dependable, a high PDR is required it is calculated in equation 2.

PDR =(N.Success Delivered Packets)/(N.Sent Packets) (2)

Where PDR: Packet Delivery Ratio, N. Success Delivered Packets: Number of Successfully Delivered Packets, N.Sent Packets: Number of Sent Packets

3) End-to-End Delay: A packet's transit time from the source node to the destination node is measured using this metric. For real-time applications like phone and video communication, a low end-to-end delay is crucial it is calculated in equation 3.

$$ED = T = \frac{1}{N}\sum_{i+1}^{n}\left(Tri - Tsi\right)\times 1000\,ms \tag{3}$$

Where ED: Average E2E Delay, i: packet identifier, Tri: Reception time, Tsi: Send time, N: Number of packets successfully delivered.

4) Routing Overhead: The extra control packets needed to create and maintain routes in the network are referred to as routing overhead. Overhead in routing can use up bandwidth and degrade network performance it is calculated in equation 4

$$RO = \frac{NP}{TP} \tag{4}$$

Where RO: Routing Overhead, NP: Number of Control Packets, TP: Total Number of Data Packets

5) Network Lifetime: Ad hoc networks are often deployed in resource-constrained environments. Network lifetime measures how long the network can operate before nodes' batteries are depleted. Maximizing network lifetime is crucial in such scenarios it is calculated in Equation 5

$$\mathrm{NL} = \frac{\mathrm{IE}}{\mathrm{AC}} \tag{5}$$

Where NL: Network Lifetime, IE: Initial Energy, AC: Average Energy Consumption per Unit Time

6) Scalability: Scalability assesses how well the network performs as the number of nodes increases. A scalable ad hoc network should maintain its performance and functionality as it grows.

7) Connectivity: The ability of nodes to maintain connections inside the network is measured by connectivity. Metrics like the average hop count or the number of divergent pathways between nodes can be used to gauge it.

8) Packet Loss Rate: The fraction of data packets that fail to reach their intended location is quantified by the packet loss rate. High packet loss might lower service quality It is calculated in Equation 6:

$$P\ LR = \left(\frac{No.SP - No.RP}{No.SP} \right) \times 100\% \quad (6)$$

Where PLR: Packet Loss Rate, No.RP: Number of received packets. No.SP: Number of sent packets

4. SIMULATION RESULTS AND DISCUSSION

We tested and compared the performance of Ad-hoc network routing protocols using graphs for each of the performance indicators as mentioned below in two situations for each protocol: (a) normal behavior and (b) under a jamming attack. We used a network simulator (OPNET) to put our suggested solution into action. We created various scenarios using seven network nodes and two nodes as jammers. We used Constant Bit Rate (CBR) traffic with a packet size of 1024 bytes for regular traffic and 1000 bytes for aberrant traffic to produce the jamming attack traffic shown in Figure 2

A. Performance Metric

This section will include four performance matrices (delay, load, throughput, media access delay, and Re-transmission attempts) with three distinct protocols, each without attack and with attack as well as four performance matrices with four different protocols.

Delay (Sec)

Represents the end-to-end delay of all the packets received by the wireless LAN MACs of all WLAN nodes in the network and forwarded to the higher layer. This delay includes medium access delay at the source MAC, reception of all the fragments individually, and transfer of the frames via AP if access point functionality is enabled. Figure 3 makes it abundantly evident that Delay is used to examine the WLAN quality over the entire network. In Scenario 1, the DSR is under jamming assault, in Scenario 2, the OLSR is under jamming attack, in Scenario 3, the TORA protocol is under jamming attack, and in Scenario 4, there is no malicious event and the network is in a normal state. The jamming attack destroys the network. The protocol most affected by delay is the Reactive Protocol DSR, and we notice the lack of effect of the hybrid protocol TORA

Load (Bits/Sec)

Represents the total load (in bits/sec) that all upper levels in all network WLAN nodes have submitted to the wireless LAN layers. A variety of variables, including the kind of apps being used, the number of

Figure 2. Simulation environment

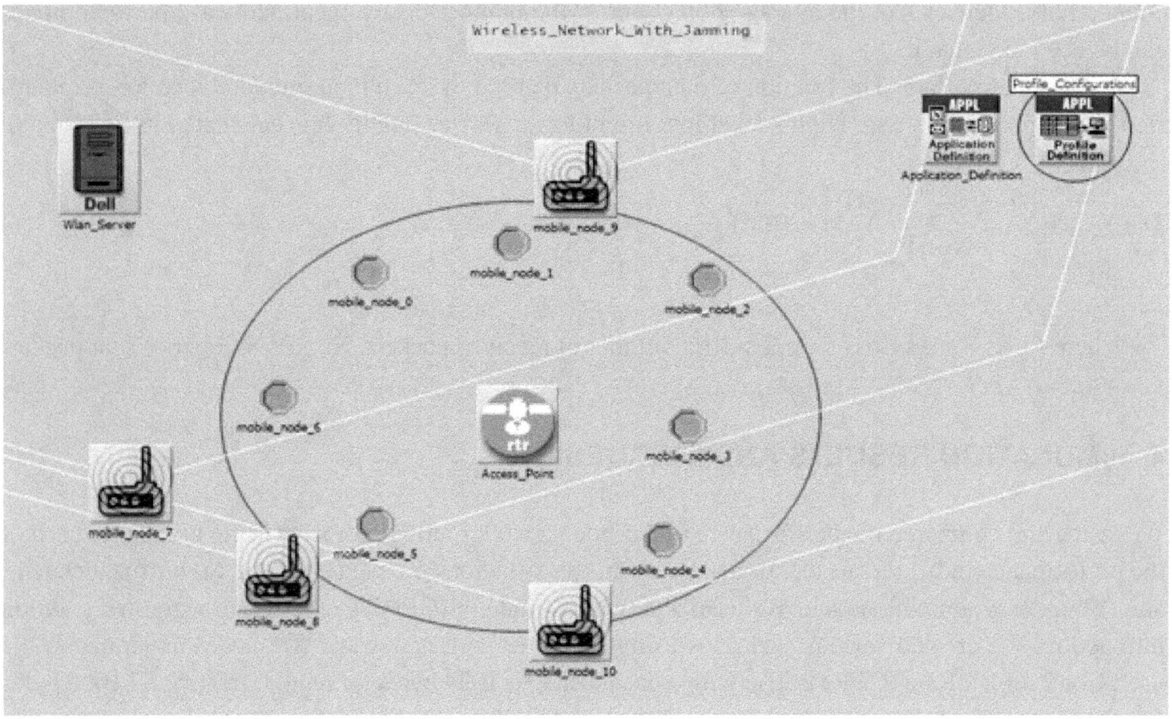

Figure 3. Delay for each protocol in different scenarios

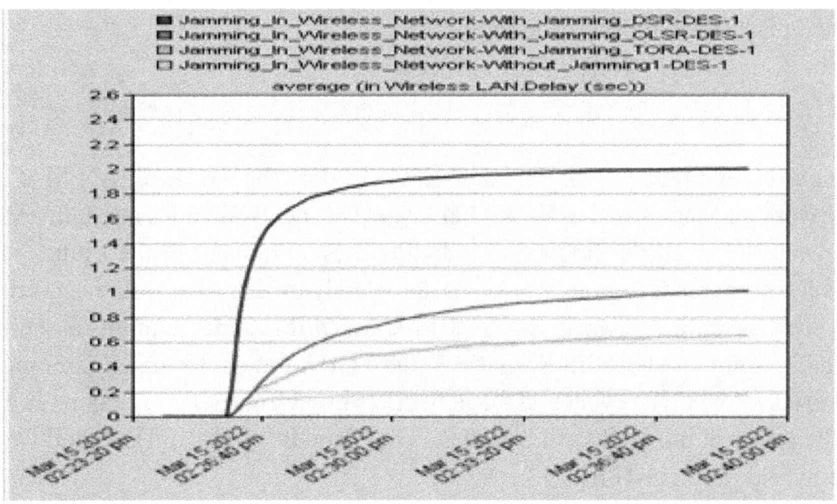

Figure 4. Load for each protocol in different scenarios

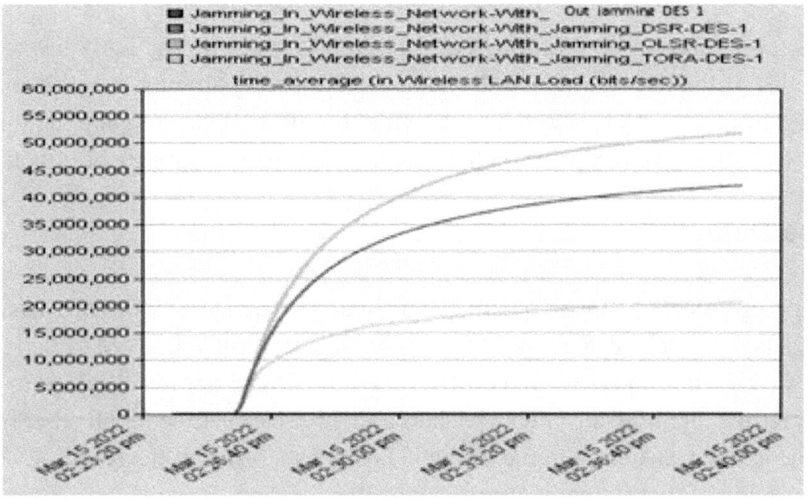

Figure 5. Throughput for each protocol in different scenarios

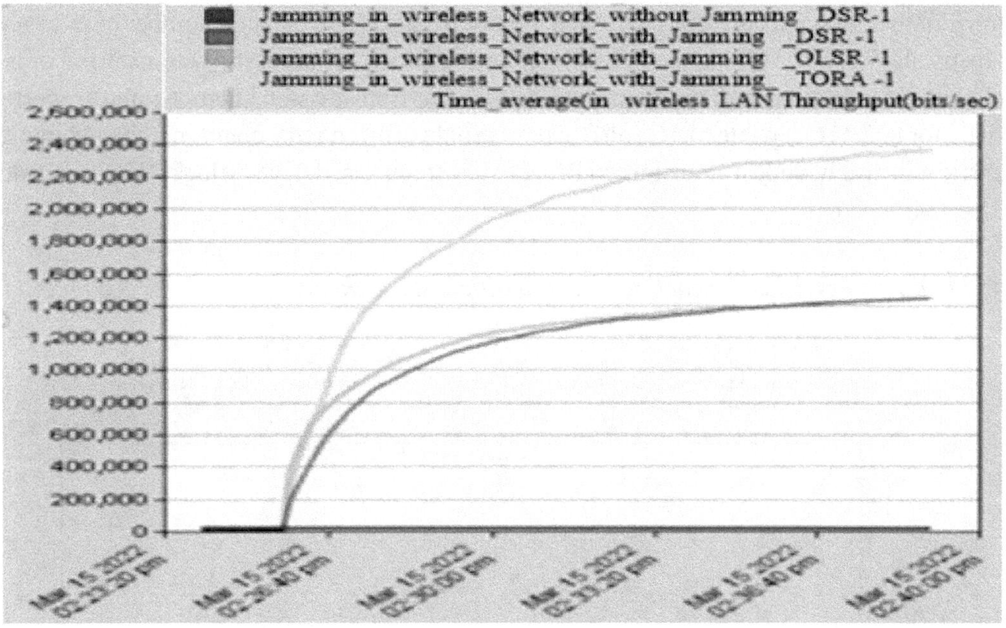

active users, and the patterns of data flow, can cause the load to change dynamically. Low network load typically denotes underutilization of network resources, whereas high network load can cause congestion, latency, and decreased performance. Figure 4 shows that when the attack starts, the WLAN network's load level increases. Compared to other protocols, the hybrid protocol is TORA.

Throughput

Represents the total number of bits (in bits/sec) forwarded from wireless LAN layers to higher layers in all WLAN nodes of the network. Once the suggested unified jamming attack is put into place, the throughput of the entire network is boosted as shown in Figure 5. If we compare the throughput in each protocol, we notice that the TORA protocol has the most significant number of effects in this case.

Media Access Delay

Represents the aggregate statistic for all queuing and contention delays of the data, management, delayed Block-ACK and delayed Block-ACK Request frames broadcast by all WLAN MACs in the network. This delay is estimated for each frame as the interval between the time the frame is added to the transmission queue—the arrival time for higher layer data packets and the creation time for all other frame types—and the time the frame is first transferred to the physical layer. As a result, if the RTS/CTS exchange is used before the transmission of that frame, it also includes the duration.

Re-Transmission Attempts (Packet)

The number of times a sender attempts to resend a specific packet and the total number of re-transmission tries made by all WLAN MACs in the network up until a packet is successfully transferred or is deleted because it has exceeded the short or long retry limit. The re-transmission attempt counts reported under this statistic for 802.11e-capable MACs also take internal collision retry count increments into account. This statistic will also include re-transmitted Block-ACK Requests, delayed Block-ACKs, and block MP-

Figure 6. Media access delay for each protocol in different scenarios

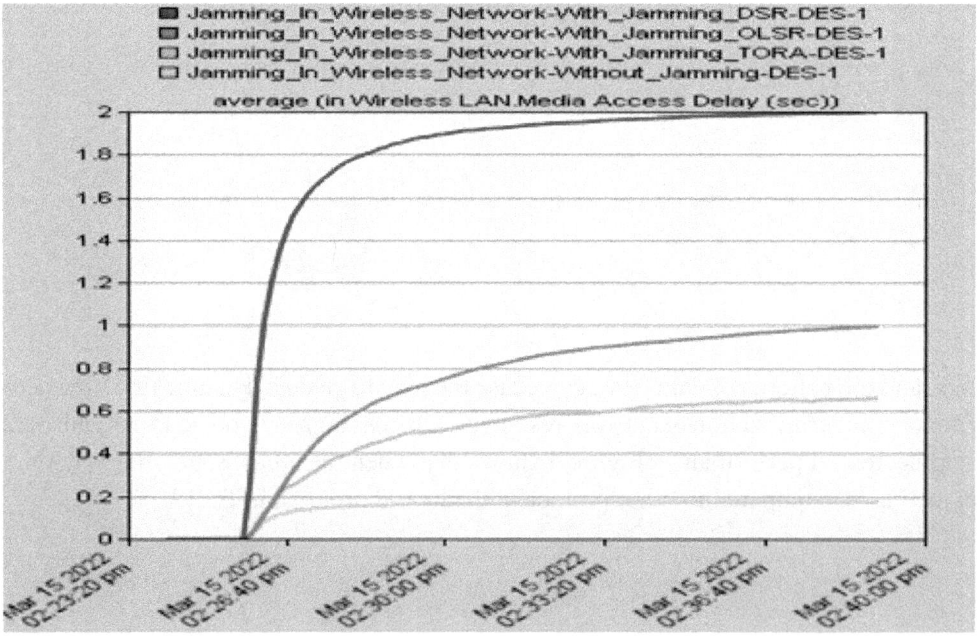

Figure 7. Retransmission attempts for each protocol in different scenarios

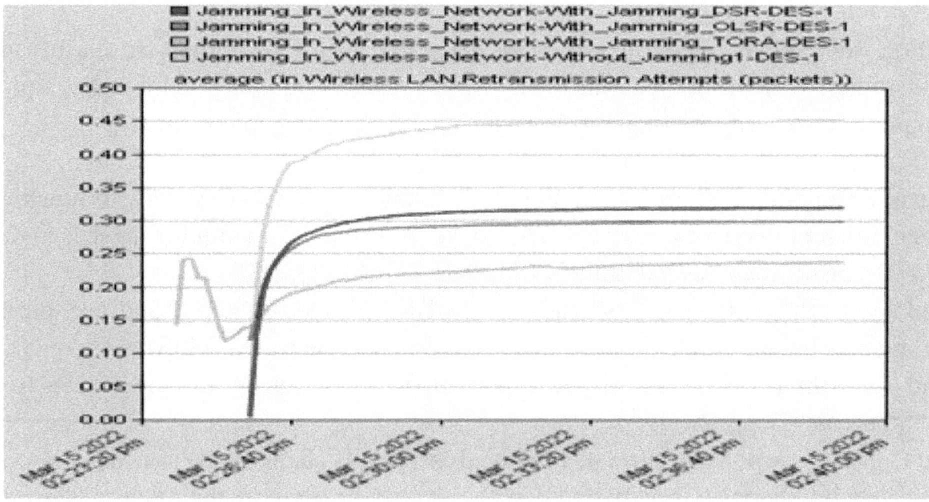

Parameters	Values	Parameters	Values
Protocols	DSR,OLSR,TORA	Mobility Speed	1-15m/s
Number of nodes	7	Simulation Time	900s
Data Rate (Bandwidth)	11mbps	Performance Parameters	Throughput, Delay, Load, Data Drop Rate
MAC Protocol	802.11	Transmit Power(W)	0.005
Simulation Area	1000 x 1000 (meters)	RTS Threshold (bytes)	1024 (bytes)

Parameters	Values	Parameters	Values
Protocols	DSR,OLSR,TORA	Mobility Speed	1-15m/s
Number of nodes	7	Simulation Time	900s
Data Rate (Bandwidth)	11mbps	Performance Parameters	Throughput, Delay, Load, Data Drop Rate
MAC Protocol	802.11	Transmit Power(W)	0.005
Simulation Area	1000 x 1000 (meters)	RTS Threshold (bytes)	1024 (bytes)

DUs that are not acknowledged in received Block-ACKs if any 11e-capable MACs use the Block-ACK mechanism. As we can see in Figure 7 in the normal mode without attack the number of re-transmission attempts is high whereas with jamming many packets are lost so the re-transmission attempts decrease.

We found that network performance significantly degraded during jamming attacks in all metrics. As the jamming signal strength grew, packet delivery ratios fell. Jamming attacks disrupted the network, increasing end-to-end delays and route-finding durations. so we need some countermeasures to enhance these problems.

B. Countermeasures Against Jamming

In this section, we explain countermeasures for expected MANET jamming scenarios, intending to inform and familiarize the reader with the most effective against jamming additionally, a proactive and adaptive approach to security is crucial in MANET due to their dynamic nature:

1) Frequency Hopping: Use frequency hopping techniques to allow devices to quickly transition between different frequency channels. This makes it difficult for jamming devices to disrupt communication on all channels indefinitely (Sharma, 2016) (Lee, 2023) .
2) Spread Spectrum Techniques: To spread the signal over a wide frequency band, use spread spectrum modulation techniques such as Direct Sequence Spread Spectrum (DSSS) or Frequency Hopping Spread Spectrum (FHSS). This makes it more difficult for signal-jamming devices to disrupt the entire broadcast (Depp, 2023)
3) Power Control: Use power control methods to dynamically change node transmission power. When nodes detect interference, they might boost their power or decrease their power. This saves energy and reduces the impact of jamming (Sedar, 2023) (López-Vilos, 2023).
4) Cognitive Radio: Use cognitive radio capabilities in nodes to intelligently choose less congested frequency bands or channels and adapt to changing network conditions. Cognitive radios are capable of detecting and avoiding blocked channels.
5) Adaptive Routing Protocols: In response to jammer attempts, use adaptive routing systems that can reroute traffic in real-time. Reactive routing protocols such as TORA are capable of adapting to changing network conditions (Zhang, 2023).
6) Physical Layer Security: To focus signals and limit vulnerability to jamming from certain directions, use physical layer security techniques like as beam-forming and directional transmitters (Arcangeloni, 2023) (Moumen, 2023).
7) Distributed Key Management: Implement secure and distributed key management techniques to guarantee communication confidentiality and integrity. This makes it more difficult for enemies to compromise the network by jamming it (Li, (2018, May).)
8) Backup Paths and Redundancy: Create numerous backup communication lines and incorporate network redundancy. This ensures that even if one path is jammed, communication can continue via alternate pathways.

C. Challenges and Limitations

There are various difficulties in simulating jamming attacks in ad hoc routing protocols. The necessity for realistic and dynamic network scenarios that effectively simulate the unpredictable nature of ad hoc networks is one of the main issues. Furthermore, it is difficult to adequately model jammer behavior and its effects on routing protocols. Furthermore, it is difficult to develop a thorough modeling framework that accounts for all potential scenarios given the wide variety of ad hoc routing protocols that are now accessible. Our study on modeling jamming attacks in ad hoc routing protocols is now in need of improvement. First, there aren't any standardized benchmarking techniques for assessing how well routing protocols operate when they're subject to jamming attacks. The capacity to effectively compare various protocols is hampered by this difference. Second, it continues to be difficult to incorporate accurate jamming attack models into simulators. Many of the currently available simulators are unable

Table 2. Comparing the proposed method to alternative methods

Simulate type	Proposed method	In (Tiloca, 2018)	In (Al-Shareeda, 2023)	In (Rani,2017	In (Salahdine, 2020)	In (Singh, 2017)	In (Rabiaa, 2023)	In (Ranjan, 2023)	In (Sharma, 2016)	In (Lee, 2023)
number of nodes	7	30/48	20,30,40,50	50	100 and 200	100 and 200	6	9	70	30
Type of attack	jamming attacks	jamming attacks	Black hole Attack	jamming	jamming	jamming	MITM	gray hole	blackhole	blackhole
Routing protocol	OLSR,RSA and TORA	AODV and OLSR	AODV	AODV	AODV	AODV	AODVUU	AODV	AODV	AODV
Environment	OPNET	NS2	NS-3	OPNET	OPNET	OPNET	OMNeT++ 4.3	Ns-2	Ns-2	Ns-2
Time of simulation	900s	100/150s	50 sec	300s	3600s	3600s	1000s	1500s	1000s	600(s)
Simulation Area	1000*1000m	750*750km	800*800m	1000*1000m	50*50 km	50*50 km 60*60 km	3*3km	2000m * 600m	800m x 800m	1000m × 1000m

to faithfully reproduce the sophistication and adaptability of the jamming methods used by attackers. Although simulation is a useful tool for researching jamming threats in ad hoc routing protocols, it does have several drawbacks. The difficulty in accurately simulating real-world settings is a serious restriction. The assumptions and simplifications that simulations rely on might not always match up with the intricacies of the physical world. Additionally, simulation scaling issues can make it difficult to investigate large-scale ad hoc networks. Furthermore, simulations might not accurately reflect the many behavioral complexities of interactions between jammers and routing protocols.

D. The Comparison of the Proposed Method With the Related Methods

Ad hoc routing protocols are a challenging but crucial study topic to simulate jamming attacks. Understanding the effects of jamming assaults on ad hoc networks and enhancing their resilience need us to address the problems, close the gaps, and accept the constraints. The achievements in this area show how important they are to improving the security and dependability of ad hoc communication. Table 2 compares the proposed method to alternative methods in our method we used three different types of conventional network protocols AODV, DSR, and OLSR were exposed to Jamming attacks on ad-hoc routing protocol environments. Were as other research used different types of protocols AODV and OLSR with different environments.

5. CONCLUSION AND FUTURE WORK

This paper has delved into the critical issue of ad hoc jamming attacks, shedding light on the effect and impact of jamming attacks for three AD-Hoc network routing protocols (DSR, OLSR, and TORA) using the OPNET simulator to evaluate the performance of under various conditions, we employed parameters including delay, load, throughput, media access delay, and re-transmission attempts then a thorough analysis of different scenarios, we have highlighted the sophistication of these attacks and their ability to disrupt communication in dynamic, self-organizing networks. In the future, we will concentrate on creative and flexible defenses to successfully recognize and counter jamming attempts and increase the network lifetime by routing the information by passing the jammed node. For future study creation of clever algorithms and machine learning models that can dynamically adapt to change jamming patterns and frequencies represents one interesting direction. To detect anomalies suggestive of jamming attacks, these systems may examine network traffic and signal properties in real-time.

REFERENCES

Abuzainab, N., Erpek, T., Davaslioglu, K., Sagduyu, Y. E., Shi, Y., Mackey, S. J., . . . Yener, A. (2019, November). QoS and jamming-aware wireless networking using deep reinforcement learning. In MILCOM 2019-2019 IEEE Military Communications Conference (MILCOM) (pp. 610-615). IEEE. doi:10.1109/MILCOM47813.2019.9020985

Al-Shareeda, M. A., Saare, M. A., Manickam, S., & Karuppayah, S. (2023). Bluetooth low energy for internet of things: Review, challenges, and open issues. *Indonesian Journal of Electrical Engineering and Computer Science*, *31*(2), 1182–1189. doi:10.11591/ijeecs.v31.i2.pp1182-1189

Aneiba, A., & Melad, M. (2016). Performance evaluation of AODV, DSR, OLSR, and GRP MANET routing protocols using OPNET. *International Journal of Future Computer and Communication*, *5*(1), 57–60. doi:10.18178/ijfcc.2016.5.1.444

Arcangeloni, L., Testi, E., & Giorgetti, A. (2023). Detection of Jamming Attacks via Source Separation and Causal Inference. *IEEE Transactions on Communications*, *71*(8), 4793–4806. doi:10.1109/TCOMM.2023.3281467

Del-Valle-Soto, C., Mex-Perera, C., Aldaya, I., Lezama, F., Nolazco-Flores, J. A., & Monroy, R. (2019). New detection paradigms to improve wireless sensor network performance under jamming attacks. *Sensors (Basel)*, *19*(11), 2489. doi:10.3390/s19112489 PMID:31159187

Depp, Z. D. (2023). *Cybersecurity in Vehicular Networks: Enhanced Roll-Jam Attack and Jamming Detection* [Master's thesis]. The Ohio State University.

Hassan, M. A., Ullah, S. I., Salam, A., Ullah, A. W., Imad, M., & Ullah, F. (2021). Energy efficient hierarchical based fish eye state routing protocol for flying ad-hoc networks. *Indonesian Journal of Electrical Engineering and Computer Science*, *21*(1), 465–471. doi:10.11591/ijeecs.v21.i1.pp465-471

Koch, T. (2019). *Developing Protocol-Agnostic Jammers Using Reinforcement Learning* [Master's thesis]. The Cooper Union for the Advancement of Science and Art.

Lee, S. J., Lee, Y. R., Jeon, S. E., & Lee, I. G. (2023). Machine learning-based jamming attack classification and effective defense technique. *Computers & Security*, *128*, 103169. doi:10.1016/j.cose.2023.103169

Li, G., Yan, Z., & Fu, Y. (2018, May). A study and simulation research of blackhole attack on mobile adhoc network. In *2018 IEEE Conference on Communications and Network Security (CNS)* (pp. 1-6). IEEE.10.1109/CNS.2018.8433148

López-Vilos, N., Valencia-Cordero, C., Souza, R. D., & Montejo-Sánchez, S. (2023). Clustering-based energy-efficient self-healing strategy for WSNs under jamming attacks. *Sensors (Basel)*, *23*(15), 6894. doi:10.3390/s23156894 PMID:37571681

Manaseer, M. S., & Younes, M. B. (2023, November). Secure Protocols in VANETs: Availability Considerations. In 2023 14th International Conference on Information and Communication Systems (ICICS) (pp. 1-6). IEEE.

Manderna, A., Kumar, S., Dohare, U., Aljaidi, M., Kaiwartya, O., & Lloret, J. (2023). Vehicular network intrusion detection using a cascaded deep learning approach with multi-variant metaheuristic. *Sensors (Basel)*, *23*(21), 8772. doi:10.3390/s23218772 PMID:37960470

Mishra, A., Singh, S., & Tripathi, A. K. (2019). Comparison of MANET routing protocols. *Int. J. Comput. Sci. Mob. Comput*, *8*, 67–74.

Moumen, I., Rafalia, N., Abouchabaka, J., & Chatoui, Y. (2023). AODV-based Defense Mechanism for Mitigating Blackhole Attacks in MANET. In *E3S Web of Conferences* (Vol. 412, p. 01094). EDP Sciences. doi:10.1051/e3sconf/202341201094

Mughaid, A., Obaidat, I., Aljammal, A., AlZu'bi, S., Quiam, F., Laila, D., Al-zou'bi, A., & Abualigah, L. (2023). Simulation and analysis performance of ad-hoc routing protocols under DDoS attack and proposed solution. *International Journal of Data and Network Science*, *7*(2), 757–764. doi:10.5267/j.ijdns.2023.2.002

Rabiaa, N., Moussa, A. C., & Sofiane, B. H. (2023). A cross-layer method for identifying and isolating the blackhole nodes in vehicular ad-hoc networks. Information Security Journal: A Global Perspective, 32(3), 212-226.

Ranjan, P., & Ranjan, R. (2023). Trust-Based DSR Protocol for Secure Communication in Mobile Adhoc Networks. In *Advances in Data-driven Computing and Intelligent Systems: Selected Papers from ADCIS 2022* (Vol. 2, pp. 167–177). Springer Nature Singapore. doi:10.1007/978-981-99-0981-0_13

Salahdine, F., & Kaabouch, N. (2020). Security threats, detection, and countermeasures for physical layer in cognitive radio networks: A survey. *Physical Communication*, *39*, 101001. doi:10.1016/j.phycom.2020.101001

Sedar, R., Kalalas, C., Vázquez-Gallego, F., Alonso, L., & Alonso-Zarate, J. (2023). A comprehensive survey of v2x cybersecurity mechanisms and future research paths. *IEEE Open Journal of the Communications Society*, *4*, 325–391. doi:10.1109/OJCOMS.2023.3239115

Sharma, A., & Kaur, D. (2016). Behavior of Jamming Attack in OLSR, GRP, TORA and improvement with PCF in TORA using OPNET tool. *Int. Res. J. Eng. Technol*, *3*(3), 191–194.

Sharma, S. K., & Chawla, M. (2023). Compatibility issues of wireless sensor network routing in internet of things applications. *International Journal of Wireless and Mobile Computing*, *25*(1), 18–29. doi:10.1504/IJWMC.2023.132400

Singh, J., & Gupta, S. (2017). Impact of jamming attack in performance of mobile ad hoc networks. *International Journal of Computer Science Trends and Technology*, *5*(3), 184–190.

Tiloca, M., Guglielmo, D. D., Dini, G., Anastasi, G., & Das, S. K. (2018). DISH: DIstributed SHuffling against selective jamming attack in IEEE 802.15. 4e TSCH networks. *ACM Transactions on Sensor Networks*, *15*(1), 1–28. doi:10.1145/3241052

Walshe, M., Epiphaniou, G., Al-Khateeb, H., Hammoudeh, M., Katos, V., & Dehghantanha, A. (2019). Non-interactive zero knowledge proofs for the authentication of IoT devices in reduced connectivity environments. *Ad Hoc Networks*, *95*, 101988. doi:10.1016/j.adhoc.2019.101988

Wang, N., Wang, P., Alipour-Fanid, A., Jiao, L., & Zeng, K. (2019). Physical-layer security of 5G wireless networks for IoT: Challenges and opportunities. *IEEE Internet of Things Journal*, *6*(5), 8169–8181. doi:10.1109/JIOT.2019.2927379

Zhang, Y., Zheng, Z., He, J., Zhao, S., Qu, Q., Shen, Y., & Jiang, X. (2023). Opportunistic Wiretapping/jamming: A new attack model in millimeter-wave wireless networks. *IEEE Transactions on Wireless Communications*, *22*(12), 9907–9922. doi:10.1109/TWC.2023.3274808

Compilation of References

Abawajy, J. H., Ninggal, M. I. H., & Herawan, T. (2016). Privacy preserving social network data publication. *IEEE Communications Surveys and Tutorials*, *18*(3), 1974–1997. doi:10.1109/COMST.2016.2533668

Abdulganiyu, O. H., Ait Tchakoucht, T., & Saheed, Y. K. (2023). A systematic literature review for network intrusion detection system (IDS). *International Journal of Information Security*, *22*(5), 1125–1162. doi:10.1007/s10207-023-00682-2

Abuzainab, N., Erpek, T., Davaslioglu, K., Sagduyu, Y. E., Shi, Y., Mackey, S. J., . . . Yener, A. (2019, November). QoS and jamming-aware wireless networking using deep reinforcement learning. In MILCOM 2019-2019 IEEE Military Communications Conference (MILCOM) (pp. 610-615). IEEE.doi:10.1109/MILCOM47813.2019.9020985

Ahamad, S., Veeraiah, V., Ramesh, J. V. N., Rajadevi, R., Reeja, S. R., Pramanik, S., & Gupta, A. (2023). *Deep Learning based Cancer Detection Technique, Thrust Technologies' Effect on Image Processing*. IGI Global.

Ahmad, J., & Hwang, S. O. (2015). Chaos-based diffusion for highly autocorrelated data in encryption algorithms. *Nonlinear Dynamics*, *82*(4), 1839–1850. doi:10.1007/s11071-015-2281-0

Ahmed, I. M., & Kashmoola, M. Y. (2021). Threats on machine learning technique by data poisoning attack: A survey. In *Communications in Computer and Information Science* (pp. 586–600). Springer Singapore.

Albladi, S. M., & Weir, G. R. S. (2020). Sarker. *Cybersecurity*, *3*(1), 7. doi:10.1186/s42400-020-00047-5

Al-Charchafchi, A., Manickam, S., & Alqattan, Z. N. M. (2020). Threats Against Information Privacy and Security in Social Networks: A Review. In M. Anbar, N. Abdullah, & S. Manickam (Eds.), *Advances in Cyber Security. ACeS 2019. Communications in Computer and Information Science* (Vol. 1132). Springer. doi:10.1007/978-981-15-2693-0_26

Alexandrov, A., Monov, V., Andreev, R., & Doshev, J. (2019). QoS based method for energy optimization in ZigBee wireless sensor networks. In *Communications in Computer and Information Science* (pp. 41–52). Springer International Publishing.

Alexan, W., Elkandoz, M., Mashaly, M., Azab, E., & Aboshousha, A. (2023). Color image encryption through chaos and kaa map. *IEEE Access : Practical Innovations, Open Solutions*, *11*, 11541–11554. doi:10.1109/ACCESS.2023.3242311

Alghamdi, B., Watson, J., & Xu, Y. (2016). Toward detecting malicious links in online social networks through user behavior. *2016 IEEE/WIC/ACM International Conference on Web Intelligence Workshops (WIW)*, 5–8. 10.1109/WIW.2016.014

AlHogail, A. (2018). Improving IoT technology adoption through improving consumer trust. *Technologies*, *6*(3), 64. doi:10.3390/technologies6030064

Alhomoud, A. M. (2021). Image steganography in spatial domain: Current status, techniques, and trends. *Intelligent Automation & Soft Computing*, *27*(1). Advance online publication. doi:10.32604/iasc.2021.014773

Ali, S., Islam, N., Rauf, A., Din, I. U., Guizani, M., & Rodrigues, J. J. (2018). Privacy and security issues in online social networks. *Future Internet*, *10*(12), 114. doi:10.3390/fi10120114

Ali, U., Sohrawordi, M., & Uddin, M. P. (2019). A robust and secured image steganography using lsb and random bit substitution. *American Journal of Engineering Research*, *8*(2), 39–44.

Alkhalili, M. M. H. (2021). Investigation of applyingmachine learning for watch-list filtering in anti-money laundering. IEEE Access, 18481–18496.

Alqarni, A. (2017). *Exploring factors that affect the adoption of computer security practices among college students*. Eastern Michigan University.

Alqasrawi, Y. (2016). Natural scene image annotation using local semanticconcepts and spatial bag of visual words. International Journal of Sensors Wireless Communications and Control, 153–173.

Alshaikh, H., Ramadan, N., & Hefny, H. A. (2020). Ransomware prevention and mitigation techniques. *Int. J. Comput. Appl*, *177*(40), 31–39.

Al-Shareeda, M. A., Saare, M. A., Manickam, S., & Karuppayah, S. (2023). Bluetooth low energy for internet of things: Review, challenges, and open issues. *Indonesian Journal of Electrical Engineering and Computer Science*, *31*(2), 1182–1189. doi:10.11591/ijeecs.v31.i2.pp1182-1189

Ameen, N., Tarhini, A., Shah, M. H., & Madichie, N. O. (2020). Employees' behavioural intention to smartphone security: A gender-based, cross-national study. *Computers in Human Behavior*, *104*, 106184. doi:10.1016/j.chb.2019.106184

Amin, S. N., Shivakumara, P., Jun, T. X., Chong, K. Y., Zan, D. L. L., & Rahavendra, R. (2023). An augmented reality-based approach for designing interactive food menu of restaurant using android. *Artificial Intelligence and Applications (Commerce, Calif.)*, *1*(1), 26–34. doi:10.47852/bonviewAIA2202354

Anderson, C. L., & Agarwal, R. (2010). Practicing safe computing: A multimethod empirical examination of home computer user security behavioral intentions. *Management Information Systems Quarterly*, *34*(3), 34. doi:10.2307/25750694

Anderson, R., & Moore, T. (2006). The Economics of Information Security. *Science*, *314*(5799), 610–613. doi:10.1126/science.1130992 PMID:17068253

Aneiba, A., & Melad, M. (2016). Performance evaluation of AODV, DSR, OLSR, and GRP MANET routing protocols using OPNET. *International Journal of Future Computer and Communication*, *5*(1), 57–60. doi:10.18178/ijfcc.2016.5.1.444

Anwar, M., He, W., Ash, I., Yuan, X., Li, L., & Xu, L. (2016). Gender difference and employees' cyber security behaviors. *Computers in Human Behavior*, *69*, 437–443. doi:10.1016/j.chb.2016.12.040

Anwar, S., & Meghana, S. (2019). A pixel permutation based image encryption technique using chaotic map. *Multimedia Tools and Applications*, *78*(19), 27569–27590. doi:10.1007/s11042-019-07852-2

Arcangeloni, L., Testi, E., & Giorgetti, A. (2023). Detection of Jamming Attacks via Source Separation and Causal Inference. *IEEE Transactions on Communications*, *71*(8), 4793–4806. doi:10.1109/TCOMM.2023.3281467

Aribake, F. O., & Mat Aji, Z. (2020). The mediating role of perceived security on the relationship between internet banking users and their determinants. *International Journal of Advanced Research in Engineering and Technology*, *11*(2).

Arif, J., Khan, M. A., Ghaleb, B., Ahmad, J., Munir, A., Rashid, U., & Al-Dubai, A. Y. (2022). A novel chaotic permutation-substitution image encryption scheme based on logistic map and random substitution. *IEEE Access : Practical Innovations, Open Solutions*, *10*, 12966–12982. doi:10.1109/ACCESS.2022.3146792

Artz, D. (2001). Digital steganography: Hiding data within data. *IEEE Internet Computing*, *5*(3), 75–80. doi:10.1109/4236.935180

Aslan, Ö. O.-O. (2021). Intelligent behavior-based malware detection system on cloud computing environment. *IEEE Access, 9,* 83252-83271.

Atacak, İ. (2023). An Ensemble Approach Based on Fuzzy Logic Using Machine Learning Classifiers for Android Malware Detection. *Applied Sciences, 13*(3), 1484.

Atri, R., Prabhu, S., & Cherady, J. (2023). Study of cyber security threats to online social networks. *AIP Conference Proceedings*, *2736*(1), 060004. doi:10.1063/5.0171142

Ayub, N., & Selwal, A. (2020). An improved image steganography technique using edge based data hiding in dct domain. *Journal of Interdisciplinary Mathematics*, *23*(2), 357–366. doi:10.1080/09720502.2020.1731949

Ayyagari, R., Lim, J., & Hoxha, O. (2019). Why Do Not We Use Password Managers? A Study on the Intention to Use Password Managers. *Contemporary Management Research*, *15*(4), 227–245. doi:10.7903/cmr.19394

Babu, C.V. SureshAndrew, S. P. (2024). Adaptive AI for Dynamic Cybersecurity Systems: Enhancing Protection in a Rapidly Evolving Digital Landscape. In *Principles and Applications of Adaptive Artificial Intelligence* (pp. 52–72). doi:10.4018/979-8-3693-0230-9.ch003

Balaji, S., & Narayanan, S. S. (2023). Dynamic distributed generative adversarial network for intrusion detection system over internet of things. *Wireless Networks*, *29*(5), 1949–1967. doi:10.1007/s11276-022-03182-8

Bandura, A. (1997). *Self-Efficacy: The exercise of control.* W. H. Freeman.

Bansal, R., Jenipher, B., Nisha, V. J., Makhan R., Dilip, Kumbhkar, Pramanik, S., Roy, S., & Gupta, A. (2022). Big Data Architecture for Network Security. In Cyber Security and Network Security. Wiley. doi:10.1002/9781119812555.ch11

Bao, W., & Zhu, C. (2022). A secure and robust image encryption algorithm based on compressive sensing and DNA coding. *Multimedia Tools and Applications*, *81*(11), 15977–15996. doi:10.1007/s11042-022-12623-7

Barati, R. (2022). Security Threats and Dealing with Social Networks. *SN Computer Science*, *4*(1), 9. doi:10.1007/s42979-022-01434-0

Barreda, A. A., Bilgihan, A., Nusair, K., & Okumus, F. (2015). Generating brand awareness in online social networks. *Computers in Human Behavior*, *50*, 600–609. doi:10.1016/j.chb.2015.03.023

Baskerville, R. (2018). Information systems security design methods: Implications for information systems development. *European Journal of Information Systems*, *27*(3), 228–244. doi:10.1080/0960085x.2017.1379649

Batskih, A. V., Drovnikova, I. G., Ovchinnikova, E. S., & Rogozin, E. A. (2020). *Analysis and classification of the main threats to information security of automated systems at the objects of informatiza tion of internal affairs bodies.* Bezopasnost Informatsionnykh Tekhnologiy. doi:10.26583/bit.2020.1.04

Belfaik, Y., Sadqi, Y., Maleh, Y., Said, S., Tawalbeh, L., & Salah, K. (2023). A Novel Secure and Privacy-Preserving Model for OpenID Connect Based on Blockchain. *IEEE Access : Practical Innovations, Open Solutions*, *11*, 67660–67678. doi:10.1109/ACCESS.2023.3292143

Bhardwaj, S., & Dave, M. (2023). Integrating a Rule-Based Approach to Malware Detection with an LSTM-Based Feature Selection Technique. *SN Computer Science*, *4*(6), 737. doi:10.1007/s42979-023-02177-2

Bhattacharya, M., Roy, S., Chattopadhyay, S., Das, A. K., & Shetty, S. (2023). A comprehensive survey on online social networks security and privacy issues: Threats, machine learning-based solutions, and open challenges. *Security and Privacy*, *6*(1), e275. doi:10.1002/spy2.275

Bhavsar, M., Roy, K., Kelly, J., & Olusola, O. (2023). Anomaly-based intrusion detection system for IoT application. *Discov Internet Things*, *3*(1), 5. doi:10.1007/s43926-023-00034-5

Bhuiyan, T., Sarower, A. H., Karim, R., & Hassan, M. (2019). An image steganography algorithm using lsb replacement through xor substitution. *2019 International Conference on Information and Communications Technology (ICOIACT)*, 44–49. 10.1109/ICOIACT46704.2019.8938486

Bilge, L., Strufe, T., Balzarotti, D., & Kirda, E. (2009). All your contacts are belong to us: automated identity theft attacks on social networks. *Proceedings of the 18th International Conference on World Wide Web*, 551–560. 10.1145/1526709.1526784

Bodeau, D. J. (2018). *Cyber Threat Modeling: Survey, Assessment, and Representative Framework*. HSSEDI.

Böhme, R., & Moore, T. (2012, October). *How do consumers react to cybercrime? In 2012 eCrime researchers summit*. IEEE.

Bojanc, R., & Jerman-Blazic, B. (2010). Information security governance framework for the public sector. *Computers & Security*, *29*(2), 176–189. doi:10.1016/j.cose.2009.10.002

Bountakas, P., Zarras, A., Lekidis, A., & Xenakis, C. (2023). Defense strategies for Adversarial Machine Learning: A survey. *Computer Science Review*, *49*(100573), 100573. doi:10.1016/j.cosrev.2023.100573

Brandao, P. R., & Limonova, V. (2021). Defense methodologies against advanced persistent threats. *American Journal of Applied Sciences*, *18*(1), 207–212. Advance online publication. doi:10.3844/ajassp.2021.207.212

Buono, L. (2014, June). *Fighting cybercrime through prevention, outreach and awareness raising*. Academic Press.

Buttan, D. (2020). *Hacking the Human Brain: Impact of Cybercriminals Evoking Emotion for Financial Profit*. Utica College.

Cadwalladr, C., & Graham-Harrison, E. (2018). Revealed: 50 million Facebook profiles harvested for Cambridge Analytica in major data breach. *The Guardian, 17*(1), 22.

Cai, H., Wang, S., Zhang, Y., Zhang, M., & Zhao, A. (2023). A poisoning attack based on variant generative adversarial networks in recommender systems. In *Advanced Data Mining and Applications* (pp. 371–386). Springer Nature Switzerland.

CarliniN.WagnerD. (2016). Towards evaluating the robustness of neural networks. *arXiv*. http://arxiv.org/abs/1608.04644

Cengiz, A. B., Kalem, G., & Boluk, P. S. (2022). Herath. *IEEE Access : Practical Innovations, Open Solutions*, *10*, 57674–57684. doi:10.1109/ACCESS.2022.3177652

Chandan, R. R., Soni, S., Raj, A., Veeraiah, V., Dhabliya, D., Pramanik, S., & Gupta, A. (2023). Genetic Algorithm and Machine Learning. In Advanced Bioinspiration Methods for Healthcare Standards, Policies, and Reform. IGI Global. doi:10.4018/978-1-6684-5656-9

Chander, N., & Upendra Kumar, M. (2023). Metaheuristic feature selection with deep learning enabled cascaded recurrent neural network for anomaly detection in Industrial Internet of Things environment. *Cluster Computing*, *26*(3), 1801–1819. doi:10.1007/s10586-022-03719-8

Chatterjee, S., Kar, A. K., Dwivedi, Y. K., & Kizgin, H. (2019). Prevention of cybercrimes in smart cities of India: From a citizen's perspective. *Information Technology & People*, *32*(5), 1153–1183. doi:10.1108/ITP-05-2018-0251

Cheddad, A., Condell, J., Curran, K., & Mc Kevitt, P. (2010). Digital image steganography: Survey and analysis of current methods. *Signal Processing*, *90*(3), 727–752. doi:10.1016/j.sigpro.2009.08.010

Chen, Y., Mao, Y., Leng, S., Wei, Y., & Chiang, Y. (2017). Malware propagation analysis in message-recallable online social networks. *2017 IEEE 17th International Conference on Communication Technology (ICCT)*, 1366–1371.

Cheng, Y., Park, J., & Sandhu, R. (2013). Preserving user privacy from third-party applications in online social networks. *Proceedings of the 22nd International Conference on World Wide Web*, 723–728. 10.1145/2487788.2488032

Chen, P. (2014). *A Study on Advanced Persistent Threats*. LNCS. doi:10.1007/978-3-662-44885-4_5

Cherry, K. (2021). *Attitudes and behavior in psychology*. Academic Press.

Choi, H.-H., Cho, H.-N., & Seo, J.-W. (2004). Risk assessment methodology for underground construction projects. *Journal of Construction Engineering and Management*, *130*(2), 258–272. doi:10.1061/(ASCE)0733-9364(2004)130:2(258)

Cho, K., B. V. (2014). Learning phrase representations using RNN encoder-decoder for statistical machine translation. *Computer Science*.

Chu, A. M., & So, M. K. (2020). Organisational information security management for sustainable information systems: An unethical employee information security behavior perspective. *Sustainability (Basel)*, *12*(8), 3163. doi:10.3390/su12083163

Çiftci, E., & Sümer, E. (2022). A novel steganography method for binary and color halftone images. *PeerJ. Computer Science*, *8*, e1062. doi:10.7717/peerj-cs.1062 PMID:36091978

Cina, A. E., Grosse, K., Demontis, A., Biggio, B., Roli, F., & Pelillo, M. (2023). Machine Learning Security against Data Poisoning: Are We There Yet? IEEE 34th International Symposium.

CinàA. E.GrosseK.DemontisA.VasconS.ZellingerW.MoserB. A.OpreaA.BiggioB.PelilloM.RoliF. (2022). Wild patterns reloaded: A survey of machine learning security against training data poisoning. arXiv. http://arxiv.org/abs/2205.01992

Cleveland, M., & Cleveland, S. (2018). Cybercrime post-incident leadership model. In *Proceeding of the 13th Midwest Association for Information Systems Conference, St. Louis, MO, May* (pp. 17-18). Academic Press.

Colicchia, C., Creazza, A., & Menachof, D. A. (2019). Managing cyber and information risks in supply chains: Insights from an exploratory analysis. *Supply Chain Management*, *24*(2), 215–240. doi:10.1108/SCM-09-2017-0289

Corre, K., Barais, O., Sunyé, G., Frey, V., & Crom, J.-M. (2017). Why can't users choose their identity providers on the web? *Proceedings on Privacy Enhancing Technologies. Privacy Enhancing Technologies Symposium*, *2017*(3), 72–86. doi:10.1515/popets-2017-0029

Crenshaw, K. (1990). Mapping the margins: Intersectionality, identity politics, and violence against women of color. *Stanford Law Review*, *43*(6), 1241. doi:10.2307/1229039

Crossler, R. E., Andoh-Baidoo, F. K., & Menard, P. (2019). Espoused cultural values as antecedents of individuals' threat and coping appraisal toward protective information technologies: Study of US and Ghana. *Information & Management*, *56*(5), 754–766. doi:10.1016/j.im.2018.11.009

Crossler, R. E., Johnston, A. C., Lowry, P. B., Hud, Q., Warkentin, M., & Baskerville, R. (2013). Future directions for behavioral information security research. *Computers & Security*, *32*, 90–101. doi:10.1016/j.cose.2012.09.010

CSAM. (2020). *How IT Can Get Employees To Engage With Your Company's Security Awareness Program.* https://inspiredelearning.com/blog/how-it-can-get-employees-to-engage-with-your-companys-security-awareness-program/

Cummings, J. N. (2004). Work Groups, Structural Diversity, and Knowledge Sharing in a Global Organization. *Management Science*, *50*(3), 352–364. doi:10.1287/mnsc.1030.0134

Cybenko, G. (1989). Approximation by superpositions of a sigmoidal function. *Mathematics of Control, Signals, and Systems*, *2*(4), 303–314. doi:10.1007/BF02551274

D'Arcy, J., & Herath, T. (2011). A review and analysis of deterrence theory in the IS security literature: Making sense of the disparate findings. *European Journal of Information Systems*, *20*(6), 643–658. doi:10.1057/ejis.2011.23

Dang, D. D. (2021). *Malware classification using long short-term memory models*. Academic Press.

Darabian, H. H., Homayounoot, S., Dehghantanha, A., Hashemi, S., Karimipour, H., Parizi, R. M., & Choo, K.-K. R. (2020). Detecting cryptomining malware: A deep learning approach for static and dynamic analysis. *Journal of Grid Computing*, *18*(2), 293–303. doi:10.1007/s10723-020-09510-6

Dastres & Soori. (2021). A review in recent development of network threats and security measures. *International Journal of Information Sciences and Computer Engineering*.

David, D. P., Keupp, M. M., & Mermoud, A. (2020). Knowledge absorption for cyber-security: The role of human beliefs. *Computers in Human Behavior*, *106*, 106255. doi:10.1016/j.chb.2020.106255

Davis, F., Bagozzi, R., & Warshaw, P. (1989). User acceptance of computer technology: A comparison of two theoretical models. *Management Science*, *35*(8), 982–1003. doi:10.1287/mnsc.35.8.982

De Bruijn, H., & Janssen, M. (2017). Building cybersecurity awareness: The need for evidence-based framing strategies. *Government Information Quarterly*, *34*(1), 1–7. doi:10.1016/j.giq.2017.02.007

Del-Valle-Soto, C., Mex-Perera, C., Aldaya, I., Lezama, F., Nolazco-Flores, J. A., & Monroy, R. (2019). New detection paradigms to improve wireless sensor network performance under jamming attacks. *Sensors (Basel)*, *19*(11), 2489. doi:10.3390/s19112489 PMID:31159187

Depp, Z. D. (2023). *Cybersecurity in Vehicular Networks: Enhanced Roll-Jam Attack and Jamming Detection* [Master's thesis]. The Ohio State University.

Determann, L. (2019). Healthy Data Protection. *Michigan Technology Law Review*, *26*, 229.

Diaconu, A. V., & Dascalescu, A. C. (2017, January). Correlation distribution of adjacent pixels randomness test for image encryption. *Proc* Rom. Acad. Ser. A.

Diaz, A., & Sanchez, P. (2016). Simulation of attacks for security in wireless sensor network. *Sensors (Basel)*, *16*(11), 1932. doi:10.3390/s16111932 PMID:27869710

Ding, J., Wang, H., & Wu, Y. (2022). The Detection Scheme Against Selective Forwarding of Smart Malicious Nodes With Reinforcement Learning in Wireless Sensor Networks. *IEEE Sensors Journal*, *22*(13), 13696–13706. doi:10.1109/JSEN.2022.3176462

Ding, J., Zhang, H., Guo, Z., & Wu, Y. (2021). The DPC-Based Scheme for Detecting Selective Forwarding in Clustered Wireless Sensor Networks. *IEEE Access : Practical Innovations, Open Solutions*, *9*, 20954–20967. doi:10.1109/ACCESS.2021.3055026

Disterer, G. (2007). A business-driven approach to information security governance. *Information Management & Computer Security*, *15*(1), 38–51. doi:10.1108/09685220710730151

Dixon, S. (2023, October 27). *Most popular social networks worldwide as of October 2023, ranked by number of monthly active users*. Retrieved from Statista website: https://www.statista.com/statistics/272014/global-social-networks-ranked-by-number-of-users/

Dlamini, S., & Mbambo, C. (2019). Understanding policing of cybe-rcrime in South Africa: The phenomena, challenges and effective responses. *Cogent Social Sciences*, *5*(1), 1675404. doi:10.1080/23311886.2019.1675404

Dushyant, K., Muskan, G., Gupta, A., & Pramanik, S. (2022). Utilizing Machine Learning and Deep Learning in Cyber security: An Innovative Approach. In M. M. Ghonge, S. Pramanik, R. Mangrulkar, & D. N. Le (Eds.), *Cyber security and Digital Forensics*. Wiley. doi:10.1002/9781119795667.ch12

Eastin, M. S., & LaRose, R. (2000). Internet Self-Efficacy and the Psychology of the Digital Divide. *Journal of Computer-Mediated Communication*, *6*(1), 0. doi:10.1111/j.1083-6101.2000.tb00110.x

Edelson, L., Lauinger, T., & McCoy, D. (2020). A security analysis of the Facebook ad library. *2020 IEEE Symposium on Security and Privacy (SP)*, 661–678. 10.1109/SP40000.2020.00084

Einwiller, S. A., & Kim, S. (2020). How online content providers moderate user-generated content to prevent harmful online communication: An analysis of policies and their implementation. *Policy and Internet*, *12*(2), 184–206. doi:10.1002/poi3.239

Engmann, F., Adu-Manu, K. S., Abdulai, J.-D., & Katsriku, F. A. (2021). Network performance metrics for energy efficient scheduling in Wireless Sensor Networks (WSNs). *Wireless Communications and Mobile Computing*, *2021*, 1–14. doi:10.1155/2021/9635958

Evsutin, O., Melman, A., & Meshcheryakov, R. (2020). Digital steganography and watermarking for digital images: A review of current research directions. *IEEE Access : Practical Innovations, Open Solutions*, *8*, 166589–166611. doi:10.1109/ACCESS.2020.3022779

Ezhilarasi, M., Gnanaprasanambikai, L., Kousalya, A., & Shanmugapriya, M. (2023). A novel implementation of routing attack detection scheme by using fuzzy and feed-forward neural networks. *Soft Computing*, *27*(7), 4157–4168. doi:10.1007/s00500-022-06915-1

Fadhil, M. S., Farhan, A. K., & Fadhil, M. N. (2021, February). Designing substitution box based on the 1D logistic map chaotic system. *IOP Conference Series. Materials Science and Engineering*, *1076*(1), 012041. doi:10.1088/1757-899X/1076/1/012041

Farhan, A., Awad, F., & Saad, S. (2017). Enhance the hiding image by using compression and securing techniques. *Iraqi Journal for Computers and Informatics*, *43*(1), 14–16. doi:10.25195/ijci.v43i1.70

Feledi, D., Fenz, S., & Lechner, L. (2013). Toward Web-Based Information Security Knowledge Sharing. *Information Security Technical Report*, *17*(4), 199–209. doi:10.1016/j.istr.2013.03.004

Fire, M., Goldschmidt, R., & Elovici, Y. (2014). Online social networks: Threats and solutions. *IEEE Communications Surveys and Tutorials*, *16*(4), 2019–2036. doi:10.1109/COMST.2014.2321628

Flores, W. R., & Ekstedt, M. (2012). A Model for Investigating Organisational Impact on Information Security Behavior. *WISP 2012 Proceedings*.

Floyd, R. W., & Steinberg, L. (1976). An adaptive algorithm for spatial gray-scale. *Proc. Soc. Inf. Disp.*, *17*, 75–77.

Franchi, E., Poggi, A., & Tomaiuolo, M. (2015). Information and password attacks on social networks: An argument for cryptography. *Journal of Information Technology Research*, *8*(1), 25–42. doi:10.4018/JITR.2015010103

Franke, U., & Brynielsson, J. (2014). Cyber situational awareness–a systematic review of the literature. *Computers & Security*, *46*, 18–31. doi:10.1016/j.cose.2014.06.008

Frimpong, S. A., Han, M., Boahen, E. K., Ayitey Sosu, R. N., Hanson, I., Larbi-Siaw, O., & Senkyire, I. B. (2022). RecGuard: An efficient privacy preservation blockchain-based system for online social network users. *Blockchain: Research and Applications*, *100111*. Advance online publication. doi:10.1016/j.bcra.2022.100111

Gangarde, R., Sharma, A., Pawar, A., Joshi, R., & Gonge, S. (2021). Privacy Preservation in Online Social Networks Using Multiple-Graph-Properties-Based Clustering to Ensure k-Anonymity, l-Diversity, and t-Closeness. *Electronics (Basel)*, *10*(22), 2877. doi:10.3390/electronics10222877

Gao, T., & Li, F. (2019, June). Privacy-preserving sketching for online social network data publication. *2019 16th Annual IEEE International Conference on Sensing, Communication, and Networking (SECON)*. 10.1109/SAHCN.2019.8824823

Gao, C., Yan, C., Adamatzky, A., & Deng, Y. (2014). A bio-inspired algorithm for route selection in wireless sensor networks. *IEEE Communications Letters*, *18*(11), 2019–2022. doi:10.1109/LCOMM.2014.2360523

Gao, H., Hu, J., Huang, T., Wang, J., & Chen, Y. (2011). Security Issues in Online Social Networks. *IEEE Internet Computing*, *15*(4), 56–63. doi:10.1109/MIC.2011.50

Gao, T., & Li, F. (2022). Machine Learning-based Online Social Network Privacy Preservation. *Proceedings of the 2022 ACM on Asia Conference on Computer and Communications Security*. 10.1145/3488932.3517405

Gera, S., & Sinha, A. (2022). T-Bot: AI-based social media bot detection model for trend-centric twitter network. *Social Network Analysis and Mining*, *12*(1), 76. doi:10.1007/s13278-022-00897-6

Goldblum, M., Tsipras, D., Xie, C., Chen, X., & Schw, A. (2023). Dataset Security for Machine Learning: Data Poisoning, Backdoor Attacks, and Defenses. *IEEE Transactions on Pattern Analysis and Machine Intelligence*, *45*(2).

Gonzalez, H., Pino, F. J., & Martinez, L. (2016). A security requirement engineering process for improving security and compliance. *Computers in Human Behavior*, *62*, 807–819. doi:10.1016/j.chb.2016.04.007

Gopinath, M. (2023). A comprehensive survey on deep learning based malware detection techniques. *Computer Science Review*, *47*, 100529. doi:10.1016/j.cosrev.2022.100529

Gove, W. R., & Altman, I. (1978). The environment and social behavior: Privacy, personal space, territory, crowding. *Contemporary Sociology*, *7*(5), 638. doi:10.2307/2065073

Grimes, M., & Marquardson, J. (2019). Quality matters: Evoking subjective norms and coping appraisals by system design to increase security intentions. *Decision Support Systems*, *119*, 23–34. doi:10.1016/j.dss.2019.02.010

Guo, L., Yao, Z., Lin, M., & Xu, Z. (2023). Fuzzy TOPSIS-based privacy measurement in multiple online social networks. *Complex & Intelligent Systems*, *9*(6), 6089–6101. doi:10.1007/s40747-023-00991-y

Gupta, A., Verma, A., & Pramanik, S. (2022). Advanced Security System in Video Surveillance for COVID-19. In *An Interdisciplinary Approach to Modern Network Security*. CRC Press. doi:10.1201/9781003147176-8

Gupta, M., Singh, V. P., Gupta, K. K., & Shukla, P. K. (2023). An efficient image encryption technique based on two-level security for internet of things. *Multimedia Tools and Applications*, *82*(4), 5091–5111. doi:10.1007/s11042-022-12169-8

Gupta, T., Choudhary, G., & Sharma, V. (2018). A Survey on the Security of Pervasive Online Social Networks (POSNs). *Journal of Internet Services and Information Security*, *8*(2), 48–86. doi:10.22667/JISIS.2018.05.31.048

Hadlington, L. J. (2018). *Employees attitudes towards cyber security and risky online behaviours: an empirical assessment in the United Kingdom*. Academic Press.

Hadlington, L., Lumsden, K., Black, A., & Ferra, F. (2021). A qualitative exploration of police officers' experiences, challenges, and perceptions of cybercrime. *Policing. Journal of Policy Practice*, *15*(1), 34–43.

Hameed, M. A., Abdel-Aleem, O. A., & Hassaballah, M. (2023). A secure data hiding approach based on least-significant-bit and nature-inspired optimization techniques. *Journal of Ambient Intelligence and Humanized Computing*, *14*(5), 4639–4657. doi:10.1007/s12652-022-04366-y

Hart, S., Margheri, A., Paci, F., & Sassone, V. (2020). Riskio: A serious game for cyber security awareness and education. *Computers & Security*, *95*, 101827. doi:10.1016/j.cose.2020.101827

Hassandoust, F., & Techatassanasoontorn, A. A. (2020). Understanding users' information security awareness and intentions: A full nomology of protection motivation theory. In *Cyber Influence and Cognitive Threats* (pp. 129–143). Academic Press. doi:10.1016/B978-0-12-819204-7.00007-5

Hassan, M. A., Ullah, S. I., Salam, A., Ullah, A. W., Imad, M., & Ullah, F. (2021). Energy efficient hierarchical based fish eye state routing protocol for flying ad-hoc networks. *Indonesian Journal of Electrical Engineering and Computer Science*, *21*(1), 465–471. doi:10.11591/ijeecs.v21.i1.pp465-471

Hazman, C., Guezzaz, A., Benkirane, S., Azrour, M., & Amaouche, S. (2024). A Collaborative Anomaly Detection Model Using En-Semble Learning and Blockchain. In Y. Farhaoui, A. Hussain, T. Saba, H. Taherdoost, & A. Verma (Eds.), *Artificial Intelligence, Data Science and Applications. ICAISE 2023. Lecture Notes in Networks and Systems* (Vol. 838). Springer. doi:10.1007/978-3-031-48573-2_37

Hearst, M. A., Dumais, S. T., Osuna, E., Platt, J., & Scholkopf, B. (1998). Platt, B. Scholkopf, Support vector machines. *IEEE Intelligent Systems & their Applications*, *13*(4), 18–28. doi:10.1109/5254.708428

Helmes, A. W. (2002). Application of the protection motivation theory to genetic testing for breast cancer risk. *Preventive Medicine*, *35*(5), 453–462. doi:10.1006/pmed.2002.1110 PMID:12431894

Hemalatha, J. R., Roseline, S., Geetha, S., Kadry, S., & Damaševičius, R. (2021). An efficient densenet-based deep learning model for malware detection. *Entropy (Basel, Switzerland)*, *23*(3), 344. doi:10.3390/e23030344 PMID:33804035

Herath, T. B., Khanna, P., & Ahmed, M. (2022). Cybersecurity practices for social media users: A systematic literature review. *Journal of Cybersecurity and Privacy*, *2*(1), 1–18. doi:10.3390/jcp2010001

Herath, T., & Rao, H. R. (2009). Protection motivation and deterrence: A framework for security policy compliance in organisations. *European Journal of Information Systems*, *18*(2), 106–125. doi:10.1057/ejis.2009.6

He, Z. M. (2021). When machine learning meets hardware cybersecurity: Delving into accurate zero-day malware detection. *22nd International Symposium on Quality Electronic De*. 10.1109/ISQED51717.2021.9424330

Hina, S., Selvam, D. D. D. P., & Lowry, P. B. (2019). Institutional governance and protection motivation: Theoretical insights into shaping employees' security compliance behavior in higher education institutions in the developing world. *Computers & Security*, *87*, 101594. doi:10.1016/j.cose.2019.101594

Hofstede, G. (1980). *Culture's consequences: Comparing values, behaviours, institutions and organisations across nations*. Sage.

Hofstede, G. H. (2001). *Culture's consequences: Comparing values, behaviors, institutions, and organisations across nations*. Sage Publications.

Hosseini, S., & Sardo, S. R. (2023). Network intrusion detection based on deep learning method in internet of thing. *Journal of Reliable Intelligent Environments*, *9*(2), 147–159. doi:10.1007/s40860-021-00169-8

Huang, K., & Pearlson, K. (2019, January). For what technology can't fix: Building a model of organisational cybersecurity culture. *Proceedings of the 52nd Hawaii International Conference on System Sciences.* 10.24251/HICSS.2019.769

Huang, X., & Wu, Y. (2022). Identify selective forwarding attacks using danger model: Promote the detection accuracy in wireless sensor networks. *IEEE Sensors Journal, 22*(10), 9997–10008. doi:10.1109/JSEN.2022.3166601

Hua, Z., Zhou, B., & Zhou, Y. (2018). Sine chaotification model for enhancing chaos and its hardware implementation. *IEEE Transactions on Industrial Electronics, 66*(2), 1273–1284. doi:10.1109/TIE.2018.2833049

Hua, Z., & Zhou, Y. (2016). Image encryption using 2D Logistic-adjusted-Sine map. *Information Sciences, 339*, 237–253. doi:10.1016/j.ins.2016.01.017

Hubbard, D. W., & Seiersen, R. (2023). *How to Measure Anything in Cybersecurity Risk.* John Wiley & Sons. doi:10.1002/9781119892335

Humayun, M., Niazi, M., Jhanjhi, N. Z., Alshayeb, M., & Mahmood, S. (2020). Cyber security threats and vulnerabilities: A systematic mapping study. *Arabian Journal for Science and Engineering, 45*(4), 3171–3189. doi:10.1007/s13369-019-04319-2

Hydara, I., Sultan, A. B. M., Zulzalil, H., & Admodisastro, N. (2015). Current state of research on cross-site scripting (XSS)–A systematic literature review. *Information and Software Technology, 58*, 170–186. doi:10.1016/j.infsof.2014.07.010

IBM. (2020). https://www.varonis.com/blog/cybersecurity-statistics/

Ikhalia, E., Serrano, A., & Arreymbi, J. (2018). Deploying social network security awareness through Mass Interpersonal Persuasion (MIP). *International Conference on Cyber Warfare and Security.*

Iqbal, N., Hussain, I., Khan, M. A., Abbas, S., & Yousaf, S. (2023). An efficient image cipher based on the 1D scrambled image and 2D logistic chaotic map. *Multimedia Tools and Applications, 82*(26), 1–29. doi:10.1007/s11042-023-15037-1

Jain, A. K., Sahoo, S. R., & Kaubiyal, J. (2021). Online social networks security and privacy: Comprehensive review and analysis. *Complex & Intelligent Systems, 7*(5), 2157–2177. doi:10.1007/s40747-021-00409-7

Jain, A., & Rajpal, N. (2016). A robust image encryption algorithm resistant to attacks using DNA and chaotic logistic maps. *Multimedia Tools and Applications, 75*(10), 5455–5472. doi:10.1007/s11042-015-2515-7

Jaradat, A. S., Nasayreh, A., Al-Na'amneh, Q., Gharaibeh, H., & Al Mamlook, R. E. (2023, November). Genetic Optimization Techniques for Enhancing Web Attacks Classification in Machine Learning. In *2023 IEEE Intl Conf on Dependable, Autonomic and Secure Computing, Intl Conf on Pervasive Intelligence and Computing, Intl Conf on Cloud and Big Data Computing, Intl Conf on Cyber Science and Technology Congress (DASC/PiCom/CBDCom/CyberSciTech)* (pp. 130-136). IEEE.

Jarvis, J. F., Judice, C. N., & Ninke, W. (1976). A survey of techniques for the display of continuous tone pictures on bilevel displays. *Computer Graphics and Image Processing, 5*(1), 13–40. doi:10.1016/S0146-664X(76)80003-2

Javed, A. (2019). *Understanding malware behaviour in online social networks and predicting cyber attack* [PhD, Cardiff University]. https://orca.cardiff.ac.uk/id/eprint/131640/

Jerlin, M. A., & Marimuthu, K. (2018). A new malware detection system using machine learning techniques for API call sequences. *Journal of Applied Security Research, 13*(1), 45–62. doi:10.1080/19361610.2018.1387734

Jeun, I. (2012). A practical study on advanced persistent threats. In *Com puter Applications for Security.* Control and System Engineering. doi:10.1007/978-3-642-35264-5_21

Jiang, J., & Liu, Y. (2022). Secure IoT Routing: Selective Forwarding Attacks and Trust-based Defenses in RPL Network. *ArXiv, abs/2201.06937*

Jiang, L., & Zhang, X. (2019). BCOSN: A Blockchain-Based Decentralized Online Social Network. *IEEE Transactions on Computational Social Systems*, *6*(6), 1454–1466. doi:10.1109/TCSS.2019.2941650

Joe, M. M., & Ramakrishnan, B. (2017). Novel authentication procedures for preventing unauthorized access in social networks. *Peer-to-Peer Networking and Applications*, *10*(4), 833–843. doi:10.1007/s12083-016-0426-7

Johnson, N. F., & Jajodia, S. (1998). Exploring steganography: Seeing the unseen. *Computer*, *31*(2), 26–34. doi:10.1109/MC.1998.4655281

Jones, C. M. (2009). *Utilising the technology acceptance model to assess employee adoption of information systems security measures*. Nova Southeastern University.

Kadhim, A. N., & Sadkhan, S. B. (2021). Security threats in wireless network communication-status, challenges, and future trends. *2021 International Conference on Advanced Computer Applications (ACA),* 176–181. 10.1109/ACA52198.2021.9626810

Kalloniatis, C., Gritzalis, S., & Kavakli, E. (2015). An information security risk management approach for protecting eHealth information. *Information Management & Computer Security*, *23*(4), 350–373. doi:10.1108/imcs-11-2014-0046

Karnin, E., Greene, J., & Hellman, M. (1983). On secret sharing systems. *IEEE Transactions on Information Theory*, *29*(1), 35–41. doi:10.1109/TIT.1983.1056621

Kaur, G., Habibi Lashkari, Z., Habibi Lashkari, A., Kaur, G., Habibi Lashkari, Z. & Habibi Lashkari, A. (2021). Introduction to Cybersecurity. *Understanding Cybersecurity Management in FinTech: Challenges, Strategies, and Trends*, 17–34.

Kaur, R., & Singh, B. (2021). A hybrid algorithm for robust image steganography. *Multidimensional Systems and Signal Processing*, *32*(1), 1–23. doi:10.1007/s11045-020-00725-0

Kayes, I., & Iamnitchi, A. (2017). Privacy and security in online social networks: A survey. *Online Social Networks and Media*, *3*, 1–21. doi:10.1016/j.osnem.2017.09.001

Ke, G. Q. M.-Y. (2017). Lightgbm: A highly efficient gradient boosting decision tree. Advances in Neural Information Processing Systems, 30.

Keserwani, P. K. (2023). An Improved NIDS Using RF-Based Feature Selection Technique and Voting Classifier. In *Artificial Intelligence for Intrusion Detection Systems* (pp. 133–154). Chapman and Hall/CRC. doi:10.1201/9781003346340-7

Khalid, O. U., Ullah, S., Ahmad, T., Saeed, S., Alabbad, D. A., Aslam, M., Buriro, A., & Ahmad, R. (2023). An insight into machine-learning-based fileless malware detection. *Sensors (Basel)*, *23*(2), 612. doi:10.3390/s23020612 PMID:36679406

Khandelwal, J., Sharma, V. K., Singh, D., & Zaguia, A. (2022). Dwt-svd based image steganography using threshold value encryption method. *Computers, Materials & Continua*, *72*(2), 3299–3312. doi:10.32604/cmc.2022.023116

Khan, K. M., & Baloch, A. W. (2014). Understanding information security compliance: A unified perspective based on institutional theory. *Information & Management*, *51*(7), 816–826. doi:10.1016/j.im.2014.06.003

Khan, R., Mclaughlin, K., Laverty, D., & Sezer, S. (2017). STRIDE-based threat modeling for cyber-physical systems. *Proc. IEEE PES Innov. Smart Grid Technol. Conf. Eur. (ISGT-Europe)*, 1–6.

Khan, R., McLaughlin, K., Laverty, D., & Sezer, S. (2017). STRIDE-based threat modeling for cyber-physical systems. *Proc. IEEE PES Innovative Smart Grid Technologies Conference Europe (ISGT-Europe),* 1-6. 10.1109/ISGTEurope.2017.8260283

Khan, S., Lloret, J., & Macias-López, E. (2015). Bio-inspired mechanisms in wireless sensor networks. *International Journal of Distributed Sensor Networks*, *11*(3), 173419. doi:10.1155/2015/173419

Khanzadi, H., Eshghi, M., & Borujeni, S. E. (2014). Image encryption using random bit sequence based on chaotic maps. *Arabian Journal for Science and Engineering*, *39*(2), 1039–1047. doi:10.1007/s13369-013-0713-z

Kilincer, I. F. (2023). *Automated detection of cybersecurity attacks in healthcare systems with recursive feature elimination and multilayer perceptron optimization.* Biocybernetics and Biomedical Engine. doi:10.1016/j.bbe.2022.11.005

Kim, H. L., Choi, H. S., & Han, J. (2019). Leader power and employees' information security policy compliance. *Security Journal*, *32*(4), 391–409. doi:10.1057/s41284-019-00168-8

Kim, J., Leem, C., Kim, B., & Cheon, Y. (2013). Evolution of online social networks: A conceptual framework. *Asian Social Science*, *9*(4), 208. doi:10.5539/ass.v9n4p208

Kitchenham, B., Pearl Brereton, O., Budgen, D., Turner, M., Bailey, J., & Linkman, S. (2009). Systematic literature reviews in software engineering – A systematic literature review. *Information and Software Technology*, *51*(1), 7–15. doi:10.1016/j.infsof.2008.09.009

Koch, T. (2019). *Developing Protocol-Agnostic Jammers Using Reinforcement Learning* [Master's thesis]. The Cooper Union for the Advancement of Science and Art.

Kontaxis, G., Polychronakis, M., & Markatos, E. P. (2011). SudoWeb: Minimizing information disclosure to third parties in single sign-on platforms. *Information Security: 14th International Conference, ISC 2011, Xi'an, China, October 26-29, 2011 Proceedings*, *14*, 197–212.

Kothawade, N., Biradar, A., Kodmelwar, K., Tambe, K. P., & Deshpande, V. (2016). Performance analysis of wireless sensor network by varying reporting rate. *Indian Journal of Science and Technology*, *9*(26). Advance online publication. doi:10.17485/ijst/2016/v9i26/91906

Kovačević, A., & Radenković, S. D. (2020). SAWIT—Security awareness improvement tool in the workplace. *Applied Sciences (Basel, Switzerland)*, *10*(9), 3065. doi:10.3390/app10093065

Krishnan, P., Jain, K., Aldweesh, A., Prabu, P., & Buyya, R. (2023). *OpenStackDP*: A scalable network security framework for SDN-based OpenStack cloud infrastructure. *Journal of Cloud Computing (Heidelberg, Germany)*, *12*(1), 26. doi:10.1186/s13677-023-00406-w

Krombholz, K., Hobel, H., Huber, M., & Weippl, E. (2015). Advanced social engineering attacks. *Journal of Information Security and Applications*, *22*, 113–122. doi:10.1016/j.jisa.2014.09.005

Kshetri, N. (2019). *Cybercrime and cybersecurity in Africa*. Academic Press.

Kumar, R. L., & Bhatnagar, V. (2008). A framework for the selection of security controls in cloud computing. In *2008 International Conference on Cloud Computing* (pp. 758–763). doi:10.1109/cloud.2008.17

Kumar, S., & Kumar, P. (2021). Privacy Preserving in Online Social Networks Using Fuzzy Rewiring. *IEEE Transactions on Engineering Management*, 1–9. doi:10.1109/TEM.2021.3072812

Kwak, Y., Lee, S., Damiano, A., & Vishwanath, A. (2020). Why do users not report spear phishing emails? *Telematics and Informatics*, *48*, 101343. doi:10.1016/j.tele.2020.101343

Kwon, O., & Johnson, M. E. (2013). Security information technology governance and cybersecurity policy compliance: An empirical study of cybersecurity governance. *Information Systems Frontiers*, *15*(2), 199–212. doi:10.1007/s10796-012-9351-1

Lai, Q., Hu, G., Erkan, U., & Toktas, A. (2023). A novel pixel-split image encryption scheme based on 2d salomon map. *Expert Systems with Applications*, *213*, 118845. doi:10.1016/j.eswa.2022.118845

Lang, J., & Ma, C. (2023). Novel zero-watermarking method using the compressed sensing significant feature. *Multimedia Tools and Applications*, *82*(3), 4551–4567. doi:10.1007/s11042-022-13601-9

LaRose,R., Rifon,N., Liu,S., & Lee, D. (2005). *Understanding online safety behavior: A multivariate model*. Academic Press.

Latif, R., Abbas, H., Assar, S., & Ali, Q. (2014). Cloud computing risk assessment: A systematic literature review. *Future Information Technology: FutureTech*, *2013*, 285–295. doi:10.1007/978-3-642-40861-8_42

Laurent. (2016). *How to Prevent Cyber Crime By Training Your Employees*. https://www.lastlinesolutions.com/how-to-prevent-cyber-crime-by-training-your-employees/

Le ToquinJ.-C. (2006). *Public-Private Partnerships against cybercrime*. https://www.oecd.org/sti/consumer/42534994.pdf

Lebek, B., Uffen, J., Neumann, M., Hohler, B., & Breitner, M. H. (2014). Information security awareness and behavior: A theory-based literature review. *Management Research Review*, *37*(12), 1049–1092. doi:10.1108/MRR-04-2013-0085

Lee, M., Kim, H., & Yoe, H. (2018). Wireless sensor networks based on bio-inspired algorithms. In *Computational Science and Its Applications – ICCSA 2018* (pp. 719–725). Springer International Publishing. doi:10.1007/978-3-319-95162-1_52

Lee, S. J., Lee, Y. R., Jeon, S. E., & Lee, I. G. (2023). Machine learning-based jamming attack classification and effective defense technique. *Computers & Security*, *128*, 103169. doi:10.1016/j.cose.2023.103169

Li, H. Z. (2019). Using deep-learning-based memory analysis for malware detection in the cloud. *IEEE 16th International Conference on mobile ad hoc and sensor systems workshops*, 1-6.

Liang, H., & Xue, Y. (2010). Understanding security behaviors in personal computer usage: A threat avoidance perspective. *Journal of the Association for Information Systems*, *11*(7), 394–413. doi:10.17705/1jais.00232

Lian, W. N., Nie, G., Jia, B., Shi, D., Fan, Q., & Liang, Y. (2020). An intrusion detection method based on decision tree-recursive feature elimination in ensemble learning. *Mathematical Problems in Engineering*, *2020*, 1–15. doi:10.1155/2020/2835023

Liao, X., Lai, S., & Zhou, Q. (2010). A novel image encryption algorithm based on self-adaptive wave transmission. *Signal Processing*, *90*(9), 2714–2722. doi:10.1016/j.sigpro.2010.03.022

Lifandali, O. A., Abghour, N., & Chiba, Z. (2023). Feature Selection Using a Combination of Ant Colony Optimization and Random Forest Algorithms Applied To Isolation Forest Based Intrusion Detection System. *Procedia Computer Science*, *220*, 796–805. doi:10.1016/j.procs.2023.03.106

Li, G., Yan, Z., & Fu, Y. (2018, May). A study and simulation research of blackhole attack on mobile adhoc network. In *2018 IEEE Conference on Communications and Network Security (CNS)* (pp. 1-6). IEEE.10.1109/CNS.2018.8433148

Li, H., Yu, S., Feng, W., Chen, Y., Zhang, J., Qin, Z., Zhu, Z., & Wozniak, M. (2023). Exploiting dynamic vector-level operations and a 2D-enhanced logistic modular map for efficient chaotic image encryption. *Entropy (Basel, Switzerland)*, *25*(8), 1147. doi:10.3390/e25081147 PMID:37628177

Li, M., Lian, Y., Zhu, J., Lin, J., Wan, J., & Sun, Y. (2024). A sampling-based method for detecting data poisoning attacks in recommendation systems. *Mathematics*, *12*(2), 247. doi:10.3390/math12020247

Lipsum generator. (n.d.). https://www.lipsum.com/

Liu, C., Zhu, T., Zhang, J., & Zhou, W. (2023). Privacy intelligence: A survey on image privacy in online social networks. *ACM Computing Surveys*, *55*(8), 1–35. doi:10.1145/3547299

Liu, G., Zhao, H., Fan, F., Liu, G., Xu, Q., & Nazir, S. (2022). An enhanced intrusion detection model based on improved kNN in WSNs. *Sensors (Basel)*, *22*(4), 1407. doi:10.3390/s22041407 PMID:35214308

Liu, Q., Xiang, X., Qin, J., Tan, Y., Tan, J., & Luo, Y. (2020). Coverless steganography based on image retrieval of densenet features and dwt sequence mapping. *Knowledge-Based Systems*, *192*, 105375. doi:10.1016/j.knosys.2019.105375

Liu, Q., Zhang, Q., Zhao, F., & Wang, G. (2024). Uncertain knowledge graph embedding: An effective method combining multi-relation and multi-path. *Frontiers of Computer Science*, *18*(3). Advance online publication. doi:10.1007/s11704-023-2427-z

Li, Y., Wang, C., & Chen, H. (2017). A hyper-chaos-based image encryption algorithm using pixel-level permutation and bit-level permutation. *Optics and Lasers in Engineering*, *90*, 238–246. doi:10.1016/j.optlaseng.2016.10.020

Li, Y., Zhang, C., Qi, H., & Lyu, S. (2024). AdaNI: Adaptive Noise Injection to improve adversarial robustness. *Computer Vision and Image Understanding: CVIU*, *238*(103855), 103855. doi:10.1016/j.cviu.2023.103855

Logeswari, G., Bose, S., & Anitha, T. (2023). An Intrusion Detection System for SDN Using Machine Learning. *Intelligent Automation & Soft Computing*, *35*(1), 867–880. doi:10.32604/iasc.2023.026769

López-Vilos, N., Valencia-Cordero, C., Souza, R. D., & Montejo-Sánchez, S. (2023). Clustering-based energy-efficient self-healing strategy for WSNs under jamming attacks. *Sensors (Basel)*, *23*(15), 6894. doi:10.3390/s23156894 PMID:37571681

Lun, Y. Z., D'Innocenzo, A., Malavolta, I., & Di Benedetto, M. D. (2016). Cyber-physical systems security: a systematic mapping study. *arXiv preprint arXiv:1605.09641.*

Lu, W., Xue, Y., Yeung, Y., Liu, H., Huang, J., & Shi, Y.-Q. (2019). Secure halftone image steganography based on pixel density transition. *IEEE Transactions on Dependable and Secure Computing*, *18*(3), 1137–1149. doi:10.1109/TDSC.2019.2933621

Machdi, A. R., & Tan, Y. (2022). Performance analysis on Wireless Sensor Network based on Zigbee Wireless Communication protocol. JREC, 9(2), 25–30. doi:10.33558/jrec.v9i2.3188

Maddu, M., & Rao, Y. N. (2023). Network intrusion detection and mitigation in SDN using deep learning models. *International Journal of Information Security*. Advance online publication. doi:10.1007/s10207-023-00771-2

Mahadik, S., Pawar, P. M., & Muthalagu, R. (2023). Efficient Intelligent Intrusion Detection System for Heterogeneous Internet of Things (HetIoT). *Journal of Network and Systems Management*, *31*(1), 2. doi:10.1007/s10922-022-09697-x

Mahindru, A., & Sangal, A. L. (2021). A feature selection technique to detect malware from Android using Machine Learning Techniques. *FSDroid. Multimedia Tools and Applications*, *80*(9), 13271–13323. doi:10.1007/s11042-020-10367-w PMID:33462535

Mahlangu, T., January, S., Mashiane, T., & Ngobeni, S. J. (2020). Data Poisoning: Achilles Heel of Cyber Threat Intelligence Systems. *Proceedings of the 14th International Conference on Cyber Warfare and Security (ICCWS 2019).*

Maitlo, A., Ameen, N., Peikari, H. R., & Shah, M. (2019). Preventing identity theft: Identifying major barriers to knowledge-sharing in online retail organisations. *Information Technology & People*, *32*(5), 1184–1214. doi:10.1108/ITP-05-2018-0255

Majeed, A., Khan, S., & Hwang, S. O. (2022). A comprehensive analysis of privacy-preserving solutions developed for online social networks. *Electronics (Basel)*, *11*(13), 1931. doi:10.3390/electronics11131931

Majid, M., Habib, S., Javed, A. R., Rizwan, M., Srivastava, G., Gadekallu, T. R., & Lin, J. C.-W. (2022). Applications of wireless sensor networks and Internet of Things frameworks in the industry revolution 4.0: A systematic literature review. *Sensors (Basel)*, *22*(6), 2087. doi:10.3390/s22062087 PMID:35336261

Mall, P. K., Pramanik, S., Srivastava, S., Faiz, M., Sriramulu, S., & Kumar, M. N. (2023). FuzztNet-Based Modeling Smart Traffic System in Smart Cities Using Deep Learning Models. In *Data-Driven Mathematical Modeling in Smart Cities*. IGI Global. doi:10.4018/978-1-6684-6408-3.ch005

Manaseer, M. S., & Younes, M. B. (2023, November). Secure Protocols in VANETs: Availability Considerations. In 2023 14th International Conference on Information and Communication Systems (ICICS) (pp. 1-6). IEEE.

Manderna, A., Kumar, S., Dohare, U., Aljaidi, M., Kaiwartya, O., & Lloret, J. (2023). Vehicular network intrusion detection using a cascaded deep learning approach with multi-variant metaheuristic. *Sensors (Basel)*, *23*(21), 8772. doi:10.3390/s23218772 PMID:37960470

Manikandan, S. A., & Kaladevi, A. C. (2017). *Privacy Protection for Online Social Network Through Third Party Application Programming Interface* (SSRN Scholarly Paper No. 3125922). doi:10.2139/ssrn.3125922

Marotta, A., Böhme, R., & Moore, T. (2012). The economics of information security investment. *ACM Computing Surveys*, *45*(4), 50. Advance online publication. doi:10.1145/2379776.2379789

Martin, L. E., & Mulvihill, T. M. (2019). Voices in education: Teacher self-efficacy in education. *Teacher Educator*, *54*(3), 195–205. doi:10.1080/08878730.2019.1615030

Matos, Rebello, Costa, Queiroz, Regufe, & Nogueira. (2022). *Bio-inspired algorithms in the optimisation of wireless sensor networks*. Academic Press.

Mat, S. R., Ab Razak, M. F., Kahar, M. N. M., Arif, J. M., Mohamad, S., & Firdaus, A. (2021). Towards a systematic description of the field using bibliometric analysis: Malware evolution. *Scientometrics*, *126*(3), 2013–2055. doi:10.1007/s11192-020-03834-6 PMID:33583978

Mauw, S., & Oostdijk, M. (2005). *Foundations of Attack Trees*. ICISC. doi:10.1007/11734727_17

McCormack, G. R., Rock, M., Toohey, A. N., & Hignell, D. (2010). Characteristics of urban parks associated with park use and physical activity: A review of qualitative research. *Health & Place*, *16*(4), 712–726. doi:10.1016/j.healthplace.2010.03.003 PMID:20356780

McFaul, M. & Bronte, K. (2019). Understanding Putin's Intentions and Actions in the 2016 U.S. Presidential Election. *Securing American Elections*, 1.

McGraw, G., Bonett, R., Shepardson, V., & Figueroa, H. (2020). The top 10 risks of machine learning security. *Computer*, *53*(6), 57–61. doi:10.1109/mc.2020.2984868

Medková, J., & Hynek, J. (2023). HAkAu: Hybrid algorithm for effective k-automorphism anonymization of social networks. *Social Network Analysis and Mining*, *13*(1), 63. Advance online publication. doi:10.1007/s13278-023-01064-1

Meister, J. A., Akram, R. N., & Markantonakis, K. (2019). Deep learning application in security and privacy – theory and practice: A position paper. In *Information Security Theory and Practice* (pp. 129–144). Springer International Publishing.

Meslie, Y., Enbeyle, W., Pandey, B. K., Pramanik, S., Pandey, D., Dadeech, P., Belay, A., & Saini, A. (2021). Machine Intelligence-based Trend Analysis of COVID-19 for Total Daily Confirmed Cases in Asia and Africa. In D. Samanta, R. R. Althar, S. Pramanik, & S. Dutta (Eds.), *Methodologies and Applications of Computational Statistics for Machine Learning* (pp. 164–185). IGI Global. doi:10.4018/978-1-7998-7701-1.ch009

Metalidou, E., Marinagi, C., Trivellas, P., Eberhagen, N., Skourlas, C., & Giannakopoulos, G. (2014). The human factor of information security: Unintentional damage perspective. *Procedia: Social and Behavioral Sciences*, *147*, 424–428. doi:10.1016/j.sbspro.2014.07.133

Milko, D. S. (2021). Threat modeling expert system: Reasons for develop ment, method and implementation troubles. Modern technologies. Systemanalysis. *Modeling*, (D). Advance online publication. doi:10.26731/1813 9108.2021.2(70).182-189 123 372

Miller, B. (2020). *15 Advantages and Disadvantages of Quantitative Research*. Academic Press.

Mishra, A., Singh, S., & Tripathi, A. K. (2019). Comparison of MANET routing protocols. *Int. J. Comput. Sci. Mob. Comput*, *8*, 67–74.

Misra, P., & Yadav, A. S. (2020). Improving the classification accuracy using recursive feature elimination with cross-validation. *Int. J. Emerg. Technol.*, *11*(3), 659–665.

Mittal, M., Kumar, K., & Behal, S. (2023). DDoS-AT-2022: A distributed denial of service attack dataset for evaluating DDoS defense system. *Proceedings of the Indian National Science Academy. Part A, Physical Sciences*, *89*(2), 306–324. doi:10.1007/s43538-023-00159-9

Moher, D., Shamseer, L., Clarke, M., Ghersi, D., Liberati, A., Petticrew, M., Shekelle, P., & Stewart, L. A.Prisma-P Group. (2015). Preferred reporting items for systematic review and meta-analysis protocols (PRISMA-P) 2015 statement. *Systematic Reviews*, *4*(1), 1–9. doi:10.1186/2046-4053-4-1 PMID:25554246

Mohurle, S., & Patil, M. (2017). A brief study of Wannacry Threat: Ransomware Attack 2017. *International Journal of Advanced Research in Computer Science*, *8*(5), 1938–1940. doi:10.26483/ijarcs.v8i5.4021

Molok, N. N. A., Ahmad, A., & Chang, S. (2018). A case analysis of securing organisations against information leakage through online social networking. *International Journal of Information Management*, *43*, 351–356. doi:10.1016/j.ijinfomgt.2018.08.013

Morison, K., Wang, L., & Kundur, P. (2004). Power system security assessment. *IEEE Power & Energy Magazine*, *2*(5), 30–39. doi:10.1109/MPAE.2004.1338120

Moumen, I., Rafalia, N., Abouchabaka, J., & Chatoui, Y. (2023). AODV-based Defense Mechanism for Mitigating Blackhole Attacks in MANET. In *E3S Web of Conferences* (Vol. 412, p. 01094). EDP Sciences. doi:10.1051/e3sconf/202341201094

Muccini, H., Sharaf, M., & Weyns, D. (2016, May). Self-adaptation for cyber-physical systems: a systematic literature review. In *Proceedings of the 11th international symposium on software engineering for adaptive and self-managing systems* (pp. 75-81). 10.1145/2897053.2897069

Mughaid, A., Obaidat, I., Aljammal, A., AlZu'bi, S., Quiam, F., Laila, D., Al-zou'bi, A., & Abualigah, L. (2023). Simulation and analysis performance of ad-hoc routing protocols under DDoS attack and proposed solution. *International Journal of Data and Network Science*, *7*(2), 757–764. doi:10.5267/j.ijdns.2023.2.002

MyCERT. (2021). Retrieved December, 20, 2021 from https://www.mycert.org.my/portal/statistics-content?menu=b75e037d-6ee3-4d11-8169-66677d694932&id=77be547e-7a17-444b-9698-8c267427936c

Naseer, H., Maynard, S. B., & Desouza, K. C. (2021). Demystifying analytical information processing capability: The case of cybersecurity incident response. *Decision Support Systems*, *143*, 113476. doi:10.1016/j.dss.2020.113476

Nath, H. V. (2014). Static malware analysis using machine learning methods. *Recent Trends in Computer Networks and Distributed Systems Security*. 10.1007/978-3-642-54525-2_39

Nawaz, N. A., Ishaq, K., Farooq, U., Khalil, A., Rasheed, S., Abid, A., & Rosdi, F. (2023). A comprehensive review of security threats and solutions for the online social networks industry. *PeerJ. Computer Science*, *9*, e1143. doi:10.7717/peerj-cs.1143 PMID:37346522

Ng, B. Y., & Rahim, B. A. (2005). A socio-behavioral study of home computer users' intention to practice security. *Proceedings of the Ninth Pacific Asia Conference on Information Systems.*

Nguyen. (2021). ZigBee based data collection in wireless sensor networks. *Int. J. Inform. Commun. Technol.*, *10*(3), 212.

Nie, B. (2022). Zigbee-based wireless sensor network energy-saving networking intelligent technology and middleware optimization. *2022 3rd International Conference on Smart Electronics and Communication (ICOSEC).* 10.1109/ICOSEC54921.2022.9951997

Nielson, S. J. (2023). Authentication Technology. In *Discovering Cybersecurity*. Apress. doi:10.1007/978-1-4842-9560-1_2

Noguerol, L. O., & Branch, R. (2018). Leadership and electronic data security within small businesses: An exploratory case study. *Journal of Economic Development, Management, IT, Finance, and Marketing*, *10*(2), 7–35.

Noor, B., & Qadir, S. (2023). Machine Learning and Deep Learning Based Model for the Detection of Rootkits Using Memory Analysis. *Applied Sciences (Basel, Switzerland)*, *13*(19), 10730. doi:10.3390/app131910730

Onumo, A., Cullen, A., & Ullah-Awan, I. (2017, August). An empirical study of cultural dimensions and cybersecurity development. In *2017 IEEE 5th International Conference on Future Internet of Things and Cloud (FiCloud)* (pp. 70-76). IEEE. 10.1109/FiCloud.2017.41

Openstego. (n.d.). https://www.openstego.com/

Ophoff, J., & Lakay, M. (2018, August). Mitigating the ransomware threat: a protection motivation theory approach. In *International Information Security Conference* (pp. 163-175). Springer.

Osman, Z., Adis, A. A. A., & Phang, G. (2017). Perceived security towards e-banking services: an examination among Malaysian young consumers. *Journal of the Asian Academy of Applied Business*, 15.

Özkaynak, F. (2017, October). Role of NPCR and UACI tests in security problems of chaos based image encryption algorithms and possible solution proposals. In *2017 International conference on computer science and engineering (UBMK)* (pp. 621-624). IEEE. 10.1109/UBMK.2017.8093481

Paek, S. Y., Nalla, M. K., Chun, Y. T., & Lee, J. (2021). The Perceived Importance of Cybercrime Control among Police Officers: Implications for Combatting Industrial Espionage. *Sustainability (Basel)*, *13*(8), 4351. doi:10.3390/su13084351

Pandey, S., Singh, R. K., Gunasekaran, A., & Kaushik, A. (2020). Cyber security risks in globalised supply chains: Conceptual framework. *Journal of Global Operations and Strategic Sourcing*, *13*(1), 103–128. doi:10.1108/JGOSS-05-2019-0042

Panker, T., & Nissim, N. (2021). Leveraging malicious behavior traces from volatile memory using machine learning methods for trusted unknown malware detection in Linux cloud environments. *Knowledge-Based Systems*, *226*, 107095. doi:10.1016/j.knosys.2021.107095

Patel, A., & Jinwala, D. (2021). A reputation-based RPL protocol to detect selective forwarding attack in Internet of Things. *International Journal of Communication Systems*, *35*(1), e5007. Advance online publication. doi:10.1002/dac.5007

Patel, N. D., Mehtre, B. M., & Wankar, R. (2023). Od-ids2022: Generating a new offensive defensive intrusion detection dataset for machine learning-based attack classification. *International Journal of Information Technology : an Official Journal of Bharati Vidyapeeth's Institute of Computer Applications and Management*, *15*(8), 4349–4363. doi:10.1007/s41870-023-01464-8

Paullet, K., & Pinchot, J. (2012). Cybercrime: the unintentional effects of oversharing information on Facebook. *Proceedings of the Conference on Information Systems Applied Research ISSN, 2167*, 1508.

Peace, C. (2017). *The risk matrix: uncertain results?* Policy Pract. Health Saf. doi:10.1080/14773996.2017.1348571

Pen, L. Z. K. X. (2022). Artocarpus classification technique using deep learning based convolutional neural network. Classification Applications with Deep Learning and Ma-chine Learning Technologies, 1–21.

Pen, L. Z., Xian Xian, K., Yew, C. F., Hau, O. S., Sumari, P., Abualigah, L., Ezugwu, A. E., Shinwan, M. A., Gul, F., & Mughaid, A. (2022). *Artocarpusclassification technique using deep learning based convolutional neuralnetwork. In Classification Applications with Deep Learning and Ma-chine Learning Technologies*. Springer.

Pham, H. C., Ulhaq, I., Nkhoma, M., Nguyen, M. N., & Brennan, L. (2018). *Exploring knowledge sharing practices for raising security awareness*. Academic Press.

Pham, T. H., Phan, T.-A., Trinh, P.-A., Mai, X. B. & Le, Q.-C. (2023). Information security risks and sharing behavior on OSN: the impact of data collection awareness. *Journal of Information, Communication and Ethics in Society*.

Pollini, A., Callari, T. C., Tedeschi, A., Ruscio, D., Save, L., Chiarugi, F., & Guerri, D. (2022). Leveraging human factors in cybersecurity: An integrated methodological approach. *Cognition Technology and Work, 24*(2), 371–390. doi:10.1007/s10111-021-00683-y PMID:34149309

Popham, J., McCluskey, M., Ouellet, M., & Gallupe, O. (2020). Exploring police-reported cybercrime in Canada: Variation and correlates. *Policing, 43*(1), 35–48. doi:10.1108/PIJPSM-08-2019-0128

Pradhan, D., Sahu, P. K., Goje, N. S., Myo, H., Ghonge, M. M. M., Tun, R., & Pramanik, S. (2022). Security, Privacy, Risk, and Safety Toward 5G Green Network (5G-GN). In Cyber Security and Network Security. Wiley. doi:10.1002/9781119812555.ch9

Pramanik, S. (2022). Carpooling Solutions using Machine Learning Tools. In *Handbook of Research on Evolving Designs and Innovation in ICT and Intelligent Systems for Real-World Applications*. IGI Global. doi:10.4018/978-1-7998-9795-8.ch002

Praveenkumar, S., Veeraiah, V., Pramanik, S., Basha, S. M., Lira Neto, A. V., De Albuquerque, V. H. C., & Gupta, A. (2023). *Prediction of Patients' Incurable Diseases Utilizing Deep Learning Approaches, ICICC 2023*. Springer. doi:10.1007/978-981-99-3315-0_4

Punt, A., Schiffelers, M.-J. W., Horbach, G. J., van de Sandt, J. J., Groothuis, G. M., Rietjens, I. M., & Blaauboer, B. J. (2011). Evaluation of research activities and research needs to increase the impact and applicability of alternative testing strategies in risk assessment practice. *Regulatory Toxicology and Pharmacology, 61*(1), 105–114. doi:10.1016/j.yrtph.2011.06.007 PMID:21782875

Qiu, J., Liu, J., Bi, Z., Sun, X., Gu, Q., Hu, G., & Qin, N. (2022). An investigation of 2D spine magnetic resonance imaging (MRI) with compressed sensing (CS). *Skeletal Radiology, 51*(6), 1273–1283. doi:10.1007/s00256-021-03954-x PMID:34854969

Quintero-Bonilla, S., Rey, T. J., & Park, A. M. (2020). A new proposal on the advanced persistent threat: A survey. *Applied Sciences (Basel, Switzerland), 10*(11), 3874. Advance online publication. doi:10.3390/app10113874

Rabiaa, N., Moussa, A. C., & Sofiane, B. H. (2023). A cross-layer method for identifying and isolating the blackhole nodes in vehicular ad-hoc networks. Information Security Journal: A Global Perspective, 32(3), 212-226.

Raff, E. F. (2021). Classifying sequences of extreme length with constant memory applied to malware detection. *Proceedings of the AAAI Conference on Artificial Intelligence*, 35. 10.1609/aaai.v35i11.17131

Rafrastara, F. A. (2023). *Performance Improvement of Random Forest Algorithm for Malware Detection on Imbalanced Dataset using Random Under-Sampling Method.* Jurnal Informatika Jurnal Pengembangan. doi:10.30591/jpit.v8i2.5207

Rahim, N. H. A., Hamid, S., Mat Kiah, M. L., Shamshirband, S., & Furnell, S. (2015). A systematic review of approaches to assessing cybersecurity awareness. *Kybernetes*, *44*(4), 606–622. doi:10.1108/K-12-2014-0283

Rahman, M. A., Islam, S., Nugroho, Y. S., Al Irsyadi, F. Y., & Hossain, M. J. (2023). An exploratory analysis of feature selection for malware detection with simple machine learning algorithms. *Journal of Communications Software and Systems*, *19*(3), 207–221. doi:10.24138/jcomss-2023-0091

Ranjan, P., & Ranjan, R. (2023). Trust-Based DSR Protocol for Secure Communication in Mobile Ad-hoc Networks. In *Advances in Data-driven Computing and Intelligent Systems: Selected Papers from ADCIS 2022* (Vol. 2, pp. 167–177). Springer Nature Singapore. doi:10.1007/978-981-99-0981-0_13

Ransbotham, S., & Mitra, S. (2009). Choice and chance: A conceptual model of paths to information security compromise. *Information Systems Research*, *20*(1), 121–139. doi:10.1287/isre.1080.0174

Rao, S., Verma, A. K., & Bhatia, T. (2021). Evolving cyber threats, combating techniques, and open issues in online social networks. In *Handbook of research on cyber crime and information privacy* (pp. 219–235). IGI Global.

Ravi, V. (2023). *Deep learning-based network intrusion detection in smart healthcare enterprise systems.* Multimed Tools Appl. doi:10.1007/s11042-023-17300-x

Report, C. D. (2021). Retrieved December, 15, 2021 from https://cyber-edge.com/wp-content/uploads/2021/04/CyberEdge-2021-CDR-Report-v1.1-1.pdf

Reza, K. J., Islam, M. Z., & Estivill-Castro, V. (2021). Privacy protection of online social network users, against attribute inference attacks, through the use of a set of exhaustive rules. *Neural Computing & Applications*, *33*(19), 12397–12427. doi:10.1007/s00521-021-05860-8

Ring, M., Wunderlich, S., Scheuring, D., Landes, D., & Hotho, A. (2019). A survey of network-based intrusion detection data sets. *Computers & Security, 86*, 147-167. doi:10.1016/j.cose.2019.06.005

Rivard, J. P. (2014). *Cybercrime: The creation and exploration of a model* [Doctoral dissertation]. University of Phoenix.

Rodrigues, A., Villela, M. L. B., & Feitosa, E. L. (2023). Privacy threat MOdeling language. *IEEE Access : Practical Innovations, Open Solutions*, *11*, 24448–24471. doi:10.1109/ACCESS.2023.3255548

Roseline, S. A. (2020). Intelligent vision-based malware detection and classification using deep random forest paradigm. *IEEE Access, 8*, 206303-206324.

Rtayli & Enneya. (2020). *Enhanced credit card fraud detection based on SVM-recursive feature elimination and hyper-parameters optimization.* Academic Press.

Ryan, M. (2021). *Ransomware Revolution: The Rise of a Prodigious Cyber Threat* (Vol. 85). Springer International Publishing. doi:10.1007/978-3-030-66583-8

Safa, N. S., & Von Solms, R. (2016). An Information Security Knowledge Sharing Model in Organisations. *Computers in Human Behavior*, *57*, 442–451. doi:10.1016/j.chb.2015.12.037

Sahoo, S. R. & Gupta, B. B. (2018). Security issues and challenges in online social networks (OSNs) based on user perspective. *Computer and Cyber Security*, 591–606.

Sahoo, S. R., & Gupta, B. B. (2019). Classification of various attacks and their defence mechanism in online social networks: A survey. *Enterprise Information Systems*, *13*(6), 832–864. doi:10.1080/17517575.2019.1605542

Sahu, A. K., Swain, G., Sahu, M., & Hemalatha, J. (2021). Multi-directional block based pvd and modulus function image steganography to avoid fobp and iep. *Journal of Information Security and Applications*, *58*, 102808. doi:10.1016/j.jisa.2021.102808

Saini, L. K., & Shrivastava, V. (2014). A survey of digital watermarking techniques and its applications. arXiv preprint arXiv:1407.4735.

Saini, V. K., Duan, Q., & Paruchuri, V. (2008). Threat modeling using attack trees. *JCSC*, *23*(4), 124–131.

Salahdine, F., & Kaabouch, N. (2020). Security threats, detection, and countermeasures for physical layer in cognitive radio networks: A survey. *Physical Communication*, *39*, 101001. doi:10.1016/j.phycom.2020.101001

Sarker, I. H., Furhad, M. H., & Nowrozy, R. (2021). Ai-driven cybersecurity: An overview, security intelligence modeling and research directions. *SN Computer Science*, *2*(3), 1–18. doi:10.1007/s42979-021-00557-0

Sasse, M., & Flechais, I. (2005). Usable Security: Why Do We Need It? How Do We Get It? In L. F. Cranor & S. Garfinkel (Eds.), *Security and Usability* (pp. 13–30). Sebastopol, CA: O'Reilly Publishing. Retrieved from https://discovery.ucl.ac.uk/20345

Schillinger, F., & Schindelhauer, C. (2019). End-to-end encryption schemes for online social networks. *Security, Privacy, and Anonymity in Computation, Communication, and Storage: 12th International Conference, SpaCCS 2019, Atlanta, GA, USA, July 14–17, 2019 Proceedings*, *12*, 133–146.

Schwarzschild, Goldblum, Micah, Gupta, Arjun, Dickerson, & Goldstein. (n.d.). Just how toxic is data poisoning? A unified benchmark for backdoor and data poisoning attacks. Arxiv.org. http://arxiv.org/abs/2006.12557

Sedar, R., Kalalas, C., Vázquez-Gallego, F., Alonso, L., & Alonso-Zarate, J. (2023). A comprehensive survey of v2x cybersecurity mechanisms and future research paths. *IEEE Open Journal of the Communications Society*, *4*, 325–391. doi:10.1109/OJCOMS.2023.3239115

Senol, M., & Karacuha, E. (2020). Creating and implementing an effective and deterrent national cyber security strategy. *Journal of Engineering*, *2020*, 2020. doi:10.1155/2020/5267564

Shah, S. S., Ahmad, A. R., Jamil, N., & Khan, A. R. (2022). Memory forensics-based malware detection using computer vision and machine learning. *Electronics (Basel)*, *11*(16), 2579. doi:10.3390/electronics11162579

Sharda, S., & Budhiraja, S. (2013). Image steganography: A review. *International Journal of Emerging Technology and Advanced Engineering*, *3*(1), 707–710.

Sharma, A., & Kaur, D. (2016). Behavior of Jamming Attack in OLSR, GRP, TORA and improvement with PCF in TORA using OPNET tool. *Int. Res. J. Eng. Technol*, *3*(3), 191–194.

Sharma, M. (2020). Image encryption based on a new 2D logistic adjusted logistic map. *Multimedia Tools and Applications*, *79*(1-2), 355–374. doi:10.1007/s11042-019-08079-x

Sharma, N. V., & Yadav, N. S. (2021). An optimal intrusion detection system using recursive feature elimination and ensemble of classifiers. *Microprocessors and Microsystems*, *85*, 104293. doi:10.1016/j.micpro.2021.104293

Sharma, S. K., & Chawla, M. (2023). Compatibility issues of wireless sensor network routing in internet of things applications. *International Journal of Wireless and Mobile Computing*, *25*(1), 18–29. doi:10.1504/IJWMC.2023.132400

Shiau, J.-N., & Fan, Z. (1996). Set of easily implementable coefficients in error diffusion with reduced worm artifacts. Color Imaging: Device-Independent Color, Color Hard Copy, and Graphic Arts, 2658, 222–225. doi:10.1117/12.236968

Shinde, R., Patil, S., Kotecha, K., & Ruikar, K. (2021). Blockchain for securing ai applications and open innovations. *Journal of Open Innovation*, *7*(3), 189. doi:10.3390/joitmc7030189

Showkat, N., & Parveen, H. (2017). Non-probability and probability sampling. *Media and Communications Study*, 1-9.

Sihwail, R. O., Omar, K., & Akram Zainol Ariffin, K. (2021). An Effective Memory Analysis for Malware Detection and Classification. *Computers, Materials & Continua*, *67*(2), 2301–2320. doi:10.32604/cmc.2021.014510

Sihwail, R. O., Omar, K., Zainol Ariffin, K., & Al Afghani, S. (2019). Malware detection approach based on artifacts in memory image and dynamic analysis. *Applied Sciences (Basel, Switzerland)*, *9*(18), 3680. doi:10.3390/app9183680

Singh, J., & Gupta, S. (2017). Impact of jamming attack in performance of mobile ad hoc networks. *International Journal of Computer Science Trends and Technology*, *5*(3), 184–190.

Singh, K. N., & Singh, A. K. (2022). Towards integrating image encryption with compression: A survey. *ACM Transactions on Multimedia Computing Communications and Applications*, *18*(3), 1–21. doi:10.1145/3498342

Singh, P. B. (2022). Performance Enhancement of SVM-based ML Malware Detection Model Using Data Preprocessing. *2nd International Conference on Emerging Frontiers in Electrical and Electronic Technologies (ICEFEET).* 10.1109/ICEFEET51821.2022.9848192

Siponen, M., Mahmood, M. A., & Pahnila, S. (2014). Employees' adherence to information security policies: An exploratory field study. *Information & Management*, *51*(2), 217–224. doi:10.1016/j.im.2013.08.006

Siva Shankar, S., Hung, B. T., & Chakrabarti, P. (2023). A novel optimization based deep learning with artificial intelligence approach to detect intrusion attack in network system. *Education and Information Technologies*. Advance online publication. doi:10.1007/s10639-023-11885-4

Song, J., & Tan, Y. K. (2012). Energy consumption analysis of ZigBee-based energy harvesting wireless sensor networks. *2012 IEEE International Conference on Communication Systems (ICCS).* 10.1109/ICCS.2012.6406192

Song, W., Fu, C., Zheng, Y., Tie, M., Liu, J., & Chen, J. (2023). A parallel image encryption algorithm using intra bitplane scrambling. *Mathematics and Computers in Simulation*, *204*, 71–88. doi:10.1016/j.matcom.2022.07.029

Song, Y., Liu, T., & Jia, W. (2021). Data diversification revisited: Why does it work? In *Lecture Notes in Computer Science* (pp. 521–533). Springer International Publishing.

Space, M. (2018). The Dark Side of Social Media: A Reality Becoming More Contemporary by the Day. *Asian Social Science*, *14*(1).

Spagnoletti, P., Resca, A., & Lee, H. G. (2015). Governance of information security: A systematic literature review. *Information & Management*, *52*(1), 24–38. doi:10.1016/j.im.2014.09.004

Srisakthi, S., & Suresh Babu, C. V. (2024). Cybersecurity: Protecting Information in a Digital World. In S. Saeed, N. Azizi, S. Tahir, M. Ahmad, & A. Almuhaideb (Eds.), *Strengthening Industrial Cybersecurity to Protect Business Intelligence* (pp. 1–25). IGI Global. doi:10.4018/979-8-3693-0839-4.ch001

Srivastava, S. K., Das, S., Udo, G. J., & Bagchi, K. (2020). Determinants of cybercrime originating within a nation: A cross-country study. *Journal of Global Information Technology Management*, *23*(2), 112–137. doi:10.1080/1097198X.2020.1752084

Steghide. (n.d.). https://steghide.sourceforge.net/

SteinhardtJ.KohP. W.LiangP. (2017). Certified defenses for data poisoning attacks. arXiv. http://arxiv.org/abs/1706.03691

Straub, D., & Welke, R. J. (1998). Coping with systems risk: Security planning models for management decision making. *Management Information Systems Quarterly*, *22*(4), 441–469. doi:10.2307/249551

Sulaiman, M. U., Waseem, M., Ali, A. N., Laouini, G., & Alshammari, F. S. (2024). Defense strategies for epidemic cyber security threats: Modeling and analysis by using a machine learning approach. *IEEE Access : Practical Innovations, Open Solutions*, *12*, 4958–4984. doi:10.1109/ACCESS.2024.3349660

Suresh Babu, C. V. (2022). *Artificial Intelligence and Expert Systems*. Anniyappa Publication.

Syed, R. & Dhillon, G. (2015). *Dynamics of Data Breaches in Online Social Networks: Understanding Threats to Organizational Information Security Reputation*. Academic Press.

Syed, R., & Dhillon, G. (2015). Dynamics of Data Breaches in Online Social Networks: Understanding Threats to Organizational Information Security Reputation. *ICIS 2015 Proceedings*. Retrieved from https://aisel.aisnet.org/icis2015/proceedings/SocialMedia/14

Sy, I., Diouf, B., Diop, A. K., Drocourt, C., & Durand, D. (2024). Enhancing Security in Connected Medical IoT Networks Through Deep Learning-Based Anomaly Detection. In S. Bouzefrane, S. Banerjee, F. Mourlin, S. Boumerdassi, & É. Renault (Eds.), Lecture Notes in Computer Science: Vol. 14482. *Mobile, Secure, and Programmable Networking. MSPN 2023*. Springer. doi:10.1007/978-3-031-52426-4_7

Szczepaniuk, E. K., Szczepaniuk, H., Rokicki, T., & Klepacki, B. (2020). Information security assessment in public administration. *Computers & Security*, *90*, 101709. doi:10.1016/j.cose.2019.101709

Tahmasbi, M., Boostani, R., Aljaidi, M., & Attar, H. (2022, November). Improving Organizations Security Using Visual Cryptography Based on XOR and Chaotic-Based Key. In *2022 International Engineering Conference on Electrical, Energy, and Artificial Intelligence (EICEEAI)* (pp. 1-6). IEEE. 10.1109/EICEEAI56378.2022.10050448

Talukder, M. A., Hasan, K. F., Islam, M. M., Uddin, M. A., Akhter, A., Yousuf, M. A., Alharbi, F., & Moni, M. A. (2023). A dependable hybrid machine learning model for network intrusion detection. *Journal of Information Security and Applications*, *72*, 103405. doi:10.1016/j.jisa.2022.103405

Tarafdar, M., D'Arcy, J., & Turel, O. (2015). The dark side of information technology: An emerging perspective. In M. M. Cruz-Cunha, I. Miranda, & P. Gonçalves (Eds.), *Handbook of Research on Managerial Solutions in Non-Profit Organizations* (pp. 266–290). doi:10.4018/978-1-4666-7401-6.ch013

Tashakkori, A., & Teddlie, C. (2003). *Handbook of Mixed Methods in Social and Behavioral Research*. Sage.

Termimi, M. A. A., Rosele, M. I., Meerangani, K. A., Marinsah, S. A., & Ramli, M. A. (2015). Women's involvement in cybercrime: A premilinary study. *Journal: Journal of Advances In Hmanities*, *3*(3).

Thomas, K., Li, F., Grier, C., & Paxson, V. (2014). Consequences of Connectivity: Characterizing Account Hijacking on Twitter. *Proceedings of the 2014 ACM SIGSAC Conference on Computer and Communications Security*, 489–500. 10.1145/2660267.2660282

Thong, J. Y. L., Hong, S.-J., & Tam, K. Y. (2002). Understanding user acceptance of digital libraries: What are the roles of interface characteristics, organizational context, and individual differences? *International Journal of Human-Computer Studies*, *57*(3), 215–242. doi:10.1016/S1071-5819(02)91024-4

Thong, J. Y. L., Hong, S.-J., & Tam, K. Y. (2006). The effects of post-adoption beliefs on the expectation-confirmation model for information technology continuance. *International Journal of Human-Computer Studies*, *64*(9), 799–810. doi:10.1016/j.ijhcs.2006.05.001

Thorat, V., Kumar, S., & Wadhwa, D. L. (2020). Extended multipath routing in zigbee which improves performance parameters. SSRN *Electron. J.* doi:10.2139/ssrn.3659913

Tiloca, M., Guglielmo, D. D., Dini, G., Anastasi, G., & Das, S. K. (2018). DISH: DIstributed SHuffling against selective jamming attack in IEEE 802.15. 4e TSCH networks. *ACM Transactions on Sensor Networks*, *15*(1), 1–28. doi:10.1145/3241052

Tsafrir, T. C., Cohen, A., Nir, E., & Nissim, N. (2023). Efficient feature extraction methodologies for unknown MP4-Malware detection using Machine learning algorithms. *Expert Systems with Applications*, *219*, 119615. doi:10.1016/j.eswa.2023.119615

Ursillo, S., Jr., & Arnold, C. (2019). *Cybersecurity Is Critical for all Organizations – Large and Small.* https://www.ifac.org/knowledge-gateway/preparing-future-ready-professionals/discussion/cybersecurity-critical-all-organizations-large-and-small

US Chamber of Commerce. (2018). *Partnering With Law Enforcement to Combat Cybercrime.* Author.

van Bavel, R., Rodríguez-Priego, N., Vila, J., & Briggs, P. (2019). Using protection motivation theory in the design of nudges to improve online security behavior. *International Journal of Human-Computer Studies*, *123*, 29–39. doi:10.1016/j.ijhcs.2018.11.003

Van Der Malsburg, C. F. R. (1986). principles of neurodynamics: perceptrons and the theory of brain mechanisms. In Brain Theory. Springer.

Van Niekerk, J. F., & Von Solms, R. (2013). Governance frameworks for information security: An introduction. *Computers & Security*, *38*, 1–7. doi:10.1016/j.cose.2013.04.001

Voloch, N., Gal-Oz, N. & Gudes, E. (2023). *A Privacy Providing Context-based Trust Model for OSN and its Relation to GDPR.* Academic Press.

Wainakh, A., Grube, T., Daubert, J., Porth, C., & Muhlhauser, M. (2019, December). Tweet beyond the cage: A hybrid solution for the privacy dilemma in online social networks. *2019 IEEE Global Communications Conference (GLOBECOM).* 10.1109/GLOBECOM38437.2019.9013901

Walker, S. H., & Duncan, D. B. (1967). Estimation of the probability of an event as a function of several independent variables. *Biometrika*, *54*(1-2), 167–179. doi:10.1093/biomet/54.1-2.167 PMID:6049533

Walshe, M., Epiphaniou, G., Al-Khateeb, H., Hammoudeh, M., Katos, V., & Dehghantanha, A. (2019). Non-interactive zero knowledge proofs for the authentication of IoT devices in reduced connectivity environments. *Ad Hoc Networks*, *95*, 101988. doi:10.1016/j.adhoc.2019.101988

Wang X, Guan N. (2023). 2D sine-logistic-tent-coupling map for image encryption. Journal of Ambient Intelligence and Humanized Computing, 14(10), 13399-13419.

Wang, F., Wang, X., Yuan, H., & Ban, X. (2023). Data poisoning attacks on traffic state estimation and prediction (TSEP). SSRN *Electronic Journal.* https://doi.org/ doi:10.2139/ssrn.4396123

Wang, B., Xie, Y., Zhou, C., Zhou, S., & Zheng, X. (2016). Evaluating the permutation and diffusion operations used in image encryption based on chaotic maps. *Optik (Stuttgart)*, *127*(7), 3541–3545. doi:10.1016/j.ijleo.2016.01.015

Wang, N., Wang, P., Alipour-Fanid, A., Jiao, L., & Zeng, K. (2019). Physical-layer security of 5G wireless networks for IoT: Challenges and opportunities. *IEEE Internet of Things Journal*, *6*(5), 8169–8181. doi:10.1109/JIOT.2019.2927379

Wang, V., Nnaji, H., & Jung, J. (2020). Internet banking in Nigeria: Cyber security breaches, practices and capability. *International Journal of Law, Crime and Justice*, *62*, 100415. doi:10.1016/j.ijlcj.2020.100415

Wang, X., Yang, B., Wang, Z., Liu, Q., Chen, C., & Guan, X. (2022). A compressed sensing and CNN-based method for fault diagnosis of photovoltaic inverters in edge computing scenarios. *IET Renewable Power Generation*, *16*(7), 1434–1444. doi:10.1049/rpg2.12383

Wang, Z., Jiang, Y., & Chen, S. (2023). Image parallel block compressive sensing scheme using DFT measurement matrix. *Multimedia Tools and Applications*, *82*(14), 21561–21583. doi:10.1007/s11042-022-14176-1

Wang, Z., Pei, H., Chen, H., Wang, C., Fang, Z., & Zhou, T. (2021). Performance study of ZigBee wireless sensor network for 500kV UHV transmission tower. *2021 International Conference on Power System Technology (POWERCON)*. 10.1109/POWERCON53785.2021.9697782

Wang, Z., Wang, Z., Zeng, C., Yu, Y., & Wan, X. (2023). High-quality image compressed sensing and reconstruction with multi-scale dilated convolutional neural network. *Circuits, Systems, and Signal Processing*, *42*(3), 1593–1616. doi:10.1007/s00034-022-02181-6

Ward, P. T. (1986). The transformation schema: An extension of the data flow diagram to represent control and timing. *IEEE Transactions on Software Engineering*, *SE-12*(2), 198–210. doi:10.1109/TSE.1986.6312936

Warkentin, M., Johnston, A. C., & Shropshire, J. (2011). The Influence of the Informal Social Learning Environment on Information Privacy Policy Compliance Efficacy and Intention. *European Journal of Information Systems*, *20*(3), 267–284. doi:10.1057/ejis.2010.72

Witman, P. D. & Mackelprang, S. (2022). The 2020 Twitter Hack--So Many Lessons to Be Learned. *Journal of Cybersecurity Education, Research and Practice, 2021*(2).

World health Orgaisation. (2009). *Human Factors in Patient Safety Review of Topics and Tools*. https://www.who.int/patientsafety/research/methods_measures/human_factors/human_factors_review.pdf

Wright, D. (2012). The state of the art in privacy impact assessment. *Computer Law & Security Report*, *28*(1), 54–61. doi:10.1016/j.clsr.2011.11.007

Wu, Y., Yang, G., Jin, H., & Noonan, J. P. (2012). Image encryption using the two-dimensional logistic chaotic map. *Journal of Electronic Imaging*, *21*(1), 013014–013014. doi:10.1117/1.JEI.21.1.013014

Wu, Y., Zhang, L., Berretti, S., & Wan, S. (2022). Medical image encryption by content-aware DNA computing for secure healthcare. *IEEE Transactions on Industrial Informatics*, *19*(2), 2089–2098. doi:10.1109/TII.2022.3194590

Wu, Y., Zhou, Y., Saveriades, G., Agaian, S., Noonan, J. P., & Natarajan, P. (2013). Local Shannon entropy measure with statistical tests for image randomness. *Information Sciences*, *222*, 323–342. doi:10.1016/j.ins.2012.07.049

Wuyts, K., Van Landuyt, D., Hovsepyan, A., & Joosen, W. (2018). Effective and efficient privacy threat modeling through domain refinements. *Proc. 33rd Annu. ACM Symp. Appl. Comput.*, 1175–1178.

Xiang, H., & Liu, L. (2020). An improved digital logistic map and its application in image encryption. Multimedia Tools and Applications, 79, 30329-30355.

Xu, G., Zhang, B., Yu, H., Chen, J., Xing, M., & Hong, W. (2022). Sparse synthetic aperture radar imaging from compressed sensing and machine learning: Theories, applications, and trends. applications, and trends. *IEEE Geoscience and Remote Sensing Magazine*, *10*(4), 32–69. doi:10.1109/MGRS.2022.3218801

Xu, Z. R. (2017). Malware detection using machine learning-based analysis of virtual memory access patterns. In *Design, Automation & Test in Europe Conference & Exhibition* (pp. 169–174). doi:10.23919/DATE.2017.7926977

Yang, Y., & Newsam, S. (2010). Bag-of-visual-words and spatial extensions for land-use classification. *Proceedings of the 18th SIGSPATIAL international conference on advances in geographic information systems*, 270–279. 10.1145/1869790.1869829

YangZ.HeX.LiZ.BackesM.HumbertM.BerrangP.ZhangY. (2022). Data poisoning attacks against multimodal encoders. arXiv. http://arxiv.org/abs/2209.15266

Yavuz, E., Yazıcı, R., Kasapbaşı, M. C., & Yamaç, E. (2016). A chaos-based image encryption algorithm with simple logical functions. *Computers & Electrical Engineering*, *54*, 471–483. doi:10.1016/j.compeleceng.2015.11.008

Yerlikaya, F. A., & Bahtiyar, S. (2022). Data Poisoning Attacks against Machine Learning Algorithms. *Expert Systems with Applications*, 208.

Ye, Z., Wen, T., Liu, Z., Song, X., & Fu, C. (2017). An efficient dynamic trust evaluation model for wireless sensor networks. *Journal of Sensors*, *2017*, 1–16. doi:10.1155/2017/7864671

Yin, Y. J.-J., Jang-Jaccard, J., Xu, W., Singh, A., Zhu, J., Sabrina, F., & Kwak, J. (2023). a hybrid feature selection method for MLP-based network intrusion detection on UNSW-NB15 dataset. *Journal of Big Data*, *10*(1), 1–26. doi:10.1186/s40537-023-00694-8 PMID:36618886

Yu, M., Tang, Z., Zhang, X., Zhong, B., & Zhang, X. (2022). Perceptual hashing with complementary color wavelet transform and compressed sensing for reduced-reference image quality assessment. *IEEE Transactions on Circuits and Systems for Video Technology*, *32*(11), 7559–7574. doi:10.1109/TCSVT.2022.3190273

Yu, W., Wei, Q., Cheng, Y., Zhou, J., & Lu, K. (2018). A multi-stage risk assessment model for information security risk management in enterprises. *Information Sciences*, *428*, 169–186. doi:10.1016/j.ins.2017.11.028

Zach, O. (2019). GDPR compliance strategies. In *International Conference on Trust, Privacy and Security in Digital Business* (pp. 23–35). Springer. doi:10.1007/978-3-030-30714-8_2

Zeadally, S., Badra, M., & Zhang, X. (2017). Intrusion detection and prevention systems in the cloud: A survey. *Journal of Network and Computer Applications*, *79*, 25–47. doi:10.1016/j.jnca.2016.11.022

Zhang, C., Sun, J., Zhu, X., & Fang, Y. (2010). Privacy and security for online social networks: Challenges and opportunities. *IEEE Network*, *24*(4), 13–18. doi:10.1109/MNET.2010.5510913

Zhang, J., Chen, B., Xiong, R., & Zhang, Y. (2023). Physics-inspired compressive sensing: Beyond deep unrolling. *IEEE Signal Processing Magazine*, *40*(1), 58–72. doi:10.1109/MSP.2022.3208394

Zhang, J., & Huo, D. (2019). Image encryption algorithm based on quantum chaotic map and DNA coding. *Multimedia Tools and Applications*, *78*(11), 15605–15621. doi:10.1007/s11042-018-6973-6

Zhang, J., Luximon, Y., & Song, Y. (2019). The role of consumers' perceived security, perceived control, interface design features, and conscientiousness in continuous use of mobile payment services. *Sustainability (Basel)*, *11*(23), 6843. doi:10.3390/su11236843

Zhang, J., Zhang, G., Huang, Y., & Kong, M. (2022). A novel enhanced arithmetic optimization algorithm for global optimization. *IEEE Access : Practical Innovations, Open Solutions*, *10*, 75040–75062. doi:10.1109/ACCESS.2022.3190481

Zhang-Kennedy, L., & Chiasson, S. (2021). A Systematic Review of Multimedia Tools for Cybersecurity Awareness and Education. *ACM Computing Surveys*, *54*(1), 1–39. doi:10.1145/3427920

Zhang, Q., & Zhang, W. (2019). Accurate detection of selective forwarding attack in wireless sensor networks. *International Journal of Distributed Sensor Networks*, *15*(1). Advance online publication. doi:10.1177/1550147718824008

Zhang, S. H., Hu, C., Wang, L., Mihaljevic, M., Xu, S., & Lan, T. (2023). A Malware Detection Approach Based on Deep Learning and Memory Forensics. *Symmetry*, *15*(3), 758. doi:10.3390/sym15030758

Zhang, S., Yao, T., Arthur Sandor, V. K., Weng, T.-H., Liang, W., & Su, J. (2021). A novel blockchain-based privacy-preserving framework for online social networks. *Connection Science*, *33*(3), 555–575. doi:10.1080/09540091.2020.1854181

Zhang, X. W. (2023). *Detection of Android Malware Based on Deep Forest and Feature Enhancement*. Academic Press.

Zhang, Y., Zheng, Z., He, J., Zhao, S., Qu, Q., Shen, Y., & Jiang, X. (2023). Opportunistic Wiretapping/jamming: A new attack model in millimeter-wave wireless networks. *IEEE Transactions on Wireless Communications*, *22*(12), 9907–9922. doi:10.1109/TWC.2023.3274808

Zhao, Y. (2021). Research on wireless sensor network system based on ZigBee technology for short distance transmission. *Journal of Physics: Conference Series*, *1802*(2), 022008. doi:10.1088/1742-6596/1802/2/022008

Zhao, Y., Chen, J., Zhang, J., Wu, D., Blumenstein, M., & Yu, S. (2022). Detecting and mitigating poisoning attacks in federated learning using generative adversarial networks. *Concurrency and Computation*, *34*(7). Advance online publication. doi:10.1002/cpe.5906

Zha, Z., Wen, B., Yuan, X., Ravishankar, S., Zhou, J., & Zhu, C. (2023). Learning nonlocal sparse and low-rank models for image compressive sensing: Nonlocal sparse and low -rank modeling. *IEEE Signal Processing Magazine*, *40*(1), 32–44. doi:10.1109/MSP.2022.3217936

Zhou, Y., Panetta, K., Agaian, S., & Chen, C. P. (2012). Image encryption using P-Fibonacci transform and decomposition. *Optics Communications*, *285*(5), 594–608. doi:10.1016/j.optcom.2011.11.044

Zhu, H., Zhao, Y., & Song, Y. (2019). 2D logistic-modulated-sine-coupling-logistic chaotic map for image encryption. *IEEE Access : Practical Innovations, Open Solutions*, *7*, 14081–14098. doi:10.1109/ACCESS.2019.2893538

Zineddine, A., Chakir, O., Sadqi, Y., Maleh, Y., Gaba, G. S., Gurtov, A., & Dev, K. (2024). A systematic review of cybersecurity assessment methods for HTTPS. *Computers & Electrical Engineering*, *115*, 109137. doi:10.1016/j.compeleceng.2024.109137

Zou, Y., Mhaidli, A. H., McCall, A., & Schaub, F. (2018). "I've Got Nothing to Lose": Consumers' Risk Perceptions and Protective Actions after the Equifax Data Breach. *Fourteenth Symposium on Usable Privacy and Security (SOUPS 2018)*, 197–216.

Zrahia, A. (2018). Threat intelligence sharing between cybersecurity vendors: Network, dyadic, and agent views. *Journal of Cybersecurity*, *4*(1), tyy008. doi:10.1093/cybsec/tyy008

About the Contributors

Mohammed Amin Almaiah is an Associate Professor in the Department of Computer Science at The University of Jordan. He has published over 95 research papers in highly reputed journals such as the Engineering and Science Technology, an International Journal, Education and Information Technologies, IEEE Access and others. Most of his publications were indexed under the ISI Web of Science and Scopus. His current research interests include Cybersecurity and Cyber-risk assessment and mobile apps.

Yassine Maleh (Senior Member, IEEE) received the Ph.D. degree in computer science from Hassan 1st University in Morocco, in 2017. He is currently a Professor in cybersecurity and a Practitioner with industry and academic experience. Since 2019, he has been a Professor in cybersecurity with Sultan Moulay Slimane University, Beni Mellal, Morocco. From 2012 to 2019, he was the Chief Security Officer with the National Ports Agency in Morocco. He is the Founding Chair of IEEE Consultant Network Morocco and the Founding President of the African Research Center of Information Technology & Cybersecurity. He is a member of the International Association of Engineers and Machine Intelligence Research Labs. He has made contributions in the fields of information security and privacy, the Internet of Things security, and wireless and constrained networks security. His research interests include information security and privacy, the Internet of Things, networks security, information system, and IT governance. He has authored or coauthored more than 100 papers (book chapters, international journals, and conferences/workshops), 24 edited books, and 4 authored books. Dr. Maleh is currently the Editor-in-Chief of the International Journal of Information Security and Privacy and International Journal of Smart Security Technologies. He is also an Associate Editor for IEEE Access (2019 Impact Factor 4.098) and a Series Editor of Advances in Cybersecurity Management by CRC Taylor & Francis. He has served and continues to serve on executive and technical program committees and as a Reviewer of numerous international conferences and journals, such as Elsevier's Ad Hoc Networks, IEEE Network Magazine, IEEE Sensor Journal, ICT Express, and Springer's Cluster Computing. He was the Publicity Chair of BCCA 2019 and the General Chair of the MLBDACP 19 symposium and ICI2C'21 Conference. He was the recipient of Publons Top 1% reviewer award for 2018 and 2019.

Abdalwali Alkhassawneh is an Associate Prof of Accounting/Accounting Information System in King Faisal University (KFU) – KSA. He holds an undergraduate degree in Accounting from Irbid University, a master's degree in accounting from Jadara University, and a PhD in Accounting\Accounting Information System from University Utara Malaysia (UUM). His teaching and research interests are in the area of Accounting, Digital Accounting and Accounting Information System. His current research involves end-user computing, adoption and usage of AIS/ISs, cloud-based technologies, digital

Technologies and electronic payment systems. He has published more than 85 refereed articles in high ranked journals such as Journal of Retailing and Consumer Services, Technology in Society, Heliyon, Cogent Social Sciences, Current Psychology, EuroMed Journal of Business, Sustainability, Frontiers in Environmental Science, Global Knowledge, Memory and Communication and Global Business Review.

* * *

Mohammed Amin Almaiah is an Associate Professor in Cybersecurity at University of Jordan. He has published over 120 research papers in highly reputed journals such as the Engineering and Science Technology, an International Journal, Education and Information Technologies, IEEE Access and others. Most of his publications were indexed under the ISI Web of Science and Scopus. His current research interests include Cybersecurity, cyber risk assessment and cyber risk management.

C. V. Suresh Babu is a pioneer in content development. A true entrepreneur, he founded Anniyappa Publications, a company that is highly active in publishing books related to Computer Science and Management. Dr. C.V. Suresh Babu has also ventured into SB Institute, a center for knowledge transfer. He holds a Ph.D. in Engineering Education from the National Institute of Technical Teachers Training & Research in Chennai, along with seven master's degrees in various disciplines such as Engineering, Computer Applications, Management, Commerce, Economics, Psychology, Law, and Education. Additionally, he has UGC-NET/SET qualifications in the fields of Computer Science, Management, Commerce, and Education. Currently, Dr. C.V. Suresh Babu is a Professor in the Department of Information Technology at the School of Computing Science, Hindustan Institute of Technology and Science (Hindustan University) in Padur, Chennai, Tamil Nadu, India. For more information, you can visit his personal blog at .

Shanmugapriya D. is the Assistant Professor and Head, Department of Information Technology, Avinashilingam Institute for Home Science and Higher Education for Women, Coimbatore, INDIA since 2001. She has more than 20 years of teaching experience and 10 years of research experience. Her areas of interest include, Cyber Security, Biometric security and Image Processing. She has executed funded projects sponsored by DRDO, DST and UGC. Currently Supervising 4 scholars at Ph.D level, she has more than 25 publications in peer-reviewed journals and Prestigious conferences . She is a Reviewer for many Conferences and Journals. She is a content Writer of Virtual Currency, Block Chain Technology and Basics of Security Auditing for SWAYAM-MOOC course on Cyber Security.

Hasan Gharaibeh received her BSc. degree in Mathematics and Statistics from Jordan University of Science and Technology, Jordan, in 2021. he is currently studying MSc in Artificial Intelligence at Yarmouk University, Jordan. His research interests include Optimization, Yolow, Medical imaging, Machine Learning, Artificial Intelligence, Machine and Deep Learning.

Ankur Gupta has received the B.Tech and M.Tech in Computer Science and Engineering from Ganga Institute of Technology and Management, Kablana affiliated with Maharshi Dayanand University, Rohtak in 2015 and 2017. He is an Assistant Professor in the Department of Computer Science and Engineering at Vaish College of Engineering, Rohtak, and has been working there since January 2019. He has many publications in various reputed national/ international conferences, journals, and online book chapter contributions (Indexed by SCIE, Scopus, ESCI, ACM, DBLP, etc). He is doing research in the field of cloud computing, data security & machine learning. His research work in M.Tech was based on biometric security in cloud computing.

Rohaidah Kamaruddin is a lecturer in Faculty of Modern Languages and Communication, Universiti Putra Malaysia and Head of Laboratory of Ethnomathematics and Didactics in Institute for Mathematical Research, Universiti Putra Malaysia. She obtained her degree from University of Kyorin, Japan, Master and PhD from Universiti Putra Malaysia. Her area of specialisation is Japanese and Malay language; and ethnomathematics.

M. Keerthika is Assistant Professor, Department of Computer Science, Yuvakshetra Institute of Management Studies and Research Scholar Department of Computer Science, Avinashilingam Institute for Home Science and Higher Education for Women. 08 Years of experience in Teaching field.

Malathi Letchumanan is a Research Officer in Institute for Mathematical Research, Universiti Putra Malaysia. She has Degree in Information Technology, Masters in Computer Science and PhD in ICT in Mathematics Education. Her area of expertise is ICT in education and cyber education.

Uma Devi M. is working as Associate Professor in the Department of computing Technologies, SRM Institute of Science and Technology having 23 + years of experience in Teaching profession. She gained good exposure and worked extensively in teaching profession with some premier Engineering colleges in India and Singapore. She completed Ph.D in Sathyabama Institute of Science and Technology in 2018, completed M.E in Sathyabama Institute of Science and Technology in 2010 and completed B.E in Manonmaniam Sundaranar University in 1996. Her area of interest is Data Mining, Information Retrieval and Mobile Application Language Learning.

Rohaila Naaz is proven academic in computer science Engineering with 10 Years of Teaching experience. Her area of Teaching includes both core subjects computer networks, Digital electeonics, computer architecture and emerging technologies subjects Blockchain Technology, Ethereum platform, web3. She is having 25 +research papers published internationally in reputed journals and conferences.

Ahmad Nasayreh was born in Irbid, Jordan in 1998. He received the B.S. degree in mathematics and statistics from Jordan University of Science and Technology, Jordan, in 2021. He is currently pursuing the M.S. degree in Artificial Intelligence at Yarmouk University, Jordan. His research interests span across artificial intelligence, with a special focus on machine learning, deep learning, natural language processing, computer vision, data science, and pattern recognition. Ahmad has made significant contributions to his field, evidenced by his publication of 18 papers related to these areas.

D. Nethra Pingala Suthishni is Assistant Professor, Department of Information Technology, Avinashilingam Institute for Home Science and Higher Education for Women, Coimbatore Tamil Nadu, India.

Sabyasachi Pramanik is a professional IEEE member. He obtained a PhD in Computer Science and Engineering from Sri Satya Sai University of Technology and Medical Sciences, Bhopal, India. Presently, he is an Associate Professor, Department of Computer Science and Engineering, Haldia Institute of Technology, India. He has many publications in various reputed international conferences, journals, and book chapters (Indexed by SCIE, Scopus, ESCI, etc). He is doing research in the fields of Artificial Intelligence, Data Privacy, Cybersecurity, Network Security, and Machine Learning. He also serves on the editorial boards of several international journals. He is a reviewer of journal articles from IEEE, Springer, Elsevier, Inderscience, IET and IGI Global. He has reviewed many conference papers, has been a keynote speaker, session chair, and technical program committee member at many international conferences. He has authored a book on Wireless Sensor Network. He has edited 8 books from IGI Global, CRC Press, Springer and Wiley Publications.

Raghavendra R. is an assistant professor at the School of Computer Science and Information Technology (CS & IT) within Jain University, located in India. In his role, he contributes to the academic and research endeavors of the institution, focusing on areas such as computer science, information technology, and related fields. His responsibilities include teaching courses, conducting research, mentoring students, and contributing to the overall academic environment of the university. As part of Jain University, known for its academic excellence and commitment to innovation, Raghavendra R likely plays a crucial role in shaping the future of computer science and information technology education in India.

Senthilkumar T. was born on 22nd July 1982 at Cuddalore, Tamilnadu. He did his school education from the State Board of Secondary Education at the Secondary level. Due to his immense interest in learning Computer Science Engineering. He opted for M.Tech (CSE) at Post graduation from SRM University. During his post graduation he gained research experience in the field of wireless communication. After completing his post graduation he joined as a lecturer in Department of Computer Science & Engineering, SRM University & continued his research in the field of wireless communication, under the guidance of Dr. S. Prabakaran, Professor, Department of Computer Science & Engineering, under the guidance of his supervisor, he has contributed to scientific research papers.

Abdelhadi Zineddine is a PhD student at the Laboratory of Innovation in Mathematics, Applications, and Information Technology (LIMATI) at Sultan Moulay Slimane University in Beni-Mellal, Morocco. He holds an M.Sc. degree in Computer Science with a specialization in Computer Networks and Telecommunications Systems from the Polydisciplinary Faculty of Sultan Moulay Slimane University, in 2021. His research primarily revolves around cybersecurity, with a specific emphasis on web security and privacy. Currently, he is focused on investigating various security aspects related to HTTPS deployment.

Index

J

L

M

O

P

R

S

T

U

W

Z

www.ingramcontent.com/pod-product-compliance
Lightning Source LLC
LaVergne TN
LVHW080645011026
849160LV00014B/1329